In the public interest

In the public interest
Competition policy and the
Monopolies and Mergers Commission

Stephen Wilks

Manchester University Press
Manchester and New York

distributed exclusively in the USA by St. Martin's Press

Published by Manchester University Press
Oxford Road, Manchester M13 9NR, UK
and Room 400, 175 Fifth Avenue, New York, NY 10010, USA
http://www.man.ac.uk/mup

Distributed exclusively in the USA by
St. Martin's Press, Inc., 175 Fifth Avenue, New York,
NY 10010, USA

Distributed exclusively in Canada by
UBC Press, University of British Columbia, 6344 Memorial Road,
Vancouver, BC, Canada V6T 1Z2

British Library Cataloguing-in-Publication Data
A catalogue record for this book is available from the British Library

Library of Congress Cataloging-in-Publication Data applied for

ISBN 0 7190 5574 1 *hardback*

First published 1999

06 05 04 03 02 01 00 99   10 9 8 7 6 5 4 3 2 1

Typeset in Ehrhardt with Syntax
by Northern Phototypesetting Co. Ltd, Bolton
Printed in Great Britain
by Bookcraft (Bath) Ltd, Midsomer Norton

To Philippa

Contents

List of figures

List of tables

Preface

A fascination with the relationship between government and industry drew me into a study of competition policy in the late 1980s. One of the stimulating aspects of competition policy is the way it encompasses so many aspects of the impact that large business corporations have on the societies in which they operate. Competition policy is certainly about efficiency and growth but it is also about equity, accountability and economic democracy. The Monopolies and Mergers Commission (MMC) has been a buffer between the formidable forces of government and of industry since 1949 and in its investigations and reports has reflected the substantial changes in competition policy over the decades. I was therefore intrigued when the Commission approached me (and others) in the spring of 1997 to canvass a history of its activities to coincide with its fiftieth anniversary. I advanced some thoughts and the Commission invited me in July 1997 to write this book.

There were two caveats from my side. First, that the scope would be wider than the MMC and would encompass the full breadth of British competition policy. Second, that this would be a fully independent scholarly study so that the Commission would attach no qualifications and place no limits on my freedom to publish. Both conditions were agreed to, and the Commission has been absolutely scrupulous in respecting my independence in the selection and analysis of material and in the conclusions drawn. It has greatly facilitated the research by allowing access to Commission records not covered by the rules of commercial confidentiality, and by facilitating access to past and present members and staff. As part of this process the Commission created a Consultative Group which has met regularly to discuss the progress of the work and to assist with access within and outside the Commission. In addition the Commission has allowed me access to its databases and has permitted a much richer appreciation of the investigation process through two initiatives. First, it sought and secured permission from the large number of interested parties to allow me to review papers from one past inquiry. Second, with the agreement of the parties, and with the encouragement of Sir Graeme Odgers, I was able to observe the hearings and the group meetings on a recent merger inquiry.

In taking this initiative the Commission has been generous in its assistance and fairly heroic in its risk taking. Opening the doors to independent researchers is a hazardous and unpredictable business. In taking this step the Commission is to be commended for a significant step towards open government. For its part, the Commission took this initiative in a genuine spirit of inquiry which is apposite for an investigatory body, a variation on *quis custodiet ipsos Custodes?* It also, however, intends that the study should have a more direct benefit in facilitating an appraisal of the Commission's record as it goes through a period of transition, and as a source of information for staff and members who might find the history relevant for the present. Again, these motives are laudable, if daunting for an author who has to cater for an extremely knowledgeable audience. It is to be hoped also that the scope and detail of this book will engage, inform and possibly even entertain some of the many businesspeople, consumers, economists and lawyers who deal with the Commission. In writing the book I have been aware of this diverse potential audience of practitioners and competition specialists, as well as my more natural academic audience of historians, political economists and political scientists. It is for this reason that academic colleagues may find this a less 'academic' book than they might have expected. I have strayed into several theoretical thickets, perhaps too many for the practitioner reader, but I have tried to keep out of the theoretical jungle. The MMC of the title metamorphosed into the new Competition Commission on 1 April 1999. This is also my cut-off date. I have retained the convention of referring to the Commission as the 'MMC' for all generic mentions in the text and there is no attempt to analyse the likely workings of the new Competition Commission Appeal Tribunals.

In acknowledging the considerable help I have received from many quarters I must start with the Commission itself and with the Consultative Group. This was Chaired by Dr Derek Morris, now Chairman of the Commission, who has been an indispensable source of encouragement. It was composed of Penny Boys, Secretary of the Commission; Margaret Bloom, Director of Competition Policy at the Office of Fair Trading (OFT); Dan Goyder, former Deputy Chairman of the Commission; and Dr Ann Eggington, Director of UK Competition Policy at the Department of Trade and Industry (DTI). The members of the Group were unfailingly helpful and the meetings have been first-rate seminars. They have read in draft form the great bulk of the book and made some remarkably constructive suggestions. However, I must repeat, the analysis, the approach and the conclusions are entirely my own and must not be taken as representing the views of the Group or individuals within it.

The three preceding Chairmen of the Commission, Sir Godfray Le Quesne QC, Sir Sydney Lipworth QC and Sir Graeme Odgers have all been kind enough to discuss the history of the Commission with me. I am particularly grateful to Sir Graeme, who was Chairman when the project got under way and was uncommonly generous with his time and encouragement. I have talked widely to the past and present staff and members of the Commission. They have invariably been positive and informative but we have followed the usual conventions of talking on a non-attributable basis. Thus, except where explicit permission has been given, they are not named in the text. It would be right, however, to thank explicitly those people who were kind enough to read and comment on draft chapters. Three people who read virtually all the drafts and who have been quite exceptionally helpful are Hans Liesner (former DTI Deputy Secretary and Deputy Chairman of the Commission); Dr Martin Howe (former MMC Economic Adviser and former Director of Competition Policy at the OFT); and Stephen Burbridge (former Secretary of the MMC). Other members who have read drafts are Dr Gill Owen, Professor John Pickering, Professor Geoffrey Whittington and Dr Arthur Pryor. The past and present staff who have read drafts are John Banfield, Charles Dhanowa, David Elliott, David Fisher, Jane Richardson and Pat Sellers. I am extremely grateful for their comments and corrections.

On the same principle, of people who have been generous enough to comment on drafts, I would like to thank Lord Borrie QC and Sir Bryan Carsberg (both former Directors General of Fair Trading), Cyril Coffin (former DTI), Elizabeth Llewellyn Smith (former DTI and OFT), Tom Sharp QC, Patrick Shovelton (former DTI) and Andrew White (OFT). I am especially grateful to Dame Alix, Lady Meynell, who read two chapters and reminded me of how differently these matters were viewed in the 1940s. Two of my colleagues at Exeter, Dr Alan Booth and Professor Bruce Doern, provided some perceptive and challenging comments of a more theoretical character, as did an anonymous reader for Manchester University Press. The project also owes a considerable intellectual debt to past collaboration with Professor Maurice Wright. Some of the early analysis and arguments were presented at a seminar at Durham University Business School to Professor Andrew Gray and his colleagues; and at a half-day seminar for staff and members of the Commission. Both occasions generated very helpful feedback. Just to compensate for the risk of parochialism I also took the opportunity to discuss the overseas perception of British policy with Margaret Sanderson at the Canadian Bureau of Competition Policy in Ottawa; with Chuck Stark and Ed Hands of the Department of Justice Antitrust Division in Washington DC; and with Hank Spier and David Smith of the Australian Competition and Consumer Commission in Canberra. These participants in the international antitrust community were most hospitable and illuminating.

The DTI has been especially helpful in the matter of archives. It very kindly allowed access to the DTI files leading up to the passage of the Fair Trading Act 1973. These proved a rich source of insight. I would like warmly to acknowledge the help of the DTI's Competition Policy Directorate and the hospitality and guidance of DTI records staff, especially Patricia West and Les

Mondry, who, as a file reviewer, helps to make history. A standard requirement of access to DTI papers is the declaration, which I am happy to make, that 'the author has been given access to official documents. He alone is responsible for the statements made and the views expressed in this publication.'

The book has been written over a truncated period of time. The pressure was eased by the help of casual research assistance from some excellent Exeter Politics students, and also by more systematic help and support from Sebastian Eyre, who was awarded his Doctorate on competition policy as this book was being completed; and from Danny Yank, my part-time research assistant whose initiative and computing skills have been invaluable. Kim Horwood and her colleagues in the MMC Library have been generous with their assistance. In the matter of time and encouragement Manchester University Press has been an understanding and congenial partner. I am most grateful for the professionalism and forbearance of everyone involved. The project would not have been feasible without study leave from my University and the tolerance of my colleagues. For 1997–98 the University provided study leave which was greatly appreciated. For 1998–99 I benefited from Economic and Social Research Council (ESRC) award R000222596, which allowed the Politics Department to provide a second year of study leave. The ESRC award also funded research assistance and was essential for the completion of the study. In addition the MMC provided financial assistance for travel and for extended periods closeted with various archives.

It should be clear from the above that this history rests on extensive foundations of evidence generously supplied. The size of the subject and the breadth of the material would have justified a two-volume study. In compressing the material I am aware that some areas, such as the economic analysis of reports and the sub-plot of resale price maintenance, have been touched on all too briefly. I am also aware that this is a history by a non-historian and also a history that has the temerity to become fully contemporary. I therefore prefer to think of the book as an extended study of policy making and administration. Given the help that this project has received, the standard formula needs to be re-emphasised. The responsibility for the analysis, the conclusions and any errors of fact in the following pages are mine alone.

Finally, my most heartfelt thanks are to Philippa, to whom this book is dedicated; and to Susannah, Laura and Verity who helped to keep the book, and the Commission, in perspective.

S.W.
Exeter
May 1999

List of abbreviations

BAA	British Airports Authority
BG	British Gas
BoT	Board of Trade
CAA	Civil Aviation Authority
CAG	Comptroller and Auditor General
CBI	Confederation of British Industry
CEGB	Central Electricity Generating Board
CIM	Commission on Industry and Manpower
CPRS	Central Policy Review Staff
DEA	Department of Economic Affairs
DEP	Department of Employment and Productivity
DG	Directorate General (of the European Commission)
DGFT	Director General of Fair Trading
DGT	Director General of Telecommunications
DGWS	Director General of Water Services
DPCP	Department of Prices and Consumer Protection
DTI	Department of Trade and Industry
ECLR	*European Competition Law Review*
EEC	European Economic Community
ESRC	Economic and Social Research Council
EU	European Union
FBI	Federation of British Industry
IC 3	Industrial and Commercial Policy Division 3 (DTI)
IM 1	Industry and Manufactures, branch 1 (BoT)
IPPR	Institute for Public Policy Research
IRC	Industrial Reorganisation Corporation
MAFF	Ministry of Agriculture, Fisheries and Food
MAR	Market to asset ratio
MC	Monopolies Commission
MinTech	Ministry of Technology
MITI	Ministry of International Trade and Industry (Japan)
MMC	Monopolies and Mergers Commission
MRPC	Monopolies and Restrictive Practices Commission
NAO	National Audit Office

NBPI	National Board for Prices and Incomes
NDPB	non-departmental public body
NEB	National Enterprise Board
NEDC	National Economic Development Council
NEDO	National Economic Development Office
OFFER	Office of Electricity Regulation
OFGAS	Office of Gas Regulation
OFT	Office of Fair Trading
OFTEL	Office of Telecommunications
OFWAT	Office of Water Services
ORRTP	Office of the Registrar of Restrictive Trade Practices
PAC	Public Accounts Committee
PIB	Prices and Incomes Board (see also NBPI)
PRO	Public Records Office
RPI $- X$	Retail price index minus X (utility price control formula)
TIC	Trade and Industry Committee (of the House of Commons)
TUC	Trades Union Congress

1

Introduction: an institutional approach to competition policy

Study of competition policy requires a willingness to engage with the intricacies of individual cases, with legal constructs and economic prescriptions, and all with an awareness of the great values of efficiency, equity and accountability in the political economy at large. The members of the MMC are required to perform these mental gymnastics on a day-by-day, case-by-case basis, and they have been fulfilling that obligation for fifty years. The requirement to grapple with detail is demanding and can produce some fascinating and counter-intuitive findings, as seen in the Commission's 419 published reports. But the requirement is not exceptional and the Commissioners have experience, tried procedures and professional staff to assist them. The real challenge lies in the second half of the job: the need to make a recommendation in each case. The test which the Commission is asked to apply is that of 'the public interest'. The task of identifying the public interest is not easy.[1] Is it economic, legal or constitutional? Is it concerned with economic growth, with industrial stability, with consumer welfare or with democratic accountability? Is it about sustaining the existing system or about instituting reforms? Is there a public interest in defending capitalism from itself?

    This introductory chapter raises these large theoretical issues and locates both the MMC and competition policy within a national economic and political context. In the study overall we will be equally concerned with the details of organisation, procedures, legislation and, to a necessarily limited extent, with the reports themselves. The study offers a history of British competition policy, mediated through the MMC, which emphasises continuity. Policy in 1997 could be traced back very clearly to the first legislation in 1948, with many of the same principles and procedures. In the field of British economic policy this is a virtually unique record. Economic policy and government engagement with

industry have been the battleground of twentieth-century British politics. Class politics, ideological party politics, and the confrontation
between capitalism and socialism, has meant that each main area of economic policy has been subject to redefinition and reconstruction which
has left the battlefield littered with organisational corpses. Table 1 gives a
sample of the main organisations and initiatives that have come and gone
over the post-war decades. The great exception to the pattern of transient
initiatives is competition policy, and the great post-war survivor is the
MMC.[2] The members of the MMC are recognisably similar people,
doing a recognisably similar job, to their predecessors appointed in 1949.
This is at once symbolic of powerful historical traditions in the institutional structure of British capitalism, and indicative of something extraordinary about the MMC itself. Many studies of organisations and
agencies focus on creation and change; this study focuses on the no less
important question of continuity. The parallels to the continuity of the
MMC are the great departments of state (or the Bank of England), and
abroad the American antitrust authorities. The MMC is the longest-
established European competition agency and it provides a fascinating
window on British competition policy, as well as a yardstick against which
to evaluate the exceptional characteristics of British capitalism.

Before embarking on a preliminary evaluation it would be as well to
outline the approach taken in this study. This is an 'institutional history'
of competition policy. In other words, it regards the policy area as being
made up of a series of organisations, enactments and interests, all bound
together by mutually understood ideas and by shared normative assumptions. The concept of an institution is used quite deliberately and specifically. It draws upon North's idea of an institution as 'humanly
constructed constraints that shape human interaction' and, although this
study does not share North's transaction cost approach, it does lean on
his ideas of historical reproduction through path dependency.[3] Thus the
common law and the family are 'institutions' but so also is company
autonomy and, arguably, competition policy itself. Institutions have
three dimensions. They are regulative (with rules and organisations);
they are normative (embodying values and ethics); they are cognitive
(built on norms and habits); and they embody incentives to co-operate.
Institutions are not organisations. Thus the study is concerned with
competition policy as a complex institution and not simply with the
MMC (or the OFT or the DTI) as organisations. This is important
because it distinguishes the approach taken here from an earlier generation of administrative histories which focused on an agency or a ministry,
and tended to give a formalistic, descriptive and often chronological

Table 1 *Initiatives and organisations in supply-side policy, 1945–98*

Date created	Industrial policy	Prices and incomes	Competition policy	Date abolished	Survivors
1946–50	Nationalised industries			1984–96	Bank of England
1946	Bank of England				MMC/Competition Commission
1949			MMC		Commission
1956			Restrictive Practices Court	1998	
1962	NEDC/NEDO			1992	
1964	MinTech			1970	
1965		NBPI		1970	
1965	DEA/National Plan			1969	
1966	IRC			1971	
1968		DEP		1970	
1970 and 1983	DTI				DTI
1973			OFT		OFT
1974	Department of Industry	Price Commission		1980	
				1983	
1975	NEB/British Technology Group	DPCP		1979	
				1983	
1984			OFTEL, etc.		OFTEL, etc.

Notes: For full names see list of abbreviations.
This is a sample only.

treatment.[4] Perhaps because such earlier studies were descriptive, and because political science has only recently rediscovered institutions,[5] there are regrettably few institutional histories of even the major units of British government. An additional and perennial obstacle is, of course, lack of access and the secrecy fixation of the British civil service. This book is therefore a relatively rare specimen of what might yet become a new species of institutional studies of British public administration and public policy.

Regardless of whether or not the approach has been 'institutional' it is striking that competition policy as a field has proved unattractive to students of public policy. Most important policy areas such as housing, environment or defence, have engendered a substantial specialist literature. Equally, other economic policy areas, including training, employment and industrial policy, have a respectable coverage. For competition policy, however, studies of 'the policy' as opposed to 'the discipline' are rare. There is a full, if recent, literature on competition law, which often strays into policy concerns; and there is an extensive economics literature which is often addressed to the economics of policy and policy reform. Curiously, however, both these literatures have shied away from questions of the administration of policy and from its politics, with the result that there has been no book on British competition policy since 1974, and no full-scale study of the MMC since Rowley's thorough and critical treatment in 1966.[6] Books by economic historians have gone some way to redress the balance[7] but there is a notable absence of books on recent policy. This book covers the full fifty-year period but it also brings the discussion entirely up to date to cover the 1998 Competition Act. In addition the two thematic chapters, on mergers and on utility regulation, deal by definition with more recent periods.

The recent tendency in policy studies to take a more institutional approach incorporates a recognition that 'history matters'. Indeed, one important variant of the approach is historical institutionalism. Hence the melding of an historical approach with a policy studies approach has the potential to provide an effective insight into current policy. The analysis thus sits on the boundary between policy studies and history. The bias, in fact, is towards recent developments and to that extent this is a study of public administration. It covers events and addresses questions which are unlikely to engage 'proper' historians for another twenty years. For these current events the participants are cautious, the debates surrounded in secrecy and the papers safely locked away. In 2029, when the unfortunate thirty-year rule will make the papers available, the definitive story of the 1998 Competition Act can be told.[8] On the other hand this study does aspire to a genuine historical treatment of the earlier period and draws on original archive material. In particular it offers the first treatment of competition policy in the late 1960s and early 1970s for which papers are just becoming available.[9] The availability of data means, curiously, that the 1950s and 1960s can be treated more thoroughly than the 1970s. Since much of the material originates in official sources there is a possibility that the analysis is over-responsive to official papers and to the memories of articulate former officials. This study does not subscribe to the approach of post-modernists who regard any reading of the historical record as relative and all interpretations as subjective.[10] Nevertheless, it has been necessary to step back from the evidence and to bear in mind that political exchanges, laws, reports and political ambitions are often relayed by officials who will put a certain 'spin' on the material; and to bear in mind also that these are often 'surface disturbances, crests of foam that the tides of history carry on their strong backs'.[11] Conventional studies of public policy are seldom sufficiently historical to identify such tides. In the fifty years of British competition policy however, covering half of the most startling century in human history, the high and the low tides should become apparent. Competition policy, as we see later in this chapter, is flowing towards the high water mark.

Understanding competition policy

The following chapters take what is in some ways a conventional approach to the study of public policy. They examine the goals of policy and the dynamics of policy making. This involves evaluation of the roles played by the main policy actors (ministers, officials, consumers, business, etc.) and examination of the pattern of power relations that appears to influence policy development. In other words, they examine whether policy is dominated by business or by officials, whether patterns of policy making could be described as corporatist or pluralist. Throughout the study we are concerned with policy outputs in the shape of legislation and administrative actions, and in later chapters an attempt is made to specify policy outcomes – a question that focuses on the impact of policy and its distributional consequences. It is to be expected that policy dynamics will have changed over the fifty-year period. Industrial politics in the 1940s and 1990s are very different phenomena. Accordingly, various efforts are made to divide the analysis into time periods where one or another model of policy or organisational influence appears paramount.

The book also adopts a less conventional approach which combines

the intensely specific with the theoretically general. The specific component involves a detailed study of the MMC. In particular, chapters 3, 4
and 5 present an analysis of the Commission. This is an approach with
some obvious advantages. The MMC has been at the centre of policy for
fifty years and, prior to the 1973 Fair Trading Act, shared policy responsibility with the Board of Trade (BoT). It is a self-evidently important
actor, and a unique one, whose mode of operation is not always easy to
understand. There is therefore an intrinsic interest in studying the Commission. There is also a more hidden benefit of great interest to an
administrative historian. It is rare for one organisation to enjoy a contin-
uous existence throughout the life of a policy. The MMC provides a
'window' on policy, or perhaps a better metaphor would be of a 'core
sample'. To illustrate the ecological conditions at any historical juncture
we can examine this core and see how the MMC was discharging its
functions. There is yet a third advantage in studying the MMC. It will
become apparent, especially in chapter 5, that the Commission embodies
a quite extraordinary continuity in organisation, in normative assumptions and even in procedures. It appears as an embodiment of policy
making by incrementalism and it allows us to trace current policy content back to its origins. Of course, organisations and procedure are
adapted and their current effect depends on an evolution of ideas and the
exercise of administrative discretion. Nonetheless, the study of historical
continuity throws a powerful light on the operation of competition policy. Ideas of policy inheritance or policy succession underline the fact
that no policy is constructed on a green field – all policies have to build
on a previous legacy of institutions, understandings and political bargains. This is especially true of an unreconstructed and complex society
such as Britain and it lends credence to the historical institutionalist view
that 'institutions connect the past with the present and the future so that
history is a largely incremental story of institutional evolution in which
the historical performance of economies can only be understood as part
of a sequential story'.[12] For North, institutions impose 'path dependence', which expresses the idea that once an economy, or a policy, is set
on a particular path it finds its choices constrained and its incentives
skewed towards staying on that path. The MMC and British competition
policy appear to provide a perfect example of the connectedness of past
and present, the incremental style of policy change and the power of path
dependence.

     If the MMC focus deals with the specific it also raises the problem
of change. It poses the question of why path dependence has been so evident in competition policy and, crudely, how on earth the MMC has

managed to survive and to continue in existence under its new incarnation of the Competition Commission from April 1999. The survival of the MMC poses a wonderful research question for organisation theorists and for political economists. The MMC has not survived on the basis of its power and influence as an organisation. It has come near to abolition on at least four occasions and has been saved by the conjuncture of external developments rather than by its own efforts. Instead, its survival owes more to its 'fit' with the expectations of officials, politicians and business. Its methods, assumptions, activities and findings appear to gel with traditional British practices. It expresses the essence of British competition policy as an institution and is well integrated with the institutional configuration of British capitalism. It is this more general question of the relationship between competition policy and the British political economy that is considered in the next section.

Competition policy and the British political economy

This section presents a sketch of arguments about the post-war British political economy that stresses its historical roots in the exceptionalism of British capitalism, and in the extension of wartime accommodation in the form of the 'post-war settlement'. It is a sketch that is necessarily abbreviated and can barely do justice to a rich and erudite literature. It seeks to locate competition policy in the context of a much broader stream of development in British economic institutions and in the processes of bargaining between them. It draws a bold parallel between the experience of the MMC and the post-war settlement itself – a parallel which not all may accept but which serves to provoke thought and to throw light on the atmosphere, the ethos, within which the institution of competition policy was conceived and nurtured.

The long-term historical background to British exceptionalism lies in two revolutions: the triumphant industrial revolution and the unfinished bourgeois revolution. As to the first, Britain was the first developer and evolved the first industrial market system which proved immeasurably superior to the craft-based, under-capitalised, small-scale, over-regulated systems of production operated by its continental rivals.[13] British industrial success did not depend on government assistance, and a system of expectations was established which regarded minimal intervention by government as normal and healthy, so much so that 'few countries have ever been more totally dominated by an *a priori* doctrine than Britain was by *laissez faire*'.[14] British industrial culture became suffused with the assumptions and virtues of the market economy, with entrepreneurial independence, possessive individualism, a sanctification of private property, and with the freedom to contract. These traits were embodied in, and defended by, family firms, relying on reinvested capital and underpinned by a company law that allowed an extreme of company autonomy.[15]

The 'unfinished revolution' was to be found in the process of transition from monarchy to liberal democracy. Unlike all other transitions from medieval society, the British revolution retained aristocratic and land-owning influences with an effect nicely captured by Marquand:

> the old liberties, the old corporations, the old, precedent-bound common law, the old houses of parliament all survived; and they ... became the conduits of modernity. The end product was a political culture suffused ... above all with the Lockean assumption that individual property rights are antecedent to society. In such a culture, the whole notion of public power, standing apart from political interests, was bound to be alien.[16]

Hence British government did not develop a concept of 'the state' in the continental tradition. British government and British officials were hesitant in the deployment of public power, recognised proper spheres of freedom and autonomy for the major groups in society, and would have regarded as quite improper the continental, Hegelian, concept of 'the interests of the state'.[17] British officials were servants of the Crown, not of the state; their function was to co-operate, bargain, balance, not to 'direct'. An important effect of this partial transition was that the manufacturing bourgeoisie were further subordinated by the continued power of commercial capital centred in the City and focused on the empire and on global trading. For Ingham this division lies at the heart of British exceptionalism.[18] Thus the unfinished revolution became embedded in British institutions. For those with a conspiratorial bent, Gowan and Left-leaning administrative theorists also suggest that the decisive factor was the development of the civil service. Although the propertied classes lost control of the House of Commons they gained control of the civil service through Gladstone's late nineteenth-century reforms. The civil service, rather than the legislature, became the guardian of traditional British market values and of the autonomy of capital.[19]

The dual impact of these revolutions was examined by Shonfield in the 1960s. In Britain he inspired what has become virtually a school of historical political economy and, while many of his specific arguments have been overtaken by events, his method and insights remain influential. In this context his views on the deployment of state power remain apposite. Talking of the immediate post-war period he observes that:

old-fashioned *laissez-faire* had gone; but the old instinctive suspicion of positive government, which purports to identify the needs of the community before the community itself has recognised them, remained as vigorous as ever. It was reflected both in the behaviour of ministers who refused to plan, and in the administrative devices invented for them by civil servants who were anxious above all to ensure that the exercise of the new powers of government did not saddle them with the responsibility for making choices, for which they might later be accountable. Administrative discretion, which is meat and drink to the French, is anathema to the British official. Of course, he has it in practice: without it a modern state could not function. But because it raises awkward problems about the division of responsibility between politicians and officials, the officials hold desperately to the pretence that they have no initiative of their own, that they are instruments only, wholly passive, in the hands of some masterminding minister. To give this pantomime verisimilitude, the powers attributed to civil servants must be seen to be kept to a minimum.[20]

Here we have the period, and the thinking, which informed the creation of the MRPC as an intermediary between Whitehall and business. An intermediary that insulated officials and which was insufficiently powerful to threaten the other main institutions within the political economy. This insight becomes even more compelling if we visualise the creation of the MRPC in the context of, and as a component of, the 'post-war settlement'.

The great producer interests of the unions and organised business had already come together in the 1930s to sanction the rationalisation of industry with the restrictive practices, oligopoly and market sharing which was to present such problems for the MRPC. The wartime collaboration of these interests produced a war economy that was remarkably successful and which forged strong links of trust and co-operation between officials, ministers and businesspeople. A shared economic victory, with unpaid businessmen working shoulder to shoulder with officials in Whitehall, generated indissoluble bonds between industry and the production departments. In planning for wartime reconstruction officials sought to extend wartime harmony and efficiency and, by 1944, 'officials had ready for Ministers' approval the concept of a unified post-war settlement, constructed so as to offer each constituent partner to a proposed political contract what it most wanted. A high and stable level of employment … became the central principle.'[21]

This idea of the post-war settlement, brilliantly explored in Middlemas's trilogy is, of course, an historian's gloss. It was not a formal creation and different authors stress different elements. At its heart was the

1944 White Paper on Employment, and the implications for industrial politics were momentous. The settlement placed senior civil servants at the centre of the post-war system of economic government, as mediators, brokers and initiators. In addition, however, it gave the main interest groups continued autonomy. 'Precisely because their co-operation was believed to be vital if government were to achieve economic growth and political stability they remained governing institutions, part of the extended state.'[22] Thus the unions and the representatives of organised business had their traditional autonomy recognised and incorporated into the system of post-war political economy. A dominant norm, tacit but ubiquitous, was the emphasis placed on the autonomy of the individual company. As we have seen, this autonomy was enshrined in company law and in the common law. The post-war settlement, posited on negotiation and voluntarism, if anything reinforced rather than threatened that autonomy. Thus the unwillingness of civil servants and ministers to supersede the settlement, to intervene didactically, to use administrative discretion and to create in Britain a 'developmental state' has been a constant source of criticism from writers on Britain's relative industrial decline.[23]

These are grand generalisations, pitched at a level of high theory: what do they imply for the more humble development of competition policy? The 1948 Monopolies and Restrictive Practices Act was a child of the 1944 Employment White Paper. The rationale for the creation of monopoly control lay in full employment. The later development of competition policy and the role played by the MMC displays persistent characteristics which appear more comprehensible when seen in the context of this link to the post-war settlement. Thus later chapters stress the role of civil servants in the BoT and the relative dependence of the MMC and the OFT. They point to the avoidance of legal process and the determined retention of room for bargaining implied in ministerial discretion. They emphasise the accommodating approach taken towards industry and the respect for reasonable business behaviour and voluntary compliance with inquiries and recommendations. Additionally they stress the tendency towards 'negotiated legislation' in which the views of business were given considerable weight.

Thus, it is argued, an appreciation of the historical peculiarities of the British political economy is essential for understanding the parallel peculiarities of competition policy. An appreciation is helpful in two further respects. First, the post-war settlement began to break down in the industrial confrontation of the early 1970s, and the concluding chapter speculates on the growth of a new settlement under New Labour. The

MMC can thus be seen in the late 1980s as a hangover from an earlier model of industrial politics, and its reform, discussed in chapter 9, can be seen both as overdue and as representative of the new settlement of explicit regulation. Second, this perspective provides a partial explanation for our central problematic: how has the MMC survived? It survived because it represented the quintessence of the post-war settlement. Its constitution and approach were entirely resonant with the traditional assumptions of British free-market capitalism and with the rationalisation of those traditions in the post-war settlement. Because of this it was accepted by the governing institutions and defended by the civil service (especially the BoT). Later organisational competitors, especially agencies of intervention and price control, were manifestations of failed attempts to supersede the settlement. They were controversial and vulnerable. What this perspective does not explain, of course, is the survival of the MMC in the 1990s and its fresh incarnation in the Competition Commission. This is a more contemporary issue which is addressed in the concluding chapter.

The changing salience of competition policy

The problems of monopoly and restrictive practices have a venerable tradition of attention from government and the law. Monopolies created scandals under Elizabeth I, and enterprising legal historians can trace common law restraint of trade cases back to 1298.[24] Indeed, the common law origins of the Sherman Act continue to provoke stimulating scholarship.[25] This legal inheritance need not detain us here. Some excellent studies in economic history review the background.[26] Three features of the pre-war situation are, however, worth emphasising. First, the courts did not recognise any great need to control restrictive practices and monopoly; if anything the legal atmosphere encouraged corporate concentration and cartelisation, giving more emphasis to freedom to contract and freedom of association. Second, however, a public concern over the 'monopoly problem' stimulated wide debate before and after the First World War. This provoked various government initiatives, including the creation of a Committee on Trusts in 1918 which was followed by the short-lived experiment of the Profiteering Acts. The debate surrounding the Committee included a proposal for an investigatory tribunal which could be seen as the seed of a prospective MMC, and a monopolies bill was actually drafted. In the atmosphere of the Great Depression the BoT backed away from this course of action. At this time free trade and a market economy provided moderating influences on restrictive practices but, and this is the third factor, that was to change in 1932 with the Import Duties Act, which ushered in a period of cartelisation and monopolisation which, in Gribbin's words, meant that 'competition in many sectors of the economy was destroyed'.[27] The years of protection followed by the direction and suppression of competition in the wartime economy meant that by 1945 the economy was dominated by cartels, oligopolies and restrictive practices which were regarded as wholly normal and were openly sanctioned and administered by government departments, trade associations and formal agreements. In this sense it could be said that the problems to be dealt with by the post-war monopolies legislation had been created by pre-war government – an argument of undue simplicity but one that would commend itself to Austrian thinkers.[28] The war altered the relationship between industry and the state in more formal and lasting ways. In an administrative expression of the post-war settlement it created 'a kind of corporativism – a tradition of close co-operation between organised industry … and the central administration'.[29] This became an established pattern of government, and a system of 'sponsorship' was created which gave each major sector of industry a 'sponsor' somewhere in Whitehall. These sponsors have not infrequently found themselves in opposition to the competition agencies.

The questions of how to create a competitive market, and the appropriate post-war structure for industry, were addressed within the BoT as early as 1941 and analysis was undertaken through the reconstruction machinery in 1943–44. The outcome was the May 1944 White Paper on Employment[30] with its commitment that 'the Government will therefore seek power to inform themselves of the extent and effect of restrictive agreements, and of the activities of combines; and to take appropriate action to check practices which may bring advantage to sectional producing interests but work to the detriment of the country as a whole'.[31] The White Paper concealed heated debate within the BoT. The seminal paper was written in July 1943 by Hugh Gaitskell and Professor George Allen. This, says Mercer, 'represented the high point of the evolution of antitrust proposals in Britain for many years to come, indeed ever since'.[32] The genius of the Paper was to link control of monopoly to the creation of employment, thus 'post-war policies for the maintenance of employment and for the control of monopoly should be clearly related to each other'.[33] The substantive economic components of the Paper were written by Allen (later to become a member of the MRPC) and the machinery section by Gaitskell (later to become leader of the Labour

Party). It was uncompromising. It reviewed the history of British experiments with the control of monopoly, referred to American experience,
and suggested a number of areas which later featured prominently in the
legislation – such as the virtues of publicity. 'In conclusion', wrote Allen,
'it should be emphasised that an attack on private monopoly is not to be
confused with an attack on private enterprise. On the contrary, private
enterprise and private monopoly are ultimately incompatible. In a democratic country, the public must be the master of industry.'[34] Such translu-
cent prose did not wholly succeed in convincing officials and ministers,
and the ensuing story, well told by Gribbin and Mercer, is of a vigorous
debate which produced a less stringent set of recommendations, followed
by delays in legislation and further compromises which resulted, eventually, in the 1948 Act.

The story of the implementation of the Monopolies and Restrictive
Practices (Inquiry and Control) Act 1948 is told in the following chapters.
The salience of competition policy fluctuated widely in public debate and
in political and economic assessments of economic policy. The salience of
the MMC fluctuated even more markedly. Competition policy was consistently overshadowed by other components of economic policy until the
late 1980s. It must, of course, be borne in mind that British policy has tolerated an extraordinary bifurcation of administration. After 1956 restrictive practices were dealt with by a legal process of a registrar and a
specialised court.[35] The court interpreted its brief strictly, which disconcerted business, and it very quickly eliminated 'old-fashioned' cartels
operated by trade associations and based on formal agreements. This area
of policy has been regarded as highly successful, although later its legal
formalism caused it to fall into disrepute. In contrast, the schizophrenic
British state continued to control monopolies and eventually also mergers through an administrative process of investigation which has no close
equivalent anywhere else in the world. Assessments of the success of this
model of monopoly control are typically far more sceptical. Most studies
of economic policy pay little attention to monopoly control and their
treatments tend to be dismissive. In the Cambridge economic history
Tomlinson dismisses the 1948 Act as 'almost worthless'.[36] Further assessments are offered in the Conclusion but, at the very least, it could not be
claimed that British control of monopolies and mergers was widely
regarded as important or successful until quite recently. Perhaps one reason for this is picked up by Tom Sharpe, who observes that:

> paradoxically a case can be made for the proposition that the UK really
> does not have an anti-monopoly policy, as the term is recognised in the

USA, Germany and the EEC. What the UK possesses is less a legal framework designed to establish standards of acceptable behaviour, to regulate
conduct, to provide remedies for those affected and, generally, to provide
some guarantees to prospective entrants in any industry that they will be
protected effectively from the anti-competitive excesses of a dominant
incumbent. What the UK possesses is a mechanism whereby certain
defects or failures in the market mechanism can be investigated and ad hoc
remedies applied.[37]

Sharpe may be overstating his case but he does succeed in emphasising
the low profile of the UK law when compared with the USA and Germany (less so in comparison with France or Italy). In Germany and in the
United States competition policy has a significance far beyond its regulatory framework or economic impact; it is a matter of high politics. It is
worth emphasising this role because it could be argued that the UK has
treated competition policy as part of a very political calculus. Instead of
using it as part of a constitutional safeguard, it has refrained from using
it and turned to alternative methods of controlling industry.

This is not to argue that politicians or the public were unconcerned
about monopoly and private economic power. If anything they were too
concerned. In a world of class politics and class parties the confrontation
between capital and labour was the basic cleavage of post-war politics,
and it eventually overthrew the post-war settlement itself. Labour's 1945
manifesto attacked 'the "hard faced men"' who 'had only learned how to
act in the interests of their own bureaucratically-run private monopolies
which may be likened to totalitarian oligarchies within our democratic
state'.[38] But the solution in 1945 was nationalisation and in the 1960s and
1970s a resort to planning and intervention. British competition policy
therefore did not assume the responsibility of undertaking front-line regulation of private economic power, nor the political salience that would
have accompanied it. This helps to explain the atypical bi-partisan nature
of the development of policy. As the following chapters reveal, competition legislation has not been regarded by politicians as urgent, and it has
invariably been enacted with bi-partisan support. The lack of political
controversy is undoubtedly a factor in the longevity of the MMC.

This situation can be compared with the position in the other major
industrialised countries. In the United States antitrust has provided the
main way in which government has regulated the private sector. It has
therefore been embroiled in debates about economic democracy and
political priorities and cannot be regarded simply as a tool of economic
policy. It is as near a part of the constitution as it could be without a formal amendment. For Germany the ordo–liberal tradition which underlies

the German social market economy gave pride of place to strong anti-cartel laws operated by an independent authority. The German cartel laws and the Bundeskartellamt again have a quasi-constitutional status outside and above the routine processes of party politics. In this respect it could be argued that Britain had more in common with France, where competition policy and law have always been overshadowed by the powerful machinery of state intervention.[39] The most important addition to the international repertoire of competition regimes is that of the European Union (EU). Because of the impact of the European competition rules on UK policy reform the genesis of the European system is discussed in chapter 9. Here, too, the European rules are multi-purpose. Certainly they are aimed at market competition and economic efficiency but their overwhelming aim has been market integration.

International comparison thus reveals an underdeveloped potential for British competition policy. It has a potential for acting to control concentration of economic power and could thus contribute to the safeguarding of economic freedom to parallel the political freedoms secured by the tenets of liberal democracy. Giuliano Amato has recently contributed a stimulating essay which helps to lift the eyes of students of competition policy from such delights as the complexities of joint ventures and the merits of vertical restraints to consider also the essential political rationale for competition policy:

> antitrust law was, as we know, invented neither by the technicians of commercial law … nor by economists themselves … It was instead desired by politicians and (in Europe) by scholars attentive to the pillars of the democratic systems, who saw it as an answer (if not indeed 'the' answer) to a crucial problem for democracy: the emergence from the company or firm, as an expression of the fundamental freedom of individuals, of the opposite phenomenon of private power; a power devoid of legitimation and dangerously capable of infringing not just the economic freedom of other private individuals, but also the balance of public decisions exposed to its domineering strength.[40]

He goes on to argue that this original desire to secure 'democratic efficiency' has gradually been fulfilled by other forces within society, especially by the countervailing power of labour, consumers, shareholders, and so on. Instead competition policy has become steadily more preoccupied with economic efficiency. This, as we shall see, is an accurate account of the move in the UK towards a policy for 'competition' as the eventually dominant component of the public interest test. As to the subordination of goals of 'democratic efficiency', there still remains a role for

British competition law to play. It is a role best exemplified by the utility regulators in the 1990s. Public outrage at the pricing, service and remuneration practices of the privatised utilities was matched only by the regulatory impotence of politicians. The response of the independent regulators, as seen in chapter 8, was to use competition to redress the balance and to control the companies. Under the new Competition Act competition will be enforced more systematically and the law will be used concurrently by the utility regulators. Thus the reversal of nationalisation has produced an appropriate renewal of the significance of competition policy. Not only has competition law been rejuvenated as a major element in government supply-side policies, it has also begun to perform a vital political role in controlling the exploitation of private economic power. If, as we have seen since the fall of the Berlin Wall in 1989, capitalism has emerged triumphant, then the classic methods employed to control capitalism on its own terms, through competition and the market, have to measure up to their increased responsibilities. In this sense British competition policy is more important than ever and will enjoy a considerable prominence as the powers under the new Act begin to be deployed. Here we see the echo of Allen's wartime observation, cited above, that 'in a democratic country, the public must be the master of industry'.

The MMC and the structure of the book

The bulk of this study is concerned with the detailed administration of competition policy rather than with grand ideas of constitutional or political theory. The main focus and organising theme is the MMC in its various guises. This means that there is a bias towards consideration of monopolies and mergers. Discussion of restrictive practices and resale price maintenance is limited.

The MMC is a difficult creature to define. Britain does not enjoy a system of administrative law, and there is no accepted framework for the creation of agencies or the definition of their powers, their independence or their accountability.[41] This chaotic eclecticism in British administration causes bemusement among continental observers and is, in truth, helpful only to those who can find advantage in exploiting ambiguity. Thus the MMC was established as 'a Commission' in the 1948 Act without any further enlightenment as to its powers and statutory status. The fact that it could 'determine its own procedures' indicated a degree of independence but there was nothing explicit. It is sometimes described as 'quasi-judicial' but the legal parallel is misleading. It is suggestive to regard it as a Permanent (Royal) Commission but its true specification is as a 'tribunal'. Unfortunately, this does not take us very much further. Tribunals are a huge and varied category of bodies, some highly legalistic, some administrative, and the Commission can be regarded as an administrative tribunal. This is important because it opposes the temptation to evaluate the Commission as an extension of the judicial system and therefore repeatedly to compare it with a court of law. This temptation was reinforced by the appointment of barristers to Chair the Commission between 1953 and 1993. Farmer observes that 'some tribunals really constitute alternatives to departmental or ministerial decision making rather than court substitutes'[42] and, with some reservations, this is where we might locate the Commission. Certainly it was designed explicitly to avoid the impression or the reality of legal process and its procedures are almost entirely administrative. Thus the Commission does not apply a legal test but makes a judgement about 'the public interest'. This judgement is made anew in each individual case. There is no formal guidance, no informal guidelines and the Commission is not bound by precedent. Of course, precedent is not ignored and nowadays it strives for consistency in its procedures and its findings but it still retains discretion in every case. This provides a constant source of criticism and controversy but the Commission is following the requirements of the 1948 Act re-stated as section 84 of the 1973 Fair Trading Act (and retained for monopolies and mergers under the 1998 Act). Section 84 is reproduced in the Appendix. It contains a list of five matters to which the Commission should have regard, of which 'promoting effective competition' is the first. But no pre-eminence is legally attached to competition and the Commission is enjoined to 'take into account all matters which appear to them in the particular circumstances to be relevant'. Here, then, we have a body of prominent, part-time people, selected for their experience and their powers of judgement, deciding on the vaguest of criteria whether certain business structures, agreements and behaviours are or are not 'against the public interest'. This is the philosopher king come to life.

In evaluating the Commission one alternative image, preferred by many members and by recent Commission chairmen, is that of an 'economic jury'. This may be a helpful metaphor but it is an inaccurate description. A jury is composed of lay people who respond to evidence presented in an adversarial court setting. Moreover, they do not define or propose a 'sentence'. In all these respects an MMC group differs. In particular the MMC investigation process is inquisitorial rather than adversarial – a factor that has caused concern and incomprehension to lawyers and businesspeople who assess the Commission as a 'court substitute' and expect to find an adversary procedure. In official parlance the Commission is marshalled under none of these terms and is categorised as a non-departmental public body (NDPB). Under civil service rules this is important because it gives the Commission additional flexibility in procedures and in staffing, but NDPB is a catch-all category and provides minimal guidance for assessing status and powers. In short, it is not possible to assess the MMC against any established yardstick drawn either from international competition law agencies, or from British legal or administrative practice. It is *sui generis*, and the following chapters build up a picture of the Commission starting from scratch.

In chapter 2 the book presents a fifty-year overview of competition policy which looks at the goals of policy, the main legislative Acts and the periods of greater prominence. Its purpose is to provide orientation for the non-specialist reader and to set the scene for later chapters, which are considerably more detailed. Chapters 3, 4 and 5 turn to the MMC and cover the main administrative aspects of its history. Chapter 3 deals with its structure and powers; 4 with the members; and 5 with its procedures and with the less tangible (but no less important) idea of its 'culture'. These three chapters seek to combine historical and contemporary material and tend to emphasise continuities and the way in which historical factors have moulded contemporary practice as an expression of 'path dependence'. In contrast, they do not contain a systematic analysis of cases undertaken and reports published. Some reports are mentioned but a full-scale analysis drawing out economic principles and lessons has not proved feasible. In compensation there are a number of good economic studies which are referred to in the text.[43] Chapter 6 presents a more detailed history of competition policy which draws on the experience of the MMC but looks at the political and economic context within which policy developed. It builds up to the passage of the key piece of legislation, the 1973 Fair Trading Act, and it offers a new historical interpretation of the Act's passage and significance. Chapter 7 picks up the thematic issue of merger control. This is a more recent competence, initiated in 1965 and unaffected by the 1998 Competition Act. It is an area of huge importance for business and for the Commission. It generates the highest profile attention and it remains very significant, notwithstanding the 1989 European merger regulation. From here the study turns to utility regulation in chapter 8. This is an even more recent area of activity dating from 1984. Utility regulation has become a central activity for the MMC and was arguably the decisive factor in explaining the Labour Government's decision to retain it as the Competition Commission. Chapter 9 reverts to a broader treatment and tells the story of the evolution of competition policy over the decades since 1973. The chapter gives some prominence to the OFT and to the theme of reform. It covers the growth of the European competence and the eventual passage of the 1998 Competition Act which (partially) reproduces a European approach in British law. In conclusion, chapter 10 returns to the arguments first outlined in this chapter and draws together the analysis from the earlier chapters. It briefly speculates on the significance of the new Act and the new Commission but is more concerned with summarising the history of competition policy in this century, rather than analysing the next.

Notes

1 There are profound philosophical and ideological issues concealed by this simple phrase. See, for instance, C. Friedrich (ed.), *The Public Interest* (New York, Atherton, 1962).

2 The MMC started life as the Monopolies and Restrictive Practices Commission (MRPC); in 1956 its name was changed to the Monopolies Commission (MC); and in 1973 to the MMC. In April 1999 it became the Competition Commission. For convenience the term MMC is used throughout the book whenever a generic usage is intended. For usage at a particular date the appropriate title at that date is used.

3 D. North, *Institutions, Institutional Change and Economic Performance* (Cambridge University Press, 1990), p. 3, ch. 11; see also W. R. Scott, *Institutions and Organizations* (London, Sage, 1995).

4 There is great value in the earlier histories such as the 'New Whitehall Series'. Much of the early literature is summarised in J. W. Grove, *Government and Industry in Britain* (London, Longman, 1962) but study of the machinery of government went out of fashion until recently. Peter Hennessy's *Whitehall* (London, Fontana, revised edn, 1990) symbolises a fresh interest in a more rounded account of the organisation, culture and power of the central executive.

5 This approach and the literature are reviewed admirably in B. G. Peters, *Institutional Theory in Political Science: The 'New Institutionalism'* (London, Pinter, 1999).

6 The 1974 study is the second edition of P. Guenault and J. Jackson, *The Control of Monopoly in the United Kingdom* (London, Longman, 1960); Charles Rowley, *The British Monopolies Commission* (London, Allen and Unwin, 1966).

7 See especially H. Mercer, *Constructing a Competitive Order: The Hidden History of British Antitrust Policies* (Cambridge University Press, 1995); T. Freyer, *Regulating Big Business: Antitrust in Great Britain and America 1880–1990* (Cambridge University Press, 1992).

8 Like most academics I would agree with Keith Middlemas that not only is the thirty-year rule for the release of public papers damaging to scholarship, it is

unhealthy for sensible policy making based on intelligent analysis of recent past policy. See K. Middlemas, *Power, Competition and the State, Volume 1: Britain in Search of Balance, 1940–61* (London, Macmillan, 1986), p. 13.

9 Here I am immensely grateful to the DTI which, as noted in the Preface, was kind enough to make available the relevant files relating to the background of the Act.

10 See R. Evans, *In Defence of History* (London, Granta, 1997) for a review of the post-modernist debate on historical method and for an attack on the post-modernists.

11 To quote Fernand Braudel's characterisation of political events, cited in P. Burke, *The French Historical Revolution. The Annales School 1929–1989* (Oxford University Press, 1990), p. 39.

12 North, *Institutions*, p. 118.

13 A classic treatment is A. Gerschenkron, *Economic Backwardness in Historical Perspective* (Cambridge, Mass., Harvard University Press, 1962); see also C. Trebilcock, *The Industrialisation of the Continental Powers 1780–1914* (London, Longman, 1981).

14 E. Hobsbawm, *Industry and Empire: An Economic History of England since 1750* (London, History Book Club, 1968), p. 195.

15 See A. D. Chandler, *Scale and Scope: The Dynamics of Industrial Capitalism* (Cambridge, Mass., Belknap, 1990); T. Hadden, *Company Law and Capitalism* (London, Weidenfeld and Nicolson, second edn, 1977); J. E. Parkinson, *Corporate Power and Responsibility* (Oxford, Clarendon, 1993).

16 D. Marquand, *The Unprincipled Society* (London, Fontana, 1988), p. 154.

17 K. Dyson, *The State Tradition in Western Europe: The Study of an Idea and an Institution* (Oxford, Martin Robertson, 1980).

18 G. Ingham, *Capitalism Divided? The City and Industry in British Social Development* (London, Macmillan, 1984).

19 P. Gowan, 'The origins of the administrative elite', *New Left Review*, 162 (1987).

20 A. Shonfield, *Modern Capitalism: The Changing Balance of Public and Private Power* (Oxford University Press, 1965), pp. 93–4.

21 Middlemas, *Power, Competition and the State, Volume 1*, p. 341.

22 *Ibid.*, p. 349.

23 The literature is very substantial. See, for instance, S. Pollard, *The Wasting of the British Economy* (London, Croom Helm, 1982); C. Barnett, *The Audit of War* (London, Macmillan, 1986); Marquand, *The Unprincipled Society*, or, most recently, W. Hutton, *The State We're In* (London, Vintage, revised edn, 1996).

24 Sir David Cairns, 'Monopolies and restrictive practices', in M. Ginsberg (ed.), *Law and Opinion in England in the 20th Century* (London, Stevens and Sons, 1959), p. 174.

25 R. Peritz, *Competition Policy in America 1888–1992* (Oxford University Press, 1996).

26 In particular Freyer, *Regulating Big Business*; and Mercer, *Constructing a Competitive Order*.

27 D. Gribbin, *The Post-war Revival of Competition as Industrial Policy*, Government Economic Service Working Paper 19 (London, Price Commission, 1978), p. 2.

28 Austrian thinkers in the Schumpeterian or Hayekian tradition tend to regard the only problematic barriers to competition to be those created by government.

29 Grove, *Government and Industry*, p. 61.

30 *Employment Policy*, Cmd 6527 (London, HMSO, May 1944); these developments

are well analysed in Middlemas, *Power, Competition and the State, Volume 1*, ch. 3; see also D. Gribbin, 'The contribution of economists to the origins of UK competition policy', in P. de Wolf (ed.), *Competition in Europe* (Dordrecht, Kluwer, 1991).

31 Cmd 6527, para 54.

32 Mercer, *Constructing a Competitive Order*, p. 57.

33 PRO, BT64/318 Memorandum by G. C. Allen and H. Gaitskell, 'The control of monopoly' (17 July 1943), summary, p. 1.

34 *Ibid.*, p. 28.

35 The standard early study is R. B. Stevens and B. S. Yamey, *The Restrictive Practices Court: A Study of the Judicial Process and Economic Policy* (London, Weidenfeld and Nicolson, 1965).

36 J. Tomlinson, 'British economic policy since 1945', in R. Floud and D. McClosky (eds), *The Economic History of Britain Since 1700. Volume 3: 1939–1992* (Cambridge University Press, second edn, 1994), p. 276.

37 T. Sharpe, 'British competition policy in perspective', *Oxford Review of Economic Policy*, 3:1 (1985), p. 90.

38 'Let us face the future', Labour manifesto 1945, in F. Craig (ed.), *British General Election Manifestos 1900–1974* (London, Macmillan, second edn, 1975), p. 123.

39 See H. Dumez and A. Jeunemaitre, 'The convergence of competition policies in Europe: internal dynamics and external imposition', in S. Berger and R. Dore (eds), *National Diversity and Global Capitalism* (Ithaca, Cornell University Press, 1996).

40 G. Amato, *Antitrust and the Bounds of Power: The Dilemma of Liberal Democracy in the History of the Market* (Oxford, Hart, 1997), p. 2.

41 For a discussion of organisational types see B. Hogwood, 'Regulatory institutions in the United Kingdom: increasing regulation in the "shrinking state"', in B. Doern and S. Wilks (eds), *Changing Regulatory Institutions in Britain and North America* (University of Toronto Press, 1998).

42 J. A. Farmer, *Tribunals and Government* (London, Weidenfeld and Nicolson, 1974), p. 3.

43 A case in point is R. Clarke, S. Davies and N. Driffield, *Monopoly Policy in the UK: Assessing the Evidence* (Cheltenham, Edward Elgar, 1998).

2

The post-war development
of competition policy

Competition policy in its American variant may have existed for over a
hundred years but its British version is much more recent. There were
certainly episodic experiments with competition policy during the first
half of the twentieth century, and Colin Baillieu rather beguilingly takes
his discussion of monopolies back to the scandals of the early seventeenth
century under the first Queen Elizabeth.[1] Nonetheless, the consistent
prosecution of competition policy is a post-war phenomenon. Of course,
it was not called 'competition policy' until rather late in its life and the
word 'competition' did not appear in a legislative title until 1980. For
much of its life policy was thought of in terms of more specific, and more
common law terms, as concerned with the issues of monopolies and
restrictive practices.

The evolution of contemporary competition policy since its origins
in the mid 1940s is interwoven with differing conceptions of how the
economy operates and with conflicts of ideas as well as political pressures
over whether, how and when government should involve itself in the
economy. This chapter plots the development of policy and in so doing
gives emphasis to the legislative landmarks and the emergence of the key
actors. It charts the various incarnations of the MMC and introduces the
changes in its role and responsibilities. It also, however, examines the theoretical rationale for the policy itself and the emergence of competition
first as one element in policy and eventually as its dominant concern. It
is evident that the coherence and integrating influence of 'competition'
as a principle of policy may be misleading. We start, therefore, with the
concept itself, before examining how it has been translated into policy.

Competition as a guiding concept

Competition is an extraordinarily broad concept that deals not only with economic behaviour but also with the fundamentals of human interaction. The contrasting principles of competition and co-operation are omnipresent in business and throughout society. They are basic to the dominant twentieth-century ideological opposition between capitalism and socialism, and to the emergent contrasts between the social organisation of 'the West' and that of 'the East'. Accordingly, the idea of competition varies in significance according to the alternative understandings of capitalism, the market and market processes. It is the principle by which Adam Smith's invisible hand operates magically to maximise welfare, and it thus takes on an almost quasi-religious significance in the understanding of markets. It is important to appreciate the complexities of competition as an idea because it colours the reactions of individuals and the goals of policy. Not all observers will regard competition as a good thing; not all will regard it as a technical economic process; and many will regard the role of competition policy as to attenuate or to channel competition, not simply to maximise it.[2]

Since competition is the dominant process of economic regulation in a market society, it is not surprising that governments have found it necessary to develop a competition policy. Given also that competition is such a broad phenomenon, it is equally unsurprising that governments have had immense difficulty in defining the goals of policy and defining suitable mechanisms to implement it. In some ways 'competition policy' is a meaningless phrase. It takes on significance only in relation to particular policy configurations and combinations of policy goals. Indeed, national variations in the nature of competition policy are built into the very language with which it is described.

The United States' language of 'antitrust' is redolent of the origins of US policy in the 1890 Sherman Act. The catalyst for action and the target of reformers was the trusts which had come to dominate the US industrial economy from the 1880s. The progressives who inspired the legislation were as interested in economic democracy, republican self-government of business and defending the 'little man' against oppression as they were in abstract competition and economic efficiency. The legislation did not become administratively effective until the 1914 Clayton and Federal Trade Commission Acts, which created an Independent Regulatory Commission to administer antitrust policy. The perception that the Sherman Act included a substantial symbolic element is reinforced by the fact that no monies were specifically allocated for antitrust activities until 1903.[3] Nonetheless, the Sherman Act was certainly forceful. It embodied a prohibition on all restraints on commerce or trade, and it did so in a common law language of 'restraint of trade' and 'monopolisation'. The

Act does not actually mention competition although the general goal was the pursuit of competition, however defined. This goal was the subject of legal argumentation in the early cases prior to 1911 which led the Supreme Court to develop a 'rule of reason' which moderated the blanket coverage of the Act to restrict it to cover 'unreasonable' restraints. In its reluctance to pursue pure competition the Court found itself defending private property rights and the freedom to contract in what was the first of multiple cycles of permissiveness and stringency in American antitrust.[4] Unfortunately there is no space to discuss the complex, fascinating and influential evolution of US antitrust, but it can certainly be argued that it was not until the late 1970s that the efficiency theories associated with the Chicago School came to dominate US federal agencies and the courts. Competition was only one basic goal of US antitrust, and not necessarily the dominant one until very recently. British policy makers have consistently looked to the United States for inspiration but have equally consistently reacted against what they have found. The first Secretary of the MRPC, Alix Kilroy, was invited to the United States in 1949 to benefit from the American example but she found it barely relevant. 'After two months in America', she later wrote, 'I had learned enough to make a thesis about the workings of the Sherman anti-trust act with its demand for competition and about their fair trade laws ... – you could lampoon them, I felt, by saying that together they meant everyone must run the race but the winner must have his head cut off.'[5] This reaction was repeated by officials, ministers and business itself over the following years.[6]

The British vocabulary talked similarly of 'monopolies' and 'restrictive practices' but it did not regard them as unlawful and was not 'anti' anything. Indeed, although nowadays these terms have become pejorative, the normative coloration was more muted in the 1940s when both monopoly and restrictive practices had proved their worth in responding to depression and mobilising for war. The term 'monopoly' is an especially curious shorthand with which the MMC has had to live. Cases of true monopoly, where 100 per cent of production is concentrated in one undertaking, are extremely rare and in principle indefensible. The MMC has in practice dealt with oligopoly. The economic illiteracy of its title underlines the way in which the MMC has found 'monopoly' not to be harmful – in cases such as flat glass or soluble coffee, where a principled stress on competition would have indicated remedial action but where an efficiency defence has been accepted. Thus British policy came late to a wholehearted commitment to competition. The focus of competition policy on 'competition'; the high salience of competition policy within the mix of economic policies; and the insertion of principles of competition into a range of unrelated policies – all these are developments of the Thatcher years. It is therefore important to set aside the preconceptions of the 1990s in evaluating earlier and more agnostic views of competition, and to appreciate that the machinery of government was designed as much to restrict competition as to encourage it.

The complexity and ambiguity of British competition agencies and law, as they stood in 1997 ahead of the Labour reforms, therefore reflected peculiar policy dynamics. The policies did not grow from a clear design or a policy vision. They were not forged in a furnace of public outrage (as in the United States); they were not imposed as part of the fruits of victory (as in Japan and, partially, Germany); neither were they conceived as part of a vision of political and economic integration (as with the European Economic Community (EEC)). Instead British policy emerged incrementally and piecemeal as a product of consensus building by a powerful civil service, heavily influenced by business lobbying, increasingly responding to developments in economic thought, and operating under a benign and exceptional mantle of political bi-partisanship. As lawyers began to get to grips with this hydra-headed creature in the 1980s they found it 'bizarre and complex', so that 'the resultant jumble of statutes bears no common style and few common policies'.[7] Competition, therefore, is a constant preoccupation of British policy but not an unambiguous goal. Indeed, given the many alternative definitions of competition that are available it is probably best to see British policy as flexibly adapting its conception of competition to the requirements of the time and to the case. In this regard it has, perhaps wisely, avoided the dogmatism of the German Kartellamt, whose purist pursuit of 'competition' has frequently been overturned by the courts and parodied by industry.[8] The evolution of concepts of competition as embodied in British policy has reflected changes in industrial circumstances and in industrial opinion, and has reflected also the evolution of political doctrine and economic thought.

The evolution of fifty years of economic thought about competition policy has had an impact which surfaces in later chapters and which has been profound. From the insights generated by Joan Robinson's work on imperfect competition published in the 1930s, through the work of Chamberlin, Coase, Galbraith, Bain, Williamson, Posner, Stigler, Bork and Porter.[9] Such names are evocative of major shifts in economic diagnoses which have fundamentally redirected competition policy and enforcement, at least in the United States. But the influence of economics and

economists is far from direct and is often unclear. In an influential summary of British policy, Hay went so far as to argue that 'economic analysis
is generally ambiguous, *a priori*, about the efficiency effects of particular
market structures and conducts'.[10] The search by administrators for some
clear and simple economic guidelines has thus proved elusive. Officials
and legislators have attached adjectives such as 'workable', 'effective' and
'satisfactory' to the concept of competition but the attempts to provide a
simple definition have proved futile. 'Competition' emerges as an area of
debate rather than a firm rule in the making and implementation of policy.

A sceptical view of competition as morally dubious and economically inefficient grew out of the depression of the 1930s and fuelled
Labour Party socialism and the programme of nationalisation. It also
generated a rationalisation movement in the private sector that provided
the dominant outlook of the 1940s. The rationalisation imperative
extended its influence into the 1960s and 1970s and was encouraged by
the government, not least through the activities of the Industrial Reorganisation Corporation (IRC) in the 1960s and the National Enterprise
Board (NEB) in the 1970s. Rationalisation as a component of industrial
policy may have lost favour since the 1970s (although not with Michael
Heseltine) but it has re-emerged in a new theoretical guise through the
emphasis on co-operation, trust and 'relational contracting' between
companies. This again calls into question a purist pursuit of competition,
so that it has been argued that 'competition law needs to be more sensitive to the possibility that apparently "collusive" arrangements promote
trust of the kind needed to enhance dynamic efficiency'.[11] With an awareness of these arguments the OFT and the MMC have seldom pursued
'competition' for its own sake. Competition has been regarded as a means
to the ends of efficiency and economic welfare. The 'efficiency defence'
which had to be created in the United States has always been an element
in British thinking.

At this point we can simply conclude that, although British competition policy has been steered steadily closer to a preoccupation with
competition, that concept in itself provides an inadequate basis for the
administration of policy and, in addition, that in the UK competition has
not been the dominant concern over the life of competition policy and
that a range of other objectives has provided inspiration and direction.

The complex goals of British policy

In the early days Alix Kilroy remarked that the MRPC 'is seen either as a body set up to condemn and suppress monopolies, or as a subterfuge under which to put the whole subject to sleep'.[12] Between these extremes lay a raft of complex and sometimes incompatible objectives. We can review them briefly, first through the lens of academic hindsight and second through analysis of the preoccupations of politicians and officials.

In his substantial comparative history Freyer adopts a wide interpretation of competition policy. He sees its role in relation to the emergence of managerial capitalism, first in the United States and then, belatedly, in the UK. The way in which competition policy attacked cartels and restrictive practices, but tended to allow mergers, means that it hastened the demise of the family-owned firm, and hastened the rise of the multi-divisional, managerially controlled corporation. In the context of this grand historical interpretation, 'British governmental policy encouraged the adoption of multidivisional management structures, especially conglomerates. Despite the high level of corporate concentration, this structure facilitated the adaptation of British big business to changing economic conditions.'[13] If Freyer sees British competition policy working in the interests of an emergent, professionalised class of corporate managers, then Mercer documents the way in which business lobbied for this outcome. Hers is a very stimulating study in which she argues that 'the history of British competition policy has little to do with the gradual enlightenment of the British public and its business leaders about the virtues of competition … Instead it is a story of power politics, special pleading and, at times, downright skulduggery.'[14] Mercer's argument is that the purpose of British antitrust policy was to weld the British economy into a new, American dominated, world order; and that business pressure was the factor which determined the nature and timing of legislation. Her study is unsurpassed for its detailed and finely contextualised account of events. Her interpretation of American influence and attempt to apply American capture theory are perhaps less satisfactory. Overall she falls towards the 'subterfuge' end of Alix Kilroy's spectrum. She sees competition policy as a way of saving capitalism from itself and as a way of pre-empting more radical attacks on private enterprise through nationalisation or planning.

Of course, officials and most politicians have not conceived competition policy in such grand theoretical terms. The immediate goals of policy are far more prosaic and derive from the political and administrative pressures of the moment. As we saw in chapter 1, the inspirational goal for the original conception of British competition policy was full employment. Subsequently a series of goals have been articulated, and it is useful to review five 'sets' of goals. These are efficiency, competitiveness, policy linkage, regulation and information.

There is no doubt that political reformers have had in mind a goal of economic efficiency as 'a prime objective'[15] in designing new policy, and equally little doubt that efficiency has been an important element in the implementation of policy. But efficiency has been conceived in terms of a general intensification of competitive pressures within the economy, and of a general attack on the complacency of monopoly and restrictive practices. As a goal of policy, efficiency has two defects: first it is analytically contested; second, it is extraordinarily difficult to measure. The quote from Hay above indicated the difficulty in deriving from economic analysis any general rules that specify how competitive behaviour or industrial structure will or will not increase efficiency. The question has, of course, been extensively debated. Thus Williamson's influential 1968 trade-off model notes gains to productive efficiency resulting from economies of scale in horizontal mergers, to be set against losses in allocative efficiency resulting from increased market power.[16] Efficiency calculations are more clear cut in cartel analysis. For politicians in the 1940s and 1950s, the advice of liberal economists that more competition would almost automatically bring better efficiency was easier to accept when the reality was of a protected, cartelised and monopolised economy that was so clearly in need of revitalisation. But even then, officials and business-people were pointing to the dangers of 'excessive' or 'cut-throat' competition; in one evocative phrase, 'the economics of the dust-bowl'. In the 1960s and 1970s the proponents of economies of scale and of research concentration, and in the 1980s the seductive arguments of the Austrians and Chicago, all combined to question the link between anything resembling a neo-classical competitive market and resulting efficiency benefits.

The pursuit of industrial efficiency in the operation of policy is a requirement of the legislation as part of the public interest test. However, the MMC has found it extremely difficult to evaluate industrial efficiency in monopoly cases and managerial efficiency in merger cases. It has made heroic attempts but has often fallen back on an agnostic stance and treated efficiency as but one element in a complex equation. Thus in only two cases from 1956 to 1976 did the Commission explicitly criticise a firm's industrial efficiency.[17] In some cases MMC groups have actually found that a principled pursuit of competition would not, on the facts of the case, be likely to increase efficiency.[18] Thus while ministers from Wilson to Thorneycroft and Heath to Ridley sincerely maintained that competition policy would yield efficiency gains, we do not find in official papers, MMC reports or OFT studies, any systematic or detailed pursuit of economic efficiency as a major (much less a measurable) goal. The question of whether competition policy as a component of broad economic policy has actually improved the efficiency of the economy is a question we return to in chapter 10.

Ministers have consistently seen a trade-off between the first goal, of efficiency through intensified competition, and a second goal of international competitiveness. Michael Porter's landmark work on *The Competitive Advantage of Nations* argued that strong domestic competition policy fostered comparative economic success[19] but his conclusions gained impact from their novelty. Until the 1980s every major piece of competition legislation was passed in the shadow of a sterling crisis (1948 the dollar shortage; 1956 the dollar blackmail over Suez; 1965 the impending Labour devaluation; 1973 incomes policy and the three-day week). Ministers and officials were far more preoccupied with the pragmatics of export earnings, big overseas contracts, the strength of sterling and international market shares than with the academic niceties of competition theory. They were attuned to the arguments of the big exporters, their trade associations and lobbyists who argued for national champions, economies of scale, strategic export planning and government support for exporters. The language is deceptive here. The idea of international competitiveness is not the same as the idea of a highly competitive domestic industry. International competitiveness is affected by exchange rates, the terms of trade, regulatory stringency, government support, size, economic diplomacy and generic policies (in education or training, for instance). While in the abstract ministers might accept that competitive domestic markets produce companies also able to compete in international markets, in practice they were, until the early 1980s, equally likely to be persuaded that domestic monopoly was a pre-requisite for international success.[20] Such arguments surfaced in a series of reports such as *Flat Glass* (the Pilkington case in 1968), the two *GEC/Plessey* reports in 1986 and 1989, the 1987 *Tate and Lyle/Ferruzzu/Berisford* mergers and the two *VSEL* merger reports in 1995, when variants on the national champion and international competitiveness imperatives were put forward. Such considerations were also at the heart of Michael Heseltine's scepticism about an active UK competition policy.

A third set of policy goals derives from linkages with other areas of economic policy. The policy linkages are made explicit in the public interest guidance for the Commission. Section 14 of the 1948 Act stressed efficiency in its first clause but also mentioned full employment, the distribution of industry and technical improvement. Section 84 of the 1973 Act shifts the emphasis in the first clause to 'promoting effective competition' but goes on to mention price levels, new techniques, regional policy and promotion of international competitiveness.

In practice competition policy has for most of its life been unusually subordinate to other policy concerns. In the 1940s and again in the 1960s priority was given within the BoT to the location of industry, and outside the BoT to the priorities of the rationalisers who put industrial consolidation ahead of competition. Up to 1953 competition policy was so hesitant as to be almost experimental. From 1964–70 and again from 1973–83 the great policy gulf was between industrial policy and competition policy. This is a constant theme in the analysis of any competition policy regime and is seen in Japan in the animosity between the Ministry of International Trade and Industry (MITI) and the Fair Trade Commission and in Europe between Directorate General (DG) III and DG IV. In the UK it was similarly institutionalised in the conflict between the fashionable and powerful machinery for industrial intervention in the Department of Economic Affairs (DEA), Ministry of Technology (MinTech), National Economic Development Office (NEDO) and IRC in 1964–70 and again with the Department of Industry, NEB and NEDO in 1974–79; and on the other hand a rather forlorn MMC and OFT responsible to the BoT and Department of Employment and Productivity in 1969–70, and to the DPCP in 1974–79. This policy clash was regularly resolved in favour of the interventionists. The 1970s also saw an association with consumer policy and price control. The creation of the OFT made an explicit and important link between competition policy and policy towards consumer protection. This link remains integral to the OFT, and successive Directors General of Fair Trading (DGFTs) have put emphasis on their consumer protection function. Later, as the economic policy emphasis shifted to the control of inflation, the MMC was seen as a potential agency of price control. Already in October 1969 the Queen's Speech had anticipated the merger of the MC and the National Board for Prices and Incomes (NBPI) (a proposal that fell at the election), and again in 1978 the Liesner Green Paper considered that there would be advantages in bringing together the MMC and the Price Commission (again the MMC was saved by a Conservative election victory). The Green Paper also marked the last confrontation between industrial and competition policy when it presented the potential for strengthening competition policy 'taking account of the need for this policy to make its full contribution to the Government's industrial strategy'.[21]

The consumer link is intriguing. One interpretation of competition policy is that it should be orientated towards consumer interests, and in the 1990s this was a constant refrain from the Consumers' Association and an explicit recommendation of the Trade and Industry Committee

(TIC), which argued that 'consideration of consumer interests be at the heart of competition policy'.[22] Consumer concerns have been prominent in OFT referrals but critics have felt that the priorities of industry have been given more prominence in OFT and MMC reports than those of consumers.[23] The consumer interest is there in theory but not sufficiently voiced in practice.[24] Here, too, is an important policy linkage, reflected in institutional design, but which has not provided a dominant goal.

It seems, then, that the 'golden ages' of British competition policy, where it was seen as major policy foci and not subordinate to other policies, were the periods 1953–64 and 1984–92. In 1953 the MC was greatly strengthened; in 1956 came the most revolutionary piece of legislation, which effectively squeezed most former cartels out of the industrial economy; and in 1964 came Heath's principled attack on resale price maintenance. All these measures were based primarily on a competition rationale. From 1984, while legislative changes were important (especially the 1980 Competition Act and the Privatisation Acts), the main shift of emphasis was associated with ministers such as Tebbit, Brittan, Ridley, Lilley and Young, who seriously believed in competition as a principle upon which to base policy. Yet legislation was slow to emerge. It is curious that eighteen years of Conservative Government (1979–97) passed without major reform of British competition policy.

The fourth policy goal is regulation. It was important for officials to have a regulatory framework in place for two reasons. The first was to avoid political embarrassment when ministers were confronted with demands for action, yet had no power to act. This was especially evident in 1948 and again in 1961–65 when merger control was introduced. The second reason was the subterfuge argument. The appearance of a machinery of control could usefully serve to head off demands for more radical action and more effective control. Mercer is quite clear that this is what both officials and business wanted in the early days. She concluded that, in 1948, 'The Monopolies Commission was to gently point out to industry where its own best interests lay.'[25] Later on, critics of the weakness of policy appeared not to realise that this was the very point. The purpose of policy was to hold the ring, to defend the system, which allowed business mainly to regulate itself, but to pick up any obvious or embarrassing anomalies or absurdities. The regime also allowed business to resolve internal disputes, and it is interesting that in MC reports greater weight tends to be given to business submissions in the form of evidence and complaints from third parties. This is what Sutherland found in 1970 when he observed that 'opposition to the merger from trade buyers or suppliers has always been given great weight'.[26] The common thread in this goal is the need to retain flexibility and to maintain ministerial discretion. As noted in chapter 1, the monopolies side of competition policy has been based mainly on administrative action – it has avoided *per se* rules and prohibitions and has minimised legal involvement. In short, it is very much a child of traditional civil service generalists. The great exceptions are the 1956 Restrictive Trade Practices Act and latterly, of course, the 1998 Competition Act.

This brings us to the fifth policy goal, the pursuit of information. Although the 1948 Act was parodied as an impossibly weak piece of legislation, it was genuinely speculative in its approach. As noted in chapter 1, the weight of business and official opinion was in favour of the established arrangements of strong trade associations, restrictive agreements, close links with sponsoring departments, and the intimacy between government and firms which had grown up in wartime. Thus the parenthetic title of the Act, Monopolies and Restrictive Practices (Inquiry and Control), was significant. BoT officials were genuinely uncertain about the merits of the practices they referred to the Commission. Would they be condemned or justified? Accordingly, the BoT's annual report noted the intention 'to build up a programme of study which will enable the Commission to bring under review ... representative examples of all the common type of restrictive practices and monopolistic influence in British industry'.[27] In practice this intention was not thoroughly pursued, and of the huge number of possible cases proposed to the BoT a very small number of often rather trivial cases were referred. Officials had hoped and expected that examination of a series of cases would generate general principles which might cohere into something like rules or guidelines. This expectation in 1949 was repeated in 1965 in relation to merger control and it has stimulated a steady stream of criticism. The competition authorities have found it impossible to establish binding guidelines. In this they have been hindered by the ultimate political and potentially arbitrary role of ministers but they have also been hindered by the commitment to the case-by-case principle and by the rejection of precedent. This is less a fault of the Commission, which did indeed propagate general principles in general reports and in addenda to merger reports, as it is a criticism of the tripartite system. Geoffrey Howe again articulated the criticism in 1992 when he observed, 'I have to tell you that I do not any longer find this imprecise state of affairs compatible with the proper operation of what we like to think of as the Rule of Law.'[28] In similar vein (and the quotes could be multiplied) the TIC remarked that 'this highlights a major weakness in the system since a decision-making authority like the MMC should be able to set out policy guidelines on competition issues and on the priority given to the public interest criteria in the Fair Trading Act'.[29] Whether the case-by-case principle is indeed so undesirable is a moot point but, as we shall see in later chapters, it is true that the raw material provided by the Commission's investigations has not generated a set of principles which could be applied to the control of various anti-competitive practices.

This is not to dismiss the role of the Commission in educating public, official (and academic) opinion. Even now it is salutary to go back to the early reports and to note the quite incredible restrictive practices operating in the 1940s. Fighting companies (to undertake predatory attacks on rivals), collective boycotts and 'kangaroo courts' to fine cartel breakers, all feature as accepted practices. Sober demonstration of the harm they could do and the unfairness they embodied was an important educative function stressed in early assessments. In a landmark survey Jewkes remarked that 'what was most significant was not the practical steps taken to increase competition but the increased understanding of the whole problem of monopoly arising out of the reports of the Commission'.[30] Allen goes further. He talks of the shock of the new policy and the educative effects of the reports: 'this psychological convulsion may be perhaps regarded as the most important result of the Commission's work in its early stages'.[31] But while this educative role may have been important even up to the 1970s, it is less clear that MMC reports produced a 'psychological convulsion' in the 1980s or 1990s. This raises the question of whether the MMC is still a body engaged in 'inquiry' and the investigation of first principles; or whether it is now examining specific cases of familiar problems and thus becoming more administrative or executive. What can certainly be said is that the Commission has moved from the occasional blockbuster report to an outpouring of reports on a series of areas. Table 2 gives a schedule of cases signed by year (rather than published) – which gives a better estimate of annual workload. It is drawn from the MMC database and presents cases by type of inquiry. The increase of output in the 1980s is quite extraordinary and is discussed further in chapter 5.

Table 2 *Reports by the MMC by year and subject, 1949–99*

Date	No. signed	Monopoly	Merger	General	Newspapers, etc.	Section 11 nationalised industries	Anti-comp.	Utility	Airport
1949	0								
1950	1	1							
1951	2	2							
1952	3	3							
1953	2	2							
1954	1	1							
1955	5	4		1					
1956	7	7							
1957	0								
1958	1	1							
1959	1	1							
1960	0								
1961	1	1							
1962	0								
1963	2	2							
1964	0								
1965	2	1	1						
1966	10	6	3		1				
1967	6	3	2		1				
1968	7	4	2	1					
1969	5	2	2		1				
1970	4	1	1	2					
1971	1	1							
1972	6	3	1		2				
1973	8	5	1	1	1				
1974	7	2	4		1				
1975	10	6	3		1				
1976	9	7	2						
1977	8	4	4						
1978	8	6	2						
1979	4		3		1				
1980	12	6	3		2	1			
1981	17	3	6	2	3	2	1		
1982	13	2	5		1	4	1		
1983	13	2	7			3	1		
1984	7		3			4			
1985	13	2	4		2	3	2		
1986	15	5	5			5			
1987	14	2	8		1	2			1
1988	16	6	4	1	1	4			
1989	24	4	13		2	2	2	1	
1990	35	4	27		1	2	1		
1991	15	6	6		1	1			1
1992	14	2	7		2	2			1
1993	21	10	2		3	2	1	3	
1994	9	5	2		2				
1995	21	3	12		1		1	4	
1996	15	0	12		2				1
1997	11	3	5					2	1
1998	10	2	4		1		1	2	
1999	3		3						
Total	419	143	169	8	34	37	11	12	5

Source: MMC database.
Notes: Newspapers, etc., includes one report on restrictive labour practices and one on broadcasting.
'Section 11' includes efficiency reports on nationalised industries and three reports providing information.
Reports analysed by date of signature up to May 1999.
Anti-comp. = report on an anti-competitive practice.
Utility = licence or price adjudications.
Airport = price control reports on regulated airports.

The development of legislation

The conventional way of recounting the history of post-war competition policy is through the series of legislative enactments. There is a conventional wisdom about the inspiration and the objectives of each Act and, indeed, they are landmarks and need to be mapped. The accumulation of Acts had produced by 1997 a very complex and unsatisfactory state of affairs. We can review developments to see how this tottering pile of legislative provisions came to be erected.

The background and content of the 1948 Act were examined in chapter 1. The subsequent major Acts are the:

- Monopolies and Restrictive Practices Commission Act 1953
- Restrictive Trade Practices Act 1956
- Resale Prices Act 1964
- Monopolies and Mergers Act 1965
- Restrictive Trade Practices Act 1968.

The above repealed, the following in effect in 1997:

- Fair Trading Act 1973
- Resale Prices Act 1976
- Restrictive Trade Practices Acts 1976 and 1977
- Competition Act 1980
- Telecommunications Act 1984
- Transport Act 1985
- Airports Act 1986
- Financial Services Act 1986
- Gas Act 1986
- Companies Act 1989
- Water Act 1989
- Electricity Act 1989
- Broadcasting Act 1990
- Water Industry Act 1991
- Railways Act 1993
- Deregulation and Contracting Out Act 1994.

This is a formidable total of twenty-one Acts, sixteen of which were still applicable in 1997. The pace of legislation had become frenetic in the late 1980s in pursuit of sector-specific regulation.

The first legislative step was taken in 1953 when the Conservative Government responded to wide criticism of the modest coverage and substantial delays of the MRPC by strengthening its organisation.

Membership was expanded to sixteen and the Commission was permitted to work in groups of not less than five. It was also permitted to appoint a Deputy Chairman but David Cairns was cautious on this score and continued to Chair all the inquiries personally. The Commission's budget almost doubled between 1953 and 1956 and the pace of work, and of reports, increased markedly. The contemporary MMC is, in fact, still operating the '1953 model'.

But the MRPC sowed the seeds of its own downfall, in two respects. First, it proved too active. The roll call of complaints has become relatively familiar and included the inquisitorial nature of the MMC investigations; the alleged lack of clarity of the case 'against' the company; the vagueness of the public interest test; the lack of a right to see third-party allegations or to reply to conclusions; the amount of money and senior management time required; and the unpredictability of the BoT response.[32] These complaints were expressed forcibly by business-people, companies and the Federation of British Industry (FBI), and they had a significant impact, especially on Peter Thorneycroft (President of the BoT, 1951–56) and Lord Kilmuir (the Lord Chancellor, formerly David Maxwell-Fyfe). Business dissatisfaction took a stronger form than mere complaints. In her extended discussion of these events Mercer argues that business 'did hamstring the administration of the Commission by the BoT' and was sufficiently agitated to persuade Thorneycroft and Kilmuir to turn to a legal solution. Kilmuir noted that business opposition to the Commission was the 'sole motive' for the 1956 Bill.[33]

The second respect is the Commission's first general report, on *Collective Discrimination*.[34] The conventional view is that the 1956 Act grew out of a gradually increasing public dissatisfaction with restrictive practices, which culminated in the analysis, presented in *Collective Discrimination*, and made legislation inevitable. Certainly the report was influential and had an impact on the form of the 1956 Act. The reference had been made in December 1952; it was signed in May 1955 and published in June. It condemned the practices it reviewed as operating against the public interest and advocated a general prohibition to be incorporated in new legislation; thus, 'we believe that all the practices falling within our reference should be prohibited by law, provision being made for exemptions on grounds which would be set out in the legislation'.[35] This is very close to the method established under Article 85 of the Rome Treaty, which the report pre-dates (although it does not pre-date the 1951 Treaty of Paris, which created the European Coal and Steel Community and has similar Articles). However, a three-page minority report, signed by three members (Sir Thomas Barnes, Brian Davidson and Professor Goodhart), was not prepared to endorse a blanket prohibition and instead advocated the principle of registration and examination. The Government followed the minority report and chose to set up legal machinery through the Registrar of Restrictive Trade Agreements and the Restrictive Practices Court. This was probably not what the Commission had envisaged; neither did it have the support of the judiciary, which 'reluctantly returned to the field of restrictive practices agreements, from which it had been painfully extricating itself for the previous sixty years'.[36] It did, however, enjoy business support and occasioned Kilmuir great satisfaction. The Act created the dual system in Britain of administrative control of monopolies and mergers, and judicial control of restrictive practices.

After decades of a permissive approach by the judiciary to restrictive practices business might have expected a lax regime to be established under the Court. There is, in fact, no particularly rigorous expectation built into the legislation, which also has a range of exceptions and loopholes inserted as a result of special pleading. In fact the Court, initially under Mr Justice (later Lord) Devlin, proceeded to bowl over restrictive agreements and to send shock waves through industry which transformed the cosy world of cartels and restrictive practices. Mercer argues that Thorneycroft may even have expected and exploited this possibility: 'it seems from circumstantial evidence that a wily devotee of competition, Peter Thorneycroft, used the businessmen's own programme against them'.[37] She also argues that the general effect was to create a vigorous regime that eliminated a huge range of restrictive practices, while creating a very relaxed regime (through the slimmed-down MC) for controlling large firms and oligopolies. Business was shocked by the former but anticipated and welcomed the latter.

The 1956 Act was regarded initially as a breakthrough and is seen as the single most successful piece of British competition legislation. The widespread cartel agreements that prevailed in British industry in the early 1950s were effectively eliminated by the mid 1960s. Cartels still exist but they are rare – or they are rarely identified – and are treated as improper and exceptional. But the RTPA was already coming under criticism even after its biggest successes. Stevens and Yamey chart the initial 'euphoric'[38] response to the Act but by 1965 were beginning to identify serious flaws in the model – in the proceedings, the findings and the impact on industry at large. Latterly the need to maintain the administration of the Act with its labour-intensive register, formalistic agreements and relatively inactive Court has been a source of immense frustration to the OFT and successive DGFTs. The picture became quite surreal after the 1988 Green Paper, which officially exposed the weaknesses of the Act to public gaze. It declared that 'the registration system will be scrapped' yet left the unfortunate OFT to administer it for a further ten years.[39]

For the MC the 1956 RTPA was little short of disastrous. It was the Commission's 'night of the long knives'. The 1953 Act was repealed and the Commission was returned to its 1948 constitution. Ten members were removed, including the Chairman, Sir David Cairns, and five of the seven members who had signed the *Collective Discrimination* majority report. While Thorneycroft did not follow his instincts and abolish the Commission it went into decline and, with very few referrals, with the elimination of group working and with a brief to deal only with large firm monopolies, it signed only six reports from 1957 to 1965. In four of those nine years it signed no reports at all.

The saviour of the MC was the 1965 Monopolies and Mergers Act. Although passed by Labour, the Act was essentially Conservative in its origins and design, and is discussed in chapter 7. The Act returned the Commission to the 1953 arrangements, with an authorised membership of up to twenty-five, up to three Deputy Chairmen and authority for group working. It extended the monopolies legislation to services and provided for the momentous new competence of merger control. In some ways the 1965 Act was an incremental development of powers. It took the important, and perhaps mistaken, step of consigning merger control to the same investigatory process, and the same public interest test, as monopolies. Several sources of concern had come together to persuade the Conservatives to legislate and to produce the 1964 White Paper which heralded the 1965 Act.[40] Thus ministers were concerned about resale price maintenance and about the competitiveness of the economy, as well as the ways in which the RTPA was being circumvented. The rapidly increasing concern about mergers and hostile takeovers probably made legislation necessary but, as chapter 7 outlines, there was a lot of hesitancy over merger control and a strong disinclination to deter 'benign' mergers. In this respect the tentative and exploratory nature of the 1948 Act was mirrored in the exploratory coloration of merger control in the 1965 Act. Certainly ministers were careful to maintain political discretion and the wide swathe of non–economic criteria embraced by the public interest test.

The early forays into merger control in the 1960s were therefore modest and, as has repeatedly been stressed, the Labour Governments were far more concerned with strategic intervention and with building national champions through the IRC (see chapter 7). The MC did, however, become significantly more active on the monopoly front and had a raft of influential references under Douglas Jay as President of the BoT in 1965 and 1966. It hence began its first engagement with industries in which MMC findings have had a profound influence on structure and development. This period saw the first engagement with flat glass, detergents and petrol retailing. Equally the reference on beer which was the first in a long drawn-out involvement with the industry, and important references on film distribution and photographic film processing. In the later 1960s the pace of references slowed but in 1969–70 the Commission made three general reports (on resale price maintenance, refusal to supply and professional services). It also produced *obiter dictum* – general comments on mergers published in June 1968 with the merger reports on the conglomerate mergers of *Unilever/Allied Breweries* and *Rank/DeLaRue* (Unilever was permitted, Rank found to be against the public interest). The general comments were most unusual. They were accompanied by suggestions for the further disclosure of information by companies and represent the MC attempting to derive general principles and to contribute to a debate about policy.

After 1970 the course of policy was dominated by the industrial policy travails of the Heath Government and by the debates surrounding the 1973 Fair Trading Act. Before the passage of the Act the Commission's workload had moderated but a trickle of monopoly references reflected the instincts of Nicholas Ridley, at that time Parliamentary Under-Secretary of State. Thus in 1971 came important references on breakfast cereals (which created a prolonged system of price monitoring) and the spectacular valium, librium reference which caused Hoffman La Roche so much money and embarrassment (hailed as a 'giant step' forward;[41] see chapter 9). After the passage of the Act, which came into force in October 1973, the picture changed. The Act is analysed in chapters 6 and 9. It created new consumer protection competencies, extended the RTPA to services, and lowered the threshold for monopoly and merger references from one-third to one-quarter of the market. A new statement of the public interest in Article 84 stressed competition but retained the all-encompassing formula that 'the Commission shall take into account all matters'. To this extent it is reasonable to describe the Act as essentially a consolidation of earlier legislation. Its true impact, however, was far more significant.

As a general principle, as outlined in chapter 1, the institutional framework which grows up around a policy area has a fundamental influence not only on the implementation but also on the content of policy. This is possibly even truer for competition policy than for direct programmes of service provision and spending. Competition policy is aimed at regulating the private sector and is permeated with discretion, judgement, lobbying and self-regulation. In some respects administration of the policy *is* the policy. (One is reminded of the serious definition of Japanese industrial policy as 'what MITI does'). From this perspective the Fair Trading Act had a huge impact by redesigning the machinery of policy implementation. The creation of the DGFT transformed competition policy by creating a consumer and competition advocate within a tripartite system and thereby modified the functions of the BoT and of the renamed MMC.

The 1970s were a difficult decade for government relations with industry. These were the 'Jekyll and Hyde years'[42] of adversary politics which saw abrupt reversals of industrial policy between governments and strong antipathies between the interventionist preferences of Labour (indeed, the directive philosophy of Tony Benn) and the free-market neo-liberalism of Sir Keith Joseph and the Tory Right. But the MMC existed on the sidelines during these conflicts. It was insulated (or marginalised) partly by virtue of its allocation to one of the smallest and least important departments into which Wilson had split the giant DTI. The MMC answered to the DPCP, and hence to Shirley Williams and Roy Hattersley. Its star was therefore linked both to the OFT and to expectations of inflation and price control. Undoubtedly an important, and even a dominant, issue in the mid 1970s, with inflation reaching 25 per cent in 1975, this preoccupation with inflation nonetheless divorced competition policy from its 'proper' concern with competitive processes and industrial efficiency. The consumer bias was accentuated under the first Director General, John Methven. His first report as DGFT noted that 'much of my time and attention has been given to the consumer affairs side of my Office', while his second report stressed negotiation and voluntary undertakings so that 'complaints about market powers can be handled without recourse to a formal and necessarily lengthy investigation by the Monopolies and Mergers Commission'.[43] In this atmosphere the MMC was handed little more than a trickle of monopoly and merger cases, and it certainly did not become a major instrument of industrial policy.

The cases that were referred to the MMC in the 1970s included important industries and serious public interest issues but they were less than central to the heart of the productive economy. The bias was towards retail, distribution and consumer services. Thus there was a raft of eleven professional service reports in 1976–78 and monopoly inquiries included frozen foods, cat and dog foods, and ice cream. With inquiries also into bread, contraceptive sheaths and ceramic sanitaryware the MMC was concerning itself with the essentials of civilised life. But again, these tended to be final product markets and, as in the 1960s, the MMC was seen as incompatible with the interventionist, rationalising side of government policy, which operated under the banner of Labour's 'industrial strategy'.

This ostensible tension between competition policy and the industrial strategy provoked the inter-departmental Liesner Committee's Green Paper on Monopolies and Mergers which reported in May 1978[44] and was followed by a Green Paper on Restrictive Practices.[45] The Liesner monopolies report was thorough and conveyed an increased scepticism about concentration and the benefits of merger, as well as the need 'to resolve apparent conflicts between competition policy and some measures adopted in furtherance of the industrial strategy'.[46] The report explored overlaps with the Price Commission and advocated a shift in the burden of proof on mergers. These proposals, including the proposed marriage with the Price Commission, are explored further in chapter 9; they fell at the 1979 election. The two reports did have a more lasting legacy. They also explored drawbacks in monopoly control and proposed a new system of control to deal with the uncompetitive practices of dominant firms more swiftly and effectively than the MMC investigations under the Fair Trading Act. In the now familiar pattern of bi-partisan legislation, the Labour proposals were adopted by the Conservatives and formed the basis of the 1980 Competition Act.

The Competition Act had some radical implications. It filled a significant loophole by targeting anti-competitive practices of individual firms. While not strictly a separate category from Fair Trading Act investigations, it could target firms rather than industries, practices rather than products, and cases of market dominance rather than formally defined monopoly. It was anticipated that it would provide a flexible tool and it generated a certain amount of angst within the Confederation of British Industry (CBI). In practical terms it gave the DGFT much more discretion and encouraged him to investigate and to negotiate voluntary (but publicised) undertakings on pain of a second-stage investigation through reference to the MMC. Again, it was anticipated that this arrangement would greatly empower the DGFT and could systematically by-pass the MMC. Finally, the Competition Act was groundbreaking in the test it applied. It was explicitly inspired by Article 85 and was targeted at conduct which is 'intended to have or is likely to have the effect of restricting, distorting or preventing competition' (section 2(1)). This is an effects-based provision, novel in British competition law, although the second stage, reference to the MMC, did again draw on the ubiquitous public interest test.

The Competition Act also contained provisions not anticipated in the closing days of the Callaghan Government. Clause 1 emphatically underlined the Conservatives' commitment to market forces by abolishing the Price Commission. But of more profound significance was clause 11, which provided for inquiries into nationalised industries. The Conservative Government lost no time in getting section 11 inquiries underway and for the MMC they proved more important than anti-competitive practices cases. The Commission dealt with only ten anti-competitive practices cases up to 1996 but with thirty-five section 11 inquiries up to 1993, by which time most of the potential clients had been privatised (see chapter 8). The experience with anti-competitive practices proved disappointing. The early cases, and especially the Raleigh case, were extensively criticised[47] and the DGFT used the Act to react to complaints rather than to evolve systematic doctrine. Some of the cases analysed were important but many were trivial and the Act was used in some respects as a poor substitute for specialised bus regulation. When the anti-competitive practices powers were repealed in 1998 Freeman and Whish observed that 'their deletion will be neither greatly noticed nor lamented'.[48]

The Competition Act did symbolise the start of an important decade which put competition policy at centre stage and generated unprecedented volumes of work for the MMC. It symbolised a shift to competition as a criterion; to a focus on nationalised industries and post-privatisation regulation; to a proliferation of duties for the competition agencies; and, most of all, it underlined the novel and principled commitment of Conservative industry ministers to liberal market competition. The MMC went from four cases signed in 1979 to twelve in 1980 and seventeen in 1981. Although 1980 was a legislative turning point, it was to a greater extent a political and a policy turning point as competition was entrenched as a central plank in the Conservative platform. The place of the MMC in this rediscovery of competition was important but not central. While the MMC was much more active it did not get its teeth into the giant monopolies until the end of the decade. Many of the cases were mergers, newspapers and small industries – what might be called 'niche monopolies'. Thus Walshe rather brutally observed that 'the picture conjured up … by this motley collection from the foothills of British industry may not seem very familiar … It would seem that monopoly policy was relatively dormant in the 1980s.'[49]

The background to the 1998 Competition Act is rehearsed in chapter 9. The great paradox of the 1980s was why the Conservatives failed to legislate to reform competition policy despite the manifest inadequacy of policy and practice. The first official step towards reform came as early as June 1986, when Paul Channon set up a review of restrictive trade practices policy; although his immediate predecessor, Leon Brittan, had also been in favour of a policy review. There then came a Green Paper in March 1988[50] and a White Paper in July 1989.[51] But progress was almost unbelievably slow. When he retired in 1992 Gordon Borrie reflected that, 'My greatest disappointment ... is the failure of the Government to strengthen the law on cartels and other restrictive trading agreements.'[52] Neil Hamilton, as junior DTI Minister, did announce comprehensive legislation in April 1993 and a draft Bill was published in August 1996, but it was not until Labour entered office that the Bill was actually introduced.

Delays in law reform on this scale are hard to explain or to justify. The course of the debate and the eventual decision to embark on a comprehensive redesign of policy are examined in chapter 9. In fact, for the MMC, there was no shortage of legislative innovation. For the Conservative Governments in the round it could be argued that reform of competition law as such was less important than the radical steps taken to liberalise markets and to increase competition across the whole economy. Into this broad agenda one would put the abolition of exchange controls and the introduction of a framework to regulate industrial relations. Indeed, it is difficult to know where to stop. Competition was introduced into financial markets, housing, health care, pensions, training – it had become a governing principle of policy innovation. The most dramatic examples of competition obsession, and here with a direct effect on the competition policy institutions, were privatisation and utility regulation. Beginning with the 1984 Telecommunications Act the industry regulators became themselves competition regulators and, as chapter 8 outlines, the regulators had been given explicit instructions to create competition. Their formal powers paralleled those of the DGFT to refer monopolies, anti-competitive practices and mergers to the MMC (indeed, reference of substantial water industry mergers is compulsory), and concurrent powers are perpetuated in the 1998 Competition Act. In addition, the MMC has taken on a new role of adjudication in respect of licence modifications. In the event of disagreement over licence changes the regulator is obliged to refer the matter to the MMC for investigation. The huge and dramatic licence cases have developed in relation to British Gas and its successors but the MMC has also been involved in water, electricity and telecommunications. By the early 1990s the relatively simple legislative framework of the 1970s was a matter of nostalgia. The responsibilities of the OFT and the MMC were to be found in the raft of sixteen Acts listed earlier in this chapter.

Landmarks in the development of UK competition policy

In retrospect 1973 was the pivotal year for UK competition policy. Partly this is due to the obvious fact that this was the year of the Fair Trading Act and the creation of the OFT; but also to be weighed in the balance is Britain's entry into the EEC on 1 January 1973. Reformers in the 1960s had examined European practice and noted with care the provisions of Articles 85 and 86 of the Rome Treaty, but the EEC policy was embryonic and weak, there was no provision for merger control and certain ministers, especially Douglas Jay, were vehemently 'anti-Europe'. Accordingly the UK went its own way. By the 1980s European competition policy was beginning to come of age, and under Frans Andriesson, Peter Sutherland and Leon Brittan as Competition Commissioners during the 1980s policy became much more effective, especially in relation to Article 85. The constitutional superiority of European law required that Britain should adjust its practices but the European impact was subtler. It challenged and inspired the UK authorities, it changed the atmosphere in which competition policy was evaluated and, perhaps most significant of all, it required British companies and their legal advisers to take competition law very seriously indeed.

The impact of 'Europe' is evaluated in later chapters, as is the development of the various competencies briefly introduced in this chapter. Here we can hazard some early speculations about the varying salience of competition policy in the UK and the role of the MMC as part of those variations. But first one important caveat. The earlier discussion is based on the 'internal' evolution of competition policy; it is inward looking. Occasionally it has been possible to locate developments in relation to the evolution of other aspects of economic policy, such as the balance of payments, industrial restructuring and inflation control. But there is insufficient space to do justice to the political or to the economic and industrial context.

In general it is not unreasonable to maintain that the need for competition policy is related to the general level of competition within the economy. Thus we saw in chapter 1 that it is widely accepted that Britain's free-trade stance prior to the 1930s made competition policy less necessary, and that the post-war policy on restrictive practices was partly necessitated by government-administered protectionism and economic controls. Over the post-war period competition policy can be related to trends in industrial concentration, changes in industrial structure (and the rise of service industries), trends in inward investment, to the liberalisation of trade, and to the growth in Europeanisation and globalisation. These trends are well treated in standard economic and political-economic texts[53] and they provide a context that should not be overlooked. Thus the trends in concentration are important both in defining a need for policy and in judging its success. Concentration provides a rough guide to trends in monopolisation, and the considerable increase in concentration during the 1970s engendered much comment.[54] Similarly, domestic concentration is of less concern in competition terms if it can be challenged by inward investment or by imports. Britain has always had a high propensity to import but the structure of imports has changed dramatically over the post-war period, away from food and raw materials towards manufactures. As successive rounds of the General Agreement on Tariffs and Trade and membership of the EEC brought tariff reductions, so a strictly domestic interpretation of competition in markets became less and less credible. Thus, over the fifty years, the application of competition policy in Britain has to be related to the nature of the problem. In 1948 the economy was monopolised, cartelised, corporatist, protected and internationally powerful. In 1998 Britain's economy might still have been monopolised but it was no longer cartelised or corporatist. It was exposed as never before to the pressures of global trade and was a medium-sized competitor in world markets.

The transformation of the domestic British economy changed the context in which competition policy worked and the problems it addressed. Could one argue that competition policy was in part the cause of that transformation? As we saw at the beginning of the chapter, Freyer does indeed argue that competition policy was instrumental in aiding the transformation of industrial structure from a family-owned model to one dominated by managerially controlled large corporations. It achieved this by attacking cartels and restrictive practices far more stringently than monopolies or mergers. The outcome was large, often conglomerate companies and the growth of aggressive management teams running multi-divisional and dominant corporations. But it is hard to argue that competition policy did much more than assist this transformation. In contrast it is not hard to find a range of academic opinion that is sceptical of the impact of policy. In fact the dominant academic view is sceptical. Morgan's conclusions are typical of mainstream opinion. He argues that significant successes were scored in the areas of restrictive practices and resale price maintenance; but that 'the record for matters within the province of the MMC is more chequered'.[55] Walshe is more critical. He doubts the lasting effectiveness even of restrictive practices measures. He suggests that the efforts devoted to competition policy have not yielded commensurate benefits and that 'after a promising, if dilatory, start in the immediate post-war period, policy was largely passive, allowing oligopolization to proceed unchecked'.[56] Hay's rather more recent assessment expresses some of the impatience almost universally felt by competition policy specialists in the early 1990s. He concludes that policy was badly designed and ineffective, that 'UK competition policy is in need of radical reform' and that 'the institutional arrangements in the UK are a mess'.[57] This is a fairly typical cross-section of views from academic economists. In chapter 10 we come back to the range of evaluations.

Thus far the discussion has been concerned with UK policy in the round and not exclusively with the MMC. In concluding we can characterise the MMC's changing role over the years, taking into account the evolution of competition policy itself but also taking account of the goals of government, the mix of economic policies and the transformation of the industrial economy. The following propositions are impressionistic and heuristic – designed to provide insights, not to present unambiguous categories.

The changing salience of the MRPC/MC/MMC

- *1949–56, experimentation and education:* genuinely speculative investigation which had a considerable effect on industrial and popular opinion, and which culminated in the *Collective Discrimination* report. Few powers, no control, but influence through reports.
- *1956–64, the wilderness years:* reduced resources, few reports, attention shifted to the Registrar of Restrictive Trade Agreements. The government dithers over reform and virtually ignores the Commission.
- *1965–71, establishing credibility:* cases beginning to make an impact, developing a voice in relation to mergers and principles of policy. Increased resources and playing a role as an antidote to the restructuring enthusiasm.
- *1972–84, marking time:* casework in the public interest, role in policy formulation reduced and policy linked to a range of non-competition issues. Significant workload but overshadowed by the OFT.
- *1985–92, renaissance:* of competition policy and of the MMC with greatly increased efficiency and workload, a new utility role. Accumulating respect, trusted to take on new roles.
- *1993–96, a threatened species:* falling under the shadow of 'Europe', dealing with a pressure towards competitiveness and with arguments for a unitary authority.

- *1997– , New Labour, New Commission:* treated very favourably in the Labour legislation. Retaining much of its old role and with major new responsibilities. Prognostications vary from a greatly increased workload and significance to a genteel decline if lawyers avoid appeal to the UK competition tribunals.

As far as the MMC is concerned the historical evolution of policy and administration is picked up over the next three chapters. In chapters 6 and 9 we come back to a broader based and more detailed analysis of the major legislative enactments briefly described above. In chapter 3 we turn to the organisation that has, for fifty years, been at the heart of policy.

Notes

1 C. Baillieu, *The Lion and the Lamb* (London, Wilfred Street for the Conservative 2000 Foundation, 1996), p. 14.

2 For a stimulating review of the 'paradoxes of competition' see T. Burke, A. Genn-Bash and B. Haines, *Competition in Theory and Practice* (London, Croom Helm, 1988), ch. 1.

3 Theodore Kovaleff, 'Introduction: symposium in commemoration of the 60th anniversary of the establishment of the Antitrust Division', *The Antitrust Bulletin*, XXXIX: 4 (Winter 1994), p. 813.

4 R. Peritz, *Competition Policy in America 1888–1992* (Oxford University Press, 1996), p. 43.

5 Dame Alix Meynell, *Public Servant, Private Woman* (London, Gallancz, 1988), pp. 260–1.

6 A noted specialist was Sir Alan Neale, a BoT civil servant and later Deputy Chairman of the Commission, who wrote a well-regarded study of the American system: A. D. Neale and D. G. Goyder, *The Antitrust Laws of the U.S.A.* (Cambridge University Press, third edn, 1980, first published 1960).

7 The first quote is R. Whish, *Competition Law* (London, Butterworths, third edn, 1993), p. 730; the second is from T. Frazer, *Monopoly, Competition and the Law* (London, Harvester Wheatsheaf, second edn, 1992), p. 4.

8 See Roland Sturm, 'The German cartel office in a hostile environment', in B. Doern and S. Wilks (eds), *Comparative Competition Policy* (Oxford, Clarendon, 1996), pp. 196–8.

9 There is a huge literature but initial surveys are offered by P. Auerbach, *Competition: The Economics of Industrial Change* (Oxford, Basil Blackwell, 1980); and D. Hay and D. J. Morris, *Industrial Economics and Organization: Theory and Evidence* (Oxford University Press, second edn, 1991).

10 D. Hay, 'The assessment: competition policy', *Oxford Review of Economic Policy*, 9:2 (Summer 1993), p. 2.

11 S. Deakin, T. Goodwin and A. Hughes, *Cooperation and Trust in Inter-Firm Relations: Beyond Competition Policy?* (Cambridge, ESRC Centre for Business Research, WP 79, December 1997), p. 31.

12 Dame Alix Kilroy, 'The task and methods of the Monopolies Commission', *The Manchester School*, XXII:1 (January 1954), p. 38.

13 T. Freyer, *Regulating Big Business: Antitrust in Great Britain and America 1880–1990* (Cambridge University Press, 1992), pp. 269, 332.

14 H. Mercer, *Constructing a Competitive Order: The Hidden History of British Antitrust Policies* (Cambridge University Press, 1995), p. 170.

15 Department of Prices and Consumer Protection (DPCP), *A Review of Monopolies and Mergers Policy*, Cmnd 7198 (London, HMSO, May 1978), p. 5.

16 See 'Introduction', in J. Fairburn and J. Kay (eds), *Mergers and Merger Policy* (Oxford University Press, 1989), pp. 8–13.

17 M. Howe, 'Efficiency and competition policy', in C. Bowe (ed.), *Industrial Efficiency and the Role of Government* (London, HMSO, 1977), p. 41; the two firms were Imperial Tobacco (MMC, *Cigarettes and Tobacco*, HC 218 (London, HMSO, 1961)) and Turner and Newall (MMC, *Asbestos and Certain Asbestos Products*, HC 3 (London, HMSO, 1973)).

18 A recent case cited in this context is *The Supply of National Newspapers*, Cm 2422 (London, HMSO, 1993).

19 M. Porter, *The Competitive Advantage of Nations* (London, Macmillan, 1990).

20 For discussion of this paradigm shift see V. Wright, 'Conclusion: the state and major enterprises in Western Europe', in J. Hayward (ed.), *Industrial Enterprise and European Integration: From National to International Champions in Western Europe* (Oxford University Press, 1995).

21 DPCP, *A Review of Monopolies and Mergers Policy*, p. 1.

22 TIC, *UK Policy on Monopolies*, 1994–95, HC 249–I (May 1995), p. xxxi.

23 Burke *et al.*, *Competition in Theory and Practice*, pp. 186, 212.

24 A criticism voiced by the National Consumers' Council, *Competition and Consumers* (London, NCC, 1995), pp. 59–60.

25 Mercer, *Constructing a Competitive Order*, p. 102.

26 A. Sutherland, *The Monopolies Commission in Action* (Cambridge University Press, 1970), p. 68.

27 BoT, *Annual Report by the BoT,1950*, HC118 (London, HMSO, 1951), p. 5.

28 Lord Howe of Aberavon, 'The birth of an office: a midwife's view', OFT, collected papers from a conference on fair trading organised at the Café Royal, London (May 1992), p. 10.

29 TIC, *UK Policy*, p. xxiii.

30 J. Jewkes, 'British monopoly policy 1944–56', *Journal of Law and Economics*, 1:1 (October 1958), p. 8.

31 G. C. Allen, *The Structure of Industry in Britain* (London, Longman, second edn, 1966), p. 70.

32 A nice early summary of criticism is given in R. Stevens and B. Yamey, *The Restrictive Practices Court* (London, Weidenfeld and Nicolson, 1965), p. 13.

33 Mercer, *Constructing a Competitive Order*, p. 109; D. Maxwell-Fyfe, *Political Adventure* (London, Weidenfeld and Nicolson, 1964), p. 261.

34 *Collective Discrimination: A Report on Exclusive Dealing, Collective Boycotts, Aggregated Rebates and Other Discriminatory Trading Practices*, Cmnd 9504 (London, HMSO, June 1955).

35 *Ibid.*, p. 86.

36 Stevens and Yamey, *The Restrictive Practices Court*, p. 19.

37 Mercer, *Constructing a Competitive Order*, p. 147.
38 Stevens and Yamey, *The Restrictive Practices Court*, pp. 6–7.
39 DTI, *Review of Restrictive Trade Practices: A Consultative Document*, Cm 331 (London, HMSO, March 1988).
40 BoT, *Monopolies, Mergers and Restrictive Practices*, Cmnd 2299 (London, HMSO, March 1964).
41 L. Rhinelander, 'The Roche case: one giant step for British antitrust', *Virginia Journal of International Law*, 16:1 (Fall 1974). The original report was 'Chlordiazepoxide and diazepam'.
42 M. Stewart, *Politics and Economic Policy in the UK Since 1964: The Jekyll and Hyde Years* (Oxford University Press, 1977).
43 Annual reports by the DGFT, 1974, HC370 (London, HMSO, 1975), p. 10; 1975, HC258 (London, HMSO, 1976), p. 11.
44 DPCP, *A Review of Monopolies and Mergers Policy*.
45 DPCP, *A Review of Restrictive Trade Practices Policy*, Cmnd 7512 (London, HMSO, 1979).
46 DPCP, *A Review of Monopolies and Mergers Policy*, p. 6.
47 See E. V. Morgan, *Monopolies, Mergers and Restrictive Practices: UK Competition Policy 1948–87*, Hume Paper 7 (Edinburgh, The David Hume Institute, 1987), pp. 30–3; J. Kay and T. Sharpe, 'The anti-competitive practice', *Fiscal Studies*, 3 (1982), pp. 191–8.
48 P. Freeman and R. Whish, *A Guide to the Competition Act 1998* (London, Butterworths, 1999), p. 111.
49 J. G. Walshe, 'Industrial organization and competition policy', in N. Crafts and N. Woodward (eds), *The British Economy Since 1945* (Oxford, Clarendon, 1991), p. 369.
50 DTI, *Review of Restrictive Trade Practices Policy: A Consultative Document*, Cm 331 (London, HMSO, March 1988).
51 DTI, *Opening Markets: New Policy on Restrictive Trade Practices*, Cm 727 (London, HMSO, July 1989).
52 OFT, *Annual Report of the Director General of Fair Trading, 1991*, HC 38 (London, HMSO, 1992), p. 12.
53 For instance, Hay and Morris, *Industrial Economics and Organization*; R. Floud and D. McCloskey (eds), *The Economic History of Britain Since 1700, Volume 3: 1939–1992* (Cambridge University Press, second edn, 1994); Crafts and Woodward, *The British Economy Since 1945*.
54 For instance, S. Prais, *The Evolution of Giant Firms in Britain* (Cambridge University Press, 1976).
55 Morgan, *Monopolies, Mergers and Restrictive Practices*, p. 54.
56 Walshe, 'Industrial Organization', pp. 374, 379.
57 Hay, 'The assessment', p. 21.

3

The MMC: structure and powers

The MMC is a distinctive and in some ways a contradictory body. It displays considerable continuity in organisation but has also adapted to a range of new obligations. What is equally interesting is that it combines extensive independence with an organisational structure and culture which is very similar to that of the traditional British civil service. It is at once an integrated part of the Whitehall machine, yet distinctively separate, thus presenting one of the several paradoxes encountered in the course of this study.

The MMC is a small organisation which has never employed more than 120 people. It is also sober and modest. It inhabits anonymous offices behind the Law Courts, its members do not trumpet their activities, its Chairmen are cautious and self-effacing in their public appearances, and discretion is taken as a dominant virtue. Traditionally press conferences were seldom held and the Commission does not embark upon debate about the content of its reports or their reception. All of these characteristics spring from a common fount – the ingrained belief that the MMC must be impartial in its approach – and sustain the appearance and the practice of strict independence. This is not only political or administrative independence; it is more properly thought of as independence of mind. Each case is different, each investigatory group has its own dynamic, each report is unique and members enter upon an investigation with no preconceptions. This is a tremendous virtue, but it can also be a handicap.

The nature of the MMC's independence, and the fashion in which it has been elevated into a primary goal, is partly a product of legislation. Equally, however, it is to do with how the organisation and its self-definition have evolved over fifty years, and with its relationship with the BoT and its successors. Organisationally the 1948 legislation was highly permissive. It gave the Commission authority to devise its own approach to investigations, to construct its own procedures, to operate in public or under oath, and to demand the production of papers and the attendance of witnesses on pain of significant sanctions (including imprisonment). Similarly the Commission was allowed extensive discretion in the style, thoroughness and, to some extent, the content of reports. But despite this procedural leeway the legislation said nothing explicitly about 'independence'. In fact it would not take a particularly partial reading of the Act to conclude (as was in fact the case) that the Commission was to be quite 'dependent' on the BoT. In its comments on the draft Bill the *Economist* had already argued that 'the powers retained by the Board of Trade are too great for the Commission to be called independent'.[1] Hence the Commission began life with an endowment that in some respects gave it considerable room for manoeuvre but in other respects provided strict restraints. The way in which discretion was exploited involved some definite choices which did not necessarily extend the Commission's room for manoeuvre. The choices were made by the early Chairmen and by the Commission's first Secretary, both responding to fairly direct promptings from ministers and officials in the BoT.

There is a long-running debate about the relative influence of structure and agency in organisations. On the structural side the MMC's duties to inquire and report tended to dictate certain organisational requirements. At the same time the people appointed and their definition of the problems would be equally, if not more, influential. The BoT was certainly well aware of the importance of people. Early BoT papers outlined the preferred qualities of the Chairman,[2] who should be 'a person of standing … with plenty of drive without being headstrong',[3] but they also wanted someone who would be biddable. Later papers, as noted in chapter 4, stressed the need to secure a competent, well known and trusted Chairman. This, together with the appointment of an able, determined Commission, pre-ordained a certain level of independence. Prominent figures are unlikely to be tolerant of official steering, and the Royal Commission parallel is suggestive. Nonetheless, it is intriguing to note how firmly the priority of independence has become embedded in the culture of the Commission, so that both structure and agency have given it a character that is 'quasi-judicial'.

There are important international parallels to the MMC's pursuit of independence. Most competition jurisdictions similarly attach ostensible independence to their competition agencies. The precursor is obviously the Federal Trade Commission, which is, by definition, an independent regulatory commission, but it is striking how that model has been followed in Canada, Australia, Japan, the UK and Germany. It is a model that became widespread in the 1990s as those many countries which adopted competition competencies did so through formally independent agencies. The main exception was the EU, and this has itself created a minor debate about the virtues of a 'European Cartel Office'.[4] The pattern is of governments anxious to distance themselves from the detailed administration of competition rules. Before embarking on speculation about the Commission's level of independence it is as well, however, to outline in detail its structure and powers. The following discussion presents a portrait of the MMC in the mid 1990s. It goes on to chart the origins of the organisation, why it grew up as it did and some of the continuing topics of debate. The major organisational turning points are then briefly touched upon before coming back to the question of independence and a discussion of the forces of change and path dependence which produced the structure which became, on 1 April 1999, the reporting side of the new Competition Commission.

The MMC in the 1990s

By the mid 1990s the MMC had become a highly professional body, in organisation more akin to a management consultancy or a merchant bank than to the leisurely investigatory body of myth and fable. Many things were recognisably the same as the early Commission, especially the size, the procedures, the legislative requirements and the public interest test; but the workload had greatly intensified, the degree of management necessary was unprecedented and a relatively stylised routine had become essential.

In March 1998 the MMC had an authorised complement of fifty members with forty members actually in post and a further thirteen members on the specialised newspaper or utility panels. The membership is analysed in more depth in chapter 4. Dr Derek Morris had taken over as Chairman in February 1998, following the early retirement of Sir Graeme Odgers. Like previous Chairmen he was the only full-time member and was aided by two Deputy Chairmen, Denise Kingsmill and Graham Corbett. The MMC has operated with three Deputy Chairmen since 1982 but the third appointment had been delayed until the Commission had a better sense of the requirements of the Competition Act.

Deputy Chairmen work three to four days per week and all the other members are part time with a notional commitment of one and a half days per week. They may engage in analysis but in practice the research and the writing are undertaken by staff under the Secretary, in 1998 Penny Boys, a grade 3 civil servant on secondment from the DTI. The role of Secretary is important. He or she is given formal standing in the Fair Trading Act and operates as the accounting officer. He or she provides the key link with officials in the DTI, and Secretaries inevitably have considerable influence over the Chairman. The effective operation of the Commission therefore rests on a good working partnership between Secretary and Chairman. To provide a snapshot of the body these partners control, we can consider the main formal aspects of the Commission and, in particular, staffing, organisation, budget, co-ordination, powers, public relations and management.

In March 1998 the MMC employed only seventy-four staff (full-time equivalent). This was the lowest number since 1979, but staff numbers are volatile and vary with the volume of inquiries. Numbers peaked at 119 in 1990 and fell as low as 33 in 1960. Staff include generalist administrators who manage inquiries and specialists who provide more technical analysis. They can be recruited directly by the Commission but the majority of senior staff come on secondment, usually from the DTI but also from the Treasury and other economic departments. The key staff are the team managers who run each inquiry and are, in effect, responsible for the MMC's only product – its reports. Team managers are senior officials (at grade 5 – Assistant Secretary – level) and are typically on secondment, although some have been with the Commission for many years.

The MMC is organised roughly on a 'staff and line' basis, with the added complication of relations between officials and members. Figure 1 places the inquiry teams at the centre of the picture since all MMC activities revolve around inquiries. A typical inquiry team will involve a Chairman, four other members, a team manager and staff from the functional divisions, almost always an accountant and an economist, sometimes an industrial adviser, and a lawyer brought in for advice as necessary. The 'team' is the working unit and it will be administered and co-ordinated by a reference secretary. Some teams have a degree of continuity but on the whole this is a classic matrix organisation, with teams broken up and reconfigured from inquiry to inquiry depending on the workload and the technical requirements. For staff as well as members, teams provide the working environment and generate intense loyalties as staff work to tight deadlines – and sometimes intense frustrations when relationships break down.

The MMC team organisation replicates the traditional civil service pattern of using specialists as advisers to the generalists who direct the investigation, balance the various inputs and draft reports. The skill of

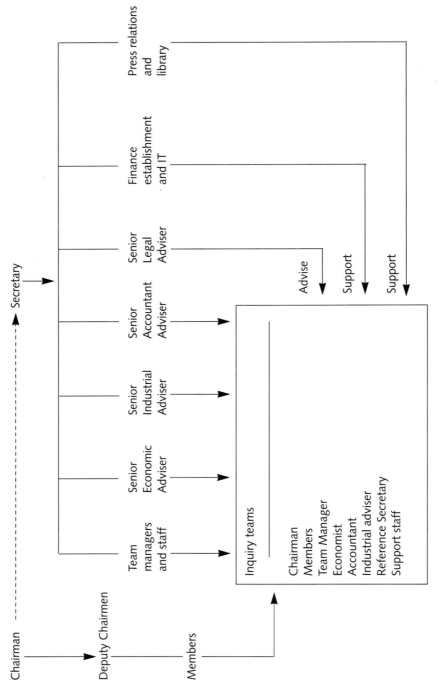

Figure 1 *The make-up of inquiry teams*

report writing is highly developed and highly valued. The make-up of the Commission staff is summarised in table 3.

Table 3 *MMC staffing, 1998*

Division	Head	Staff
Secretary	Penny Boys	
Secretariat	David Fisher	19
Finance and information	Tim Head	16
Personnel	John Dyble	2
Accountants	Tim Head	6
Economists and statisticians	Geoffrey Sumner	6
Industrial advisers	Clive Rix	3
Legal advisers	Jane Richardson	3
Team managers and inquiry staff	John Banfield	23
	Margaret Smith	
	Clive Brewer	
	Alan Williams	
Total		78

Source: MMC, *Organisation Chart and Index to Services* (MMC, Internal Document, September 1998).

Specialist accountants have been employed since 1949 but the other specialisms came later. The first economists were employed in 1971, a formal group of industrial advisers from 1980 when staff were taken over from the Price Commission, but no legal specialists until 1982 when Noel Ing joined the Commission as its first and distinguished legal adviser. Formerly Chairmen such as Sir Ashton Roskill had regarded themselves as 'their own legal adviser', and this limited recourse to legal staff under-lines the non-legalistic nature of the Commission's procedures. Nowa-days in-house lawyers advise on every inquiry, and their role will become more substantial under the new Competition Act, but they are not part of the core investigatory team. Economists, on the other hand, are absolutely central to the inquiries. The relatively late development of a cadre of economic advisers is rather surprising and, when first appointed, they were regarded with great suspicion by the other staff. This speaks of a body in which pragmatism and attention to the specifics of the case were more highly valued than economic skills. The increased prominence given to economists (including the appointment of an economist as Chairman) reflects the increased salience given to competition as a guiding principle. The heads of the specialist divisions are important Commission advisers[5] but the decisive moulding of reports remains in the hands of the team managers.

The inquiry process provides the basic management unit for planning and budgeting, as well as organising. Since the MMC started publishing audited accounts in 1997 it has also released the costs of inquiries – virtually all MMC costs are attributed to inquiries. A merger inquiry is unlikely to exceed £0.5 mn in total cost; utility licence inquiries are more expensive, perhaps up to £0.8 mn, while the monopoly inquiries are likely to cost over £1 mn. The blockbuster *Domestic Electrical Goods* inquiry (technically eight references) cost a massive £3.7 mn. The total budget for 1997–98 was £6.6 mn, which is appreciably less than the OFT's at £20.2 mn. On the other hand, the competition policy sections of the OFT account for only 39 per cent of its costs (£7.9 mn) so, in broad terms, the MMC costs a little less than the competition policy activities of the OFT. (The net cost to the Treasury is substantially lower. The OFT collects fees to cover all aspects of merger investigations.) The accounts also reveal the relatively low level of expenditure on outside consultants and show excellent 'value for money' from members whose total remuneration (excluding Chairmen) was only about £600,000. The Chairman himself received £107,000 in 1996–97 (plus pension contributions), while the Deputy Chairmen received between £45,000 and £55,000. The Secretary earned £73,000 and seven officials received salaries of over £50,000 on standard civil service scales calibrated to the DTI's job evaluation system.[6]

Co-ordinating the Commission presents its own distinctive problems. The unpredictability of the workload is a constant challenge and various devices, such as reserve panels of members and calling part time on panels of retired staff, have been used. Some forewarning is provided by forecasts from the OFT and by Commission attendance at Mergers Panel meetings, but it is difficult to look more than a few weeks ahead. This also makes it difficult to allocate Chairmen and members to groups while still securing the right combination of skill and experience. Co-ordination of work in progress to provide support for inquiry Chairmen and to maintain consistency of approach across inquiries is also important. Under Sir Godfray Le Quesne a steering group operated but it discussed mainly administrative matters. During Sir Sydney Lipworth's Chairmanship from 1988 the remit was extended to cover discussion of inquiries. The group consisted of the Chairman, three Deputy Chairmen, three senior members and the Secretary. The intention was not to influence individual groups but to enhance consistency by comparing notes and 'reading across' principles and problems between groups and their Chairmen. Sir Graeme Odgers replaced the steering group with a Deputy Chairman's Group, which included the three Deputy Chairmen, the Secretary and the Chief Legal Adviser. Derek Morris perpetuated this arrangement. But here the motif of independence surfaces again. The Chairman is independent of the DTI but cannot him- or herself influence the deliberations of groups. In turn Deputy Chairmen often have a difficult task in securing unanimity within a group and dissenting reports are not unusual. As part of this debate on the content of reports the relationship between the staff and the group is complex. While the Secretary has his or her own sphere of responsibility, and in some administrative matters is responsible to officials in the DTI as well as to his or her Chairman, the individual team managers work very closely with their inquiry Chairman in a relationship that is more like a minister/civil servant pattern. The team manager has been described as 'the chairman's aide-de-camp'[7] but, as the 'Yes Minister' genre illustrates, the permanent official who originated the papers often has more influence than at first appears. How much of a report is due to the members and how much to the staff? A perennially interesting question to which we return in chapter 5.

Since the bulk of the MMC's work consists of acquiring and digesting information its organisation reflects these requirements. The procedures for inviting the submission of data are reviewed further in chapter 5, which also emphasises the problems of confidentiality. One striking feature of the process is that the Commission is reactive – it reacts both to the reference process from the OFT and the DTI, and to the information provided by companies. On the whole the process of data acquisition is co-operative. A distinction is frequently drawn between agreed mergers – where companies will race to get information to the Commission quickly – and monopolies where they have no such incentive. But the difficult customers such as Hoffman La Roche are rare.[8] Thus the Commission operates by persuasion and it has only once employed its powers to compel companies to provide people or data (see p. 122). Penalties for wilful destruction of documents or false statements are significant (up to two years' imprisonment), but again they have never been used. Such penalties have certainly been considered. There are cases well known within the Commission of executives who have blatantly lied at hearings, but the Commission has felt that adversary proceedings would be unproductive. It is only in respect of judicial review that legal considerations have had a substantial impact.

This emphasis on co-operative relations with companies under investigation militates in favour of a generous degree of transparency. If companies have a good idea of what the Commission wants and why, they will be in a better position to co-operate. Similarly, if senior company executives have an appreciation of, and even a sympathy for, the MMC approach it will help smooth inquiries and will consolidate the credibility of the competition policy regime. Historically, however, this area of transparency has been one of the Commission's Achilles heels. Up to the mid 1980s the Commission was among the least transparent agencies in Whitehall. The BoT ceased to publish an annual report in 1973, the Commission did not engage in public pronouncements, its procedures were unique and Godfray Le Quesne, like many barristers, paid very little attention to the press. A senior official who joined in the mid 1980s recalls it as a 'murky' body; a senior member talked of 'the mystique' of the Commission at that time.[9] The response of the partnership of Sydney Lipworth (Chairman from 1988) and Stephen Burbridge (Secretary from 1986) was to launch a communications strategy and to summarise the MMC's doctrines and procedures in an accessible form.

The new approach drew on an important investigation of opinion formers' understanding of the Commission which was conducted in the early months of 1988. A substantial interview survey of 140 opinion formers produced a profile of the MMC that was in some ways gratifying but in others worrying. There were some warm comments about fairness, objectivity, independence and competence; but also some negative views about speed, consistency, accessibility and the abilities of junior staff. The survey revealed some serious misunderstandings. Thus, for instance, a third of respondents thought that the MMC could institute its own investigations and, extraordinarily, a fifth thought it could act in mergers on behalf of target companies at their request. On independence only 22 per cent said that 'independence from government pressure' applied a great deal to the MMC and 26 per cent of industrialists thought it did not apply at all. This was worrying in relation to other organisations with which the MMC was compared in the survey. The proportion of respondents who thought that a great deal of independence from government pressure was enjoyed by the Advisory Conciliation and Arbitration Service was 52 per cent; for the Council of the Stock Exchange 46 per cent; and for the OFT 34 per cent. All were therefore seen to be materially more independent than the Commission. The survey also showed a considerable variation among opinion formers. Academics and MPs had the highest opinion of the MMC; trade unionists and the media the lowest. Politicians felt that it was entirely free from government pressure; more conspiratorially minded trade unionists felt that it was subject to a great deal of pressure. The survey identified the old bugbear of speed as the single most important problem facing the Commission. It presented a frank analysis and argued that the Commission should work more quickly and emphasise its independence from Whitehall, the DTI and the OFT. It concluded that 'opinion formers suggested that the MMC could improve its standing ... by having a more public persona in the form of a visible and vocal Chairman. It was also suggested that other officials "come out of their shell" and have more personal contact with those who have to deal with the MMC.'[10] The new Chairman and the Secretary responded to this analysis and embarked on a programme of greater openness and engagement which went some way to changing the image of the Commission in the 1990s, and perhaps improved effectiveness by improving transparency and therefore compliance.

The first manifestation of this new openness was an annual review covering 1988 which was launched with a press conference that was to become an annual event. The Commission also produced a booklet entitled 'The role of the MMC'. A senior official recalls that the DTI greeted these initiatives 'with shock and horror', and that the OFT was also scathing.[11] Sydney Lipworth's Introduction to the 1988 review struck a self-confident note; his 1989 Introduction was even bolder. It commented on law reform and trailed one of his preoccupations – the concentration of powers in European merger control. He then commented on leveraged bids and on 'reciprocity' (code for the Lilley Doctrine). This was unaccustomed openness for the Commission and was followed by a valuable booklet on 'Assessing competition' and even by a video. At the same time the Chairman gave high profile press interviews, and pictures of him against the backdrop of the Law Court spires became a familiar feature of the financial press. By the mid 1990s, then, the MMC was a more open, less mysterious body. The spirit of debate received a boost under Derek Morris's Chairmanship, starting with the first ever public release of an issues letter in May 1998. The inquiry on UK share underwriting, Chaired by Denise Kingsmill, involved a great many parties. Since the issues letter was in any case subject to wide circulation the Commission issued it as a press release. The seven-page letter summarised the monopoly findings, public interest issues and hypothetical remedies. The initiative received favourable press coverage[12] and was followed by publication of the issues letter in the majority of subsequent monopoly and merger inquiries. On the mobile phones inquiries, also in 1998, the Commission experimented with a joint hearing in which several parties gave evidence and listened to the evidence of others, thus allowing a more collective appreciation of the problems. With its new role as a Competition Commission in the offing it seemed that the MMC was beginning to explore a world in which official secrecy was beginning to look old fashioned as well as counter-productive.[13]

In one further way the MMC of the 1990s had moved on from the creature of the 1980s. The 'new public management' has had a significant effect on British administration. The most obvious change is the creation of the 'Next Steps Agencies' through which the majority of British central administration is now undertaken. Allied to this is a fresh emphasis on performance measurement, value for money, contracting out, market testing and generally the principles of modern management in a market setting.

In fact the Commission was beginning to improve its internal management just as the Ibbs report on *'The Next Steps'* was being published in 1988.[14] The DTI has periodically undertaken management reviews of the Commission in line with a commitment to review NDPBs every five years. The 1986 review pre-dated much of the Conservatives' management reforms but in the summer of 1993 Price Waterhouse was commissioned to review the MMC. Its threefold brief was to assess action following the 1986 review; to examine the burden on companies which had experience of the MMC; and to examine arrangements for achieving value for money. In practice the company concentrated on value for money. The report was thorough, although there must be reservations about the ability of a firm of management consultants properly to appraise a body of this sort; and also concern about the accountability to the public of its doing so. Reviews take two or three months, are undertaken by staff with no proven experience, findings are not published, and reviews tend to produce a formula approach. The Price Waterhouse report gave the MMC a clean bill of health. It conceded, magisterially, that *'we have concluded that the MMC is effective in its role as an investigatory body'* and observed that 'most parties consulted commented that *within the current policy and statutory framework* the MMC carries out its responsibilities in an *independent, professional and fair manner'*.[15] Quite how the firm could have reached the first conclusion is unclear, but no doubt the Commission was gratified to receive the seal of approval.

The Price Waterhouse report made a series of recommendations which have gradually been put into effect and have amended the MMC's work and accountability. Thus the Commission produces accounts and more detailed costings by inquiry. It has also improved liaison with the OFT and has instituted a system of post-inquiry feedback from companies. On the whole, however, the changes have been incremental. There have also been some fundamental recommendations, very much in accordance with the current management formulae in Whitehall, which stressed contracting out and market testing.[16] In pursuit of current policy, endorsed by Michael Heseltine, Price Waterhouse recommended the extraordinary step of contracting out the whole conduct of an inquiry. It suggested a pilot exercise with one inquiry to 'benchmark' future contracting out. The group of members would be retained but in the more extreme version all the staff work would be undertaken by private contractors. The MMC explored this proposal at some length. The problems of contracting out were considered – including the gradual development of public interest judgements, consistency, confidentiality, trust, cost and the omnipresent judicial review. Senior Commission members felt that the Price Waterhouse report had displayed a lack of understanding of how the Commission worked and that contracting out, even if technically feasible, would result in flawed and delayed reports. These views were put candidly to the Price Waterhouse team and an extended staff report was considered by the full Commission. As a result very little changed and, in retrospect, a senior official expressed a view of the contracting out proposal that must have been widespread in the Commission. It was, said the official, 'absolutely nuts'. Another proposal that fell foul of the MMC's norms of independence was the proposal that the Commission should negotiate a 'framework document' with the DTI in the same way as Next Steps Agencies. This would be a contract defining its duties and performance measures. But, as MMC officials were quick to point out, framework documents imply a relationship of subservience (of principal and agent), and the whole MMC rationale had become its independence – for which the Price Waterhouse report praised it. The proposal was not followed up and the MMC retained its traditional relationship with the DTI. It is, in a sense, an 'agency' of the DTI but it has not become an executive or Next Steps Agency.

Rather than a framework document the MMC has an annually negotiated 'Memorandum of Understanding' with the DTI which is quite elaborate. It includes a code of practice for members and defines the MMC's tasks as fourfold:

- 'to produce thorough, accurate, fair, consistent, realistic and vigorously argued reports' (a formidable list of adjectives),
- 'to give persons who may be affected by findings of the MMC a fair opportunity to present their case',
- 'to complete each report within the deadline',
- 'to maintain their independence'.[17]

Thus the norm of independence is accepted as a prime objective. To say that the MMC is 'jealous' of its independence is an understatement. It is an issue about which members and Chairmen care deeply. In relation to inquiries and reports real independence from the OFT and the DTI is as near absolute as anything ever can be in British government. Chairmen, Secretaries and officials from the other bodies are unanimous on this score. Whether independence more broadly construed, from politicians and through appointments to the Commission, is quite so absolute is less certain. It might be noted that nowhere in the 1973 Act is 'independence' mentioned as such. It is implied in the nature of the membership, the tests applied and the requirement of fairness. Equally, however, the Act gives the Secretary of State power to limit references (in other words, to set the terms of reference). He or she can also give directions as to procedures (section 8(3)), and section 15 of schedule 3 provides that 'a group shall comply with any special or general directions ... given to the Commission by the Secretary of State'. The DTI has never used these powers, and did not use them to impose either the Tebbit Doctrine in respect of giving priority to competition or the Lilley Doctrine in respect of foreign state-owned takeover bidders. In formal terms, however, the 'independence' of the Commission is as fragile under the 1973 Act as it was under the 1948 Act, not as watertight as some have come to believe. Independence has been fought for and created by a process of negotiation and determination. It is, perhaps, its very fragility that has raised it so high in the MMC's pantheon.

The evolution of the MMC as an organisation

The degree of continuity that is evident in many facets of the MMC is seen also in its organisation. Procedures are dealt with in chapter 5 but here it is interesting to trace the organisational arrangements back to 1948, to review the extent to which they have evolved, and to identify turning points where change could have been (but often was not) undertaken.

The main feature which conditioned the early organisation was the commitment to agnostic investigation. The Commission was conceived as a vehicle of inquiry; it was investigating and reporting rather than implementing or regulating and can be seen as the nearest thing in Britain to a permanent Royal Commission. Its investigations were agnostic. There was no presumption of fault and in official circles there was genuine curiosity as to what the Commission would discover and recommend – both factually and in respect of the public interest. It was thought

that much of this investigatory work would fall to the members themselves. The members would meet collectively as a Commission of eight
people but clearly they needed staffing and research support. This support could have come from a variety of sources – the private sector, acad-
emia, professional firms, and so on. The BoT papers considered these
options but eventually proposed the appointment of civil servants to the
senior positions, serving on a three-year secondment and drawn from the
BoT. It was recognised that specialised accounting support would be necessary and it was suggested that 'one accountant' be put on the permanent staff. For legal advice the Commission would go to the BoT
Solicitors Department. There was no great enthusiasm for the employment of an economist but, if the Commission wanted a research economist, 'he should be easily come by – adequate young economists are
cheap and plentiful'.[18]

This choice of civil service staffing was momentous. The official
paper (written by the ubiquitous Ronald McIntosh[19]) noted that the civil
service was 'the obvious place' from which to recruit staff, but also
observed that

> the only objection to a civil service staff is that the Commission may seem
> to be too much in Whitehall's pocket. This objection cannot be altogether
> dismissed, especially as we are to have an ex-Civil Servant as Chairman
> and perhaps a Vice Chairman also, it is important that the Commission
> should be and should seem to be independent and its success or failure
> may depend on the extent to which it can persuade those affected that its
> opinions are its own.[20]

The Chairman was Sir Archibald Carter (former Permanent Secretary at
Customs and Excise); the Vice Chairman (exceptionally also full time)
was Sir Harold Saunders, the BoT's former Comptroller of Patents.
McIntosh was clearly identifying a real problem. The BoT's inclination
to appoint its own people went unchecked by Sir Archibald, who met
McIntosh in November 1948 and confirmed that 'he would like to get
virtually all his staff from the Civil Service but thinks that one of the
members should be brought in from outside in order to avoid the accusation that the Commission is completely in the pocket of Whitehall'.[21]
The word 'completely' is revealing. Sir Archibald was also sympathetic
to recruitment mainly from the BoT. Here the die was cast. The MMC
was set on the path of close personnel links with the BoT. Civil service
staffing had two practical side effects. First, civil servants on secondment
would be steeped in BoT attitudes, policies and preferences. Moreover,
since they would return to the Board they might be expected to see their

work in the context of the Board's overall priorities rather than strictly in line with MMC concerns. Second, there was a risk that the BoT would send staff not of the highest calibre, because they were dull, disillusioned or nearing retirement. This could not help being a difficulty, especially if the MMC was itself regarded as inactive, of low prestige and not the place for ambitious civil servants. Here, too, is a lasting source of concern. One MMC official recalled that in the periodic 'tea parties' held with the DTI Permanent Secretary in the 1980s typically half the time was spent talking about staff – and how to get the right people. A former Chairman commented wryly that it had sometimes seemed that 'bright young people thought that a year in Carey Street would do them no good at all'.[22] The evidence is contradictory. The 1988 survey of opinion formers relayed a complimentary image of the staff. Senior staff were thought to be very good. On the other hand the CBI expressed the view in 1991 that its members were worried about the calibre of MMC staff. In evidence to the same Committee Sir Gordon Borrie also said firmly that sometimes he could not get adequate staff at the OFT on civil service pay scales.[23]

The question of the calibre of staff applies to specialist advisory staff as well as to seconded civil servants. The Commission has argued that in the 1980s – when the workload increased, the challenge became more exciting and competition policy increased in significance – then there was little difficulty in securing good quality staff. But in the 1950s and 1960s that was far from the case. Writing in 1965 Rowley recorded that companies and trade associations 'were critical of the staff of the Monopolies Commission. They considered that the staff were poorly qualified for the task in hand, and in particular that they were deficient in knowledge of economics, statistics and commerce.'[24] He continues in this vein and concludes with 'ample cause for concern'. This 1960s critique is hardly surprising. From 1986 to 1993 the annual ratio of staff to reports signed was never more than 7:1; from 1957 to 1964 it had never been less than 35:1. In the 1960s the Commission was stagnating and staff were under-employed. Rowley was therefore drawing conclusions at a low point in the Commission's history, but that is not to say that the calibre problems are ever easily or totally solved. In particular it is difficult to secure top-class professionals (such as lawyers and accountants) at civil service salaries, and there is a constant niggle of criticism from companies, outside lawyers and the members themselves about the Commission's ability to secure and retain high calibre staff. Indeed, better career structures for staff was cited as one of the reasons in favour of the single competition authority canvassed by the TIC in 1991. In this context it is interesting that the 1995 TIC inquiry was more critical of members than of staff, confirming the impression that the calibre of MMC staff in the 1990s was seen to be high.

Turning from staffing to organisation, the Commission could focus its attention on inquiries. It did not need a prosecuting branch since it was not required to generate cases and has no powers of entry and seizure. It was decided that hearings should be private, there would be no submission of evidence under oath and no cross-examination; thus the machinery of a court was not necessary. These decisions reflected the preferences of Sir Archibald Carter and Alix Kilroy, and the civil service stamp appeared in the process of inquiry organisation. The staff side of the inquiries was led by a Principal (nowadays a grade 5 team manager) who was a traditional administrative generalist. His or her abilities could be directed to organising, drafting and advising members on 'the public interest'. This pattern has been sustained. Today's team managers are more likely to have professional qualifications (as economists or scientists) but they are essentially generalists in the civil service open structure. The relationship in the 1990s is still that of a symbiosis between staff and members, although the balance of research and drafting has undoubtedly moved towards the staff. At the MMC's inception it was envisaged that the members would undertake actual investigation, and so it proved. A BoT stocktaking in 1950 observed that 'the Commission's present view is that two or three Commissioners are required personally to direct the fact finding process in each case and to present the factual material to their colleagues for judgement'.[25] The members were therefore taking a more specialist interest than is nowadays the case. In an organisation chart of 1948 vintage the present MMC structure is clearly similar but the BoT official who drew it up envisaged a line responsibility between specialist members and specialist staff. At this time a staff complement of twenty-three was envisaged, rising to a maximum of thirty-three including junior staff.

Three other features of the 1948 model are significant. First is the question of leadership. Great importance was attached to the appointment of the Chairman but his or her formal powers were and are minimal. He or she has no formal role in the appointment of members to the Commission or the nature of the references made (although informally, of course, he or she has had a part in both over the years). When the Commission met as a single body the Chairman did have more power to control the inquiry process and the shape of the report. But under group working his or her sole statutory power is through appointing the members of the group. The Chairman can join the deliberations of a group of which he or she is not formally a member (as can other members), and at

times has done so. But any attempts on the part of the Chairman to intervene would be resisted and resented. In this sense the Commission is col-
legial, although it is a fragmented collegiality since the Commission has
not had a truly collective identity since the 1960s.

Second, is the the question of penalties. The 1948 Act required the
Commission to consider what action might be taken to remedy mischiefs.
Whether or not action was actually taken was entirely up to the BoT. The
Board was empowered to make orders to prohibit agreements but it had
only limited powers to control single firm monopolists by prohibiting
some forms of behaviour. More significant powers, including compulsory
divestment, arrived with the 1965 Act. In any event, this separation of
powers allows the MMC a glorious irresponsibility. It does not have to
implement what it recommends, although remedies are nowadays discussed with the OFT and with the companies, and the Commission has
an eye to feasibility. The important point, however, is that the Commission's job is finished when the report is delivered to the DTI. It does not
have to monitor the negotiation of remedies, the policing of continuing
remedies (such as price controls) or the past experience to inform future
recommendations. Some might argue that this represents a weakness in
the system but organisationally it allows the MMC to focus exclusively
on current inquiries. Instead the prime sanction which officials envisaged
for the Commission was publicity. The efficacy of publicity and its
allegedly salutary effect on British companies were stressed in official
papers, in public debates and in discussion with American trade negotia-
tors from 1943 onwards.[26]

The emphasis put on publicity by the BoT and the Commission
itself is indicative of official thinking at the time. It means that the effectiveness of the Commission cannot be judged by its detailed impact but
rather by its influence on prevailing norms in industry and the course of
industrial self-regulation. In her review of the early years of the Commission Alix Kilroy noted that 'throughout runs the conception that
publication of the facts is basic. You may have noticed that only one Order
prohibiting the practice of an industry has yet been made [; others] have
amended their arrangements voluntarily in accordance with the Committee's recommendations.'[27] This seems nowadays too trusting and
almost naïve. Nevertheless, when the very first report, on the *Supply of
Dental Goods*,[28] was published on 14 December 1950 the public debate
was animated. In an impassioned letter to *The Times* the President of the
Dental Goods Association complained that 'The difficulty is that the
commission is both prosecutor and judge – a prosecutor who need not
disclose the charge or tell the accused what evidence is being collected

against him, and a judge whose decision is final and binding from which a party aggrieved has no appeal.'[29] As a result of the report the debate on restrictive practices intensified, and public and industrial opinion was undoubtedly affected.

It was this emphasis on publicity and industrial attitudes that was stressed by Jewkes in one of the first influential reviews of the Commission's work. Jewkes also presented the sceptical perspective on the Commission, pointing out that in comparison with US antitrust the British efforts 'may appear very much as a small-scale, half-hearted and casually informal approach to a problem of great magnitude. The total annual cost of the Monopolies Commission has never exceeded about £100,000.'[30] Jewkes's rendering was not entirely a caricature. Observers noted the delays in passing the legislation and the modesty of the provisions themselves. Labour's 1950 manifesto affirmed that 'the Government will also take practical steps to prevent monopolies from continuing to exploit the public. The Monopolies Commission has been established to expose anti-social restrictive practices.'[31] But against the weight of established restrictive practices and industrial monopoly was counterposed what? An investigatory commission employing 'an accountant'. The juxtaposition was almost ludicrous and was picked up by the *Economist*, which observed, almost sarcastically, early in 1950 that the Commission 'has organised itself in a modest way, aquiring civil servants, statisticians, executive officers, clerks and typists to the number of 37. This team cannot clean out the whole stable.'[32] The contrast was not lost on Harold Wilson and his officials at the BoT. A review of the Commission in 1950–51 appeared belatedly to recognise that the Government had created an unduly weak creature. Pressure was put on Carter and Kilroy to speed up investigations, and when the first report was published in December 1950 Wilson conceded in his statement to the House that progress had been disappointingly slow.

When Labour lost office in October 1951 it had at least created a machinery for beginning to address issues of competition policy. Chapter 2 reviewed some of the later structures that were established on this narrow foundation. Here we go on to look at the organisational development of the Commission itself.

Organisational growth: four weddings and a funeral

In chapter 2 an initial attempt was made to identify the various changes in the salience of the MMC and competition policy in the form of a

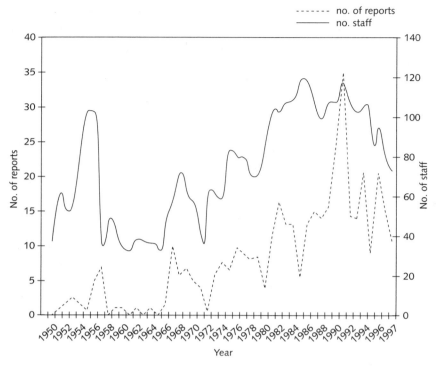

Figure 2   *Staffing and reports, 1949–97*

sequence of historical periods. The changing salience of the Commission
has been reflected in the number of reports published and in the size of
the organisation. Figure 2 presents a graph of staffing and reports which
shows considerable volatility over the years but also allows the identifica-
tion of major turning points. As far as the organisation is concerned there
has been one significant setback and four episodes of expansion. Because
organisational expansion has been associated with new legislation it has
anticipated the historical periods reviewed in chapter 2. We can express
the changes, in the title of a popular film, as 'four weddings and a
funeral'.[33] They took place as follows:

- wedding 1, 1953, followed by a period of 'experimentation and education'
- funeral 1, 1956, followed by 'wilderness years'
- wedding 2, 1965, followed by 'establishing credibility'
- wedding 3, 1973, followed by 'marking time'
- wedding 4, 1980, followed by 'renaissance'
- wedding or funeral? 1996, followed by the new Competition Commission.

The relevant legislation was reviewed in chapter 2, and the passage of the Acts is analysed in more depth in chapters 6 and 9. Here we are concerned simply with the effect on the MMC as an organisation.

The Commission enjoyed a period of prominence and success in 1953–56 when the 1953 Act created the first 'wedding' by allowing group working, three Deputy Chairmen and a membership of up to twenty-five. The passage of the 1956 Restrictive Trade Practices Act brought this period of achievement to a rather sudden end with the 'funeral' – the decimation of the Commission in 1956. The interesting question from 1956 onwards was whether the Commission would be abolished or used as a vehicle for further major initiatives. In the event the 1965 Monopolies and Mergers Act placed merger control with the MMC. As argued in chapter 8, this was by no means an obvious or uncontroversial choice. It had the effect of rescuing the MC from the obscurity into which it had fallen under the preceding Conservative Governments. The extent of Conservative neglect can be deduced from the staffing level, which plumbed an all-time low of thirty-three in 1960. This was no accident. In 1960 a paper by the Parliamentary Secretary to the BoT, John Rogers, sought approval from the Cabinet's Economic Policy Committee for new references to the MC. He noted that 'Last year the then President of the Board of Trade proposed to the Committee at its meeting on the 16th March 1959, that the Commission be placed on a care and maintenance basis. The Committee then decided that no public impression should be created that the Commission was being placed formally on such a basis.'[34] The long drawn-out official efforts to rescue the MC are analysed in chapter 6; the eventual outcome was an increase in staffing in 1965 and the prominence associated with merger control, and hence the second wedding.

As noted in chapter 6, responsibility for the MMC had been transferred to the Department of Employment and Productivity in October 1969 but plans to merge the Commission with the NBPI had been pre-empted by the June 1970 election. This was the background to the third wedding. For a short period the Commission became deeply involved in policy formulation. Sir Ashton Roskill met the new Secretary of State, Robert Carr, within a month of the election and went on to maintain frequent contact with Carr and with Ronald McIntosh, who by this time was the Under-Secretary in charge of competition policy. Together they devised plans for a new Competition Commission that would greatly expand the MMC, would give it general research and intelligence functions, and, above all, would incorporate a Registrar who would initiate references. The initiative was submerged in the reorganisation which set up the giant DTI in November 1970 and the pace slowed. Chapter 6 reviews in detail the manoeuvring which led to the all-important Fair Trading Act which received Royal Assent in July 1973. The Act was light years away from the discussions that Roskill had begun with Carr three years earlier. The MMC's formal responsibilities barely changed, and this was a low-key wedding which brought a modest increase in staffing. The newly created DGFT became the dominant figure.

The fourth wedding was a longer drawn-out ceremony. The early 1980s saw an increased salience given to competition policy and a greatly increased workload for the Commission. The Competition Act of 1980 was significant, but less for the idea of the short, sharp 'anti-competitive practice' referrals and more for the section 11 references on investigation of nationalised industries. The question of state-owned monopolies and their exclusion from the Monopolies Act had been raised in 1948. It was one of the issues addressed by officials in 1970, but the power of reference of nationalised industries had been retained by ministers who barely used it. In 1980 the Commission's competence was extended unambiguously into the public sector. The track record established by section 11 inquiries is explored in chapter 8 and was followed by a new role in the regulation of the privatised utilities. This new programme of work proved extremely important for the MMC. Partly for this reason staffing increased substantially over the 1980s, setting the scene for the increased professionalisation and influence of the Commission noted earlier in this chapter. Whether recent developments and the creation of the Competition Commission will constitute a wedding or a funeral as far as the reporting side of the MMC is concerned is a matter we turn to in chapter 9 and in the concluding chapter.

Organisational form

In significant respects the organisation of the MMC has been shaped by its tasks. Functional explanations in this vein are well established in organisation theory and appeal to common sense.[35] Thus the team working and the matrix organisation allow the Commission to respond flexibly to a series of self-contained but unpredictable inquiries. The relative lack of specialisation among team managers and the use of generalist-type civil servants also reflect the variety of potential inquiries and have the virtue of allowing the team managers to work – as the phrase has it – 'in the mind' of the Chairman and group members. The pressures on time and the need to produce an identifiable product (the report) on schedule have produced taut, focused support staff and a sophisticated system of back-up – traditionally from typists, nowadays from information technolog staff.

This, however, is a rather mechanistic approach. Economic research could be conducted by a variety of other means and the Commission could have chosen different organisational arrangements. Recent research on public sector organisations emphasises a 'bureau shaping' approach which hypothesises that senior officials seek to maximise their non-pecuniary rewards when making organisational choices. The bureau-shaping theory suggests that officials are concerned to maximise the 'core budgets' (that proportion which is spent on running costs) and also to maximise the time spent on policy work. The contrast is between management work, which is typically regarded by British civil servants as tedious and unrewarding, and policy work, which is intellectually challenging, important and involves contact with politicians. The proposition is that collectively senior civil servants design organisations so as to increase their budgetary and policy utilities. This approach seems well suited to explaining the development of Next Steps Agencies, where policy work has been retained in Whitehall and the management delegated to the Agencies.[36] It might also be applied to competition policy, where much of the 'management' of policy has been delegated to the OFT and the MMC. We return to this theoretical perspective in chapter 9 but, at this point, looking at the MMC, the key influences in the organisational history of the organisation have come from the civil service through the guidance of the BoT, the choice of a BoT Secretary and the character of those individuals. The Secretaries are listed in table 4.

Table 4 *Secretaries of the MMC, 1949–96*

Dame Alix Kilroy	1949
William Hughes	1952
J. Pimlott	1955
A. Gilbert	1956
Moria Dennehy	1965
Eric Phillips	1969
Yvonne Lovat Williams	1974
Jack Gill	1979
Neil Burton	1984
Stephen Burbridge	1986
Tony Nieduszynski	1993
Penny Boys	1996

Source: Who's Who entries.
Note: All the above officials were appointed from the BoT and the DTI at the rank of Under-Secretary (grade 3).

It is clear that in 1949 the then Chairman was willing to give his Secretary her head on organisational matters. Her decisions cast a long shadow and are still discernible in the contemporary organisation of the MMC. Dame Alix, the first Secretary, made choices that were congenial to a civil service mode of administration. There is no doubt that she regarded the MC as an important and potentially influential body but she was also a loyal and ambitious BoT civil servant who fully intended to reach the top (as did her close friend and colleague, Dame Evelyn Sharp). Latterly, at each major turning point, strong Secretaries from the BoT tended to stick to precedent, and for similar reasons. In fact it is striking how influential civil servants were posted into the Commission at major turning points. Alix Kilroy was one of the main architects of the 1948 Act and one of the most able officials of her generation. She moved into the Commission to implement the legislation. The pattern was repeated in 1965 when Moira Dennehy similarly joined the Commission as Secretary after the 1965 Act which she had a big hand in creating. It is indicative that in 1973 Frank Glaves-Smith, one of the main originators of the 1973 Act, went not to the MMC but to the OFT as Deputy Director General (to be followed in 1981 by Elizabeth Llewellyn-Smith, another respected official). Later influential Secretaries included Jack Gill in 1979, Stephen Burbridge, whose partnership with Sydney Lipworth from 1988 to 1993 helped to mould an impressive Commission; and from July 1996 Penny Boys, whose DTI links helped project MMC preferences into the design of the Competition Act.

The MMC has not been reluctant to accept BoT officials as Secretary. There are clear advantages in recruiting an able official, and even clearer gains from securing an official with good links within the BoT. Under the new Competition Act the Secretary will now be appointed by the Secretary of State rather than by the Commission,[37] but the modern recruitment process is more open with the vacancy advertised within Whitehall. In earlier days the process could be opaque. A senior Commission member recalls that when Jack Gill was appointed in 1980 the Permanent Secretary, Sir Kenneth Clucas, had said, in effect, 'you have a lot of work coming your way, you need a first-rate Secretary and – if you trust me – I will find you one'. And he did.[38] The contribution of Secretaries to the success of the Commission should not be under-rated. As noted above, the leadership of the Commission rests on a partnership. In a rare testament a press comment on Stephen Burbridge's retirement asked, 'whatever will the Monopolies and Mergers Commission do without Stephen Burbridge? [He] was known as the power behind the throne at the MMC for his sturdy input into many of the reports.'[39] Secretaries are also important for contributing to the internal debates about policy change and new legislation. Certainly Eric Philips was closely involved with the internal Whitehall deliberations over the 1973 Act and Penny Boys played the same role in the development of the 1998 Act. But as well as the advantages conveyed by their civil service connections, successive Secretaries have also brought the civil service organisational baggage.

In its organisational form the MMC has looked very much like part of the traditional civil service. The civil service approach is designed to present to ministers (or in this case members) a balanced, pragmatic interpretation of 'the public interest'. Civil servants are not dogmatic, they value judgement and consultation; they are sensitive to nuance and to the preferences of other departments. Thus civil service methods have sustained a Commission that has always behaved in a reasonable and measured manner. Senior BoT/DTI officials could be expected to appreciate this approach, which could be contrasted with the legal evangelism of the US Antitrust Division, the economic dogmatism of the German Bundeskartellamt or the pursuit of integration seen from the European DG IV activists. Neither is the MMC approach the only method to have been attempted in Britain. Alternatives could be seen in the Profiteering Acts of 1919 and in the methods used by the NBPI and the Price Commission. Their alternative approaches are discussed in chapter 5.

Conclusion

The MMC is in essence a regulatory agency. Its success does not depend on the budget it controls or on an extended organisation to implement administrative programmes. Instead its significance is related to the rigour of its processes, the quality of its reports and the respect with which it is held. In turn this directs attention to the quality of the members and the staff, and at the way in which the Commission projects itself in the business community.

The question of the membership is explored in chapter 4. As regards staff it is difficult to undertake an evaluation. So much evidence is impressionistic or anecdotal. There has been sufficient criticism over the years to suggest that calibre has sometimes been disappointing. This would constitute an absolutely fatal weakness, and one of the MMC's prime organisational priorities has to be the attraction, retention and development of outstanding support staff. But what sort of staff? The seniority of staff seems right. There are a good number of 4 and 5 grade staff (specialist and Assistant Secretary rank), and in this respect the

Commission is rightly 'top heavy'. The question of specialism is more problematic. Should the Commission have given more responsibility to its legal and economic staff over the years? Was it wise to retain separate hierarchies for economists and accountants? Should it, in particular, have elevated its economic analysis and sought out leading scholars to inform its analysis? These are questions to which we return in the Conclusion.

An even more vexing question is the MMC's relative lack of powers and dependency on the DTI. It is dependent for its budget and partly for its staffing. Moreover, it is dependent on references from the Secretary of State and, since 1973, from the DGFT and the utility regulators. When reports are completed the initiative again moves back to the DTI and the OFT. These relationships are explored in more depth in chapters 6 to 9, but they have meant that it is difficult for the Commission to develop a 'voice', either about general issues of competition policy or about specific investigations. In speaking out, Chairmen and members have been aware of the risk of comments being interpreted as criticisms of the OFT or the DTI. This has made them cautious, perhaps too cautious, and it certainly makes it difficult for the MMC to project the image which would contribute to its own standing. Which returns us to the question of independence.

The MMC's commitment to its independence is total. By now this is second nature but historically the Commission had to fight for its independence. Much of the idiosyncrasy of the MMC stems from this desire to create and protect independence, in particular its limited contacts with the OFT and the DTI, its intense reluctance to discuss reports and the way in which they may be implemented, its 'clean sheet' approach to new investigations, and its willingness to pursue logic to produce surprising conclusions in its reports. It has paid a price for the organisational arrangements which protect independence. The MMC is undoubtedly insular and inward looking. It operates according to its own standards and heavily discounts external criticism. The staff stick very closely to the specifics of current inquiries and are reluctant to generalise. In some respects it is a monastic organisation with a well-developed culture of keeping outsiders at arm's length.

The price the MMC pays for this stance is to be misunderstood. It is a problem that has lessened over the past decade but the MMC is still a conundrum to many observers. A second price is more worrying and possibly dysfunctional for the UK competition policy regime. It is the self-imposed vow of silence which the Commission has collectively taken over the development of policy. Again, this may be changing, particularly in respect of utility regulation, but the fact remains that the MMC has accumulated an extraordinary store of knowledge, experience and ideas over its fifty-year history. Its staff and members could have made an immensely valuable contribution to the debates on many aspects of industrial structure and the conduct of policy. But they have rarely done so.

Notes

1 *Economist* (3 April 1948), p. 536.
2 This book follows the MMC's own legally derived convention of using the word 'Chairman' regardless of the gender of the individual.
3 PRO, BT64/251, 'Possible Chairman of a Restrictive Practices Panel and Commission' (10 February 1947), addressed to Miss Kilroy who notes, 'personally I am inclined to favour Sir Cecil Weir for the Commission. He would certainly make the Commission acceptable to industry and (I think) be amenable to general policy directions.' For the actual appointment see chapter 4.
4 S. Wilks and L. McGowan, 'Disarming the Commission: the debate over a European Cartel Office', *Journal of Common Market Studies*, 33:2 (June 1995).
5 See the profile of the Commission's specialists in the MMC *Annual Review 1996* (London, MMC, 1997), pp. 14–16.
6 Detail from MMC, *Annual Review and Accounts 1997/98* (London, MMC, 1998), pp. 44–5.
7 Interview with a senior MMC official.
8 In the valium and librium case, published in 1973, Hoffman La Roche was notoriously uncooperative, a matter discussed more fully in chapter 9.
9 Interviews with a former senior official and a former senior member.
10 The Harris Research Centre for the Central Office of Information, Report on Perceptions of the Monopolies and Mergers Commission (unpublished, March 1988), p. 26. Note that no consumer bodies were surveyed.
11 Interview with a former senior official of the MMC.
12 MMC Press Release (11 May 1998). See also *Financial Times* (12 May 1998).
13 The Competition Commission launched a consultation paper on transparency in June 1999 as a preface to formalising some of these initiatives.
14 Efficiency Unit, *Improving Management in Government: The Next Steps* (London, HMSO, 1988).
15 MMC archive, EF842/1, Price Waterhouse, 'Monopolies and Mergers Commission: financial management survey draft report' (12 November 1993).
16 See Cm 1730, White Paper, *Competing for Quality, Buying Better Public Services* (London, HM Treasury, November 1971); Office of Public Services and Science, *The Government's Guide to Market Testing* (London, OPSS, 1993).
17 MMC, Memorandum of Understanding (15 January 1996), para. 2.
18 PRO, BT64/506, 'Monopolies and Restrictive Practices Commission staff (provisional proposals) p. 3', almost certainly by R.R.D. McIntosh (8 November 1948).
19 Sir Ronald McIntosh is probably the leading example of a BoT civil servant whose distinguished career was intertwined with the history of the Commission. He resurfaces at several later points in the book.

20 PRO, BT64/506, p. 1.

21 *Ibid.*, note of a meeting with Sir Archibald Carter to discuss the 'Staff (Provisional Proposals)' (16 November 1948).

22 Interview with Sir Godfray Le Quesne.

23 TIC, *Takeovers and Mergers: Minutes of Evidence*, 1990–91, HC 226x (London, HMSO, 1991), p. 282, evidence by John Banham and comment by Robin Maxwell-Hyslop.

24 Charles Rowley, *The British Monopolies Commission* (London, Allen and Unwin, 1966), p. 58.

25 PRO, BT64/4159, 'The problem of operating the Monopolies Act', paper by officials, unsigned and undated, but late 1950.

26 See T. Freyer, *Regulating Big Business* (Cambridge University Press, 1992), p. 262.

27 Dame Alix Kilroy, 'The tasks and methods of the Monopolies Commission', *The Manchester School*, XXII (1 January 1954), pp. 55–6.

28 *Report on the Supply of Dental Goods*, 1950–51, HC18 (London, HMSO, 1950).

29 Letter to *The Times* (15 December 1950), J. M. Hooker, President, Association of Dental Manufacturers and Traders of the UK.

30 J. Jewkes, 'British monopoly policy 1944–56', *Journal of Law and Economics*, 1 (October 1958), p. 6.

31 F. Craig, *British General Election Manifestos 1900–1974* (London, Macmillan, second edn, 1975), p. 155.

32 *Economist* (16 March 1950), p. 609.

33 A successful, beguiling, very English and low budget Oscar-winning film of 1994 starring Hugh Grant.

34 PRO, CAB134/1687, Cabinet Economic Policy Committee (19 May 1960). The 'then President' in March 1959 was Reginald Maudling.

35 See R. K. Merton, *Social Theory and Social Structure* (Glencoe, Free Press, second edn, 1957); T. Parsons, *Societies: Evolutionary and Comparative Perspectives* (Englewood Cliffs, Prentice Hall, 1966).

36 See O. James, 'Explaining the Next Steps in the Department of Social Security: the bureau-shaping model of central state reorganisation', *Political Studies*, 43:4 (December 1995).

37 The 1948 and 1973 Acts provided for the Commission to appoint its own Secretary, subject to the approval of the Secretary of State.

38 Interview with a former senior member of the Commission.

39 *Daily Telegraph*, diary (19 January 1993).

4

The members of the MMC

It has been universally claimed by both sides of industry and by all Parties in the House (and I have said from the Front Bench that the Government entirely agrees) that the Commission stands or falls even more than most bodies of this kind by the quality of its membership and particularly of its Chairman.

Harold Wilson, July 1948[1]

The choice of a Commission to implement competition policy reflected uncertainty about the goals of policy, caution about the determination with which it would be pursued, and concern for the relationship of government with the business community. The Commission that was created is a constantly changing body of part-time Commissioners with only one full-time member, the Chairman. The part-time principle has considerable benefits. The members are independent, they bring a range of experience and cutting-edge professional competence, they reassure important user constituencies, and they formulate an impartial view of 'the public interest'. The part-time principle is fundamental to the Commission and observers generally do not make sufficiently clear that every MMC report emerges from a unique group of members. Part-time membership has created a very distinctive organisation in which the members themselves are at once the essence of the Commission and yet semi-detached from it. The part-time principle has provoked repeated criticism and is one of those elements of MMC continuity that has been maintained, even when the original rationale has faded. It has become an institutional norm and its continuation now rests on precedent and on a new rationale of impartiality, rather than the old rationale of developing policy.

The old rationale, as conceived by the BoT in the 1940s and in the Commission in the early 1950s, was that part-time members would provide the set of policy priorities that government had signally failed to provide. Sir Archibald Carter accordingly told a Select Committee in

1953 that his personal view was that 'a large part of the Commission ought to consist of people of whom it is true that the Commission's work is not their main work ... It seems to me that at the moment we are rather like a jury and I would have thought that until Parliament, anyhow, frames the outline of policy about these things, it ought to be kept that way.' His argument was that the broad 'public interest' test required a mix of independent professionals to form a judgement. But he went on to concede that 'there is no doubt at all that it would go much faster with a smaller Commission, all the members of which were whole-time' and that, 'if you once get Parliament laying down some broad principles about these things, it would probably work with a smaller body with whole-time members'.[2] Since nowadays speed is stressed and the criteria for judgement have been clarified by theory, by precedent and by the prominence attached to competition, then the old rationale looks less persuasive. The new rationale is about competence, accountability and due process. The part-time principle is maintained by the 1998 Competition Act, which also provides that members can be appointed simultaneously as 'reporting panel' members (the traditional function) and as 'appeals panel' members (the new appeal tribunals). This opens up the likelihood that lay members will sit on the new three-person appeal tribunals, thus giving the principle and the membership a new significance.

The Commission is an extraordinary body, long lasting and quite unique. This chapter reviews the recruitment of members and Chairmen over the fifty-year period. It analyses their background, their qualifications and their contribution to the inquiry process. The discussion also deals with the nature of leadership within the Commission and the organisational and judgemental influences which the members have exerted.

The nature of the Commission

As noted in chapter 2, the term 'Commission' carried very English connotations of a body along the lines of the great investigatory Commissions of the High Victorian period. But the MMC is more than a Royal Commission. It has taken on a succession of tasks, its actions may have a direct administrative effect, it operates in groups and its members are paid. Nonetheless, the closest parallels likely to illustrate the choice of members are either that of the Royal Commission, with its associated ideas of fairness, expertise, status and a 'catalytic' function,[3] or the less legalistic type of administrative tribunal. The parallel, applied to the choice of members in the early days, suggested the perpetuation of one of the ruling principles of nineteenth-century government – the influence of the talented gentleman amateur. The employment of 'the great and the good' in public office became a principle of British government with its Justices of the Peace, Aldermen, administrative boards and even its MPs, most of whom enjoyed private means of support. The echoes of that approach to administration were certainly still reverberating in Whitehall as the MRPC was being designed.[4] The internal papers took a more tri-bunal-type approach and drew parallels with the British Electricity Authority, the Coal Mines Reorganisation Committee and the Import Duties Advisory Committee. These organisational options were second nature to the officials involved and were congenial to Harold Wilson, a great believer in the virtues of British institutions.

The MMC was therefore one of a band of administrative agencies whose growth generated some concern from the 1950s (the Franks Committee) to the 1990s (the Nolan Committee).[5] It is almost impossi-ble to point to general principles or characteristics of tribunals, which vary to a bewildering extent in their membership, staffing, legalism and independence.[6] At a general level the features of ministerial appoint-ment, a civil service staff and non-legal but formal procedures are widely shared by other tribunals. The principle of ministerial appoint-ment in particular caused concern in 1955 and again in the 1990s when, as a result of the Nolan report, Whitehall shifted the appointment process for all such bodies to one based on transparency and indepen-dent assessment.

The Commission as a concept thus had a mixed parentage which included traditional administrative practice as well as a conscious response to new problems. The membership has been the subject of wide interest and of public relations material. In the years up to March 1998 the BoT and its successors had appointed 187 people to the MMC – but had appointed only eight Chairmen, and it is the Chairmen with whom we start.

Leadership and the Chairman

The Chairman is absolutely central to the character and the success of the Commission. The Chairman deals with ministers and provides the public face of the Commission, but he or she also influences the inquiry process in three fundamental ways. First, he or she will influence the choice of new members. They are selected by the DTI but the Department takes

note of the wishes of the Chairman and has often accepted sensible recommendations (particularly in respect of renewals of office). Second, he
or she assembles the membership of groups. This is the Chairman's only
formal source of power and it is an important skill to assemble an effective
group. When the Commission is hard pressed the Chairman may have little room for manoeuvre and he or she will certainly accept the advice of
the Secretary, but there is significant influence at work here. Third, his or
her role as Chairman of an inquiry is important and he or she will tend to
take on the high profile cases. Prior to the appointment of the first Deputy
Chairman in 1967 the Chairman had Chaired the vast majority of
inquiries. Subsequently the task has been shared but the Chair of each
inquiry team is the dominant player. In more subtle ways the Chairman
influences both the internal workings of the Commission and its external
reception. The fact, for instance, that barristers Chaired the Commission
for forty years from 1954 to 1993 has somehow been taken as representative of legal pretensions whereas, in fact, the Commission is one of the
least legalistic of bodies in the procedures it follows, the tests it applies, the
limits on precedent and the non-adversarial approach.

The eight Chairmen of the Commission since its creation are listed
in table 5. The dominance of lawyers is marked. Each Chairman has
made his distinctive contribution, although Cairns's influence was cut
short by the reorganisation of 1956 and Levy presided over a period of
quietitude. The impact of the first Chairman, Sir Archibald Carter, is
important for the procedural precedents which he created, and we should
examine the direction of this initial path.

Securing a Chairman for this new and experimental body did not
prove easy. In 1948 sound and prominent public figures were in short
supply. The BoT got the process under way in March, when the task was
entrusted to R. C. Bryant, an Assistant Secretary working to Alix Kilroy
(to become Dame Alix in January 1949). Bryant's opening memo argued
that:

> The Commission should be small and its membership knowledgeable,
> active and sufficiently well-known to industry already to enjoy from the
> beginning some goodwill. If it were possible a Commission composed of a
> Chairman and two other members would be the best choice; the smaller
> the Commission the more likely it is that decisions will be unanimous and
> that a clear body of doctrine would emerge. The Chairman ought to be a
> full-time working Chairman and in fact the Managing Director. If possi-
> ble he should be in the early fifties. He must be untainted by restrictive
> practices. He ought not to be a lawyer (since we want to keep the Com-
> mission free from even the suspicion of employing the apparatus of the
> law). The best choice would probably be a civil servant already known to

Table 5 *Chairmen of the MMC, 1949–99*

Chairman	Occupation	Appointed to Commission	Appointed Chairman	Age appointed	Age retired	School	University
Sir Archibald Carter	Civil servant	1949	1949	62	66	Eton	Trinity, Camb.
Sir David Cairns, QC	Lawyer	1954	1954	52	54	Bede	Pembroke College, Camb.
Richard Levy, QC	Lawyer	1956	1956	64	73	Hackney	London
Sir Ashton Roskill, QC	Lawyer	1960	1965	63	73	Winchester	Exeter, Oxf.
Sir Godfray Le Quesne, QC	Lawyer	1975	1975	50	63	Shrewsbury	Exeter, Oxf.
Sir Sydney Lipworth, QC	Lawyer/ business	1981	1988	57	62	S. Africa	Witwatersrand
Sir Graeme Odgers	Business	1993	1993	59	63	S. Africa	Gonville & Caius, Camb.
Dr Derek Morris	Economist	1991	1998	52	–	Harrow Grammar	St Edmund Hall, Oxf.

Sources: annual reports and *Who's Who.*

Note: The age appointed is the appointment to the Chairmanship, not to the Commission.

and trusted by a fair section of industry. The other two members again should preferably be drawn from outside industry or trade unionism and might be half-time.[7]

A month later Alix Kilroy confirmed in a note to James Helmore, the Permanent Secretary, that 'I agree very much with Mr Bryant's description ... of the desirable qualifications of the Chairman',[8] and she suggested four names. But translating the design into practice proved demanding.

Miss Kilroy's minute came back the same day with a note from Harold Wilson, then President of the BoT. He was an omnipresent influence on the Commission and he recommended a further two names. Over the next six weeks none of these nominees were willing to accept. Lord Justice Cohen was also approached but turned down the offer. By 18 June Alix Kilroy's memo to Wilson summarising the lack of progress was signed 'two of your humble and distraught servants'.[9] Seven further candidates were considered and the post was offered to Lord Brand and to Sir David Maxwell-Fyfe – an extraordinary step since he was a Conservative MP (later Lord Kilmuir). In virtual desperation the BoT turned to that archetypal Whitehall fixer, Sir Edward Bridges at the Treasury, who recommended the Permanent Secretary for Commonwealth Affairs, Sir Archibald Carter.

The Chairman was at first sight an unlikely choice. An Old Etonian, he graduated from Trinity, Cambridge to run first India and then the Board of Customs and Excise (he was Permanent Secretary for India in 1936 and spent much of his career in the India Office). His views both on members and procedure were influential and one can speculate that the Commission would have developed quite differently if another candidate had accepted the appointment. Carter's first meeting with Wilson on 26 November 1948 confirmed Commission membership and indicated that he would like to hear formal evidence in private and probably under oath. He was adamant that he wanted a small Commission but he also wanted a representative from industry (which the officials had so far avoided). He felt that there was a good case for having 'a representative of the Board Table' on the Commission and officials were deputed to approach Josiah Wedgwood.[10] The partnership between Carter and Kilroy established the early pattern of working. Alix Kilroy noted that 'he led his team of many talents with a light rein and he left the staffing and running of the office and the preparation of documents to me'.[11] A striking feature of this process of creating the Commission was its bi-partisan nature. Not only was the Conservative shadow minister Maxwell-Fyfe actually asked to Chair the Commission, Wilson constantly involved him in discussion and notified him of approaches to Josiah Wedgwood and Frederick Grant inviting them to become members. This pattern would not have surprised Mercer, who has also analysed this early history.

In Mercer's stimulating reading of events she sees business influence as dominant. She argues that Wilson and his officials had made repeated concessions to business and the FBI. Maxwell-Fyfe she portrays as 'a mouthpiece for business in Parliament'.[12] She sees business influence in the idea of the investigative principle, the independent Chairman, the part-time principle, and restrictions on the BoT's powers of reference to the Commission. In short she sees the 1948 Act, and the Commission's design, as strongly influenced by industrial interests. There is undoubtedly something in this but it might be more accurate to suggest that the BoT was protecting its own intimate connections with organised business. Certainly officials retained a healthy suspicion of industry. They specifically ruled out an industrialist as Chairman and a paper late in 1948 noted that, as far as members were concerned, 'industrialists are pretty well ruled out as a class because all, or almost all, are connected either directly or indirectly with monopoly or with arrangements of some kind involving restrictive practices'.[13] Indeed, the very memo from Kilroy to her Permanent Secretary which Mercer cites in support of her argument that the BoT 'wanted a Commission that would command the confidence of industry'[14] also notes that 'it would be almost impossible to find an industrialist who was not committed one way or the other in the matter of restrictive practices'.[15] This does not speak of an official kow-towing to industry and we have seen that it was not until the meeting with Carter on 30 November that it was conceded that an industrialist should be appointed to the Commission. Mercer is undoubtedly correct in stressing a close relationship with industry, but her argument that the BoT itself was 'captured'[16] can be taken too far. Civil servants were equally concerned, in time-honoured Whitehall fashion, to secure a Commission in which members 'should have first-rate minds, capable of reaching a balanced conclusion'.[17]

Mercer's other preoccupation in analysing the creation of the Commission is American influence. The Americans were very keen indeed to export antitrust principles, to open up markets and to encourage a vigorous competition policy across the industrialised world. The necessity of placating the Americans was constantly in ministerial minds. In 1948 (and again in 1965 when competition policy was strengthened) the Americans held the purse strings and had sterling at their mercy. Now and again this imperative surfaced in the official papers. Thus in a long letter to Stafford Cripps, the Chancellor, in which Wilson is persuading him to

'release' Sir Thomas Barnes as a potential Chairman, Wilson ends his
missive with the thought that:

> With a new drive on productivity in hand it seems to me vital that we
> should not appear to be half-hearted about the Monopoly Commission.
> And the Americans have an interest in our activities on Cartels! At the
> official level they have been flattering about the Bill (as have also the
> Canadians) but they will undoubtedly take the appointment we make for
> Chairman as the true indication of our real intentions in this sphere.[18]

Both Carter and Kilroy visited the United States (separately) in 1949.
Alix Kilroy's visit was intense, with a three-month programme of meetings including one with William Clayton, then Under-Secretary of State.
But she proved a difficult convert for the American antitrust evangelists
and concluded that 'the philosophy behind the American legislation ...
was basically so different that their experience would have no practical
bearing on the working of our young legislation'.[19] There is no hint in the
papers that officials were consciously motivated by a need to respond in
any detailed way to American pressures or that those pressures took the
form of direct intervention. Alix Kilroy herself recalled no hint of a
detailed American agenda at work – this was domestic policy evolved for
domestic reasons and she did not consider the American interest.[20] It may
have been diplomatic to present the policy abroad in a favourable light
but there were also strictly practical reasons to visit North America.
Thus McIntosh minuted the view that 'there are no end of snags in
monopoly investigations and I think the Chairman ought, if he can manage it, to go to Canada to get practical tips from Fred McGregor. He
wouldn't get much benefit from Washington but tactically ... a courtesy
visit might pay dividends. Sweden is for later on, I think.'[21]

This review of early appointments shows the government selecting
an independent, high calibre leadership, but one steeped in civil service
norms. While they took proper note of industrial interests and foreign
models, they set the Commission on its own independent path. With the
possible exception of Richard Levy, who was sixty-four when appointed
and suffered ill health during his term as Chairman, the succeeding
appointments were all strong leaders who brought, however, quite different perspectives to their role. From 1954 to 1981 the government
appointed senior barristers, QCs steeped in a legal tradition. If one were
looking for evidence of the old boy network then the fact that all four
practised at either the Middle or Inner Temple would appear overly coincidental. Ashton Roskill and Godfray Le Quesne both treated the Commission as something approaching a court of law in that they emphasised

a formal procedure, a strict application of the case-by-case principle, a low public profile and a strict observation of the separation of powers within the tripartite system. Their strengths lay in their absolute and irreproachable integrity, their independence of mind and their confident exercise of authority. Sydney Lipworth, although also a QC, was an extremely successful entrepreneur in the life assurance industry. This gave him great credibility with industry (he went on to become Chairman of Zeneca). His instincts were to let the light in, to explain and to justify the Commission in a far bolder and outgoing fashion. In many ways he was the creator of the 'modern' Commission. In earlier times recruitment to the Chair was rather informal. Godfray Le Quesne recalls being approached by the DTI Deputy Secretary, Patrick Shovelton, 'out of the blue' but at the suggestion of Geoffrey Howe; and Sydney Lipworth prevaricated for at least a year before accepting a ministerial offer of the Chairmanship. Later both Graeme Odgers and Derek Morris were selected through a more objective process of advertisement and selection, and Graeme Odgers is adamant that he did not even meet Michael Heseltine until after he had been selected through a search process. Both of them were well attuned to the realities of government–industry relations, Graeme Odgers through working as the Director of the DTI's Industrial Development Unit in the exciting times of the mid 1970s; Derek Morris as Economic Director of the NEDO in the early 1980s. Both built on the Lipworth legacy to create a body that is managerially more professional, is aware of its duty to communicate, and is more willing to express its priorities inside and outside Whitehall. Both have also been very aware of the need to reinforce the collegiate culture of the Commission, and at this point we should introduce the *corps de ballet* – the members.

The members: characteristics and trends in appointment

Between January 1949 and March 1998 187 people were appointed to the MRPC and its successors. In some ways they live up to the stereotype of British appointment to public institutions – 'the great and the good' of the industrial and professional worlds. On the whole they have been middle aged (or retired), middle class and male. There are some surprises in the list. Some extremely eminent members have co-existed with those considerably less eminent. Writing in 1966, at the end of the Commission's 'wilderness years', Rowley rather brutally observed that 'The Board of Trade has failed to make sufficient impact in its appointments to the Monopolies Commission. Many existing members are not well known, especially outside their specialist fields. The Monopolies Commission can scarcely aspire to a position of real significance unless the nature of its membership is transformed.'[22] Rowley's view that members, while they were good, were not sufficiently 'great' does point up a dilemma. Membership of the MMC is not a sinecure. From its inception the BoT was anxious to appoint people of real expertise who were prepared to work. As early as 1950 a BoT review of the Commission observed that 'a vast amount of work falls on the Commissioners – more, in Dame Alix's view, than they ever bargained for'.[23] This pattern has continued, and the BoT's ability to recruit extremely able people who are prepared to work hard for relatively modest recompense is a testament to a spirit of public service. As the work intensified in the 1980s, and as time limits were steadily truncated, so the pressures on members, staff and collegiality began to threaten traditional patterns of working. If it had the choice the MMC could be expected to maximise application, even at the expense of eminence, in its preferences on members.

Co-existing with expertise and standing in the choice of members is their ability to work reliably as a team. In a particularly astute early recommendation Alec Cairncross observed that, 'it matters much more what kind of man you can find than whether he is an academic economist … The final choice of members of the Commission would have to depend … at least as much on the personality of the candidate as on their professional qualifications.'[24] This quintessentially British approach comes to life in the marginilia scribbled by officials against the names listed in Bryant's paper on possible candidates. Thus Sir Sam Brown is described as 'v. good chap. Any amount of common sense. A hard worker', whereas another KC is dismissed as 'v. tedious', another as 'dreary' and yet another with a simple but emphatic 'NO'. Joan Robinson, felt by some to be too far to the Left, is blessed with the compliment that 'we have found her to be an extremely good committee member'.[25] As recently as 1998 a Commission official noted that 'in my view, it is members' personal qualities – in particular open-mindedness, and a propensity as well as the ability to probe analysis and argument – which are most important'.[26] Such are the timeless requirements of Commission construction.

Characteristics

The public record allows us to analyse the basic patterns of Commission appointments and to draw some tentative conclusions. Table 6 analyses appointments in five-year periods from 1949 to 1998. These data are drawn mainly from public sources and are not based on a survey or

Table 6 Members of the MMC, 1949–99: by year of appointment

Period	No. appointed	Female	Appt. age	Ret. age	Civil service	Trade union	Lawyer	Econo-mist	Account-ancy	Industry	Finance	Consult-tant	Consumer rep.	Co-op.
1949–54	18	1	53	59	3	3	4	3	1	2	1			
1955–59	8		59	66		1	1			4				
1960–64	7		59	66	1		1	1		4				
1965–69	25	1	54	60	3	2	3	6		4	2	3		1
1970–74	11	3	50	57		1	2	1		5	1			
1975–79	18	3	51	64	2	3	1	3		5	1	1	1	2
1980–84	28	1	55	60	1	2	3	3	2	11	3	1		
1985–89	19	1	55	62	1	2	1	4	1	8	1	1		
1990–94	24	6	54	n/a		1	1	4	1	11	4	3		
1995–98	29	7	52	n/a	5	2	4	3	5	5	1	1	3	
Total	187	23			16	17	21	28	9	59	14	10	4	3

Sources: annual reports BoT/OFT, MMC biographical details, *Who's Who* and *Debrett's*.

Notes: Some of the columns do not add across as it has proved impossible to obtain data on a very small number of members. Members are allocated by main occupation.

The 'Industry' column includes lawyers and qualified accountants in companies.

The 'Consultant' column included 'think tank' people.

The 'Co-op.' column comprises representatives of the co-operative movement.

The 'Appt. age' and 'Ret. age' figures are the average for all the people who were appointed in that time period, *not* those who retired in the period.

n/a = not available (members not yet retired).

extensive interviews. Allowance must therefore be made for over-simplification. We deal first with gender.

Gender

Rather shockingly only twenty-three women have ever been appointed as members, thirteen of these since 1990. The second (1965–68) was Dame Alix with a fresh incarnation at the MMC, but from 1952–65 and 1968–72 there were no women on the Commission. By the 1960s this gender imbalance excited a modest hint of concern in the BoT. Its paper of December 1964 on the expanded Commission devotes a whole paragraph to the role of women. After discussing Scotland, Ireland and Wales officials note that 'we must also aim at getting at least one woman onto the enlarged Commission. In the Commission history, there has been only one female member… We must now make a deliberate effort of policy to achieve a better balance.'[27] The paper, addressed, ironically, to Elizabeth Llewellyn-Smith, provided 113 possible names but only two women, with the extraordinary note that 'two women are included – an economist and one from commerce; they have been chosen on merit'.[28] It was over twenty years before this 'deliberate effort of policy' began to yield results. While the BoT has never aimed to create a 'representative' Commission, the absence of women could be taken to exclude a significant consumer voice. More speculatively, this might have affected the conduct of group debates and produced a 'clubbish' atmosphere.

Age

The youngest ever appointment to the Commission was Valerie Marshall in 1976 at the age of thirty-one. The oldest member was Sir Robert Clayton, who retired in 1989 aged seventy-four. Along this spectrum appointments are typically made from the mid 40s onwards. By this time people have proved their worth, established a reputation and presumably gained sufficient seniority to earn part-time secondment. This applies especially to economists and lawyers, for whom a spell at the Commission can also be a good career move. Appointments of people in their thirties are still exceptional. The first came in 1976 and there have been only four in total (or five including Gill Owen, who was appointed to the Utilities Panel aged thirty-eight before being transferred to full membership). A regular pattern of recruitment is of people retiring from their main occupation. Appointment of people aged sixty or more is marked in the late 1960s and again in the late 1980s. Post-retirement appointment of industrialists but also of civil servants is almost inevitable if the Commission is to recruit top-flight people and is probably also welcome, provided a balance can be maintained.

The analysis in table 6 shows that the Commission has never been a gerontocracy (although it came dangerously close in the early 1960s). It also, however, shows a membership resolutely of the 'fifty-something' generation in a pattern that has barely changed over fifty years. The Commission was reasonably youthful on appointment but steadily aged up to 1965, when the expansion following the 1965 Act brought in young men. The period of consistently youthful appointments was the early 1970s in parallel with the new legislation and the creation of the OFT. From then on average ages crept up again, especially into the late 1980s when the Commission saw a number of retired businesspeople appointed in their sixties and serving into their seventies. Recent younger appointments take the average age down to exactly the same level as in 1954. There is a slight correlation between the proportion of industrialists appointed and the age profile. The BoT has consistently found it difficult to prise leading executives away from their companies during their peak career years of forty-five to sixty. At the same time it is slightly regrettable that the under forty-five age group has been so sparsely represented. There are, of course, exceptions which indicate the possibilities, such as the recent appointment of Richard Rawlinson in 1998 aged forty, or several people who have made more of a 'career' at the Commission as a member and then as Deputy Chairmen, such as Richard Smethurst (thirty-seven when appointed in 1978) and Dan Goyder (forty-two in 1980).

The period of appointment of Commission members has become normalised as a three-year term, typically renewed once. The six-year tenure allows members to build up significant expertise and allows a good degree of continuity with a rotating membership. In earlier years the pattern was more erratic. The averages thus conceal some remarkable cases of longevity, colleagues that became almost fixtures within the institution. Table 7 indicates that the record for perseverance is held by Dan Goyder but with a number of others serving extended terms. In total sixteen members have served for twelve years or more but Dan Goyder and Peter Dean seem to be the last cohort of such stalwarts. The present membership is retiring more routinely and there is no one to challenge the record holders. Perhaps this indicates a Commission in which the work of members has become more routinised and less personalised.

Education and social standing

There is no doubt that members of the Commission have been prominent in their chosen fields. In some cases, however, their fields (of accountancy or law, for instance) may have made them less than public figures. In other

Table 7 *Longest-serving members of the Commission*

Member	Length of service (years)	Period	
Dan Goyder	17	1980–97	(Deputy Chairman from 1991)
Peter Dean	15	1982–97	(Deputy Chairman from 1990)
Edgar Richards	15	1965–80	(Deputy Chairman from 1974)
Roger Falk	15	1965–80	
Professor Tibor Barna	15	1963–78	
Sir Ashton Roskill	15	1960–75	(Chairman from 1965)
Brian Davidson	14	1954–68	

Source: annual reports by the BoT/OFT.

cases, in the fields of commerce, industry and the City, it has proved less easy to recruit leading figures. The BoT had enough experience of refusals to remark in 1965 that 'we have restricted the choice to substantial people, but those who are *too* heavy in weight … have not been included'.[29] Scrutiny of the backgrounds of members conveys an initial Establishment profile but overlaid with a tone of meritocracy. The social background can be judged by the educational record.

In schooling there was quite a dramatic shift in the 1980s. In earlier years there was significant recruitment from the great public schools (Eton, Rugby and Winchester) and, up to 1984, fully 42 per cent of members had attended a major public school. From 1985 the position changed radically, and between 1985 and 1998 only 10 per cent of members had a public school background. This may reflect trends in society, the increased number of women members or the anti–Establishment bent of the Thatcher years. It has given the Commission a new and more egalitarian face. It is a different picture at University level, although it is striking that only 128 of the 165 members who provide details took degrees (see table 8). The trade unionists, the practical businesspeople and the soldiers are supplemented by the solicitors and the chartered accountants who chose the professional rather than the University route. But here the British establishment does seem to recur.

Thus 52 per cent of those with degrees took them at Oxbridge and 73 per cent in the magic triangle of Oxford, Cambridge and London. Historically about 40 per cent of all members have had an Oxbridge background. This has barely changed over recent years, so that from 1949–84 57 per cent of the Commission had degrees from either Oxbridge or London; from 1985–98 the figure remained precisely the same. In very

Table 8 *Educational background of Commission members*

University	No.
Oxford	33 (5 New College)
Cambridge	33 (6 Trinity)
Oxbridge	66
London	28 (13 LSE)
Outside London	20
Scottish	9
Overseas	5
University degree	128
Professional qualification	14
No qualification	23
Total	165

Sources: Compiled from *Who's Who, Debrett's,* Commission biographical data and personal correspondence. Data for some members were unavailable.

recent years there has been a reduction in people with no qualifications and the representation of a slightly larger range of universities. The bias towards the traditional social Establishment has disappeared but there remains a strong meritocratic element in recruitment with a marked partiality for the traditional Oxbridge graduate and the perhaps more egalitarian products of the University of London. It remains a picture of responsible, hard-working people, appointed for their application, not as a glossy façade – perhaps not that dissimilar to the patterns seen in recruitment to the civil service itself.

The policy in 1965, as today, was to get the 'right' people and yet there remains a feeling of the civil service recruiting, if not in its own image, at least to its own prejudices. In his memo of February 1965 R. F. Allen notes: '*Industrialists* (1) we have narrowed this wide field by looking for some evidence of intellectual penetration, as well as impressive personality. We have excluded export salesmen and other purely "executive" types (in the civil service use of the word).'[30] This reference to 'executive types' is redolent of a superior, almost patrician, civil service attitude which was to be bitterly criticised as the Fulton report of 1968 provoked an outpouring of concern. What is clear is that BoT civil servants had considerable freedom in influencing the selection of members. They may have made many sensible choices but the system was based on an 'old-boys' network' which was ripe for reform in the 1980s.

Occupation

The most intriguing aspect of the members is the mix of skills and experiences which they bring. Papers identified potential candidates by occupational background and by 1965 the BoT was talking of the 'balance' of the Commission.[31] The dominant concern was the expertise necessary to the nature of the investigations. Civil servants were therefore initially interested in lawyers, accountants, people from the City, patent specialists, economists (grudgingly) and civil servants (naturally).

Alongside expertise, however, was a concern with the public image of the Commission and its likely reception by business. The function of 'legitimation' is seldom spelled out but underlies the frequently expressed concern that members should be substantial, responsible and well known. The wider public image has also been important, so that members should not be too closely associated with potential targets for investigation. It is interesting that there was no discussion of appointing 'ordinary' people who might represent a public or consumerist view. Neither in 1948–49, nor in 1964–65, did the BoT apparently consider how the consumer, the housewife, the small businessperson, could be represented on the Commission, although an August 1965 paper does talk of 'general interest' candidates, of whom Dame Alix Kilroy and Roger Falk (a management consultant) were felt to be representative.[32] There was also an interesting exchange of correspondence between Sir Richard Powell (Permanent Secretary at the BoT) and his opposite number at the Department of Education and Science, Sir Herbert Andrew, who recalled a conversation about appointments to the Commission. 'I said that one or two school heads might be very suitable people (not to look at mergers but for cases where you want a consumer viewpoint).'[33] He volunteered five names, including Miss Fordham from Catford Comprehensive, but the idea did not find favour. The first consumer specialist was not appointed until 1980 in the shape of Peter Goldman, a long-time Director of the Consumers' Association (and former Conservative parliamentary candidate). It seems that although the 'public interest test' was at the centre of the Commission's mission, it was not to be decided by 'the public'.

The role of lawyers is interesting. It was felt in 1949 that the Chairman should not be a lawyer. The value of lawyers was in their intellectual predispositions and forensic skills as much as in their knowledge of the law (although there was a preoccupation with patent law). Thus a summary paper observes that, 'a good lawyer's knowledge of the rules of evidence and his habit of testing it will help to keep the Commission on the rails: his refusal to reach a conclusion until the evidence has been heard is equally valuable'.[34] This emphasis on skills was repeated in 1964–65 when Miss Llewellyn-Smith's team at the BoT noted that, 'lawyers on the Commission carry a particularly heavy burden in the way of examination of witnesses'.[35] This emphasis is curious. The Commission is certainly inquisitorial but it does not operate on the basis of adversarial cross-examination so that the need for the barrister's approach would probably not be recognised by the majority of today's members. In the event Roskill over-rode the BoT recommendations, chose his own lawyers and two barristers were appointed (Roche and Barrowclough[36]), thus tending to underline the forensic role of lawyers on the Commission at that time and demonstrating the ability of a determined Chairman to influence the composition of the Commission.

Although lawyers have been prominent on the Commission they have been outnumbered by economists, who have been possibly more influential. One would not have guessed this in 1948 when the BoT's Bryant observed that the Commission could 'employ an Economic Adviser on a part rather than a full-time basis. It is probably better to have the Economist as an adviser and not as a member of the Commission, since this is a subject on which economists are apt to hold fanatical views which might lead to minority reports.' This rather patronising (if percipient) observation was taken up by Alix Kilroy, who asked Alec Caincross (then Senior Economic Adviser at the BoT) 'what would the world of economists think to a Commission without an economist member?', allowing Cairncross, also percipiently, to reply that, 'I doubt whether economists hold more "fanatical" views of monopoly … They sometimes have a better understanding of industrial organisation and a clearer conception of the public interest', going on to say that, 'I should also be disposed to take a more charitable view of minority reports … we have had reason to be thankful for minority reports.'[37] Thus Joan Robinson was added to the Commission, the first of twenty-eight economists to be appointed up to March 1998. The economists became more influential with the appointment of Tibor Barna, Aubrey Silberston, Basil Yamey and Roger Opie in the 1960s, and it would nowadays be impossible to imagine a Commission without them.

Even more striking than the long march of the economists through the Commission is the takeover by business. From the mid 1950s, under Conservative Governments, substantial numbers of businesspeople began to be appointed. They have been the largest group on the Commission since that time, and accounted for about half the membership during the 1980s. The appointment of businesspeople is linked to the 1956 Restrictive Trade Practices Act and the general reduction in anti-competitive practices across the economy. In the 1940s officials had felt that virtually all prominent businessman were associated with the sort of monopolistic practices with which the Commission was designed to deal. The 1956 Act took the control of restrictive practices away from the Commission and, by 1965, the incidence of restrictive practices and the power of trade associations had been much reduced. When the Commission was expanded in 1965 officials therefore accepted the case that 'the bulk of the Commission's membership must be expected to be made up of people with a variety of business, commercial and similar experience'; indeed, they accepted that 'it will not be possible to avoid everyone who has some connection with restrictive practices or monopolistic industries'.[38] Thus the list of 113 names included 46 'industrialists' plus another 21 'Scottish businessmen'. The list does still, however, show a sensitivity to possible anti-competitive biases. Thus Lewis Robertson, who was considered 'very able', was 'ruled out because of his activities in support of restrictive practices in the jute industry' – which curiously did not prevent him being appointed in 1969 for a seven-year term. There were also several industrial accountants on the list, and here the sins of their employers were held more systematically against them. Thus R. G. Leach is 'rejected because of his close association with Ranks', E. H. Davison 'ruled out because of Courtaulds' position on textiles' and P. V. Roberts, 'Director of Imperial Tobacco. Ruled out because of his company's monopoly position.'[39]

By the summer of 1965 BoT thinking had evolved. It was now of the view 'that the representation of industrialists is rather too high',[40] perhaps responding to the Labour preferences of the President, Douglas Jay. In part they responded by expanding the range of appointees to include businesspeople by another name, for instance, Tony Richards, a stockbroker (who became a Deputy Chairman in 1974), and the first management consultants (Roger Falk, Thomas Bowman and John Gratwick). The general business category therefore began to expand beyond the traditional manufacturing sector to include retail, services, consultancy and finance. This reflected structural changes in the economy and also the expansion of jurisdiction in the 1965 Act to cover services. If we accept a broad definition of 'business', table 6 shows that of the 181 appointees who can be identified by occupation up to March 1998, 82 were from 'business' (58 traditional, 14 finance, 10 consultancy/think tanks). This is 45 per cent of the total, with peaks of business appointments in the early 1960s and again from the early 1980s and especially in the early 1990s. The detailed appointment pattern is interesting, especially if it is correlated to the party politics of government. This is illustrated in table 9 and expanded on below.

Table 9 *Trends in business and union appointments to the Commission*

Period	Total appointments	Business	%	Trade union and co-op.	%	Government
1949–54	16	2	13	3	19	Lab./Cons.
1955–59	6	4	67	1	16	Cons.
1960–64	7	4	57	0	0	Cons.
1965–69	24	9	37	3	13	Lab.
1970–74	10	6	60	1	10	Cons.
1975–79	18	7	39	5	28	Lab.
1980–84	27	15	56	2	7	Cons.
1985–89	19	10	53	2	11	Cons.
1990–94	24	17	71	1	4	Cons.
1995–96	17	5	29	1	6	Cons.
1997–98	12	2	17	1	8	Lab.

Sources: as table 6.

Note: 1997–98, people appointed under the new Nolan procedure.

The counterpart of businesspeople in the old world of the 'two sides of industry' were the trade union members. Although the Commission is often seen as dominated by lawyers as many trade unionists (together with co-operators) as lawyers have been appointed over the years. This has clearly reflected union lobbying, to which Labour Governments have proved most susceptible. Thus the BoT noted in 1964 that 'the TUC [Trades Union Congress] have registered a mild complaint that their representation since the reduction in the Commission's size has been disproportionately cut down'. It goes on to note that 'it is necessary to depend largely on recommendations from the TUC, which are often not very exciting'.[41] It circumvented potential TUC dreariness by proposing Sydney Robinson, who was suggested by the Minister of Labour and by the current unionist on the Commission. Some awkwardness ensued when the TUC General Secretary, George Woodcock, refused to endorse Robinson, and proffered his own shortlist. The BoT conferred with the Ministry of Labour, which was insistent that the TUC should not be given the power to nominate members to public bodies, and the appointment of Robinson (President of the National Union of Boot and Shoe Operatives) went ahead.[42] He served for twelve years (and died in post). Mr Robinson notwithstanding, of the seventeen trade union appointees, at least nine have served on the TUC General Council and appear to reflect the trade union Establishment.

In this occupational review two groups initially favoured in 1949 seem subsequently to have done less well. Over the years some very eminent former civil servants have been appointed to the Commission, but very few of them, and more by Labour than by Conservative Governments. The Commission kicked off in 1949 with two senior officials but the BoT appointed only another fourteen up to 1998. Within this cadre four were Permanent Secretaries, nine had their knighthoods and all came in after retirement, putting them at the top of the age range. As might be expected, the majority were from the BoT/DTI but the really striking feature is their prominence within the Commission. Six civil servants have been Chairman or Deputy Chairman, giving the civil service group disproportionate influence. It seems, however, that numerically the civil service is making a comeback. Five civil servants (four from the DTI) have been appointed since 1995, with three in 1998 alone. The recent past is thus seeing a move away from business appointments and back to officials, although the officials nowadays tend to have a greater practical familiarity with industry through secondments, consultancies and board positions.

The other group favoured in 1949 was accountants. It was felt that examination of industrial structure and efficiency required a good familiarity with costing systems and company accounts. The least controversial member of the first Commission was Richard Yeabsley FCA, who was already Accountant Adviser to the BoT. But it was another twenty-five years before a second practising accountant in the shape of Jeremy Hardie was appointed (in 1976). He became Deputy Chairman in 1979, followed by his Deloittes partner David Richards in 1978. In very recent years accountants have come back into fashion but this lacuna remains puzzling, even if one makes allowances for the quite substantial number of business appointments with accounting qualifications.

In summarising the significance of occupation within the Commission membership, several conclusions can be drawn.

First, the Commission has not been dominated by lawyers. They have been outnumbered by economists and have been chosen for their clarity of thought and for their procedural instincts as much as for their substantive knowledge of the law.

Second, the Commission has not been a colony of the BoT. In absolute terms former civil servants have been outnumbered by economists, lawyers and even trade unionists. Ex-officials who have joined the Commission have been few in number but historically tended to take prominent positions.

Third, it has been felt necessary to appoint a steady stream of Establishment trade unionists. Appointees such as Alex Ferry and David

Hammond have played a full and valued role but this is the only group consistently appointed to represent a lobby.

Fourth, there has been a steady build-up in business membership, which has become the dominant element within the Commission. This was particularly true during the late Thatcher years. Since nearly half of all appointees have been 'from business', one might expect a positive reception within the business community.

Fifth, there have been few consumer appointees until very recently.

Sixth, the Commission and the DTI have established genuine 'balance' in Commission membership over the years. There have been changes but they are variations on the theme of expertise and professional skills. One challenge is to reproduce that balance within groups.

Seventh, the traditional pattern is appearing less dominant in the 1990s. The influx of new knowledge professions (consultants and think tanks), of consumer interests and of those working in a range of service industries, has made the Commission a more disparate and a much less 'Establishment' body.

Geography: the tartan token

There has been a curious pre-occupation throughout the life of the Commission with Scottish representation. This may be a characteristic common to all national bodies, and it reflects the power of the Scottish Office, but the BoT has been anxious to include Scots on the MMC. Quite why this should be essential has never been spelled out. The rules of competition, accountancy or corporate strategy cannot be so different north of the border, so expertise is not the criterion. It might be argued that the public interest is different in Scotland, which was certainly a factor in some of the Scottish merger cases of the early 1980s, but the question of legitimating the Commission to the Scottish business community is presumably the unspoken rationale.

The Scottish dimension surfaced in Alix Kilroy's April 1948 minute to her Permanent Secretary in which she notes that 'it will be necessary to offer the Scottish Office the chance of making suggestions for Members of the Commission (they were very keen on making a proposal for the Resale Price Maintenance Committee)'.[43] In fact the Scottish Office suggestions were not taken up but the BoT pursued Thomas Knox who held a Chair in Moral Philosophy and who was also associated with Lever Bros, of whom McIntosh remarked, 'I believe (but I am not sure) that Levers can be regarded as a "good" monopoly.'[44] Good monopoly or not, the BoT failed to recruit him but at the last minute came up with a

Scottish barrister, Gordon Stott (at forty by far the youngest of the first Commission), who had not featured in any of the earlier discussions. Perhaps his main qualification was his nationality. The Scottish dimension was re-emphasised in the 1960s when a memo confided that 'the field of industrialists is more difficult and it is specially difficult to get younger men or to secure a Scot'.[45]

The concern with Scotland is noteworthy given the relative inattention devoted to the other regions. The December 1964 paper had also noted that 'we ought perhaps to consider finding one member from Wales, and try to avoid having all the other members from the South East'.[46] But no obviously 'Welsh' member seems to have been appointed until David Jenkins in 1993 (General Secretary of the Wales TUC). The reference to the 'South East' emphasises a feature of the many public bodies which are based in London, and the MMC shares a pronounced Home Counties bias. This is a practical matter. The BoT noted in 1964 the absence of a representative from Northern Ireland but also noted that, 'it would probably be a hopeless task to find a suitable person who could put in the necessary time in London'.[47] Similarly, when considering lawyers, the Chairman veto'd one BoT suggestion, 'about Mr Pearson he felt that it might be a mistake to appoint a busy solicitor with his practice in Manchester: he had found that geographical remoteness could cause problems'. The idea of Manchester being 'remote' has a quaint metropolitan eccentricity. It was certainly not remote from business, from restrictive practices or from the origins of capitalism itself. In what was clearly a frank discussion with officials, Roskill also commented at length on the Hon. T. G. Roche, who 'might introduce a discordant note with his uncompromising, not to say rude, personality and inability to suffer fools'. Roskill felt that he could 'live with this problem' for the sake of Roche's experience (with the Restrictive Practices Court), his ability and his good standing in the business world (his only fear was that 'he might be thought too closely identified with the "business" as opposed to the "consumer" interest of the Commission').[48]

The BoT thus displays a lingering yearning for geographical representation which is really only expressed through the 'Scottish member'. The case for regional representation has to be mainly political or presentational rather than substantive, and this, with the trade union members, is an example of the representational principle in appointment to set alongside expertise. The principle persists and may now seem wise in the light of political devolution. In the 1999 Commission the two Scottish members are the Scottish solicitor Robert Bertram and Peter Mackay, who is the first former Scottish Office official to join the MMC. Hence

Edinburgh becomes an honorary extension of the Home Counties, but not Cardiff or Belfast.

Politics

From the beginning the Commission was conceived of as a politically neutral body, but it could not escape the pressures of the political context (as with trade union members) or the biases of ministers. It is clear that ministers have had decided views. Officials take the lead but ministers may intervene. Conventionally, a proposed new member will have 'a chat' with the Commission Chairman and a more formal interview with the minister, the Parliamentary Under-Secretary. Each member will have his or her own story of the meetings with (for instance) John Redwood or Neil Hamilton. In the life of the Commission a number of members with clear political affiliations have been appointed. In the early days, curiously enough, they were Liberals, with the past Chairman of the Scottish Liberals appointed in 1956 (Dr Leonard Gray). Indeed, the Chairman, Sir David Cairns, was a prominent Liberal and former parliamentary candidate. From the Labour side the trade union and co-operative members had obvious political sympathies and in more recent years Conservative activists have begun to appear. Former Conservative candidates or declared supporters include Peter Goldman (1980), James Ackers (1981), Bernard Owens (1981), Colin Baillieu (1984), Catherine Blight (1990) and Richard Prosser (1993), as well as a number of 'think tankers' such as Graham Mather (1989 and now a Conservative Euro-MP) and Ann Robinson (1993). The list is not exhaustive and, without impugning the impartiality of the individuals, it does seem that ministers were veering dangerously close to politicisation. Thus one senior civil servant noted that, in his view, DTI ministers did use appointments to influence the balance of opinion within the Commission, and another noted that officials did sometimes find that they had to resist the proposed appointment of people who were too close to the Conservative Party. Resistance tended to be successful but could cause arguments.[49] In fact there must have been some concern from about 1985 that the combination of Conservative activists and libertarian economists might have put too political a slant on the composition of the Commission (see the discussion of Commission reports in the early 1990s in chapter 9). It would be surprising if the Commission had been able to escape the trends of political fashion and Conservative success, but it is an interesting question as to how the free-market Conservatism of the 1980s might have affected the way the groups defined their public interest judgements.

Some more systematic evidence of political influence comes from the statistics on business and trade union appointments noted in table 9. The time periods approximate to periods of Conservative and Labour Governments. The statistics are crude and subject to time lags (hence a member appointed in 1976 may first have been proposed in 1974), but they do indicate the sorts of appointment that ministers were willing publicly to endorse. There is a marked correlation. Labour Governments appoint trade unionists, Conservatives appoint business people. This is hardly a revelation but it should temper the formula claims from the Commission and the DTI that appointments are strictly neutral. It is simply impossible to exclude party political influence (neither is it necessarily undesirable). The bias was particularly striking from 1980–94 but has broken down in 1995–98. Recent appointments of business people have fallen to an historic low, which presumably denotes a correction, a reaction to the over-indulgence of the early 1990s and a re-creation of the Commission's 'balance'.

The specialist panels

Agitation in the early 1960s, including a report from the Royal Commission on the Press,[50] concerning control of the press led to special provisions in the 1965 Act to evaluate newspaper mergers. This is an interesting sub-plot within the Commission's public interest work since the rationale for controlling newspapers has less to do with economic efficiency or exploitation and more to do with the freedom of the press, sustaining national control and maintaining an open democratic process. Many countries have similarly restrictive provisions in their competition laws which are also often linked to a 'cultural' argument (Canada's desire to keep the United States at bay is a prime example). Politicians have a keen interest in the press and Douglas Jay was instrumental in creating the press provisions in the 1965 Act. Enoch Powell once observed that 'for a politician to complain about the press is like a ship's captain complaining about the sea',[51] but when control of the press is concentrated perhaps there is cause for concern. The Fair Trading Act provides for mandatory reference of a merger if the purchaser already controls a daily circulation of over 500,000. The Secretary of State can make an exception if the titles are under economic threat, and this device was used, very controversially, to allow News International to take over *The Times* in 1980 and *Today* in 1987. It is interesting that one of the few defeats for the 1998 Competition Bill in the Lords should be over newspaper pricing and the allegedly predatory tactics used by *The Times* and other papers under Rupert Murdoch's control.[52] To provide for a knowledgeable group of members, who may be called upon at short notice, the Act provides for a Newspaper Panel from whom members can be drawn to supplement a group composed in the normal way. The first Newspaper Panel of nine people was created in 1965. Members were selected less for their economic expertise than for their knowledge of the newspaper industry, and Douglas Jay had clear preferences, especially Lord Francis-Williams, who had been a prominent participant in the Bill proceedings in the House of Lords. Jay consulted Lord Devlin, then Chairman of the Press Council, who turned down the offer of an appointment but recommended his Vice Chairman, Henry Bate. Devlin's judgements were very much what officials would have been expected to endorse. Bate, he stressed, was 'intelligent and objective'; Donald Tyerman, former editor of the *Economist*, was 'first class and never speaks unless he has something to say' – praise indeed.[53]

The principle of specialist panels was invoked following privatisation. A Telecommunications Panel was created in 1985 and Water and Electricity Panels in 1991. The Commission is required to appoint from one to three members of the panel to any licence modification reference or for a water price adjudication. Here again the specialist members will join a conventional MMC group but, as discussed in chapter 8, the relatively low level of utility regulation references means that they have been somewhat under-employed and the size of the panels has been reduced. Now and again members have made the transition to regular membership (Sir Ronald Halstead from the Newspaper Panel in 1991; Gill Owen from the Utility Panels in 1996), but on the whole they have served their terms solely as panel members. It is not entirely clear why such panels were regarded as necessary, especially since there are no panels for gas or railways. Expertise is certainly important but the MMC has not opted for specialisation among members and here conflicts of interest become more likely. One possibility is that Whitehall sponsoring departments pressed for specialists in whom they would have more faith. The panels have been retained but the 1998 Utilities Consultation Paper made it clear that the MMC would be required to take the sensible step of concentrating the specialists into a single Utilities Panel (see chapter 8).

The job of the member

Over the life of the Commission the only full-time members have been the Chairmen (with the sole exception of Sir Harold Saunders, 1949–54). The Deputy Chairmen typically served half-time and the majority have

been 'regular' members serving on a part-time basis. The DTI's consultative document on mergers in 1988 stressed members' 'current experience of the outside world', but also recommended variable periods of
part-time employment moving away from the standard one and a half
days per week. Following the paper the DTI increased the maximum
number of members to fifty[54] but retained the norm of one and a half days.
In 1990 the Commission introduced the category of 'reserve' members.
These tend to be members who find the time commitment difficult. They
are only paid when they are actually working on an inquiry (at the rate of
one day per week) and they will feel less of an obligation automatically to
agree to serve. In 1999 almost half of the Commission members were
serving on a 'reserve' basis.

The practical meaning of 'part time' is variable. At some points,
when the workload is light, members can go for months without being
called upon; at other times the demands are barely manageable. The con-
tracted commitment of one and a half days per week could be seen as 30
per cent of a normal working week, for which regular members in April
1997 were paid £14,731, an annualised rate of around £49,000. This is
not over-generous – a salary equivalent to that of a junior main board
director of a small to medium-sized company or that of a senior professor. Members do not take the job for the money. Both the time commitment and the relative pay scales have remained at similar levels over the
years although it is interesting to note that the differential relative to the
Chairman has grown larger.

The BoT has considerable discretion as to periods of appointment
and renewal. Under the 1948 Act members were appointed for up to five
years, amended to three to seven years under the 1965 Act and up to five
years again in the 1973 Act. There is no age limit and no restriction on
reappointment, so members can serve for extended periods. The size of
the Commission and turnover of members means that it really cannot
develop a collective identity and, while they will know all their colleagues,
members will have served on inquiries with only a limited number of
them. Things were very different in the early days when 'The Commission' was an organic body which met collectively for all inquiries. The
contemporary member of the Commission is therefore a slightly isolated
member of a fragmented body and his or her main contacts will be with
the administrative staff, with the present small group with whom he or
she is working, and with the Chairman or Deputy Chairman of that
group. In the 1960s and 1970s things were reputedly even worse. Sir Ashton Roskill appeared to discourage the expression of collective views by
the Commission and it met very rarely as a full body. Nowadays more

effort is made through seminars, feedback meetings and social meetings to bring members together and to discuss current issues and theoretical developments. All the same, the experience of working with today's Commission is not particularly glamorous or well resourced. Members do not have offices at New Court, itself an undistinguished building. They attend the Commission mainly for hearings and group meetings, and make only sporadic use of the library and databases. Although this style of working appears congenial to many members it does have implications for the coherence and collegiality of the Commission. Morale could certainly become an issue, especially since members work hard.

From its earliest days the Commission has taken its work extremely seriously and has aspired to produce reports that are as definitive as possible. If the BoT appoints leading experts it must expect them to deploy their expertise but, as we saw earlier, members of the first Commission found themselves taking on rather more work than they expected. In one of his first meetings with Harold Wilson Sir Archibald Carter noted, almost plaintively, that 'the members wished to read, and if they were to consider the position fully could hardly avoid reading, a very large volume of papers about each industry referred to them'. This helped to account for the time delays so that the Chairman estimated that each reference would take at least fifteen months.[55] The work pressures are hardly alleviated by the unpredictability of references and the safeguards perceived to be necessary to avoid possible conflicts of interest. Unpredictability means that the staff find it difficult to do very much background work before a case arrives, and the regular members have no opportunity. References can be exceedingly complex. In the *GEC/Plessey* merger inquiry, to take a random example, members had to be sufficiently expert in the arcane world of armaments procurement to be taking evidence, within weeks, from Sir Arnold Weinstock, from the Permanent Secretary of the Ministry of Defence and from assorted Admirals. On the *Milk Marque* monopoly case, members with no prior knowledge of European agricultural policy and the complexities of foodstuffs marketing had to become expert within months.

Specialisation is made more difficult by the rules on conflict of interest, which mean that knowledgeable members may not be able to serve. Any member who has a financial or personal interest in an industry must be excluded on grounds of natural justice to avoid any hint of bias. Thus financiers may have difficulty in looking at City dealing rules, and former oil executives are likely to be excluded from energy inquiries. The increased preoccupation with judicial review has reinforced this concern and means that a hint of conflict of interest can exclude valuable members. The MMC has, in the words of Lord Nolan, 'some of the strictest rules in government circles on conflict of interest'.[56] For instance, the rules obviously exclude members with a shareholding in a company subject to inquiry, but they have been tightened up also to exclude those with any shareholding in the industrial sector. Chairman Sir Graeme Odgers actually switched all his investments into government bonds. The rules have become so tight as to verge on the absurd and some members certainly find them irksome. In this the Commission is at the mercy of the courts. The risk is that an MMC report and its findings could be struck out in its entirety if a member were found to have any interest in the outcome. On this Counsel have advised that there is no *de minimis* rule and that the courts may regard apparent bias as just as important as actual bias.[57] The Commission therefore veers on the side of caution.

Once in place members work hard, and recent members work harder than their predecessors, at least as measured by cases completed. Analysis shows that a member can expect to work on fifteen to twenty cases over his or her period of appointment, figures which have become more consistent during the 1980s. There has also been a steady increase in the number of cases dealt with by any one member each year. In the relaxed 1950s a member might only do one case a year, in the 1960s two a year, nowadays it is three. The increase reflects a higher number of smaller cases (mergers, Competition Act cases and newspaper mergers) but it also reflects the 'speed-up' from 1987 (see chapter 5). Of course, these averages conceal extreme variations. The cases themselves are often incomparable, so that huge investigations such as *Beer* (1989), *Gas* (1993) and the immense *Domestic Electrical Goods* (1997) can hardly be regarded in the same light as a provincial newspaper merger. Similarly, some members have served for only a short period while others have taken many cases over many years. More in a spirit of illustration rather than trying to establish any 'order of merit', it is nonetheless interesting to note the huge contributions made by some members, as seen in table 10. It is these members who might be thought to represent the weight of continuity within the Commission and who could be thought to have moulded the procedures, and perhaps the contents, of reports. Some of the names are to be expected, the Chairmen and Deputies; others have been the 'cannon fodder' of the Commission in the 1960s and 1980s, people such as the economists Basil Yamey and Tibor Barna, industrialists such as Fred Bonner, Bernard Owens and Patricia Mann, or the trade unionist Sydney Robinson. The table indicates the crucial importance of the Deputy Chairmen, a role which has given rise to a measure of collective leadership.

Table 10 *The 'Top Twenty' members of the Commission by cases undertaken*

Name	Appoint-ment	Chaired	Served	Total	Years served	Cases per year
Sir Godfray Le Quesne	1974	59	1	60	13	4.6
Dan Goyder	1980	26	29	55	17	3.2
Peter Dean	1982	32	18	50	15	3.3
Sir Ashton Roskill	1960	45	2	47	15	3.1
Sir Sydney Lipworth	1982	30	17	47	12	3.9
Bernard Owens	1981	7	36	43	12	3.6
Basil Yamey	1966	0	38	38	12	3.2
Roger Falk	1965	0	37	37	15	2.5
Tibor Barna	1963	1	34	35	15	2.3
Sydney Robinson	1966	0	34	34	12	2.8
Richard Smethurst	1978	10	22	32	11	2.9
Holman Hunt	1980	19	12	31	11	2.8
Colin Baillieu	1984	1	30	31	9	3.4
Alex Ferry	1986	1	30	31	8	3.9
Patricia Mann	1984	1	29	30	9	3.3
John Sadler	1973	0	30	30	13	2.3
David Richards	1983	25	4	29	7	4.1
Frederick Bonner	1987	0	28	28	6	4.7
Hans Liesner	1989	26	2	28	8	3.5
Lief Mills	1982	1	24	25	9	2.8

Sources: annual reports and MMC database at February 1998.
Note: the list is strictly indicative; it makes no allowances for the type of case.

The Deputy Chairmen

The Commission has suffered periodic and intense criticism for the length of its inquiries. It argues that the investigations and judgements which it is required by statute to make necessitate a relatively prolonged inquiry. But procedural issues have also caused delay, one of them being the requirement under the 1948 Act for the whole Commission to conduct each inquiry.

Sir Archibald Carter met Harold Wilson at several points during 1950 to discuss the delays which were preventing Wilson from making new references. Carter said they could only deal with two, Wilson had in mind at least five.[58] Several ways out of the impasse were debated. These included increasing both the size of the Commission and its staff, creating more full-time members, dividing up the work between the 'factual' and the 'public interest' elements of the inquiry, and working in much smaller groups. The difficulty of splitting into groups was that the Commission was itself divided on the nature of its role. Some members felt extremely uncomfortable with the case-by-case approach and these members might have been concerned that a sub-group might put forward a report with which they disagreed. In the event two members did enter a reservation in the first report (on *Dental Goods*) in which they noted that the malpractices found there were common across industry. Thus, Wilson told the House, 'they point out that, as is common knowledge, similar practices are carried on in other industries and that it is purely fortuitous that this industry should have been investigated first by the Commission'.[59] Their objections were overcome and it was agreed to expand the Commission and to create two 'informal' Deputy Chairmen who would do the bulk of the work on the fact finding with a small group of members, before putting the material to the whole Commission for the 'public interest' stage. Thus C. N. Gallie, a trade unionist, and Gordon Stott, the Scottish barrister, agreed to become half-time with an increased salary. These arrangements were formalised in the 1953 Act, which provided for three permanent Deputy Chairmen and the ability to work in groups. The new arrangements came under the control of Sir David Cairns, who took over from Carter as Chairman in January 1954. But while he began formally to divide the work into groups he did not seek appointment of any Deputy Chairmen and instead Chaired them all himself. Groups were abandoned with the 1956 Act, which reinstated a smaller, single-Chaired Commission. The Deputy Chairmen idea thus went into suspension.

The 1965 Act revitalised the Commission with Deputy Chairmen on exactly the 1953 model. Ashton Roskill had agreed to take on the Chairmanship from December 1965 but, like Cairns, proved cautious about deputies. In a meeting with the BoT in October 1965 he observed that 'he would prefer to continue with the ad hoc arrangements whereby members of the Commission are asked to lead groups'. He thought that only two of the current Commission members would make suitable Chairs and in one case, that of Bernard Miller, he was a relatively junior member 'whose appointment might cause jealousy among other members'.[60] The BoT went along with the Chairman-elect's preferences and the first formal Deputy Chairman was eventually appointed in 1967 in the form of Sir Henry Hardman, former Permanent Secretary of the Ministry of Defence. The Commission managed with one Deputy

Chairman until 1974, when a second was appointed, but did not move to appoint a third until October 1983, when the current pattern of a Chairman and three Deputy Chairmen became established.

As table 11 indicates, there have been sixteen formally appointed Deputy Chairmen up to 1999. It is hard not to believe that their individual style, talents and interests have had some influence on the cases they have heard and, of course, the constant problem of maintaining consistency between groups has been intensified. Table 11 shows the process of 'balancing' at work. There has been some preference for civil servants and there has consistently been an industrialist as one Deputy Chairman but also a good representation of economists with the appointment of younger economists in the 1970s. In addition the legislation allows for any member to Chair a group and, especially where the pressure of work is intense, experienced members of the Commission still occasionally take on the role of group Chairman.

Members' motivations

As chapter 5 goes on to discuss, the role of Chairmen in inquiries is complex. They have to manage self-confident colleagues who are not cyphers but are successful professionals with decided views. As the Commission has grown, and turnover increased, to be a member of the Commission is not as exceptional as twenty years ago. On the other hand it is more important, and to be a member of a high profile inquiry takes members dangerously close to becoming national figures. After the extraordinarily sensitive *BSkyB/Manchester United* merger report was published, for instance, *The Times* ran a picture and profile of the five-person group.[61] But members do not join for the sake of publicity. They join to undertake an important and fascinating job and do so, it seems, mainly from a sense of public service. The pool of potential recruits appears to be large. When membership was openly advertised as part of the Nolan reforms in 1997–98 there were over 700 applicants for the 12 posts actually filled.

For members the work discipline comes from the cases which are, almost by definition, complicated. It comes also from internal peer group pressure and from 'the management', which expects members to conform to standard practices. As Sir Graeme Odgers remarked, 'I am very upset if an individual member misses a major hearing.'[62] Despite the work pressure, members find the job quite fascinating. A past member found it 'the most interesting thing I have ever done – I would be willing to pay to do it'.[63] The sense of intellectual excitement and the opportunity to

Table 11 *Deputy Chairmen of the Commission*

Name	Appointment	To Chair	Cases Chaired	Age appointed	Age retired	Occupation	School	University
Edgar Richards	1965	1974	10	53	68	finance	Harrow	–
Sir Henry Hardman	1967	1967	1	62	65	civil servant	Manchester Central	Manchester
Sir Alexander Johnstone	1969	1969	11	64	71	civil servant	Heriot	Edinburgh
Sir Max Brown	1975	1976	5	61	67	civil servant	New Zealand	Clare, Cambridge
Hon. John Eccles	1976	1980	12	45	54	industrialist	Winchester	Magdalen, Oxford
Jeremy Hardie	1976	1980	10	38	45	accountant/economist	Winchester	New College, Oxford
Richard Smethurst	1978	1986	10	37	48	economist	Liverpool College	Worcester, Oxford; Nuffield, Oxford
Dan Goyder	1980	1991	26	42	59	lawyer	Rugby	Trinity, Cambridge
Holman Hunt	1980	1985	19	56	67	industrialist/consultant	Queen's Park, Glasgow	Glasgow
Sir Alan Neale	1981	1988	12	63	67	civil servant	Highgate	St John's, Oxford
Peter Dean	1982	1990	32	43	58	industrialist/lawyer	Rugby	London
David Richards	1983	1983	25	55	62	accountant	Highgate	Fellow of the Institute of Chartered Accountants
Hans Liesner	1989	1989	26	60	68	civil servant/economist	Germany	Bristol; Nuffield, Oxford
Derek Morris	1991	1995	9	46		economist	Harrow Grammar	St Edmund Hall, Oxford; Nuffield, Oxford
Graham Corbett	1997	1997		63		industrialist/accountant	Stowe	Fellow of the Institute of Chartered Accountants
Denise Kingsmill	1997	1997		50		lawyer		Girton, Cambridge

Sources: annual reports BoT/OFT; *Who's Who*; MMC database (at February 1998).

apply skills and test ideas comes through regularly in members' assessments. In addition there can be very rewarding group dynamics. A new member observed, with some surprise, how the ideas of people from different backgrounds managed to 'gel'; and a past member observed that, 'although members of the Commission only get to know each other well during the course of the inquiry, there was a surprising level of camaraderie which was most enjoyable'.[64] Of course, the picture is not all rosy. Relationships with staff, with other members and with Chairmen generate friction and the process of reaching a consensus on an inquiry can be tense (see chapter 5). Despite this the Commission has established a high degree of collegiality.

The inquiry material is exceedingly sensitive, both politically and 'price sensitive' (a health warning that appears on most inquiry papers, meaning that public release of the information could affect share prices). But leaks are extremely rare and, when leak inquiries have been instituted, the source has tended to be politicians who sometimes reveal findings inadvertently. A good lunch with an astute journalist can be dangerous. There are no recorded instances of leaks being traced to Commission members (although there have been hints[65]) and only one recorded case of a member being dismissed. The case was that of Brian Davidson, a long-serving industrialist who was removed in 1968 by Tony Benn after his company, Bristol Siddeley, was found to have made 'exorbitant profits' on government contracts.[66] The traditional appointments process thus appears to have secured members who have been talented, upstanding and public spirited. Commission employment does not offer large material inducements and for many younger members there can be a substantial opportunity cost. Some business people, such as John Sadler, have been allowed generous leave of absence by their employers (John Lewis in that case) although others also find that their knowledge of the Commission can be fed back to employers to improve regulatory compliance. But the traditional process has not been beyond criticism, and the potential for undue 'old boy' networking and for quixotic ministerial appointments led the DTI to endorse the new Nolan procedures quickly and wholeheartedly. The Nolan procedures require open advertisement, transparent interviewing and oversight by an external assessor.[67] They do slow down the appointment process and introduce their own biases through, for instance, the use of 'appointment consultants'. The first tranche of twelve Nolan appointees arrived at the Commission in 1997–98. They were politically neutral people with a professional background. Only four were under fifty and the flavour was 'technocratic', the only surprising element being the large proportion of former civil servants.

Conclusion

The review of the pattern of membership underlines the importance of the Chairman and the Deputy Chairmen in providing leadership, continuity and consistency. The part-time principle makes it difficult for members, individually or collectively, to influence the broad direction of the Commission as a whole. The members appear in a good light as a committed body of people who display considerable dedication and give, on a crude measure, remarkable value for money in respect of their time, skill and experience. The market value of their work would be considerably in excess of their salaries.

The members provide expertise, sometimes of a quite exceptional standard. Their experience also perhaps explains the difficulty of making younger appointments. All the same, there is clearly a case for appointing more people in their thirties. The DTI has responded to changes in the economy by appointing, in recent years, a far wider spectrum of members including more women (and a female Deputy Chairman), more representatives of the consumer viewpoint and people from a range of service industries. The appointment of industrialists is important in maintaining business confidence and also for leavening a theoretical approach with practical insights. Sometimes poachers do make good gamekeepers.

The distinctive aspect of the employment of part-time members is seen in the synthesis of the inquiry process. This is, as one member remarked, 'incredibly British'.[68] Members work with staff in a process which draws on decades of experience and which succeeds in producing a synthesis of analysis and judgement; of technical skills and original questioning; of staff advice and members' decisions. It would be difficult to design such a system from scratch and members are drawn into the process in a fashion that exhibits collegiality and mutual respect. Whether the process produces the 'right' verdicts; whether the balance of members creates a Commission that is too tolerant of business, are questions we can return to later in the study. At this point we can simply observe that the Commission has created a defensible model. In 1953 Sir Archibald Carter speculated that the 'public interest' would eventually become clear enough to be codified by Parliament.[69] That point has not been reached and is in fact a philosophical impossibility. The members of the Commission still could not construct an agreed definition of the 'public interest' but they think they know it when they see it and the Commission procedures are there to aid their perception. In chapter 5 we turn to those procedures.

Notes

1 PRO, BT64/482, 'The Monopolies Commission: membership and organisation', letter from Harold Wilson, President of the BoT, to George Isaacs, Minister of Labour (27 July 1948).

2 Sir Archibald Carter, Sixth Report from the Select Committee on Estimates, *Monopolies and Restrictive Practices Commission*, 1952–53, HC 177 (London, HMSO, 1953), p. 8.

3 Richard Chapman, 'Commissions in policy making', in R. Chapman (ed.), *The Role of Commissions in Policy Making* (London, Allen and Unwin, 1973).

4 See T. J. Cartwright, *Royal Commissions and Departmental Committees in Britain: A Case Study in Institutional Adaptiveness and Public Participation in Government* (London, Hodder and Stoughton, 1975), ch. 5 for the balance of criteria typically used.

5 *Report of the Committee on Administrative Tribunals and Inquiries* (Franks Committee), Cmnd 218 (London, HMSO, July 1957); *Report of the Committee on Standards in Public Life* (Nolan Committee), Cm 2850 I (London, HMSO, 1995).

6 See R. Wraith and P. Hutchesson, *Administrative Tribunals* (London, Allen and Unwin, 1973).

7 PRO, BT64/482, minute by R. C. Bryant, 'The Monopolies Commission: membership and organization' (31 March 1948).

8 *Ibid.*, minute 8.

9 *Ibid.*, minute 18.

10 PRO, BT64/508, 'Monopolies and Restrictive Practices Commission: discussions with Chairman', note by R. R. D. McIntosh on meeting between the President and the Chairman, 30 November 1948, with Miss Kilroy and Sir James Helmore also present.

11 Dame Alix Kilroy, *Public Servant, Private Woman* (London, Gallancz, 1988), p. 255.

12 H. Mercer, *Constructing a Competitive Order: The Hidden History of British Antitrust Policies* (Cambridge University Press, 1995), p. 99.

13 PRO, BT64/482, item 63, attribution lost but probably Bryant.

14 Mercer, *Constructing a Competitive Order*, p. 101.

15 PRO, BT64/482, minute 8, Kilroy to Helmore.

16 H. Mercer, 'The Monopolies and Restrictive Practices Commission, 1949–56: a study in regulatory failure', in G. Jones and M. Kirby (eds), *Competitiveness and the State* (Manchester University Press, 1991), p. 92.

17 PRO, BT64/482, paper 62.

18 *Ibid.*, paper 38, Wilson to Cripps (18 August 1948).

19 Kilroy, *Public Servant*, p. 266.

20 Interview with Dame Alix Kilroy (Lady Meynell) (October 1997).

21 PRO, BT64/482, minute 47 (15 October 1948).

22 Charles Rowley, *The British Monopolies Commission* (London, Allen and Unwin, 1966), pp. 56–7.

23 PRO, BT64/4159, 'The Future of the Monopolies Commission', note by Industry and Manufactures, branch 1 (IM 1A) following up the President's meeting of 24 April 1950.

24 PRO, BT64/482, minute 4 (6 April 1948).

25 All *ibid.*, paper 62, MRPC members.

26 Personal correspondence.

27 PRO, BT258/1646, paper 11, membership of the MC (29 December 1964).

28 *Ibid.*, note 17 (4 February 1965).

29 *Ibid.*, note 17.

30 *Ibid.*, note 17.

31 *Ibid.*, paper 11.

32 *Ibid.*, paper 60 (4 August 1965).

33 *Ibid.*, letter from Sir Herbert Andrew (27 April 1965).

34 PRO, BT64/482, paper 54 by R. R. McIntosh, 'Monopolies and Restrictive Practices Commission: membership' (15 October 1948).

35 PRO, BT258/1646, paper 11.

36 PRO, BT258/1649, note by D. C. Hartridge of meeting with Roskill, 14 October 1965. This looked very like the old-boys' network in operation. Roche and Barrowclough were both public school Oxford men who (like Roskill) both practised in the Inner Temple.

37 PRO, BT64/482, exchange of minutes (31 March to 6 April 1948).

38 PRO, BT258/1646, paper 11, paras 15 and 17 (29 December 1964).

39 *Ibid.*, paper 17, paper from R. F. Allen (4 February 1965).

40 PRO, BT258/1647, paper 60 (4 August 1965).

41 PRO, BT258/1646, paper 11.

42 PRO, BT258/1650, exchange of correspondence between Llewellyn-Smith and the Ministry of Labour, plus note to the President from IM2 (15 December 1965).

43 PRO, BT64/482, minute 8 (30 April 1948).

44 *Ibid.*, paper by McIntosh (15 October 1948).

45 PRO, BT258/1647, paper 60, 'new members for the MC' (4 August 1965).

46 PRO, BT228/1646, paper 11, para. 20.

47 *Ibid.*, paper 11, para. 19.

48 PRO, BT258/1649, minute from D. C. Hartridge to Mr Glaves Smith re a visit from Mr Roskill to the Secretary (14 October 1965).

49 Interviews and personal correspondence.

50 *Royal Commission on the Press, 1961–62, Report*, Cmnd 1811, 1961–62 (London, HMSO, 1962).

51 From a *Guardian* article by Enoch Powell (26 April 1984).

52 See Lords debate of Monday 9 February 1998. The Government lost the vote on an amendment which prohibited a newspaper 'eliminating competition'.

53 PRO, BT258/1647, letter from Devlin to Jay, President of the BoT (26 July 1965).

54 By statutory instrument in 1989. See also DTI, *Mergers Policy* (London, HMSO, 1988), p. 21.

55 PRO, BT64/4159, minutes of a meeting between the President of the BoT and the Chairman of the MC (30 June 1950).

56 Opening remarks in *Evidence to the Nolan Committee on 'Standards in Public Life'*, Cm 2850–II, Vol. 2 (London, HMSO 1995), p. 477.

57 Correspondence with Commission official.

58 PRO, BT64/4159, minutes of meeting (30 June 1950).

59 Harold Wilson, President of the BoT, statement to the House (15 December 1950) reported in the BoT, *Monopolies and Restrictive Practices Act, 1948, Annual Report for the Period Ending 31 December 1950* HC 118 (London, HMSO, 1951), pp. 7–8.

60 PRO, BT258/1649, note by D. C. Hartridge to Mr Glaves Smith (14 October 1965).

61 *The Times* (10 April 1999). The group was Derek Morris, Gill Owen, David Hammond, Nicholas Finney and Roger Munson. Their unambiguous rejection of the takeover was implemented by Stephen Byers, Secretary of State for Trade and Industry.

62 Sir Graeme Odgers, *Evidence to the Nolan Committee*, p. 484.

63 Interview with a former (academic) member of the Commission.

64 Interview and personal correspondence (with a former civil servant and an industrialist).

65 Hennessy notes an insider dealing inquiry within the DTI in 1986 which included the MMC. P. Hennessy, *Whitehall* (London, Secker and Warburg, 1989), p. 378.

66 See *The Times* (26 April 1968).

67 Office of the Commissioner for Public Appointments, *Guidance on Appointments to Public Bodies* (London, OCPA, July 1998).

68 Interview with a former member of the Commission (September 1998).

69 Carter, Sixth Report from the Select Committee, p. 5.

5

Procedures and the culture of the Commission

Sir Ashton Roskill, Q.C., refuses to talk about the philosophy of the Monopolies Commission, of which he is Chairman. 'It is enshrined in the reports ... You must read these. Each case is different.'

The Times, 28 September 1967

It is what you might call a type of jury system, certainly an experienced and high quality jury system. It is on the basis of their knowledge, their experience that they make these judgements which are particular to the case.

Sir Graeme Odgers, Chairman MMC, February 1995[1]

It is a curiosity that the procedures of the Commission have changed less than its workload or the scope of its formal responsibilities. This procedural continuity is important in three respects. First, there is the obvious question of whether procedures with their origins in the 1940s are still appropriate for the first decade of the twenty-first century. Second, the possibility that procedures may fundamentally affect outcomes. This is the question of means and ends: do the means chosen affect the ends? Third, study of the procedures can reveal much about the culture of the organisation. In particular it is revealing of the values and norms cherished by the Commission and the forms of authority which it accepts and exerts. The procedural questions are neither marginal nor technical. They lie at the heart of an understanding of the Commission.

The procedures were designed in the first three years of the life of the Commission and are still recognisable in today's practice. They responded to the early definition of the requirements of the MMC's task. These requirements were internal but also reflected the external environment, and can be summarised as follows:

Internal

- a case-by-case approach
- the need to be fair and even handed
- a full investigation of the facts
- the need to inform part-time members
- an agnostic test based on 'the public interest'
- the need to answer legislative requirements such as the stipulations to 'reach definite conclusions' and to 'specify the particular effects adverse to the public interest'.[2]

External

- no ability to influence the type of case or workload
- no control over the appointment of Commissioners
- no obligation to follow up reports.

The concept of the full, agnostic investigation was intrinsic to the 1948 Act. Some of the procedural choices could be taken to be pre-determined by that and later Acts, but on the whole the procedures were developed within the organisation and reflected an extensive discretion allowed by the legislation. Once procedures were established they proved remarkably impervious to change. Thus many of the early choices about hearings were still in place up to 1998–99, when some substantial procedural innovations began to be introduced. Hearings are formal but not legalistic; there are no oaths and no cross-examination by other parties. They have not been held in public so that the Commission usually sees only one party at a time and does not make all evidence available to other parties as a matter of course. Similarly, practices such as the 'putting back' of evidence to parties for them to check have consistently been maintained.

The Commission's autonomy over its own procedures does need to be recognised as part of a larger procedural complexity which involves the other two agencies within the tripartite system. The system has been criticised over the years for apparent duplication and dislocation between the agencies. Thus the MMC is often accused of duplicating the initial investigation by the OFT; and the DTI is often felt to be re-analysing the material in MMC reports and is certainly, with the OFT, criticised for not implementing MMC recommendations. We look more deeply at relations between the agencies in chapters 6 and 9. This chapter concentrates on the MMC.

The MMC procedures have not always met with complete approval. In response to the very first report (on *Dental Goods*) a pained letter from the President of the Trade Association complained that 'the commission is both prosecutor and judge'.[3] Forty-five years later the TIC was relaying identical criticism from industry, noting that 'companies have also complained of their lack of access to information and restrictions on their ability to challenge evidence against them'.[4] There has been consistent pressure from companies and their legal advisers for a process of 'pleading' which has been consistently resisted. All the same, it is remarkable that the investigatory procedure initially devised to deal with cartels and trade associations should then be applied to single-firm monopolies, to oligopolies, to mergers, to anti-competitive practices, to the efficiency of nationalised industries, and to the conformity of companies with regulatory licences. And in each instance variants of the 'public interest' test have been employed. It is helpful to dwell for a moment on the theoretical approach to explaining such continuity.

Historical continuity and path dependence

The survival and organisational continuity of the MMC provide material with which to explore two intriguing questions within organisation theory. The first is the question of path dependence and institutionalisation introduced in chapter 1. The second is the conditions for organisational survival. We return to these questions at the end of this section after an initial review of the insights that organisation theory might provide for understanding the Commission.

Organisations mould the behaviour of those who work within them in a number of ways. They do so by regulating behaviour through rules; by imposing social obligations through normative pressure; and by providing automatic expectations through a cognitive framing of reality. In constructing these processes an organisation builds up a repertoire of standard procedures, explicit values and tacit norms which begin to give it a 'character' that is more than the sum of its parts. Organisations develop preferred ways of undertaking their tasks and solving problems which, at the extreme, can amount to policy preferences.

These properties of organisations are increasingly recognised, and indeed exploited, through mission statements and explicit attempts at cultural manipulation. BP has one sort of organisational culture, Microsoft quite another, and such contrasts extend into government. Thus the DTI, the Ministry of Defence and the Department of Social Security have different cultures which reflect their history and functions. It would not be unreasonable to suggest that the MMC is sufficiently distinctive and long-standing to have evolved its own organisational characteristics or 'culture'. Many divisions and agencies within Whitehall certainly have peculiarities but these are a sub-set of a larger departmental or Whitehall culture. In the case of the MMC, however, it has considerable autonomy, a unique relationship with its members, and a distinctive task which has allowed it to develop distinctive characteristics. Indeed, as a 'Commission' possessed of a considerable practical independence, its autonomy is an essential part of its function and the development of cultural as well as administrative independence is not unnatural.

On this basis we can turn to the question of how organisational characteristics are created. The conception and birth of an organisation will equip it with functions, rules, a new staff and characteristics that reflect the time and the origin of the ideas and the staff. The MMC was conceived in 1944 and 'born' during 1948–49. Its origins were in the British civil service of the 1940s, from which all of its first complement of staff came, as well as its two full-time Commissioners. The early decisions about organisation, staffing and procedures could be said to provide a set of precedents or a 'genetic code' which to some extent pre-determined later developments. Some organisations move quickly away from their early origins and are 'redesigned' over the years. This is less true of government bureaucracies, which tend to exhibit greater inertia which is reinforced by continuity of staffing and their unique exercise of legal authority. Students of organisations note a general tendency for routines and procedures to become sanctified by practice so that procedural requirements become 'infused with value'.[5] Thus new generations of staff regard the existing procedures both as normal, taken for granted; and as embodiments of an accumulated wisdom. Procedures become embedded in a familiar process of goal displacement which makes it more important for the organisation to follow the 'correct' procedure than to achieve the 'correct' outcome.

Of course, procedural continuity has great virtues and is indispensable. It incorporates known and successful methods which can be followed routinely, thus cutting down the transaction costs of having constantly to reconsider how to approach repetitive problems. Familiar procedures also allow the organisation to engage smoothly with clients and other government agencies. They provide predictability and facilitate co-ordination. Organisations and their staff follow the standard procedures because this is what the rules require, because this is what colleagues expect, and because no other course of action occurs to them – this is the 'natural' thing to do.

It is familiar organisational pathology for procedures to become outdated or less relevant as organisations face constant challenges of adaptation. Flexibility is rendered more difficult as organisations take on characteristics of 'institutions'. When norms and procedures take on a value of their own they become institutionalised in a process which Selznick eloquently described in a classical treatment:

> Institutionalisation is a process. It is something that happens to an organisation over time reflecting the organisation's own distinctive history, the people who have been in it, the groups it embodies and the vested interests they have created, and the way it has adapted to the environment. In what is perhaps its most significant meaning 'to institutionalise' is to infuse with value beyond the technical aspects of the task in hand.[6]

This book does not suggest that the MMC is an 'institution', it is too small and too much a part of the wider UK competition policy institution. But it does suggest that the goals and processes of the Commission have become institutionalised. In Selznick's formulation they have become imbued with an intrinsic value which may not be wholly necessary for the technical aspects of the task in hand.

The importance of institutionalisation goes hand in hand with the more recent idea of path dependence introduced in chapter 1. Early choices about goals, methods and values establish normative patterns which begin to determine later choices by foreclosing some options and giving prominence to others. The easy example is the QWERTY keyboard, which was originally designed to avoid key jams on mechanical typewriters but is now used, quite inappropriately, on all computer keyboards 'because it's there'. There is simply too wide an acceptance to allow the development of an alternative standard.[7] More profound arguments are developed by North, who argues that 'history is a largely incremental story of institutional evolution',[8] and for whom the sequential development of policies and solutions reflects pre-determined 'paths' whose broad direction is a function of earlier decisions.

Path dependence is nicely exemplified in British competition policy and in the tests and procedures operated by the MMC. We have seen how successive innovations in policy and legislation drew upon the MMC as a tool of implementation – because it was there, was available and was accepted. What is even more striking is that in every case legislation adopted a public interest test and the standard MMC procedural approach. The public interest test was applied to monopolies, then to mergers (in 1965), to anti-competitive practices (section 6(5)c of the 1980 Act) and, extraordinarily, to the efficiency of the nationalised industries (section 11(1) of the 1980 Act). Even in the case of regulated industry licence modifications a convoluted version of the public interest test was used. This was one aspect of Stephen Littlechild's seminal 1983 report that was ignored. He had recommended that the public interest test be abandoned in the 1984 Telecommunications Act.[9] This repeated resort to a public interest test reinforced the inclination in the Commission to retain traditional procedures for the simple reason that these procedures are targeted at the public interest judgement.

As noted above, this level of continuity is in itself interesting. There have been many studies of the emergence of organisations but very few of their persistence over time.[10] The survival of the MMC in a relatively unchanged form is one of the central concerns of this study. From an organisational perspective the staff and members would be expected to fight for survival for strictly instrumental reasons – to protect their positions and incomes. But from an institutionalist perspective survival is loaded with additional importance. Survival becomes a struggle to protect a set of values along with the organisation itself. The role of the leadership of an organisation is to articulate and defend those values. This chapter explores the evolution and defence of such values and identifies some of the key organisational features of the Commission.

The production line

The task of the MMC is simple: the investigation of matters referred by the DTI, the OFT and the regulators, and the production of reports. Accordingly, the procedures, goals and values of the Commission have grown up around the investigation and reporting process. By the end of 1998 the Commission had produced 417 reports (see table 2).

The early procedural arrangements were designed by the first Secretary, Alix Kilroy. The arrangements she devised reflected three aspects of the 1948 Act: the agnostic public interest test; the publication of the report in full; and the requirement that the Commission include 'a survey of the general position in respect of the subject matter of the investigation, and of the developments which have led to that position'.[11] She designed the procedures to operate through four stages. First, an informal stage in which the Commission had a general discussion with the parties, visited sites and formed a view about what facts needed to be collected. Second, the long 'factual' stage in which the Commission confirmed that the reference met the test of one-third of market share and restriction of competition. This culminated in a 'clarification hearing' in which the parties were invited to accept the facts. In the third stage the Commission formed a view about the public interest and held a further hearing based on a formal public interest letter and written responses from the parties, which would normally be represented by counsel. The fourth was the report stage, which included conclusions and proposed remedies.

The outcome of this process has been the most remarkable series of studies of industrial and commercial sectors. The Commission's reports are almost academic in their approach and are unrivalled in their thoroughness and authority. The early reports were exceedingly detailed and conveyed the historical development of the sector. For instance, the fourth report, on *Insulated Electric Wires and Cables*, published in 1952, ran to 170 pages with detailed appendices and, along the way, noted that the first use of permanent insulated wire was in 1816 in 'glass tubes ... rendered watertight by sealing wax'.[12] Such historical colour is still used to inject interest into reports. The *Fine Fragrances* report of 1993 observes that 'perfume containers were made in ancient Egypt, Persia, Greece and Rome'.[13] The detail contained in the reports and the time required to collect the information have been the perennial subject of criticism. Alix Kilroy herself agreed that the requirement for a survey of the general position 'makes the enquiry so long in time and the reports so long in extent. Even without it the Commission would no doubt have felt it to be necessary to include a good deal of the descriptive matter about the industry but I doubt if much history would have found a place.' The thorough analysis has made the reports valuable to academics but it is doubtful that they have been deeply or widely analysed as part of the public debate. Dame Alix also noted, with surprise, that 'both the Commission and its staff thought that its reports would be the subject of critical and detailed scrutiny from industry, economists and politicians, and that they would produce hostile comments. Neither of these expectations has been realised.'[14] Despite the drawbacks of long and elaborate reports, section 54(2) of the Fair Trading Act reproduced section 7 virtually word for word and ensured that the tradition of full contextual description would be sustained. As noted in chapter 6, the Commission had a substantial impact on the Act and did not lobby against this continuity.

Investigation and report

The procedures used by the Commission in order to fulfil its duty to 'investigate and report' are in a direct line of descent from those devised by Dame Alix. In this section we summarise the current procedures with the caveat that important changes were taking place during 1998–2000.

The first step is to identify the staff team, centred on a team manager, and for the Chairman to appoint a group of members. Ideally a 'shadow' team will be created on the basis of forewarning from the DTI or the OFT, and a little preliminary research and monitoring of the press can be set in train, but little material action can in practice be taken until the reference actually arrives. At this point the Commission will absorb material from the OFT as to the analysis it has undertaken and the reasoning behind the reference. This will usually come through meetings between officials, through the transfer of files, review of the OFT file or, in a recent innovation, through a more structured 'presentation' by OFT staff to the group of members. This interface has regularly aroused criticism of duplication, and staff on both sides will privately concede that historically it has often been less than satisfactory. At the same time, the Commission is wary of being unduly influenced by OFT views and certainly does not see itself as working to an OFT 'brief'.

The next stage is for the reference secretary immediately to publicise the reference and organise a standard mailing to all the interested parties. This mailing announces the Commission's investigation and solicits evidence and views from all and sundry. It is a very open process and Commission staff encourage the broadest possible submission of evidence. Once the scope of the investigation becomes clearer the staff will consider whether any further investigatory techniques might pay off. Specific questionnaires may be devised, staff may undertake surveys and, if specialist help is required, consultants may be employed. Thus, on *New Motor Cars* in 1992 Ludvigson was engaged to survey car prices across Europe in a huge study reproduced in over 300 pages of the eventual report which gave the most brain-numbing detail of car specifications and prices.[15] In the case of *Domestic Electrical Goods* a novel technique was employed which drew on a team of thirty-six part-time (and mainly retired) officials who conducted face-to-face interviews with retailers.[16] In cases which involve allegations of anti-competitive practices the big problem is to secure concrete complaints. Trade partners are often extremely hesitant to level allegations of (for example) refusal to supply, discriminatory rebates, market sharing or covert price fixing. Allegations made on a confidential basis are of limited use. They need to be put to the misbehaving party in order that they can know the case against them and to allow them to respond.

This factual stage can produce huge volumes of evidence, all of which must be absorbed and which will be acknowledged in the final report. At the same time the accountants, economists and (often) the industrial advisers will be conducting analyses of costs and prices, market and market shares, of corporate strategy and profit profiles. These studies require flexible abilities among the staff, who need to develop real expertise over a very brief period in relation to an industry and a market with which they may have had no previous experience. The *Domestic Electrical Goods* inquiry was the largest ever undertaken by the Commission up to that point. It illustrates the extent of information which the staff and group had to digest; a volume of material which pushed the Commission very close to the limit. It involved:

- group meetings   88
- papers considered by the group   950
- postal questionnaires to suppliers   130
- postal questionnaires to dealers   5,000
- interviews with small retailers   650
- site visits (staff and members)   70
- hearings   50
- total cost   £3.65 mn

The group of seven, Chaired by Hans Liesner, had to ask for two extensions and reported after twenty-four months. It required two team managers and up to seven reference secretaries. Subsequently members felt that the eight references on which the inquiry was based might have been narrowed to make the undertaking more manageable.

This information is invariably gathered voluntarily. The Commission has quite extensive powers to demand information and to require company officials to appear to give evidence. Further, it can take criminal proceedings against those who deliberately provide false or misleading information and, when requesting information, it makes clear that there are penalties for misleading the Commission. But the cases in which powers to compel evidence have actually been used are extremely rare. They were considered in the Hoffman La Roche case in the early 1970s but otherwise have only been used once over the last twenty years – in the *Solicitor's Estate Agency Services in Scotland* inquiry in 1997 (where they proved so cumbersome as to be of little use – they were also used technically in *Private Medical Services* to overcome a duty of confidentiality). The reluctance to use powers is indicative of a preference for a co-operative and voluntaristic relationship with industry but it may put the Commission at a disadvantage with cynical transgressors. It does not help that there are no powers to 'raid' premises and no powers to secure information outside UK jurisdiction. Most companies can see the advantages in a co-operative approach although some are perversely hostile and offensive (as seen again from some parties in the *Domestic Electrical Goods* inquiry).

An intriguing aspect of data collection is the site visit. In 1953 Sir Archibald Carter told a Select Committee that 'they are really only go, look and see by way of background',[17] but the Commission has religiously sustained the practice. Rowley noted that members complained that the site visits were boring and time consuming[18] but that is certainly not the impression given by recent members. Indeed, in one rather surreal instance the visit was portrayed as an unwarranted perk when Commission members attended the Manchester United v. Leeds match at Old Trafford on the *BSkyB* inquiry.[19] Members maintain that visits are extremely valuable and one remarked that 'they are absolutely integral to the whole process'.[20] Visits provide an opportunity to deal informally with the parties and give the companies a golden opportunity to get their views across. This is the only point in the process where the company is in charge, although sometimes they are oddly unguarded and do not exploit the opportunity. Site visits perform three functions. First, they demonstrate a serious concern to engage with the facts and indicate to companies that the particularities of their case are being taken seriously. Second, they give the members a genuine flavour of the company, the activity and the culture of the organisation. The impact made, for instance, on members by visits to animal waste rendering factories, or the 1989 visit to Belfast to investigate bus services, was profound. Members argue that it would have been impossible to do justice to these industries without an appreciation of their activities on the ground. Third, site visits help to provide cohesion for the group and bind members together in a shared experience. They provide a rich seam of folklore within the Commission, with tales of teetotal evenings on a casino inquiry, or participation in live radio on the *Capital Radio* inquiry. Site visits thus lubricate group discussions and the formal hearings in a very productive fashion.

Much of the procedural cycle revolves around the 'hearings' in which the group meets interested parties. The early distinction between clarification hearings (to check the facts) and public interest hearings (to explore issues) is no longer made but both requirements are still fulfilled by hearings. The hearings process is extremely flexible. It does not follow court procedures and in British law there are no detailed administrative law procedural requirements. Essentially the Commission conducts four types of hearing. First there is the 'informal' hearing with the OFT which nowadays is likely to involve members; and at the end of the inquiry the group will (if an adverse finding is in prospect) have a 'remedies' hearing with the OFT to discuss how possible remedies might be regarded and implemented. Second, there are formal hearings to clarify the group's understanding of the facts and the nature of the problems. It will be necessary to have 'main hearings' with the parties under investigation and possibly 'third-party hearings' with other interests who may be able to make or substantiate allegations. The hearings are not designed to elicit detailed factual material but to pursue points, solicit opinions and clarify the views of the group. There is also a presentational aspect, especially with third-party hearings; justice requires an opportunity to present material to the Commission.

The clarification of the case then leads into the central hearing, which is the 'public interest' hearing based in monopoly cases on the 'issues letter'. This letter can be very substantial and is intended to put to the investigated companies the whole range of possible public interest issues which the group has identified. These could run from excessive profit to predatory behaviour, and it allows the parties to rebut possible issues. As the Commission puts it, in a monopoly investigation, 'the monopolists are given a month to prepare their answers to the letter, after which they may be invited, separately or together, to attend hearings with the group'.[21] The public interest hearing is immensely important. The parties' legal advisers will invariably attend but the burden of the answers will be taken by senior executives, usually the Chief Executive. Answers can be revealing, and demeanour and dynamics are important. Executives who appear shifty, autocratic or aggressive can materially damage their case. Similarly, legal advisers who hector or lecture the group can prove counter-productive. The folklore recounts memorable experiences with, for instance, Sir Arnold Weinstock in the *GEC/Plessey* merger case, with Brian Souter in various *Stagecoach* cases, or well-known lawyers who have taken a patronising tone.

The fourth type of hearing deals with remedies and may well come at the end of the public interest hearing. For cases where the issues of remedies may be complex it is usual to invite the investigated parties back to discuss their potential responses to hypothetical proposals. This is a very elusive and ambiguous process because the group cannot reveal its findings and cannot be specific about a possible remedy package. The discussion is conducted in wholly hypothetical terms which leaves plenty of room for confusion and which must send many company executives away both baffled and frustrated.

The conduct of hearings is evocative of the style of the Commission, which Opie characterised as 'low key and dignified – there is no room for fireworks and histrionics'.[22] In this respect the Commission's style has changed little over the years although proceedings have become somewhat less forbidding. Under Godfray Le Quesne hearings were fairly formal with a barrister's preferences for procedural niceties. The Chairman and the legal adviser would dress formally and the atmosphere would be more court-like. From 1988 the Commission made a deliberate attempt to move away from this 'mystique' to an atmosphere more like that of a Select Committee inquiry. Nowadays hearings are relatively informal. There is room for polite jokes but also a remarkable degree of courtesy. Witnesses are welcomed, introduced, some Chairmen will take the trouble to shake them all by the hand, and the purpose of the meeting is outlined. The Chairman of the group will organise the proceedings and lead the questioning, working from a brief provided by the team manager. The Chairman's style can be quite variable. Some Chairmen have totally dominated the proceedings, have followed their own line of questioning and allowed very little opportunity for other members of the group to participate. Others have been more liberal, followed their brief and allocated lines of questioning to members. Unsurprisingly, members prefer the latter style, but in either case the role of the Chairman is demanding. He or she must absorb absurd amounts of material, be in command of the proceedings and pursue questioning in a careful fashion. Questions must not convey the impression that the Commission has already made up its mind or convey personal bias. Either possibility could give rise to judicial review, which the Commission is on the whole anxious to avoid. Within the bounds of legitimate expectations each group has discretion to organise its own procedures.

In hearings the staff members of the inquiry team will attend and the inquiry team manager will sit with the Chairman to advise on questions and follow-up. Often the Commission Secretary will also attend. The role of the staff has been a source of contention. In one of her few criticisms of the early Commission Dame Alix remarked that:

> Our practice at Public Interest hearings was for the staff to prepare questions to be put to witnesses but for them to be asked only by members of the Commission. I found this galling at my rank and also inefficient. The Commission's questions constituted the only cross-examination of witnesses and were based on a close study of the facts ... it was extremely frustrating when the point of our questions was not appreciated and they didn't get asked.

She 'could never get the Chairman to agree to' her participation in questioning[23] and it remains the practice that the staff, including the Secretary, do not speak in hearings, with the exception that the Commission's legal staff may sometimes speak. Some current staff are untroubled by this, others take exactly the same view as Dame Alix and share her frustration. Some staff would take a very extreme view and regard part-time members as 'superfluous'. This perspective would stress the benefits of far fewer full-time members and more involved staff, thus producing (they would argue) a tighter, quicker and more professional reporting process. From the other side of the divide it is evident that most members would resist any significant involvement of staff in the questioning. Members stress the importance of hearings and the value of the contributions made by members. One commented that this is 'the one occasion when the members are in control',[24] and it provides an opportunity for staff as well as witnesses to judge how the members' thinking is evolving. This difference of views goes to the heart of group dynamics. It is, after all, members who have to arrive at the judgement.

The hearings process provides the theatre of the Commission and is the only point at which company executives and lawyers see the members in action. It is, therefore, a fertile source of anecdote and (possibly apocryphal) stories. Lawyers and corporate executives complain of members who seem bored or inattentive at key junctures. Other members and staff have stories of some members (and even Chairmen) who in the past tended to 'nod off' during long answers. But such stories are atypical. Members take hearings very seriously. Roger Opie recalled that 'to me, as a Commissioner, the hearings were instructive, fascinating, revealing and informative, indeed great fun'.[25] Nowadays they are sober, measured and sometimes exhausting; 'fun' would not be the first word to come to mind (especially for witnesses) and would certainly not be the impression that the Commission wishes to portray. But do they yield results? The Commission does not take evidence on oath and the proceedings are not adversarial yet the questioning does, say participants, get results. Companies take them hugely seriously and it is quite usual for their legal advisers to organise 'dummy hearings' to allow executives to practise. Despite this, one senior member observed that he was 'often astonished at how honest and truthful businessmen can be'. When they are not, one member observed that 'I would not like to be cross-examined by Dan Goyder' and another emphasised the necessity of going through the transcripts with great care.[26] The public interest hearing provides a chance to test the rigour of the parties' arguments and can decisively change the outcome of the inquiry.

Group dynamics

It is a cliché that all groups are different. Each Chairman will have his or her own approach to selecting groups but one earlier Chairman certainly took the approach of seeking to balance known views within groups, matching, for instance, right- and left-wing views. This Chairman felt that vigorous group discussion was important and that doctrinaire or pre-conceived views would almost always break down when faced with practical questions in vigorous debate. Once group working was re-introduced in 1965 the size of groups showed a steady reduction. In the 1960s and 1970s groups tended to be composed of seven or eight members (including the Chair). During the 1980s the normal complement was cut to six and from 1990 onwards it was not unusual to have a group of five, and sometimes even four, members. These figures apply to all inquiries. The Commission does not alter group sizes to reflect the nature or importance of the inquiry. Conducting work in small groups puts more weight on the commitment of individuals and one of the few sins that causes real resentment is habitual absence. There are examples of members who missed so many meetings that they had to be excluded from the final vote and signature – on the grounds that they could not properly have considered the arguments. The Chairman is empowered to add members to the group at any point in its deliberations, but this would have to be done with the agreement of the parties and would be difficult after the main party hearings.

A group will vote on its conclusions; there is no requirement of unanimity. To reach a conclusion a simple majority is adequate and the Chairman has a second or casting vote in the event of a tie. But if the report is to be used as the basis for DTI action through order-making powers a two-thirds majority is necessary, and in this respect the Chairman of the group does not have an additional vote. Hence a dissenting view by two people in a four- or five-person group can disarm the DTI and the OFT. Group discussion is therefore conducted against the possibility of dissenting views and minority reports. Dissenting voices are respected within the Commission by members and by staff, provided they are not frivolous. Staff will help draft the notes of dissent and the 1948 Act provided that they should be included in the published report.

This is not to suggest that group meetings are always calm and dispassionate. Voices will be raised, very rarely tables will be banged and, individually, there are some bitter feelings over some minority reports. But the tone and the culture are overwhelmingly of mature analysis and debate, respect for the views of others, and give and take. A Chairman will do his or her best to talk members round but appeals to the facts, to goodwill and to collegiality are more important than horse trading. Independent, part-time members are immune from material inducements.

The preferences of, and leadership from, the Chair is a key factor. The Chairman will consult through the Deputy Chairman's group and can draw on the views of the team through the team manager. Also important, however, is the nature of the staff analysis. In preparing background material, analysing data and questionnaires, and producing market analysis, the staff play a vital interpretative role. It would be unnatural for staff not to form their own views and to build them, consciously or unconsciously, into the analysis. Over the recent past the Commission has aimed for collegiate working between staff and members but there is some recent sense that some of that community may have broken down. Members have observed that staff sometimes bridle at questioning of their work by non-specialist members and one observed that, 'I have found myself wondering whether the report is a report of the members or of the staff.'[27] But these things are very subjective (and perhaps vary with inquiries), so that other members have suggested that members' views are nowadays more rather than less dominant.[28] Some members take a very 'hands on' approach and are quite willing to re-write staff drafts. In some cases, however, the increased use of small groups may mean that there is insufficient specialised expertise among the members, thus raising the salience of staff work.

Overall, then, group dynamics lead to a debate over judgements and a likelihood of compromise. Ambiguities or inconsistencies in reports can therefore reflect a genuine disagreement between members. The more visible side of disagreements is notes of dissent, which sometimes extend into substantial minority reports. Notes of dissent are far from exceptional and can be quite crucial. For instance, going right back to 1956, six of the eight members of the *British Oxygen* monopoly inquiry wrote addendums in disagreement and two voted formally against the public interest finding. The two trade unionists in the group argued that the remedies were inadequate; one industrialist and one civil servant argued that the profits were not excessive; and an industrialist and an economist said that it all depended on regional pricing. This sent, it might be imagined, mixed signals to the BoT, which was itself extensively criticised for not controlling more effectively a situation in which 'B.O.C's profits have been unjustifiably high for an almost complete monopoly facing a limited financial risk.'[29] A more recent example is found in Patricia Hodgson's note of dissent in the *Powergen/Midland* and *National Power/Southern* merger reports in 1996. Here the Commission recommended approval, with safeguards. Ms Hodgson wrote a seven-page dissent arguing against the mergers and the Secretary of State, Ian Lang, did indeed prevent them.[30]

Analysis of MMC voting patterns on reports reveals some fascinating trends. Table 12 indicates that up to 1997 15 per cent of reports were signed in the face of one or more members voting against the conclusions or the remedies. In all these cases members have indicated the cause of their disagreements through a note of dissent. Table 12 also indicates that the 1950s and 1960s were the periods of most dissent, with well over one-third of all reports including 'votes against'. More recently the pattern has settled down and votes against are much rarer although they still run at about one in ten of all reports. Over the whole period statistics indicate that, of the sixty-two reports with adverse votes, twenty-five were monopoly cases, thirty-three mergers and four were 'others'. This is, respectively, 18 per cent of the monopoly cases, 21 per cent of the merger cases and 4 per cent of the 'other' cases. Table 13 gives a breakdown of these overall figures for the last three decades. A very clear distinction is emerging between merger cases – where a dissenting voice is quite likely; as against monopolies – where they are becoming less frequent; to the 'other' category of airports, utilities and newspaper mergers, where there have been no adverse votes for over ten years.

Table 12 *Minority reports and votes against group findings, 1950–97*

Year	Number of reports signed	Number with votes against	%
1950–59	23	9	37.5
1960–69	32	14	43.7
1970–79	65	8	12.5
1980–89	144	15	10.4
1990–97	141	15	10.6
Total	405	61	15.0

Sources: MMC reports and MMC database.

Table 13 *Adverse votes by type of report, 1970–97*

	1970–79	1980–89	1990–97
% of reports with adverse votes	12.5	10.4	10.6
% adverse in monopoly cases	14.0	3.0	9.0
% adverse in merger cases	15.0	19.0	22.0
% adverse in other cases	0.0	5.0	0.0

Sources: MMC reports and MMC database.

Of course, each adverse vote tells a story. Just to pick up some of the curiosities of the process, in only five out of these sixty-two cases did the Commission fail to secure a two-thirds majority for the group finding. The last was in 1985 when the *BBC/ITP* Competition Act inquiry tied three–three and the Chairman's casting vote decided the case as not against the public interest. Earlier examples include the *Nabisco/Huntley & Palmer* merger in 1982, which was allowed by a three to two majority, and the *Babcock/Herbert Morris* merger in 1977, where the group recommended against the merger by three to two but the Secretary of State allowed it on the grounds of an insufficient majority. An even odder case was the *Charter Consolidated/Anderson Strathclyde* merger in 1982, which is one of only two cases in the MMC's history in which the Chairman was in the minority (the other being the *Babcock/Herbert Morris* merger in 1977). Godfray Le Quesne and S. R. Lyons signed a note of dissent approving the merger although the group rejected it with a sufficient majority of four to two. In the event the Secretary of State allowed the takeover, which prompted an application for judicial review as well as an angry response from Professor Andrew Bain who, as a result, resigned from the Commission. In very recent cases disagreements have been registered as 'a view' or 'a supplementary note', chiefly because they are concerned more with proposed remedies in merger cases than with the public interest finding.[31]

Votes of dissent are driven by the circumstances and dynamics of the case. There may be the occasional member who dissents on grounds of principle but there have been no persistent dissenters. The record number of votes of dissent is four, held by Professor Tibor Barna. Since 1973 no member has dissented more than twice. There is a slightly clearer pattern in the professional background of members who dissent. Crudely, industrialists, economists and lawyers are more likely to dissent (in that order). Of the seventy-five dissenting votes that it has been possible to identify by member and profession, twenty-seven came from industrialists (broadly defined to include finance), twenty-one from economists and ten from lawyers. Given that industrialists are by far the largest group on the Commission it appears that, *pro rata*, economists are the most likely group to enter notes of dissent. This bears out precisely the early predictions of BoT officials who anticipated that the more 'fanatical' economists would engage in dissent. In contrast, the civil servants and the accountants are far less confrontationist. In the whole history of the Commission only one professional accountant has signed a note of dissent – perhaps an indicator of a pragmatic profession.

The obligation for groups to vote, and for their votes to be made public, attests to the independence of the Commission and its individual members. In practical terms it also underlines the futility of trying to impose standard doctrines or strict observation of precedent. A group is independent. It may be Chaired by a Deputy Chairman or a senior member and its report is its own work. Even if the Commission as a whole had endorsed a particular doctrine it could not 'impose it' on a group where three strong-willed members (in a group of four) could get their way.

Inquiry dynamics and type of report

Although the methods are common to all inquiries there is no doubt that inquiries vary widely in time, ease and complexity. At one end of the spectrum are the newspaper mergers, which are typically settled in less than three months; at the other end there are the large complex monopolies which can still take eighteen months. Apart from the obvious criterion of size, the factors that affect the nature of the inquiry include the extent of the reference and the degree of co-operation received. The Commission is bound by the parameters set by the DGFT in a monopoly reference and by the Secretary of State in a merger reference. For monopolies this can be especially important. References can vary from the whole industry to some aspect of the industry. Alternatively, the reference may specify a particular practice to do with (say) pricing or supply. The OFT will always ask for the Commission's comments on the framing and wording of the reference, although the concern is with clarity rather than substance.

Once the Commission embarks on an inquiry the extent of co-operation or hostility can be quite variable. For an agreed merger the parties will rush to provide all necessary material and will collate and volunteer data in order to secure a speedy resolution. For monopolies, however, there is much less incentive to co-operate, and the Commission has consistently complained of the length of time it can take to obtain the necessary information. In the valium case, for instance, Hoffman La Roche was notoriously obstructionist. The Commission had to threaten orders and complained in the report that, 'we asked the company to obtain ... certain details of the Group's trading ... The Group refused to supply us with this information.'[32] This illustrates the regular problems of dealing with multinationals although, in this instance, it did Roche little good. The report was damning and the company was compelled to make swingeing cuts in its prices. Much more recently some of the manufacturers in the *Domestic Electrical Goods* inquiry were less than co-operative (including Japanese firms) and, even where there is no overt hostility, constant badgering from the Commission staff may be necessary. The case of hostile takeovers is also interesting. The target party will see the MMC investigation as a tool in the takeover battle and may have lobbied strenuously for a reference (one of the few times where constituency MPs may be influential in the reference process). It will therefore bias its evidence to fight the takeover and may try to string out the process if delay appears to suit its ends. There are wry anecdotes, for instance, of a target company which pitched all its evidence towards a public interest detriment then, when the Board decided to accept the bid, promptly re-presented the data to 'prove' that there would be no harm to the public interest. As a result of such episodes, there is a strong sceptical, or even cynical, streak in groups.

These characteristics of inquiries may have some bearing on outcomes but it would be hard to suggest any systematic effect. Merger inquiries are more dramatic and urgent, monopoly inquiries somewhat more cerebral, and utility cases tend to be dominated more by technical material. Neither does the type of inquiry determine a particular form for the report. Reports have a fairly consistent structure of summary, conclusion and recommendations, background, the parties, the market, views of third parties, views of main parties. This model has become quite stylised although the number and precise content of chapters will be adapted to the case under investigation. In recent years the conclusions chapter has been brought to the front of the report, in order to make it more accessible. There is some penalty of duplication of material but most readers need only absorb the summary and conclusions to grasp the substance of the report.

Constraints: time, confidentiality and judicial review

The practicalities of researching and writing MMC reports are dominated nowadays by a pressure on time, by a ubiquitous concern with confidentiality and by an awareness of the risk of judicial review. Each of these factors has a strong influence on the reporting process and it is interesting to consider whether they also have an effect on the content and reception of reports.

Time

The issue of time, specifically the length of time taken from the date of reference to the publication of the report, is probably the longest-standing area of criticism of the Commission. From the very beginning the BoT developed grave concerns about the pace of investigations. Of course, allowances could be made in the early days for a novel task and an untried Commission. Dame Alix proved a staunch defender of her system and observed in her 1952 London School of Economics seminar that 'the Commission have been criticised for slowness. I hope that anyone who has persevered to the end of this paper will be more inclined to wonder at their speed in getting through so many complicated investigations in the space of only 3½ years.'[33] But the torrent of criticism from the serious press, from business and from MPs led to the passage of one of the shortest yet most significant Acts in the history of UK competition legislation, the little-noted Monopolies and Restrictive Practices Commission Act 1953. This four-clause Act expanded the Commission from ten to twenty-five members, allowed the appointment of up to three Deputy Chairmen and set up the system of group working. The Commission was empowered to work in groups of not less than five members. Any member of the Commission could be appointed to Chair a group and members could be added. Groups would settle their own procedures and their reports would have the status of full Commission reports. Matters could be settled by a vote but a new provision was introduced requiring a two-thirds majority if the BoT were to be empowered to take action to implement the report.

The BoT did increase the membership, some important references were made (e.g. medical gases and tyres) and the Commission enjoyed a brief period of striking success. In 1956 seven reports were published. As we saw in chapter 4 Sir David Cairns was cautious in the introduction of group working. He created eight groups composed of eight to ten members and, extraordinarily, he Chaired each group personally. This provided consistency across groups but must have been impossibly demanding and must have operated as a bottleneck. In 1956, of course, the Commission was cut back and returned to the '1948 model' of working as a full Commission.

The continuities here are quite remarkable. In 1965 the Monopolies and Mergers Act re-instated the '1953 model' of group working and it was perpetuated in the 1973 Fair Trading Act and the 1998 Competition Act. Not only were the substantive provisions retained (such as the two-thirds majority) but even the wording of rather obscure sections was clung to. Thus section 3(7) of the 1953 Act provides that 'nothing in the foregoing provisions shall be taken as preventing any such group, or member thereof, from consulting any other member of the Commission with respect to any matter or question with which the Commission is concerned'. This is interesting since it defends the idea of the entire Commission as a cohesive and collegiate body. In practice, over recent times, this philosophy has found only limited expression. Members are reticent about current inquiries and it would be unusual for a member to discuss the group conclusions with other non-group members ahead of publication. This is not a formal rule, it is a cultural phenomenon. The freedom to discuss has been retained in the 1998 Competition Act, which says in schedule 7, paragraph 18(3) that 'nothing in sub-paragraph (1) is to be taken to prevent a group, or member of a group, from consulting any member of the Commission with respect to any matter or question with which the group is concerned'. This reproduction of phrasing over forty-five years is a celebration of the power of precedent and legal inertia. It is simultaneously impressive and horrifying. It reflects a view that the prevailing system was working well and a strong reluctance on the part of the MMC and the DTI to 'open the box' of the Fair Trading Act for the 1998 Act. Whatever the reasons, it illustrates the elements of continuity in competition law which feature so frequently in this book. Few would deny that the Commission practice of working in groups affects the content, the findings and the impact of reports. Yet history reveals that the '1953 model' of group working was set up for reasons of procedural expediency – to increase output and cut down reporting times. The impact on the nature of the Commission's task and the problems of establishing consistency across groups were not systematically considered. This provides an important example of procedures influencing outcomes.

The Commission can only have been pleased with the content of the 1965 Act although it must have been concerned about the sustained criticism which surrounded the debate. The major official papers and a large number of parliamentary interventions were consistently critical of time delays, and in this respect the Commission had become something of a laughing stock. No reports were published in 1962 and the report on *Electrical Equipment for Mechanically Propelled Land Vehicles* had taken five years ten months to signature and six years eight months to publication in December 1963. Reform was essential and this period presents an unusual example of members of the Commission themselves pressing for procedural reform. Their lobbying was expressed through Sir Laurence Watkinson. He had joined the MC in 1960 after serving in the BoT and as a Deputy Secretary in the Ministry of Fuel and Power. Contemporaries described him as one of the most creative BoT officials of his generation and he had been one of Hugh Dalton's group set up to evaluate the Gaitskell/Allen paper on 'The control of monopoly' in July 1943; indeed, he drafted the first official assessment.[34] His Whitehall contacts put him in a good position to lobby and in July 1964 he was given a draft of the outline provisions of the Bill – probably improperly since he was at that time simply the Chairman of the London Electricity Consultative

Council and no longer a civil servant. On this basis he produced a six-page review of how the Commission would work which he circulated to Moira Dennehy at the BoT and to some leading economists (including Brian Reddaway at Cambridge) before discussing it within the Commission. He spoke for a group of members and made some very practical points about improving the work of the Commission. He was well disposed towards the idea of a registrar of monopolies who, he thought, could do a good job in digging up the facts and past history, much of which he regarded as 'wasting time'.[35] Sir Laurence, or 'Wattie', talked regularly to Moira Dennehy and in April 1965 noted that 'First, I think that a thorough overhaul of staff and methods of working is needed and secondly, that the task will be impossible without the right Chairman.' He went on to complain that the staff were too set in their ways but that Roskill (who was already a Commission member) would have the right approach to reform:

> I had half an hour with him by Regents Park lake on Friday and tried him out on the theme – what do you think is wrong with the Commission, why do we take so much time, and is all this researching into the past necessary and so on? In the result I was very satisfied that he was sound on these matters – indeed, his views are very much in line with Bernard Miller's ... and with my own.

Wattie went on to ask if the BoT was doing enough to recruit Roskill as Chairman and identified the 'good guys' on the Commission (Bernard Miller, Alastair Bruce, John Smith and Brian Davidson – mainly businessmen) who, he said, should suggest new names for an expanded Commission. He was willing to threaten resignation. 'I feel with respect I must warn you that if we do not get a first rate Chairman ... you will not be able to keep first class members on the Commission. I think you will know what I mean.'[36] It seems that Wattie got his way on the matter of the Chairman and Sir Laurence served until 1968, including working on the first merger inquiry. He was, however, rather less successful on the question of time delays and procedures.

The Commission did not take the opportunity to streamline its operations. Reports were still slow to emerge and criticism remained intense. Thus, by 1972, the *Economist* was observing that 'the proceedings of the present Monopolies Commission are turning into a joke ... only when a bomb is lighted beneath it does the Commission act with anything approaching speed.'[37] The pattern of relatively leisurely production of reports continued throughout the 1970s, which is odd. The Commission could clearly have speeded up its procedures. In August

1969 Anthony Crosland, as President of the BoT, had raised the issue in the National Economic Development Council (NEDC) and pointed out that the *Rank/De La Rue* and *Unilever/Allied Breweries* merger inquiries had been dealt with in four months.[38] The delays speak of a problem of lax management within the Commission and of expectations which were still creating dissatisfaction into the 1980s. When Stephen Burbridge joined the Commission as Secretary in 1986 he found universal criticism about delays from virtually everyone he and the Chairman met, and at every conference they attended. The *White Salt* monopoly report published in 1986 had taken nearly three years, and the new Secretary pressed the Commission to address the issue. As part of the appraisal the Commission arranged the report on perceptions of the Commission discussed in chapter 3 which identified as the main weakness of the MMC the length of time taken to produce reports.

The Commission became committed to speeding up the investigatory process and made a start with mergers. Cases such as *BET/SGB* and *Norton Opex/McCorquodale* were completed in four and a half months but the real turning point came in 1987 with the *BA/BCal* merger which Lord Young asked to be completed in three months. Young noted that he used 'the simple expedient of asking the retiring Chairman to do it. Perhaps he was slightly demob happy, but he agreed on the spot.'[39] Under Godfray Le Quesne's Chairmanship the three months was achieved and it became the benchmark. From 1987 the Commission pursued inquiries with a fresh urgency so that normal time periods (to signature) have now come down to three months for mergers, nine months for monopolies and six months for utility inquiries. The 'norm' reflects experience in the mid 1990s but exceptional cases such as *Domestic Electrical Goods* do occur. The reference from the OFT or the DTI will stipulate an inquiry period and groups are reluctant to seek extensions. The processing of reports by the OFT and DTI adds another month to nearly all cases and perhaps more for large monopolies with complex remedies.

Thus the traditional picture of a leisurely 'academic' approach to the production of reports has been replaced by a taut and rigorous procedure in which prompt reporting is given priority and the expectation is that deadlines will be met. In practice staff seek to produce a first draft of the 'conclusions' chapter as early as possible in the inquiry programme, which helps to focus the process. Information technology has clearly helped. The staff can work on-line and multiple drafts are much easier to produce. But there may also be an impact on substantive content. There is always the risk that time pressure will restrict the breadth of evidence collected or the range of options considered.

Confidentiality

A second procedural constraint is the concern with confidentiality, both of evidence submitted and of the content of reports prior to publication. Companies are rightly preoccupied with the disclosure of confidential information, and the extent and detail of MMC inquiries inevitably yields large amounts of information which would be of value to commercial rivals. Thus, from the earliest days, the Commission and the BoT were anxious to assure companies that evidence would be treated in the strictest confidence. Indeed, this was a pillar of the voluntaristic approach. Companies are far more likely to volunteer information if they are satisfied about confidentiality. These assurances have taken three forms. First, that the Commission will not normally disclose confidential information given by one party to another party during the conduct of the inquiry – either in writing or orally during hearings – except after consultation. Second, that restrictions apply so long as the business is carried on. Third, that confidential material will only be included in the report if it is essential for understanding but that if such information is regarded by parties as potentially damaging it may be excised by the DTI from the published version of the report.

Legislative safeguards of this sort are usual in commercial law. Section 17 of the 1948 Act prohibited disclosure of information unless it was necessary for the 'proper performance' of the Commission's duties. This was reproduced in section 133 of the 1973 Fair Trading Act and bolstered in sections 82 and 83 concerning the inclusion of material in reports. The 1998 Competition Act continues such safeguards in sections 55 and 56. There are various gateways which allow material to be used to facilitate inquiries or for restrictive practices purposes. There is no absolute guarantee of confidentiality but companies are assured in letters seeking evidence that 'the MMC are under strict legal constraints about the disclosure of information which they obtain in the course of their investigations'.[40] In its internal procedures the Commission takes great care to ensure that commercially sensitive information provided by one company is not included in material sent to another company for checking.

Disclosure safeguards are clearly necessary but it does sometimes feel that the confidentiality tail is wagging the investigatory dog. The necessary information may circulate adequately within government but the level of secrecy restricts the amount of information available to other interested parties and to the public. The question of excisions from the published version of the MMC report is a constant source of irritation. The DTI is under a duty to remove confidential information if pressed by parties where they feel that the balance of the public interest is against publication. The DTI receives extensive requests which are time consuming and which it tends to resist. Nonetheless, members occasionally feel that excisions have been made far too freely. Some members certainly felt that about the *Domestic Electrical Goods* inquiry and *South West Water Service's* price review is another mentioned in this context. The South West inquiry dealt with the determination of a dispute over a quinquennial price review and involved detailed examination of capital and financial projections. Even though the material was undoubtedly delicate it is still extraordinary to see whole chapters with virtually every figure removed, in this case by the Secretary of State for the Environment. This meant that the published report was of limited use as a precedent.[41]

Limits on disclosure operate for as long as the business is carried on. It is historians rather than the Commission that might regret this expunction from the historical record. The disclosure limitations in section 133 have no time limit and the public records doctrine is that such records need never be deposited for public access so that they are removed from public records scrutiny and protection. This seems indefensible. It provides greater protection for information disclosed under these provisions of commercial confidentiality than Cabinet records or matters relating to national security or the royal family. We can, apparently, read about who authorised the British H-bomb programme or about the abdication of King Edward VIII, but not about the restrictive practices operated by the British Oxygen Company in the 1950s or the monopolistic techniques employed by Dunlop in the same period. The 1998 Act is no less restrictive and continues to close off from public gaze and scholarly analysis a raft of fascinating material. Moreover, the rigour of these provisions seems hardly compatible with recent undertakings on the freedom of information. The 1997 Labour White Paper promised a radical new approach to access to public records.[42] It is unfortunate that commercial confidentiality under the competition laws should be quite so defensive.

In this area of confidentiality we see again a striking historical uniformity, with current policy perhaps unduly propelled by the momentum of past concerns. During debate in 1948 it was the Lords that put most stress on confidentiality. Lord Balfour, in a somewhat scaremongering speech, suggested that 'there is no power to prevent the Commission putting into their report all sorts of confidential trade secrets. The only bulwark we have against possible severe injury being caused to commercial interests is reliance on the Board of Trade.' In response the Government spokesman, Viscount Addison, confirmed the BoT safeguard and observed that 'it would never enter the heads of the Board of Trade to injure the public interest by injuring the interests of the firm concerned'.[43] It might be thought, fifty years later, that the MMC could similarly be trusted to exercise such judgements, as do other bodies such as the Audit Commission.

Judicial review

The third area of constraint on the Commission's procedures has come more to the fore over the past fifteen years and is the question of judicial review. A Treasury Solicitor's Department guide to judicial review published in 1987 was entitled 'The judge over your shoulder',[44] and this has become an apt image for Commission work. There have been an increasing number of cases of judicial review. Members and staff have become constantly aware of the risk, and are proud of the fact that up to 1999 the MMC had never lost a case.

Judicial review was simplified by the 1976 Report on Remedies in Administrative Law,[45] which brought a new procedure in 1977. The principle is simple. The High Court is available to review decision making under administrative law but will limit review strictly to the legality of procedures. It does not attempt to consider the merits of the case or to 'retry' any given decision. The Court will consider whether decisions were illegal (lack of jurisdiction or *ultra vires*), irrational (abuse of discretion), or procedurally improper (violation of the rules of natural justice). The most common type of application is on procedural grounds and the Court is typically asked to quash an action and refer it back to the Commission (or the Secretary of State) for reconsideration. In practice, however, judicial review is a minimal form of constraint. The tests for irrationality are extreme and the requirements of natural justice are simple – that there should be no bias and there should be a fair hearing. The courts tend to support reasonable decisions by responsible public bodies. All the same, the incidence of judicial review rose sharply during the 1980s, particularly in respect of disputed mergers where the stakes were high. The incidence of applications for review reflected an increasing awareness of public law remedies together with a tactical desire to show shareholders that something was being done. From 1986 to 1991 six merger decisions were challenged and over the period 1974–96 there were thirteen applications against MMC decisions.

Early studies of the Commission are innocent of mention of judicial review. The first case was *Hoffman La Roche* in 1974, which went to the House of Lords and in which Lord Diplock confirmed that the

Commissioners had a duty to observe the laws of natural justice. The next did not come until the 1983 *Anderson Strathclyde* case in which the Court confirmed that the Secretary of State was not obliged to block a merger, despite a 4:2 majority from the group to that effect. In the 1986 *Argyll* case the Court did feel that the Chairman had gone beyond his powers in laying aside the first bid by Guiness for Distillers; still, Sir John Donaldson, in a spirited judgement, stressed the virtues of good public administration 'concerned with substance rather than form',[46] and found for the Commission. In the 1987 *Matthew Brown* case Mr Justice Macpherson stated that the Commission

> has a discretion which is broad and should not be prescribed or inflexible. The concept of fairness is itself flexible and should not be subject to the court laying down rules or steps which have to be followed. The question in each case is whether the Commission has adopted a procedure so unfair that no reasonable Commission or group would have accepted it.[47]

In the later *Stagecoach* case Justice Collins adopted a slightly less stringent test, namely one of fairness, but still found in favour of the Commission.[48]

The number of applications for judicial review declined rapidly in the 1990s and there were none between 1996 and 1999. The reason was fairly obvious: 'the message of recent case law is that the scope for judicial review of the decisions of the competition authorities is very limited indeed'.[49] Responsible advisers will warn clients against applying for judicial review but that does not remove the obligation on the Commission to be aware of the risk and to be scrupulous in its procedures. Indeed, hints or even threats of resort to judicial review, which nowadays come with almost every inquiry, keep the issue alive. At the same time, Commission staff can find reassurance in judgements. In the 1996 *Service Corporation* judgement Mr Justice Brooke observed sympathetically that 'the existence of an external timetable, which is now much tighter than it used to be in relation to the duties of the Commission, places an even greater strain on it in carrying out its very difficult statutory duties'.[50] The judges are understanding, but whether the Commission can maintain its 100 per cent record both on future Fair Trading Act cases and on cases before the appeal tribunals is a matter of speculation. That it has been so successful thus far is perhaps not so surprising because the Commission's traditional assumptions have stressed a fair and even-handed approach which has always 'built in' natural justice to standard procedures. Thus Commission lawyers feel that although judicial review is a constant background concern it should not be a cause for hesitancy or timidity.

Whether the Commission does remain unaffected by the threat of judicial review is less certain. It is possible to detect a defensive reflex which is seen in the comments of Chairmen and members and also seen in the growing length of reports. Chairmen and team managers are most reluctant to be required to go back over procedures and evidence, and the threat of litigation could lead to counter-productive formalism and defensiveness.

The procedures and the culture

In his first Chairman's Introduction to the MMC *Annual Review*, Derek Morris reflected on the fifty-year legacy and picked out some 'core values' which he felt the Commission should sustain.[51] The values he picked out – independence, integrity, rigour, thoroughness and collegiality – are essentially procedural values. Such values are also reflected in the MMC's formal objectives. The Commission is not formally enjoined to pursue competition, efficiency or legal correctness; the watchwords are 'independence' and 'fairness'.[52]

It is apparent from the earlier discussion that the pursuit of these values has informed the design of the organisation and its procedures over a fifty-year period. By now they have become sufficiently well established to become cultural norms within the Commission. The culture of the Commission is detached, agnostic, intellectual, collegiate and balanced. Each of these adjectives reflects procedural characteristics. The detachment comes from the division of powers within the competition regime and the fact that each report is episodic. The Commission has no lasting responsibility for an industry or a company. The agnostic element comes from the spirit of objective inquiry which rejects doctrinaire preconceptions or the application of objective rules. The Commission does not take sides, it investigates, it does not prosecute. The intellectual element arises from an eclectic commitment to analysis in which a range of possibilities needs to be weighed. The atmosphere of the seminar room or the common room is more accurate than that of the 'office', and this is reflected also in collegiality. The members are equals and there is nowadays little hierarchy. Similarly, staff are senior, work in teams, and make equal contributions to the process of analysing and theorising. Decisions emerge, they are not imposed, and procedures are designed to facilitate the formulation of collective views. Finally, the Commission is balanced. It consults widely, is open to all arguments, and wishes above all to be, and to be seen to be, 'fair'.

If this is a fair picture it could be said to reflect the genetic origins of the Commission. These cultural characteristics are redolent of the strengths of the traditional British civil service, which was such a clear influence on and in the first Commission. The same adjectives – detached, agnostic, intellectual (or at least cerebral), collegiate and balanced – became terms of abuse and were attacked in the civil service, initially by Fulton, later by Thatcherite critics such as Hoskyns, and more recently by the prophets of the 'new public management' such as Osborne and Gaebler.[53] But if those cultural norms were steadily less relevant to an executive civil service applying professional skills in a market economy they might still be valuable in an administrative tribunal. The task of the MMC is to pursue what Geoffrey Vickers called 'the art of judgement', a very British approach to administration.[54] If the Commission has retained civil service norms, it is hardly surprising. In a more formal way it still pursues what the civil service always saw itself as pursuing, namely 'the public interest'. One might suggest that the Commission has refined and consolidated a very powerful culture which is a sub-culture of the traditional British civil service, perpetuated at a time when that culture of origin has undergone extensive criticism and adaptation.

The culture which has evolved is in many ways a remarkable achievement. It has not been 'imposed' by the BoT/DTI, it is something that has been created by the Commission and has been accepted by the wider world of Whitehall, the professions and business. The Commission is often criticised but its procedures are respected, its thoroughness admired and its impartiality unquestioned. In conversation, lawyers will express irritation and exasperation but they concede that the Commission does a difficult job with integrity. Officials in the OFT and in the DTI are consistently willing to let the MMC get on with the job in its own way. In this fashion the MMC and its procedural preferences have taken on a constitutive role in the system. It is beyond serious criticism, like a force of nature; one may complain about the weather but it is a fact of life. But this normative success and cultural self-confidence are relatively recent. It post-dates the 1973 Fair Trading Act and probably dates from the early 1980s. During the dismal days of the late 1950s and early 1960s the Commission was not held in high regard and, as late as 1968, a *Times* leader remarked on 'that potentially valuable but heartily disliked body, the Monopolies Commission' about which 'it is fair to say that in the last year or two the Commission has not always succeeded in maintaining the necessary degree of confidence'.[55] For extended periods the Commission was besieged and there is about it still echoes of an inward-looking, self-referential character which tends to judge its output by internal standards rather than by the standards of a misinformed outside world.

The distinctive culture of the Commission has been created by senior staff and perpetuated through recruitment and the consolidation of internal norms. For Sir Archibald Carter (steeped in the proprieties of the India Office) and Dame Alix Kilroy, the best of the civil service values identified above were second nature. They had no wish to create a court of law, a body of evangelical prosecutors, or a process of technical evaluation of economic welfare or industrial efficiency. They were comfortable with the processes they devised, which were ethically sound and intellectually satisfying. Recent work on how bureaucracies structure their responsibilities stresses this urge at the senior level to pursue a work environment that is stimulating and satisfying.[56] In the jargon this is known as 'bureau shaping', and it is plausible to argue that successive Chairmen and Secretaries have 'shaped' the Commission to accord with their own sense of what is both right and fulfilling.[57] Thus the five Chairmen who followed Sir Archibald from 1954 to 1988 were all lawyers. Their contemporaries in the Commission observe that these lawyers were temperamentally inclined to the 'natural justice' approach initially created. They were used to the case-by-case principle and reinforced the cultural traits noted above. Under these Chairmen the Commission became an insular and self-absorbed organisation of high moral integrity and with an almost monastic attitude to the outside world of business and commerce. Monastic not only in its serious and austere working style, but also in what appeared at times to be a vow of silence. Ashton Roskill was often described as 'self-effacing',[58] and one former senior staff member recalled that Godfray Le Quesne was almost impossibly reticent about his public life and, indeed, that he probably only ever made two speeches as Chairman.[59]

The preferences of Chairmen and Secretaries have been consolidated by the recruitment process. As seen in chapter 4, members are selected for their substantive ability and collegiality rather than for their outspoken views or public prominence. Since they are also part time they are unlikely to challenge the prevailing norms and procedures. If dissatisfaction sets in, 'exit' rather than 'voice' is a far more likely outcome.[60] In other words, members would be more likely to resign or not to seek reappointment rather than to engage in vocal protest. Similar considerations apply to some of the Chairmen. Ashton Roskill, Sydney Lipworth and Derek Morris all became Chairmen only after extended periods as members (see table 5); long enough for them to have accepted the procedures.

The pattern is more marked for Deputy Chairmen. Before the current Nolan appointments (of Graham Corbett and Denise Kingsmill) it was usual for Deputy Chairmen to be selected from long-serving members (see table 10). This pattern has militated against radical change or challenge to the prevailing norms.

When it comes to staff the key appointment of Secretary has always been from BoT/DTI Under-Secretaries who may have strong managerial views but who would be unlikely to supersede well tried and embedded procedures. At the important level of team managers the Commission generates great loyalty and has employed a number of long-serving staff. They are the guardians of the agnostic investigatory process, and when new team managers come in on secondment from other departments they adopt the familiar way of working. Thus a new team manager from outside will rely on the internal guidance handbooks and on other staff, typically the reference secretary, who will 'know the ropes'. Reflecting on the experience of joining the Commission, one team manager observed that 'I was a bit befuddled when I first came here. There is a lot of history to this place. A lot of procedure, precedents and the right way of doing things.'[61] Thus new staff are socialised into existing methods of working and they absorb the values along with the procedures. A former team manager made observations that would have pleased any Chairman – 'they aim to be thorough, careful and completely independent, they stress complete fairness, give all parties an opportunity to have their say, to follow up guidance on this from members'.[62] The procedures have become sanctified by tradition. In our earlier terminology they have been 'institutionalised' and given a value beyond the technical necessities of the task. Moreover, they are normalised by the continuing commitment to the 'generalist' approach.

As noted in chapter 3, the Commission employs accountants, economists, lawyers and industrial advisers in functional divisions, but the pivotal players, the team managers and reference secretaries, are generalists. They rely upon the traditionalist generalist skills of intelligence, analytical ability, judgement and co-ordination. They are not doctrinaire and, while they draw upon economic analysis, they are not applying economic tests. The team managers therefore perpetuate the traditional civil service values noted above. This is worth stressing because of its implications for the economists. For over twenty years the Commission managed without economists. In 1968 *The Times* noted that 'Roskill sees "a good investigating mind" as the chief requirement for Commission staff. He does not think there is a need to hire men experienced in industry, or with specialised knowledge of some branch of it.'[63] When economists were first appointed in the early 1970s some of the generalists were so hostile to them that they actively sought to exclude them by, for instance, refusing to circulate economists' papers.[64] Things soon changed and the economists became central team members but still as specialists. They tend to be able industrial economists and are not likely to pursue purist lines (unlike economist members, who sometimes do). This presents something of a contrast with the OFT, where the organisation can be more partisan in favour of competition and where economists are more in the ascendant. It also provides a contrast with more recent developments in the United States where, it has been argued, the increased salience given to economists post-1985 has changed the culture of the Federal Trade Commission quite decisively.[65]

At this point it is productive to ask whether this is the only conceivable way in which the Commission could execute its responsibilities. Are there alternatives?

One obvious source of comparison is practices in other competition regimes but overseas competition agencies should be assessed in the context of their particular political economies and administrative traditions. In looking to UK models a body such as the National Audit Office (NAO) (now the Audit Commission) offers an intriguing parallel, explored in chapter 8. Perhaps a closer parallel is with the Prices and Incomes Board (PIB), which operated from 1965–70; or the Price Commission, which operated from 1973–79. The parallels are even more suggestive when it is recalled that there were proposals at the end of each decade to merge the MMC first with the PIB and then with the Price Commission. These two price control bodies both extended their interests beyond the technicalities of price increases to look at the underlying causes, which included efficiency, corporate strategy, competitive conditions and abuse of market power. Each of them undertook investigations, produced and published reports, and developed investigatory practices which can be compared directly with those of the Commission. In addition, both bodies became very active. Their activities influenced many sectors of the economy and they produced very substantial numbers of reports – 170 in six years for the PIB; 96 in about four years for the Price Commission.

The PIB was created as a Royal Commission in 1965 but was converted on to a statutory basis in 1966. It was wound up by the Conservatives in 1970 and was extensively influenced by its flamboyant Chairman, Aubrey Jones, to the extent that the organisation was shaped around him. It was an investigatory body which worked rather like the MC on the basis of references from the DEA and the Department of Employment and Productivity (DEP). It employed its own staff and published reports which it did not have the responsibility of implementing. It relied on a mixed body of full-time and part-time commissioners, between nine and fifteen people in all. It took evidence, conducted its own research and purported to be an expert judge, looking at prices as well as wages. In contrast to the MC it reported quickly, did not attempt complete consultation and kept its reports deliberately short. It was more cohesive and more disciplined than the Commission and, for instance, published no minority reports. Like the MC it operated on the basis of co-operation from the firms and other parties involved and it had few powers to demand evidence. Unlike the MC it was committed to generating its own information by employing the skills of its staff, by the use of consultants and by extensive shopfloor contact, so that 'what was important was its refusal to be bounded by the limits imposed by following traditional lines of inquiry'.[66] Expressed simply in terms of the volume of investigations, its performance was impressive. It seemed to demonstrate that it was not necessary to be hyper-cautious. Inquiries could be inventive, controversial views could be put forward, firms would still co-operate and things could be done much more quickly.

Of course, the PIB, like the later Price Commission, was at the heart of counter-inflation policy, and thus at the centre of political attention. It was, in reality, a highly political creature whose reports sometimes side-stepped issues to avoid giving hostages to fortune. Companies had a great incentive to co-operate in order to secure price increases but on the whole industry disliked the Board intensely. The dislike arose from the whole conception of price control but industry also reacted against a relative lack of consultation and the evangelism of the Board and its staff, which could manifest itself in what appeared almost capricious treatment of companies.[67] The PIB had a principled commitment to incomes policy and the ideological and theoretical baggage that went with it. In particular it was committed to a 'new' prices and incomes policy based on productivity bargaining. This put the emphasis on industrial efficiency and a tripartite dialogue that sought to identify common interests and to mobilise a spirit of co-operation to increase efficiency. It had strong union support and some prominent trade union members. In his invaluable study Allan Fels thus talks of 'the NBPI's preconceived policy objectives' and dryly observes that 'it could not be contended that the NBPI was an organisation free from dogma and drawing its conclusions from the result of disinterested inquiries'.[68] While the MC could be expected to reject the dogmatic element within the PIB's procedures it might have felt stimulated by its procedural activism. It could hardly avoid the PIB example because some MC references overlapped directly with PIB work and, in one or two instances, there were near conflicts, as with bank charges and mergers. Certainly Fels thought that 'the [Monopolies] Commission has ... some lessons to learn'.[69] Outside parties in government and the media also drew parallels which were unflattering to the Commission, and a merger of the two bodies, as proposed by Barbara Castle in 1969, would have seen the MC submerged within the much larger PIB, as noted in chapters 2 and 6. Hugh Stephenson summarised contemporary perceptions of the position early in 1970, before the election, in an article that picks up the procedural, as well as the substantive, contrast:

> As the Monopolies Commission moved increasingly beyond the strict confines of technical monopoly into more complex areas of restraint of competition, there was a growing overlap between their work. The way in which the Monopolies Commission operated, with its legalistic forms and its dependence on oral and written evidence, was increasingly unsuited to the technical and industrial questions involved. The decisions of the Commission appeared to outside observers to have an unsatisfactory degree of arbitrariness about them. For all these reasons a merged body, using the working methods of the old P.I.B., does seem the best solution.[70]

Stephenson's obituary proved premature. The May 1970 election resulted in the prompt demise of the PIB and instead saw the eventual passage of the Fair Trading Act analysed in chapter 6. But of course the Conservative 'U turn' of 1972 saw a return to incomes policy and to a new body in the shape of the Price Commission.

In a replay of the 1960s the Price Commission initially operated the price code under the various stages of the disastrous Heath incomes policy. Under Labour its role was maintained but it also began to investigate particular firms and industrial sectors following 'references' from the DPCP, initially headed by Shirley Williams and from 1976 by Roy Hattersley. Again the reference and investigation process had strong similarities to the MMC, and the Price Commission also dealt with nationalised industries. In 1977 the Price Commission Act extended its powers and allowed it to undertake investigations into price rises on its own initiative. The pace of investigation intensified, as indicated in table 14, and the Price Commission began to look more like the MMC. Thus, for the sectoral examinations, the Price Commission operated in response to references from the Secretary of State and investigated with a whole range of economic policy objectives in mind. Price investigations had a time limit of three months, sectoral examinations took longer and the reports went to the Secretary of State to consider action. There was again a growing overlap between the tasks and the investigations of the two Commissions. The Price Commission was to be found examining sectors which had formerly been the subject of MMC reports. More directly the Price Commission was looking at the efficiency and pricing behaviour of individual firms in industries also subject to MMC inquiries.

Table 14   *Reports by the Price Commission, 1974–79*

Year	Total	References from DPCP	Own-initiative price investigations	Sectoral examinations
1974–77	31	31	–	–
1978	44	2	30	12
1979	21	–	14	7
Total	116	33	44	19

Source: Price Commission Quarterly Reports, e.g. *Report for the Period 1 August to 31 October 1979*, session 1979–80, HC 301 (London, HMSO, 1980).

The Price Commission was very high profile and substantial in size. It employed 500 to 600 staff and its reports extended widely. In 1978 it published forty-four reports while the MMC published only four. The January 1979 MMC petrol report attracted criticism, not least from the DGFT, who expressed 'disappointment'.[71] Thus the weight of opinion was again unfavourable to the MMC, with a fresh prospect of submergence in a merger. This time the obituary was written by the *Economist*, which noted that

> the monopolies commission is floundering … the government has found a more effective inquisitor, the price commission … the price commission, rightly, has turned its eyes increasingly to anti-competitive practices and market structures … What Britain needs is an aggressive and politically independent competition authority incorporating both the commissions and the office of fair trading.[72]

Again, procedurally, the Price Commission was demonstrating a vigorous, questioning and far brisker approach, which Roger Opie likened to the MMC's merger inquiries rather than those into monopolies. Opie was a member of both Commissions and speaks approvingly of the collegiality of the Price Commission which met as a full Commission (in 1979 of fifteen people) at least weekly. This was in stark contrast to the MMC which, he says, only met twice as a full Commission in all his fourteen years of service.[73]

Again the obituaries were premature. History repeated itself as an incoming Conservative Government abolished the Price Commission and, again, the MMC experienced a revival. Some Price Commission staff joined the MMC and had an effect on procedures and norms, especially in relation to the nationalised industry work which the MMC took on under section 11 of the 1980 Competition Act. In general, however, it is difficult to detect any significant re-appraisal by the MMC of its procedures as a result of the challenge and the example of alternative investigatory bodies. The PIB and the Price Commission produced more results, much more quickly, but were trapped in the flaws of incomes policy and were heartily detested by industry. They met an early death while the MMC survived. The MMC's culture and procedures appeared therefore to have passed the basic Darwinian test of evolutionary success.

It seems, then, that the procedures of the Commission up to 1998 established a striking continuity. There were relatively few challenges from within the Commission, and the example of the PIB and the Price Commission indicates that the Commission was reluctant to adapt its procedures in response to external challenge. This procedural continuity reflected what might favourably be called a 'cultural resilience'. Less favourable terms would be insularity, stubbornness or plain hauteur. One does see in the detachment of the Commission a rather pained self-righteousness in which members and staff used to dismiss external criticism as misplaced or misinformed. Often the Commission was quite right. It was in possession of the full facts and criticism could be misinformed or tendentious. But equally, sometimes it was wrong, and it was not good at admitting when it was wrong. Partly this inability to engage in self-criticism is structural. Even when members privately concede that they disagree with the approach of a particular report, they find it hard to express open criticism of colleagues in the group concerned. It is even harder to express public criticism, which would be frowned on most severely by colleagues and which might jeopardise the authority of the Commission (and nowadays would have implications for judicial review). Without consciously endorsing the principle the Commission does appear to operate something akin to the idea of 'collective responsibility'. The danger here is the possibility of developing an insular, self-referential spiral of conceit.

This takes the argument back to the earlier discussion of organisation theory and institutionalism. The Commission has developed comprehensive and stylised procedures, and has evolved a strong and resilient culture. The danger is that the procedures become an end in themselves and that the culture repels valid criticism. This argument about the 'conceit' of the Commission and its procedural and organisational continuity should not be taken as a diagnosis of stagnation. Clearly the Commission of 1999 is very different from that of 1949. The Commission has adapted and in many ways done so successfully. Some of the adaptations are formal, some are to do with attitudes and 'culture'. The main adaptations are seen in the nature of the leadership of the Commission, the role of the staff, the emphasis on prompt reporting, and the practical narrowing of the public interest test to emphasise competition. This ability of the Commission to graft new roles on to existing procedures is striking but elusive to analyse. It requires a broader appreciation of how the 'institution' of competition policy has evolved over the decades and of the differing duties and expectations it has placed upon the Commission.

The procedures and the culture: an assessment

The MMC is a unique body, both internationally and nationally. No other competition system has an administrative tribunal of this sort. The dominant procedural characteristic is the 'case by case' principle. Once this was established and codified in the system of group working many procedural and substantive results followed. Once it is accepted that each case is different, and that it is adjudicated by a group of Commissioners who are also in each case different, there then arises the central paradox of the Commission – which is that, even after over 400 investigations, no codified rules have been developed about the acceptable and the unacceptable features of monopolies and mergers. This question of precedent and consistency is ubiquitous, and it is argued in the concluding chapter that the case-by-case principle may be an under-emphasised strength of the British system. But it also follows that the case-by-case principle elevates the importance of procedure and culture. Cases are not routine; the methods by which decisions are reached are of the essence. To some extent the 'medium is the message' – the procedures are the Commission.

To extend this idea a little further it needs to be appreciated what stands behind the reports of the Commission as their authority. What, in other words, 'legitimates' the Commission's findings? It is not public policy – the public interest test is too amorphous and, in any case, the Commission is supposed to be independent of government. It is not substantive law – the Commission does not, and has never pretended to, apply legal tests. Neither is it 'economics'. Economic theory is a tool but neither economic welfare nor competition has been employed as a universal test, partly because economic theory is itself contested and ambiguous, and partly because a strict economic calculus does not encompass important social, efficiency or stability issues which groups regard as important. And what about the groups themselves? While Commissioners are often eminent and typically respected, their judgement alone would not be a sufficient justification for reports. Equally eminent businesspeople, economists and politicians can be ranged against Commission findings. So, we are left with the conclusion that reports are justified and legitimised through the procedures that produce them and the values which they embody. The Commission has to be fair, thorough, rigorous and competent. If it fails in these procedural requirements its external stock will fall and its future will be placed in doubt.

Lastly, however, 'the procedures are the purpose' because only by procedural means can a group come to a judgement. Inquiries go through a cycle of defining issues, forming views, exploring avenues, undertaking analysis, and finally the formulation of a judgement. Ideas have to be formed, tested, debated and amended in an intimate process of dialogue and digestion which does not happen instantly. Conclusions mature over months and gestate in the medium of the procedural routines. The procedures produce the judgements and it follows therefore that to change the procedures might well change the judgements. Commissioners, even Chairmen, come and go, but the procedures and the culture of the Commission have exhibited only a gradual evolution. The Commission does not have a 'policy' but it certainly has a culture, which provides a more transparent window on to its activities than any appeal to official guidance.

Notes

1 Sir Graeme Odgers, oral evidence to the TIC, Fifth Report from the TIC, *UK Policy on Monopolies*, 1994–95, HC 249 I, Minutes of Evidence (London, HMSO, May 1995), para. 18.
2 See section 54 of the 1973 Fair Trading Act.
3 Letter to *The Times* (15 December 1950).
4 TIC, *UK Policy on Monopolies*, p. xxiii.
5 R. Scott, *Institutions and Organizations* (London, Sage, 1995), p. 58.
6 P. Selznick, *Leadership in Administration* (New York, Harper and Row, 1957), pp. 16–17.
7 See P. David, 'Clio and the economics of QWERTY', *American Economic Review*, 75 (1985).
8 D. North, *Institutions, Institutional Change and Economic Performance* (Cambridge University Press, 1990), p. 118.

9 S. Littlechild, *Regulation of British Telecommunications' Profitability* (London, DTI, February 1983), p. 7.

10 There have been many theories about how organisations seek to survive but few practical studies; see W. R. Scott, *Organizations: Rational Natural and Open Systems* (Englewood Cliffs, Prentice Hall, third edn, 1992), pp. 24–5, 117–18. For an exception see the classic P. Selznick, *TVA and the Grass Roots* (Berkeley, University of California Press, 1949).

11 Section 7(1) of the Act.

12 MRPC, *Report on the Supply of Insulated Electric Wires and Cables* (London, HMSO, June 1952), p. 15.

13 MMC, *Fine Fragrances* (London, HMSO, 1993), p. 3.

14 Dame Alix Kilroy, 'The task and methods of the Monopolies Commission', Seminar on Problems in Industrial Administration, London School of Economics (December 1952), pp. 9 and 1.

15 See the MMC report on *New Motor Cars*, Cm 1818 (London, HMSO, 1992), Vol. 2, appendix 8.1.

16 MMC, *Domestic Electrical Goods: II. A Report on the Supply in the UK of Washing Machines, Tumble Driers, Dishwashers and Cold Food Storage Equipment*, Cm 3676, vol. II (London, Stationery Office, 1997), appendix 6.3.

17 Sir Archibald Carter, oral evidence to the Select Committee on Estimates (May 1953), para. 131.

18 C. Rowley, *The British Monopolies Commission* (London, George Allen and Unwin, 1966), p. 83.

19 'Old Trafford trip was not a junket says commission', *Express on Sunday* (6 December 1998). The Commission was obliged to point out that this was standard procedure.

20 Interview with a former member of the Commission.

21 *MMC, The Role of the Commission* (London, MMC, 3rd edn, 1990), p. 11.

22 R. Opie, 'A perspective on UK competition policy', in C. Moir and T. Dawson (eds), *Competition and Markets* (London, Macmillan, 1990), p. 86.

23 Dame Alix Meynell, Public Servant, Private Woman (London, Victor Gollancz, 1988), p. 261.

24 Interview with current and former members of the Commission.

25 Opie, 'A perspective', p. 83.

26 Interviews with former members of the Commission.

27 Private correspondence of a former member of the Commission.

28 Interview with a serving member of the Commission during 1998.

29 *Report on the Supply of Certain Industrial and Medical Gases*, 1956–57, HC 13 (London, HMSO, 1957), para. 261.

30 This was a wounding episode which also saw the reports leaked to the *Economist* shortly before publication; 'Britain's electricity shocker', *Economist* (13 April 1996), pp. 15, 27–9. See *PowerGen and Midlands Electricity*, Cm 3231 (London, HMSO, April 1996). Note of dissent by Ms P. A. Hodgson, pp. 45–51.

31 See the dissents by David Newbery in *Bass, Carlsberg and Carlsberg–Tetley. A Report on the Merger Situation*, Cm 3662 (London, Stationery Office, 1997); and by Martin Cave in *The Peninsular and Orient Steam Navigation Company and Stena Line: A Report on the Proposed Merger*, Cm 3664 (London, HMSO, 1997).

32 MMC, *Chlordiazepoxide and Diazepam*, HC 197 (London, HMSO, April 1973), p. 44.
33 Dame Alix Kilroy, 'Tasks and methods', p. 11.
34 See D. Gribbin, 'The contribution of economists to the origins of UK competition policy', in P. de Wolf (ed.), *Competition in Europe: Essays in Honour of Henk W. de Jong* (Dordrecht, Kluwer, 1991), pp. 155–6.
35 PRO, BT258/1955, 'Preparation of legislation', Sir Laurence Watkinson, The Monopolies Commission: some thoughts (6 August 1964).
36 *Ibid.*
37 *Economist* (11 March 1972), p. 86.
38 *The Times* (7 August 1969).
39 Lord Young, *The Enterprise Years* (London, Headline, 1990), p. 253.
40 Extract from the format of an MMC standard letter (1996).
41 MMC, *South West Water Services Ltd: A Report on the Determination of Adjustment Factors and Infrastructure Charges for South West Water Services Ltd* (Birmingham, OFWAT, 1995); see especially chs 6, 7 and 8 dealing with capital investment, operating expenditure and financial projections. The only table in ch. 7 with any figures deals, aptly enough, with 'discoloured water'.
42 Cm 3818, *Your Right to Know: Freedom of Information* (London, Stationery Office, December 1997).
43 House of Lords, *Hansard* (13 July 1948), cols 808–9.
44 Treasury Solicitor's Department, 'The judge over your shoulder', for official use only (second edn, 1993).
45 Law Commission, *Report on Remedies in Administrative Law*, Cm 6407 (London, HMSO, 1976).
46 *Regina v MMC, ex part Argyll Group plc* (1986), ER 257, p. 266.
47 *Regina v MMC, ex part Matthew Brown plc* (1987), ER 463, p. 469.
48 See *Butterworth's Competition Law Encyclopedia* (London, Butterworths, updated, issue 24), ch. 18, X/1203.
49 S. Hornsby, 'Judicial review of decisions of the UK competition authorities: is the applicant bound to fail?', *ECLR*, 14:5 (1993), p. 186.
50 Judgement in the High Court, *Regina v MMC and the Secretary of State for Trade and Industry ex parte Service Corporation International* (15 February 1996), unreported, copy, p. 10.
51 MMC, *Annual Review 1997–98* (London, MMC, 1998), p. 3.
52 See MMC, Memorandum of Understanding with the DTI (15 January 1996), p. 1.
53 See Peter Hennessy's discussion in his splendid *Whitehall* (London, Secker and Warburg, 1989), ch. 5.
54 G. Vickers, *The Art of Judgement* (London, Chapman and Hall, 1965).
55 *The Times* (23 December 1968). Another highly critical piece from this era is M. Peston, 'A new look at monopoly policy', *Political Quarterly*, 41 (1970).
56 For an exploration of the motives of senior officials see R. D. Denhardt, *In Pursuit of Significance: Strategies for Managerial Success in Public Organisations* (London, Harcourt Brace, 1993).
57 See P. Dunleavy, *Democracy, Bureaucracy and Public Choice* (Brighton, Harvester Wheatsheaf, 1991) and the discussion in P. John, *Analysing Public Policy* (London, Pinter, 1998), pp. 129–36.

58 For instance, *The Times* (30 October 1969).
59 Interview with former senior official of the MMC.
60 See Albert Hirschman, *Exit, Voice and Loyalty* (Cambridge, Mass., Harvard University Press, 1970).
61 Interview with a team manager (1997).
62 Interview with former team manager (1998).
63 *The Times* (28 September 1968), profile of the Commission.
64 Correspondence with a former economic adviser.
65 M. Eisner, *Antitrust and the Triumph of Economics: Institutions, Expertise and Policy Change* (Chapel Hill, University of North Carolina Press, 1991).
66 A. Fels, *The British Prices and Incomes Board* (Cambridge University Press, 1972), p. 233.
67 *Ibid.*, p. 52.
68 *Ibid.*, pp. 86, 242.
69 *Ibid.*, pp. 54–5, 235.
70 H. Stephenson, 'Monopolies: machinery but no policy', *The Times* (23 January 1970).
71 *Ibid.*
72 'Sleeping Cerebus: Britain's monopolies commission is not doing its job', *Economist* (13 January 1979), p. 60.
73 Opie, 'A perspective', p. 86.

6

The Fair Trading Act and the British model of competition policy

British competition policy is based upon a series of norms and a set of organisations that comprise a striking institution. It offers a unique and rather idiosyncratic model of how to operate competition policy. British officials and politicians consciously rejected an American model (in 1948) and a European model (in 1973) and created a tripartite system. This chapter reviews developments between the 1940s and 1973, when the tripartite model was put in place. Chapters 7 and 8 deal with two areas that became increasingly important after 1973 – mergers and utility regulation – and in chapter 9 we come back to the more general development of policy after 1973. Since the MMC is but one of several competition policy agencies its role can only be evaluated in the context of the regime as a whole. The modern British regime, even after reform in 1998, rests on the foundations of the Fair Trading Act 1973. In addition to analysing the origins of this Act this chapter also undertakes a wider evaluation and considers the broader contextual relationship between the government agencies and the business community up to the mid 1970s. It is beyond question that business firms and their representatives had a striking impact on the regime – both in the design of legislation and in the intensity and direction of implementation. The chapter therefore seeks to place the MMC in a double context: that of government and that of industry.

Models of policy making

There are a variety of ways of modelling the relationship between the actors in the system in order to distinguish which are most influential. These models rest on interpretations of the distribution of power within the competition policy regime, although they also have relevance for explaining how competition policy affects other aspects of the British political economy. Such models are not a luxury, they are essential for making sense of how policy operates. It is evident that the multiple actors in competition policy depend upon, and react to, the activities of others. No one actor has complete control of the policy area, every actor develops strategies for dealing with the other players. Any analysis which ignores these verities, or which in a reductionist fashion attempts to explain by economic or legal principles alone, can be particularly unhelpful. Political analysis is even more important in the British case because it is dealing with a political system. The whole British approach has rested ultimately on the operation of ministerial discretion, a phenomenon that cannot be analysed other than with political tools.

There are six models of economic policy making which have a potential purchase. They are sketched here and returned to in the conclusions to this chapter and to the book.[1] These interpretations are not mutually exclusive or exhaustive, but they do provide some help in making sense of the purpose and effect of policy.

Pluralism and liberal democracy

The first model is quasi-constitutional and, like much constitutional theory, is something of a straw man, comparable to the theory of perfect competition in neoclassical economics. The 'pure' theory of democratic government suggests that ministers and officials register the plurality of interests and demands expressed by society and through Parliament, and devise balances and compromises to satisfy the majority while protecting the minority. Applied to competition policy it suggests that the DTI is neutral, that it registers and balances views on competition policy, and that it responds to public wishes. This is not a realistic model but it still has power in public expectation and political debate. There is a sense that the DTI 'ought' to conduct itself in this fashion.

Neo-pluralism: vested interests and policy networks

A more sophisticated and realistic version of the pluralist ideal is presented by models of policy networks. These models suggest that public policy making is segmented and that for each sector a number of 'core actors' emerge. These are agencies or groups that have a vested interest in the field, which develop expertise and which deploy valued resources. In order for policy to be made these agencies must co-operate, recognise their dependence on one another, and strike bargains that are at least minimally acceptable to all core actors. The implications of this would be that the competition policy sector is identifiable and is populated by core actors – the DTI and the OFT, (more peripherally) the MMC, the CBI and the European Commission, and (episodically) perhaps the TUC, lawyers, parliamentary committees and bodies such as the Consumers' Association. Neo-pluralism therefore recognises the complexity of policy making and also caters for the professionalised and organised nature of contemporary politics. The more satisfactory versions of the policy network approach in addition recognise the importance of ideas, as norms, which grow up and provide coherence across a well-established policy sector.

Corporatism

Corporatism describes a system in which the major producer interests – organised business and organised labour – are able to speak comprehensively for their constituencies and can use their disciplined control over their members to negotiate agreements with the other incorporated partners. Policy is then made by negotiation and accommodation between peak organisations and government but in the pursuit of, or at least in the name of, national interests. Classic corporatism was associated with fascism but contemporary, democratic, neo-corporatism is a far more benign system which is usually associated with the organised capitalism of Germany, Austria and Sweden. In the UK, tripartism and the NEDC offered a pale shadow of corporatism and Middlemas talks of 'corporate bias' in his account of industrial politics. By this, however, he means reciprocal arrangements between essentially independent representatives of industry, labour and the state;[2] not the sort of integrated disciplined compacts found in continental corporatism. In Britain clearer corporatist arrangements could be seen at the sectoral level in, for instance, pharmaceuticals or agriculture, where the ministry, the companies and the workforce operated a closed, self-supporting system which negotiated the future of the industry.

Regulatory capture and the power of business

In a capitalist economy, where economic success is derived from the efficiency and prosperity of private sector companies, it is rather obvious that economic policy will seek to foster and encourage business success. This inevitably means giving considerable weight to business lobbying and the expression of business interests. Indeed, some theorists suggest that this structural feature of capitalist society will always guarantee business a privileged position in the design and operation of policy.[3] Business may, however, acquire excessive political power. It may distort policies, exploit vulnerable groups within society, and may pursue support and subsidy rather than efficiency and competitiveness. It is not hard to visualise circumstances in which business interests and national interests diverge. This provides a core dilemma for those who operate competition policy: when to support business and listen sympathetically to business interests; and when to control business and reject tendentious special pleading?

In this setting competition policy plays a vital role in establishing a normative framework within which industry operates. But it would be logical for organised business interests to seek to influence the content of that regulatory framework. This could be in respect of the prevailing ideas about the goals of policy, in respect of detailed legislative provisions, and in respect of policy implementation through the agencies and the courts. A well-developed critique of 'regulatory capture' has emerged which suggests that business lobbying can become so effective that regulations are actually developed under business pressure to serve business interests. Regulations which control competition and protect existing companies by, for instance, creating barriers to entry, will become a target of business strategy. This is more plausible at the sectoral rather than the national level; nonetheless, some observers have interpreted the evolution of British competition policy in the light of efforts to cater to business interests, to respond to business demands, and to privilege business in the operation of policy.

Bureaucratic power: the administrative state

Rather as a counter to theories of business dominance an alternative viewpoint is offered by diagnoses of administrative dominance. This viewpoint suggests that senior civil servants are in effective control of the machinery of government. They dominate policy making by developing legislative options and by the use of discretion in implementing policy. They can utilise secrecy, information, permanence, patronage and bureaucratic networks to influence politicians towards their desired policy goals. Bureaucratic power is found when the state is strong and ministers weak or transient. In the field of British competition policy this view has something to offer. Officials have been central to the policy-making process and have dominated aspects of it, but their relations with business and with ministers have to be analysed more closely before coming to conclusions about the extent of bureaucratic power.

New institutionalism and historical continuity

Contemporary society and government are complex, extensively organised and difficult to change. Existing policies and institutions are interconnected and represent the culmination of past compromises and negotiations. As argued in chapter 1, politics and policy making do not take place on a clean sheet but work with and through existing institutions which structure ideas and behaviour. The new institutionalism explicitly recognises the possibility of change and conscious institutional design. It shares with the traditional approaches of historians an awareness that history is important, and that past administrative arrangements not only have a great inertia, but that they help to define and influence policy developments in a process of 'path dependency'. Institutions construct a social reality for policy makers which is very difficult to change. Major change and redesign of policy do take place. Policies such as housing and energy are almost unrecognisably different from the position thirty years ago. In competition policy the major enactments brought significant change but the extent of historical continuity has also been striking. In retrospect only the legislation of 1956 and 1998 has been truly 'revolutionary'. All the other developments, including the Fair Trading Act, have essentially been adaptations reflecting the persistence of pre-existing ideas and organisations.

It would be surprising if any one of these highly simplified models 'fitted' British competition policy over its fifty-year history. The new institutionalism has informed the approach taken in this study, and ideas drawn from the policy network approach have also been used. In the following discussion it will further be seen that there is evidence to support some aspects of the 'business power' position, but also evidence to support theses of 'bureaucratic power'. We come to make more formal assessments in chapter 10, but the peculiarities of competition policy do also conjure up a more 'old-fashioned' view of policy making. Competition policy is rather esoteric, difficult for lay people to grapple with. It is not a spending programme and so does not generate intensive, self-interested lobbying, and neither is it ideological in a party political sense. Views about competition and competition policy split within, rather than between, parties. For all these reasons the political salience of competition policy has been low and it has developed in the classic British policy style of 'incrementalism' and civil service dominance. Incrementalism is a stalwart of earlier generations of policy studies and is a cornerstone of decision theory. It suggests that policy is typically made by incremental change to existing arrangements and that changes are prompted and tested by 'partisan mutual adjustment'. In other words, if interested parties can all agree on the changes they are accepted. The test of good policy is agreement rather than technical correctness.[4] This model was always felt to be a good description of the typical pattern of British generalist policy making. At times it has been a perfect description of competition policy making.

The origins of the UK model

The wartime origin of the 1948 monopolies legislation was reviewed in chapter 1. The shortest section of the seminal, sixty-two-page Allen/Gaitskell memorandum was drafted by Hugh Gaitskell and titled 'The machinery of control'. It advocated an investigatory 'Statutory Commission on Restrictive Practices' and argued that the major decisions 'cannot be withdrawn from the sphere of Ministerial responsibility. In almost every case, questions of economic policy – sometimes of very high policy – are bound to be raised, and on these, it is suggested, only ministers can decide.'[5] The young Gaitskell (still only thirty-six) was a principal assistant secretary at the BoT. He was yet to begin his parliamentary career and had entered the wartime civil service from a lectureship in economics at the University of London, where he had latterly converted from socialism to an evangelical Keynesianism. His advocacy of political and hence administrative discretion was attuned to the idea of a benign, interventionist state and it became a hallmark of British competition policy.

The journey from the Allen/Gaitskell memorandum to the 1948 Act was tortuous. Helen Mercer emphasises the role of American influence, the linkage to the pursuit of full employment, and the use of a 'business veto' exercised by permanent civil servants.[6] The delay in legislation she attributes to the priorities of Hugh Dalton as the Coalition President of the BoT, who was more interested in the location of industry. When legislation on monopolies and restrictive practices was eventually enacted it was, nonetheless, recognisably the descendant of Gaitskell's proposal. With his views shaped by the pre-war and wartime intimacy between government and industry he visualised each sponsoring department enforcing competition policy in 'its' industries, but based on the information and proposals of the new Statutory Commission. In the event the new MRPC was very firmly the creature of the BoT, although the 'competent authorities' empowered under the Act to implement MRPC reports included the full range of sponsoring departments.

The new Commission was weaker than Gaitskell, Allen and their economist allies would have preferred. But the model always envisaged a partnership between the Commission and the relevant government departments and, in assessing the operation of the Act, equal attention needs to be paid to ministers and officials in the BoT and its sister departments. In many ways the BoT was in control of the Commission. In addition to the powers of reference, appointment and execution reviewed in earlier chapters, the Board also retained powers in section 8(6) to give 'general directions' on procedures and powers. This watchdog was to be kept on a short leash so that, as argued in chapter 3, the carving out of an area of independence has been one of the Commission's major achievements. The question of appointments was reviewed at length in chapter 4. Here we concentrate on the early pattern of referrals, on the follow-up by government, and on the dynamics of the relationship between the Commission, the BoT and organised industry.

Mercer's thorough analysis of the period up to 1956 is instructive. She paints a picture of a policy and a Commission that were almost wholly ineffective in their material impact on industries and the conduct of economic policy. The blame she lays squarely at the door of the BoT, which was, in turn, the target of remorseless and powerful business lobbying. Business developed an intense hostility to the Commission which, as she rightly remarks, could be taken as a badge of success. There is little hint that the Commission itself bowed to industrial lobbying, but the BoT did. Thus, she argues,

> the hostility of businessmen to the Commission was a constant threat to the working of the Act. This hostility smouldered as the Commission kept the issue of restrictive practices constantly before the public and published some reports highly critical of business methods. This hostility hamstrung and immobilised the work of the Board of Trade in administering the Commission and made the work of the Commission economically irrelevant, leading to the eventual demise of the tribunal procedure itself.[7]

Business used high level political contacts, conducted press campaigns and used powerful arguments of national security, international competitiveness and national employment. Mercer charts in some detail the success of these methods in avoiding referrals of many large monopolistic industries, and in heading off significant action following reports.

The problem lay with BoT civil servants, who were placed in a virtually impossible dilemma. The post-war settlement rested on the willing co-operation of firms and businesspeople in an atmosphere of compromise and reason, with a strict avoidance of legal process. All industries were subject to 'sponsorship'. They had (and still have, after a brief interruption in the late 1980s) specific sections of Whitehall taking responsibility for their well being – thus shipping and aviation with the Department of Transport; defence industries with the Ministry of Defence; agriculture and food with the Ministry of Agriculture, Fisheries and Food (MAFF), and so on. Officials ran the risk of antagonising their industrial clients, and destroying carefully cultivated relations of trust, if they supported the reference of an industry or firm to the Commission. Strict promotion of competition within industry logically demanded a considerable degree of 'disengagement' of government from industry. This came briefly in 1970 but was not seriously introduced into British government until the mid to late 1980s and would have been virtually inconceivable to officials of the 1940s and 1950s. Thus an early BoT paper observed in 1950 that the change in relations may actually have reduced the ability of government to moderate restrictive practices through traditional means: 'before the Monopolies Act existed, it was our usual practice on receipt of complaints about restrictive practices to take the matter up with the trade association concerned ... Since the passing of the Act we have discontinued this practice.'[8] Officials were inhibited about commenting on practices in case they appeared to endorse them prior to an MRPC inquiry, but neither were they willing to 'grass' on their industries to the Commission.

Officials were extremely knowledgeable about their industries and about rampant monopoly and restrictive practices. Thus the first paper outlining possible references to the Commission identified ten industries for the first programme of references. The list was based on a review of literally dozens of possibilities generated by the production departments and by early complaints received during 1948. Officials were well aware of the workings of the monopolies and cartels. They had details of the key agreements, were aware of high profits and understood the inter-penetration of domestic and international cartels. Complaints cited included those from the Co-operative Societies about the bizarre collective boycotts they suffered (specifically in newspapers); from South African companies (over electric cables); from the New Zealand Government (over heavy plant); and from the Bank of England (over foreign exchange payments in the matches cartel).[9] The problem seemed only partially to be lack of knowledge of the facts or the effects of cartels, but rather what to do about them. In this light references to the Commission could be seen more as the stimulation of debate rather than the investigation of facts.

The Commission received six references at the beginning of 1949 and steadily worked through nine of the ten cases on the BoT's initial list, not finishing until 1957. The early 1950s saw the beginnings of a problem which was to plague the BoT/DTI until 1973 and subsequently caused difficulty for the OFT, namely the reluctance to make monopoly references. The BoT had to engage in complex negotiations in Whitehall about many potential references. Without making too much of 'corporatist' relations between government and industry, the picture that emerges is of government departments themselves standing as a bulwark against the development of a more competitive economy. Departments would really only agree to a reference if there was dispute within an industry (such as building contractors complaining about rainwater goods) or if there was some government self-interest (the cost of cables to the Post Office, or – later – the cost of tranquillisers to the NHS). The BoT itself was not innocent in these Whitehall debates. Internal papers regularly show the monopolies division appealing to other divisions to come forward with possible references. This syndrome extended into the 1970s and might be familiar to today's officials who are not necessarily willing to encourage the OFT to pursue references. Barbara Castle provides a beguiling vignette of the problem in her diaries. Control of monopoly policy shifted from the BoT to the DEP in 1969. Castle noted that when they suggested referring jam and marmalade, 'Cledwyn Hughes said the marmalade people, Robertsons & Co, had been wonderfully co-operative and it would be a "gratuitous" reference ... I blew my top.' Six days later she notes that:

> total frustration awaited me at Industrial Policy Committee on references to the Monopolies Commission ... Harold Lever had produced a wholly negative paper, listing about ten suggestions, only to turn every one of them down. John Silkin reported he could find nothing in the building field. I tried to get them to go nap on three: wallpaper, electrical cables and china clay, as outstanding cases of dominant market power, but Harold Lever resisted every one of them ... Eventually, keeping my temper with difficulty I had to adjourn the meeting ... As Edmund Dell put it to me. 'People have been saying to me what a pity it is that monopoly policy has passed from the Board of Trade, which is competition-minded, to DEP, which is protectionist. How they would laugh if they could hear this discussion'.[10]

Policy on referrals was thus far more sensitive and conflictual than the rather bland statements of government policy implied. Not only did it fail to reflect any consistent approach to sectors or issues where monopoly was a consistent problem, the sheer paucity of references was an embarrassment. This was accentuated by the huge number of potential cases which were broadcast right up until 1973 by a section in the BoT annual reports which reviewed suggestions and requests for references. These annual reports were a further example of the 1948 Act's affection for publicity as a discipline in its own right and they provide a roll call of potential monopoly abuse. Added emphasis was given to the contrast between actual and possible references in April 1970 when, in response to a parliamentary question from Joel Barnett, Edmund Dell (as Minister of State at the DEP) listed an extraordinary 156 companies which held half or more of the British market. Only ten of these had been investigated by the Commission since 1965.[11] This was the visible face of the internal Whitehall battle for referral.

The difficulty of making references was matched at the other end of the process by a lack of effective action in implementing the recommendations made in Commission reports. The BoT did show some determination in seeking to follow up reports but faced intense industry opposition. Mercer's review of cases up to 1955 confirms that in all but one case either no action was taken or the BoT negotiated voluntary undertakings of limited effectiveness. She rubs salt in the wound by arguing that even the most momentous reference of the period, the *Collective Discrimination* reference of December 1952, was made only to avoid having to take more deliberate action on the Lloyd Jacob Committee report. This Committee on resale price maintenance had reported in 1949 and recommended abolition of collective resale price maintenance. Business opposition had prompted the incoming Conservative Government to postpone the issue using the device of the MRPC general reference on the most common and unpopular practice – collective boycott.[12]

The evolving relationship between the BoT and the Commission must be seen as a component of the broader and more volatile relationship between government and industry. The immediate post-war years saw the corporatist, protectionist instincts which had been embedded in the wartime management of production coming under steady assault. Liberal economists and many BoT officials were scornful of the old, cosy, protected and unadventurous attitudes they encountered in business, but they still needed business co-operation. The hostility of business to the Commission became something of a totem for relations between organised manufacturing and government. In facing up to this reality BoT and its ministers virtually 'gave up' on the MRPC during 1954–55. The early hopes that reports would exercise a demonstration effect were not being borne out. General principles were not emerging, companies and cartels were not obviously amending their practices, and each report was a battle in an endless war of attrition. It was almost as if the Commission were faced with a wall of monopolies and restrictive practices. If each report could be likened to a brick, and if those bricks could be extracted from the base of the wall, then there was the prospect of the whole wall collapsing. That was the demonstration and deterrence argument. But what in fact was happening was that the bricks were coming from the top of the wall, lowering it almost imperceptibly and holding out the prospect of decades of work before the wall could be removed. So, argues Mercer, as reviewed in chapter 2, Peter Thorneycroft ambushed industry with the Restrictive Trade Practices Act. Its hostility to the Commission had persuaded the FBI that an alternative judicial approach would be preferable. In the event it was far worse (at least for trade associations and the industrial traditionalists). The Commission had achieved its purpose, but not in the way originally conceived. It had publicised abuses, educated the public, focused the official debate, and helped Thorneycroft dig an elephant trap into which the FBI cheerfully stepped. At this point it seemed to many within the BoT that the Commission's work was over. It would keep ticking over, with perhaps two monopoly references a year, but it was likely to have so little work that the BoT concluded that it needed only a part-time Chairman.[13]

This perspective on the early years of the Commission stresses its educative effect and its impact on public opinion. As earlier chapters have pointed out, orthodox thinking in the 1950s continued to emphasise the merits of co-operation, economies of scale, concentration of national resources and a general scepticism about competition. If the 'free traders' in the BoT were willing to pursue competition for its own sake then the other departments in Whitehall were virtually in opposition. During each batch of legislation departments lobbied hard to exclude their industries from the Acts. As the nationalisation of the 1940s and the cartelisation of the 1950s gave way to the planning and rationalisation of the 1960s, so the arguments within Whitehall became more stylised and departmentalised. Pressures to water down competition policy became part of the high politics of industrial planning and were expressed at the highest levels. Under Labour from 1964 the creation of the DEA and the whole machinery of indicative planning pitched the rationalisers against the unfashionable proponents of competition within the BoT. Thus, in October 1965, barely a month after the euphoric launch of the National Plan, the dynamic First Secretary, George Brown, then at the height of his power, could be found writing to Douglas Jay at the BoT about the 'possible hampering effects of the restrictive practices legislation on our efforts to increase industrial efficiency and lower costs'. His letter rehearsed the specifics of the soap and detergent industries and declared that, 'while we all recognise the importance of competition in the drive to improve industrial performance and lower costs, the Government through its support for the little Neddies has also, rightly, recognised the scope for improvement through co-operative effort'.[14] Officials in the Board grudgingly acknowledged that they would have to compromise with the DEA and would have to concede consultation over prospective merger references.[15]

The first twenty years of the operation of competition policy established a set of relationships which exhibited considerable staying power. They also created the conditions and many of the assumptions which underlay the 1973 Fair Trading Act. The heart of policy and administration lay in the Industries and Manufactures Directorate of the BoT, which in turn was divided into five to eight divisions, each under an Under-Secretary. IM 1 was initially responsible for administering the 1948 Act and was a major division within the BoT hierarchy. Many of the significant officials within the Board spent periods in IM 1; people such as the future Permanent Secretaries, Frank Lee and Peter Carey. The division also provided a vocation for some officials who came back again and again in their careers to grapple with the problems of competition policy; officials such as Frank Glaves-Smith, Elizabeth Llewellyn-Smith and Ronald McIntosh, who was a Principal in IM 1 in 1949 and who features prominently later in the chapter. It is these officials, anonymous to the public, only shadowy figures to the mass of businesspeople but known to be the pivotal figures by Whitehall insiders, who really dictated the course of policy. But they, in turn, were subject to a range of conflicting pressures which they balanced pragmatically in the traditions of British administration.

The BoT officials were dealing with four sets of constraints over the period. They dealt with collegiate pressures, with political pressures, with economic uncertainty and with business relationships. The collegiate pressures with the 'Whitehall village' were part of the fabric of civil service life. In respect of references and the development of policy, IM 1 officials had to deal with colleagues in the Board, in sponsoring departments, in the Foreign Office (over extra-territoriality and treaty obligations), in the Treasury (over inward investment), and later in the DEA, MinTech and the DEP over control of the policy itself. The conventions of Whitehall made compromise and accommodation essential, and some of the more puzzling absences of references, for instance, can only be explained by power relations within Whitehall. Thus the Transport Department was a notorious defender of shipping and the shipping conferences, while the Ministry of Fuel and Power successfully fought off references of the hugely unpopular petrol distribution 'tied garage' system.[16] One of the most difficult areas was agriculture, where the MAFF defended farming industries and interests with an utter predictability and shamelessly cited the National Farmers' Union and the need to placate farmers in its inter-departmental correspondence.

A second routine constraint came from the need to accommodate ministers and their political preferences. In the period up to 1974 the BoT was relatively lucky in its Presidents. With eleven ministers over twenty-three years turnover was high, but not as bad as the frenetic 1980s. Moreover, several of the Presidents were substantial figures who took a real interest in monopolies and restrictive practices, most notably Harold Wilson (1947–52), Peter Thorneycroft (1951–57), Edward Heath (1963–64), Douglas Jay (1964–67) and Anthony Crosland (1967–69). The main problem was in sustaining interest in a policy area which was not central to party doctrine, was essentially a long-term and technical area, and which did not (until merger control arrived) have great potential for popular appeal and headlines. Time and again the direction of initiative came up the organisation from active officials, not down from concerned ministers. This problem was seen especially in the early 1960s where Frederick Erroll seemed incapable of securing agreement on a policy to control mergers.

A genuinely more difficult area of constraint within the Board was intellectual uncertainty. Even by the early 1960s there was almost nothing in the prevailing economic debate or the platforms of the two major parties to justify a principled commitment to the strengthening of competition policy. The parties were neutral on the question of monopoly. Tracts advocating a more liberal pursuit of competitive forces (such as the 1963 Poole Committee report) could be trumped by others advocating support for industrial co-operation and the responsible company (as in the Bow Group report).[17] Leading industrialists and Conservative thinkers were evaluating the 'new capitalism' based on corporate social responsibility, technocratic managerial partnerships and the evolution of a corporate society.[18] Economists were celebrating the new technocracy and the potential for planning offered by Keynesianism and indicative planning. This was the era of Shonfield's *Modern Capitalism* (1965) and of Galbraith's *New Industrial State* (1967). In his Reith lectures Galbraith declared British monopoly laws to be 'a charade', and in characteristic style maintained that 'in fact, oligopoly is combined, in one of the more disconcerting contradictions of economic theory, with efficient production, expansive output, and prices that are generally thought rather favourable to the public. The consequences of oligopoly are greatly condemned in principle and greatly approved in practice.'[19] Officials were uncertain that attacks on monopoly and promotion of competition were the right way to pursue goals of increased efficiency, technical progress and expanded share of world markets. Neither had the competition specialists provided any firmer guidelines. Stevens and Yamey noted that even the *Economist* had complained that the Restrictive Practices Court was over-emphasising competition. Their somewhat sceptical treatment of the Court denied the possibility of developing consistent judicial principles by which to judge restrictions on competition.[20] Even such a Commission stalwart as Professor George Allen, well thought of in the BoT, was asserting in his widely used textbook that 'there can be little doubt that competition of the classical kind plays a much smaller role today than in the early years of the century'.[21] When the 1945 Act had been passed it had proved impossible to define with legal precision the specific problems with which it had to deal. The parliamentary draftsmen had devised the compromise, and clumsy, phrase of 'the conditions to which the Act applies', and Parliament had insisted upon a public interest clause that was only marginally more definitive. By the mid 1960s the problems had become clearer, there were *per se* prohibitions operating against collective resale price maintenance, but the precise targets of competition policy remained ambiguous and the very principles of policy were being challenged by progressive opinion. The challenges were coming not least from the reformist writings of the President of the BoT himself, Tony Crosland, whose views on the more benign face of organised capitalism had created such a stir in the Labour Party.[22] In these circumstances it is perhaps unsurprising if officials felt rudderless.

Neither did business have a clear view of how and whether competition policy should be operated. This introduces the fourth restraint, the preferences of business. The FBI lobbied hard, and sometimes very successfully, against aspects of the operation of monopolies and restrictive practices policy. At the official level the BoT people were often highly critical of business and often unsympathetic but, nonetheless, the record indicates a sustained willingness to cater to FBI/CBI preferences. A rather stark example occurred in 1956 when the Board was considering a replacement for Sir David (Scott) Cairns, who was determined to give up the Chairmanship when the Commission was downgraded. The search was prolonged and the Board insisted upon a lawyer, which was what the FBI wanted. Scott Cairns had suggested Sir Richard Yeabsley, an experienced and respected accountant who had served on the Commission since 1949. He was fifty-eight and wanted the job. In a devastating minute Sir Frank Lee observed that:

he signed the majority report of the Monopolies Commission on collective discrimination and the Lloyd–Jacob report on resale price maintenance, and for these reasons among others he is, I think, not entirely *persona grata* with industry. He also has a distinct predilection for recommending price control and future reports of the Commission on monopolies of scale might, under his guidance, present a series of rather embarrassing recommendations for us.[23]

This episode provides an example of calculated BoT manipulation of the Commission. Added poignancy is attached to this vignette by a later minute, also by Lee, which records Sir Richard's visit to Lee's office after the announcement that Richard Levy QC was to be appointed Chairman (at the age of sixty-four). Yeabsley had been desperately keen to become Chairman and was not prepared to serve as an ordinary member; 'he was not to be persuaded by anything that I could say, though he said rather wistfully that he hoped the President and I would not think that he was taking up his attitude out of resentment or pique'.[24] Lee added (perhaps guiltily) that 'the loss of his services will be severely felt', but industrial preferences had taken precedence. Here the BoT at the highest level was anticipating business reactions, giving some substance to theories of business power or capture. This bowing to industrial wishes caused problems even when business had a clear view of what it wanted, but frequently it did not. Before turning to the creation of the 1973 Act we should consider the changing business views on the form of competition policy.

Business views of monopoly and restrictive practices policy, 1945–70

It is easy to be critical of business attitudes to competition and competition policy. The cynics observe a systematic hypocrisy in which business pays lip service to competition while seeking remorselessly to suppress it. It is even easier, from the standpoint of the liberal 1990s, to condemn the restrictionism of the 1940s which resonated into the 1970s. On closer inspection it is indignation rather than hypocrisy which emerges from business debates in the FBI/CBI and in business evidence to the Commission. In the early investigations businesspeople did not seek to hide the presence of restrictive practices; they defended and even celebrated them. Restrictive agreements were felt to provide counter-cyclical stability, rising quality, technical development, falling prices and better performance in overseas markets (exactly the same arguments were used in Japan where, perversely, they appeared to be justified). Jewkes pointed to 'the almost pathological dread of surplus capacity in the minds of British businessmen in the years between the wars'.[25] Witnesses advanced confident and often eloquent arguments to the Commission, only to have them discounted against a yardstick of robust liberalism. Hence 'British industrialists responded to the work of the Monopolies Commission with a mixture of pained surprise, exasperation and indignation'.[26] This provided the attitudinal backdrop to the business support for the judicial approach in the 1956 Act discussed in chapter 2.

The FBI monitored the progress of the Act carefully through its Working Committee on Restrictive Practices. In 1956–57 the Committee organised informal meetings between representatives of the first eleven industries to come before the Restrictive Practices Court. In one such meeting the Chairman, Sir Herbert Hutchinson, who also represented the Corrugated Paper Association, opened by suggesting that it was 'important that the first industries should not take up a defensive, but a confident, posture'.[27] The representatives discussed the best approach to the Court – how to present the cases and mobilise evidence – and discussed how the Registrar and the judges were behaving. But by the end of 1958 the initial confidence had turned to depression. The Court struck down the agreements in the first three cases – *Chemists* (November 1958), *Yarn Spinning* (January 1959) and *Blankets* (March 1959). Throughout 1959 critical judgements caused the collapse of cases and generated a torrent of abandoned agreements.[28] Business faith in the legal process had been confounded and later in the 1960s, when the CBI Trade Practices Committee was meeting to take stock of the legislative position, it found itself much more positively inclined towards the Commission. At a Working Party meeting in August 1966, 'it was generally agreed that industry had been wrong in asking for a court to hear Restrictive Practices and there must therefore be extensive explanations as to why this was wrong and to show that the Monopolies Commission procedure was better'.[29] The more positive view of the MC held across industry also reflected the modernising strain within business debate which now placed more emphasis on competition, but a competition qualified by the commitment to indicative planning made in the FBI Brighton Conference of December 1960. The early 1960s saw the rise of what Boswell and Peters call the 'revisionist'[30] faction among industrial leaders. They saw business as a responsible social partner in the pursuit of national economic objectives – especially price restraint and growth. The revisionists were in favour of responsible organised negotiation and co-operation, and they came to dominate both the FBI and the new CBI created in 1965. The revisionist perspective was held, for instance, by Norman

Kipping, the Director General of the FBI, who argued for a statesman-like balancing of national interests on the part of business.[31] This reinforced a co-operative style of negotiation and lobbying, based still on a careful independence of industry (not on corporatist integration) but with an expectation that business views would be advanced and would be heeded by government. The posture of responsible engagement by industry was an extension of the post-war settlement, and was seen at the beginning of the decade in the discussions over indicative planning and the creation of the NEDC, and at the end of the decade in connection with incomes policy and price restraint. In relation to competition policy it allowed business to place more faith in the government's view of 'the public interest' (since it helped shape it) and therefore in the discretionary machinery of which the MC was a part. But business support for the revisionists was not universal. Boswell and Peters define two alternative perspectives: the 'reconstructionists', who pursued a more radical transformation of the business role towards a more subordinate and 'socially responsible' posture; and the 'liberationists', who pursued a vision of business pre-eminence based on a freeing of markets and assertion of business values.[32]

Thus, although the business revisionists were in the ascendant, business did not speak with one voice. In addition to the varying theoretical or philosophical views held by business leaders, the interests of their companies differed radically. The divisions between small and large business, between retailers and producers, between manufacturers and the City, all produced understandable differences of views on competition policy. Such divergencies were amplified when policy was extended to cover service industries in the Acts of 1965 (for mergers and monopolies) and 1973 (for restrictive practices). The introduction of merger control also increased the stakes and began to excite City interests as it gradually dawned on business what a significant change the modest 1965 Act had in fact constituted (see chapter 7). Moreover, the FBI/CBI as organisations were not well equipped to formulate decisive views, to communicate them unambiguously or to control their members. Grant notes that the CBI was more an 'umbrella' than a 'peak' organisation and its ability to mobilise membership and reconcile business disagreements was decidedly limited.[33] Despite these weaknesses the FBI/CBI carried the most weight in government and had the most influence over the development of competition policy. This could be seen as a major defect in policy making. Ministers and officials were dealing with a flawed partner and may have received conflicting or confused messages about what industry wanted or would tolerate.

There is no doubting the access of the CBI to officials and ministers prior to the 1980s. For instance, when Barbara Castle became Secretary of State for Employment and Productivity in April 1968, 'at my suggestion Harold and I met Stephen Brown, President of the CBI. I can't have them saying my first act in my new office was to snub the CBI.' She also noted the remarkable 'quadripartite' meetings held informally in her office between John Davies (CBI), George Woodcock (TUC), Aubrey Jones (PIB) and the Minister. This was 'real' discussion, unencumbered by the diplomacy of the NEDC, 'all on first name terms and very relaxed'.[34] The CBI's thinking on competition policy was undertaken through the Legal Department and through the Trade Practices Policy Committee, with a membership of about twenty-five business leaders. In the mid-1960s the membership was almost exclusively from large manufacturing companies and the attendance at a typical meeting was a roll call of 'monopolists' – or at least oligopolists, most with firsthand experience of the MC. At a June 1966 meeting the twenty participants included representatives from Shell (in the Chair), BICC, Dunlop, Imperial Tobacco and ICI.[35] Hardly a congregation likely to worship at the altar of competition.

By the mid 1960s business opinion had evolved towards a more tolerant attitude towards a competition policy, but had evolved some decided opinions about the most preferable content of policy and the agencies through which it should be implemented. In the wake of the 1965 Act the time was ripe for a more comprehensive appraisal of policy. This took the form of debates within CBI committees and pressure for law reform. The debate became focused on the future of the MC and how it should be strengthened – a process that culminated ultimately in the Fair Trading Act of 1973, and it is to the genesis of this pivotal piece of legislation that we can now turn.

The creation of the Fair Trading Act

The 1973 Fair Trading Act is a deceptive piece of legislation. It dominated British competition policy for twenty-five years but it signified both more and less than at first appears. It was less significant in that its substantive contribution to the design of policy was minimal. Essentially it was a consolidating statute which re-enacted the principles, methods and powers of the main extant legislation. For the MMC its direct impact was slight. The MMC's functions and methods were unchanged. The Fair Trading Act gave it a new name, new partners and revised public interest guidance. On the other hand, it was more significant in creating a dedicated agency and a spokesman responsible for articulating competition concerns. The impact of the legislation should be assessed with regard to the way in which the DGFT and his Office exploited their position, rather than with regard to the stipulation of new principles or objectives of policy.

The Fair Trading Act could be portrayed as a gradual and almost inevitable policy development. Nothing could be further from the truth. It was the third of three radically different attempts at legislation and its genesis was marked by virtually every variety of political uncertainty, including elections, ministerial reshuffles, inter-departmental in-fighting, lobbying, expediency and accident. It constitutes a classic study in pragmatic policy making, of 'muddling through' in a process dominated and energised by officials in the DTI who responded, more or less ably, and more or less willingly, to the political pressures placed upon them. The story can be told in three stages.

From the Commission on Industry and Manpower (CIM) to the new Competition Commission

The late 1960s were interesting times for members of the MC, and positively exciting for its Chairman. Exciting, but not enjoyable. Sir Ashton Roskill found himself embroiled in a maelstrom of political and economic dispute. A Wykhamist and a barrister, Roskill had a haughty disdain for the press and did not relish his high public profile or his regular pictures in the serious press, where he often appeared, with a rather pained expression, alongside the PIB Chairman, Aubrey Jones. The contrast was eloquent. Jones, an accomplished and enthusiastic media performer, would appear on TV programmes such as the 'Money Programme' singing the praises of an expanded PIB, while Roskill was actually reported as 'not being enthusiastic' about expanding the powers of the Commission.[36]

Roskill and the Commission found themselves a shuttlecock in a classic Cabinet game. The BoT (under Tony Crosland from 1967) was quite keen to strengthen pro-competition policy. The DEA, in alliance with the NEDC and the CBI, was concerned to lift the constraints on industrial co-operation which it believed were imposed by the restrictive trade practices legislation. Meanwhile, Barbara Castle, who had become Secretary of State for Employment and Productivity in April 1968, was working with the PIB to control prices as part of the all-important prices and incomes policy, and she wanted to extend her control.

The CBI's Trade Policy Committee had created a lobbying position during 1966–67 based on papers from John Methven which argued for the abolition of the Restrictive Practices Court and instead for an administrative tribunal to replace both the Court and the MC. Methven was then with ICI's legal department and was the key member of the CBI working party on antitrust reform. He consulted officials at the DEA and included their comments in his papers to the working party.[37] An alliance was created which combined pressure from the DEA and the Neddy machinery within Whitehall, and the CBI outside, which succeeded in persuading the BoT to pass a limited Restrictive Practices Act in 1968. The Act brought information agreements into the remit of the Restrictive Practices Court, a long-standing BoT priority, but it also provided powers to exclude agreements which increased efficiency or cut prices, which was the CBI's target. The clauses gave ministers discretion to exempt agreements which met industrial policy or prices policy ends. They were actually little used but the CBI had gained some modest success through the 1968 Act. In contrast, it found itself on the losing side in the more important battle over the CIM.

As we have seen, the BoT faced a problem in defining a coherent economic purpose for the competition regime. The early merger reports had generated industrial and academic criticism (see chapter 7), and a blatant contradiction existed in the work of the IRC in encouraging strategic mergers. Similarly the NEDC machinery was creating agreements that could be seen as restrictive, while the new theories of industrial organisation reinforced the Government's agnostic stance over monopoly. In pursuit of a rationale the BoT commissioned Alister Sutherland's review of the Commission's reports[38] and undertook a full-scale internal review which was expected to produce a White Paper in the summer of 1968.[39] As we saw in chapter 5, the PIB empire was generating an alternative investigatory machinery and an alternative economic rationale based on productivity improvements and industrial efficiency as a way to moderate price increases. The Government's reaction to these theoretical and organisational challenges provoked a rare expression of public criticism from Commission members. Writing in *The Times* Maurice Corina quoted various members of the Commission who voiced (anonymously) great concern over the role and future of the body. Thus, 'another member commented: "We are not being taken seriously" … He was worried the Government had been turning a distinguished authority into an "exercise in public relations"'.[40] It might have come as some consolation to Commissioners that Peter Jay was writing in December that, although the White Paper had been delayed, 'the Board of Trade has now almost won its battle over the future of the Monopolies Commission'.[41] Further consolation was provided in July 1969, when Tony Crosland sought to increase the attractiveness of Commission work by giving members a 95 per cent pay increase – taking the pay of part-time members from £1,000 to £1,950. But in that same month Barbara Castle recorded in her diary that the Cabinet Committee on Economic Strategy had confounded Jay's prediction and endorsed a paper on the Future of the Monopolies Commission by an official committee, Chaired by Ronald McIntosh, who was, by now, a Cabinet Office Deputy Secretary. The paper argued for a merger between the MC and the PIB, and thereby the creation of a new Industrial Commission. It had been vigorously opposed by Crosland and the BoT but Castle was all in favour, believing that it would make it harder for a future Conservative Government to abolish the PIB. There then ensued a further battle over who should be responsible for the Commission. Wilson came down in favour of his old friend Barbara Castle and moved Tony Crosland to Environment in his Cabinet reshuffle of 5 October, which also abolished the DEA and allocated BoT's industrial functions to an expanded MinTech under Tony Benn. This cleared the way for the creation of a new CIM based on a merger (really a hostile takeover) of the PIB and the MC and under the control of the DEP. It was announced in the Queen's Speech on 30 October 1969. In her robust style Castle noted that her press secretary, Bernard Ingham (an historical curiosity), 'is terrified lest we shan't be able to convince the press that our Department is competent to deal with monopoly policy. Oh yeah? If I can't make more use of the new body than the Board of Trade has with the Monopolies Commission, I'm not the girl I think I am.'[42] The DEP quickly moved to publish a White Paper on the CIM in December 1969. It would have created a formidable interventionist agency. The CBI was extremely apprehensive as to how it might behave in the hands of a forceful leader such as Aubrey Jones and opposed the Bill fiercely. The Bill had its second reading in February and was scheduled to go into Committee in June. At this point electoral politics intervened. The polls were unanimously in Labour's favour and Harold Wilson chose to go to the country on 18 June 1970. The universal expectation was that Labour would be returned to office but that was not to be. Ted Heath and the Conservatives were victorious with a safe thirty-seat majority.

These were the days of 'adversary politics' in which the two main parties took doctrinally opposed stands on issues of micro-economic policy. Accordingly the incoming Government pursued its declared policy of 'disengagement' by promptly abolishing the NBPI and the Consumer

Council. This was followed in 1971 by the repeal of the Industrial Reorganisation Corporation Act. The manifesto had declared (rather vaguely) that 'we will pursue a vigorous competition policy. We will check any abuse of dominant market power or monopoly, strengthening and reforming the machinery that exists.'[43] Since the MC was now the only player left on the field it became the centre of attention. Robert Carr had become Secretary of State for Employment and Productivity, and he and Ronald McIntosh (who had moved to the DEP) embarked on a remarkable honeymoon with the Commission.

Within a month of the election, on 9 July, the DEP team, including Carr, McIntosh and Frank Glaves-Smith, met Sir Ashton Roskill. The Government's attitude towards the Commission was extremely warm. Roskill felt that instead of an independent registrar (as suggested in the 1964 White Paper) he

> had considered that a better course might be to provide the Commission with a strong secretariat and an investigating staff able to examine complaints, consider the details of all proposed mergers and act as a permanent watchdog in the consumer's interest. On the basis of what was found, it would be then for the Commission itself to recommend cases for reference.[44]

He added that with an additional two full-time Chairmen the Commission could manage twenty references a year. Officials worked on these proposals and continued to liase very closely with Roskill and with Eric Phillips, the Secretary of the Commission. There were regular meetings, sometimes over lunch, as the ideas matured about the new 'Competition Commission'. Roskill had strong views and wanted a possible registrar of monopolies to be a member of the Commission rather than an official. The DEP briefed the CBI, which was quite happy with the proposals, but more sceptical views were heard from elsewhere in Whitehall and were expressed in the Official Committee on Competition and Incomes which McIntosh Chaired. The production departments were generally unenthusiastic about strengthening the Commission and MinTech people spoke seriously of abandoning merger control.[45]

By September 1970 a formal paper had been prepared for Cabinet suggesting a new Competition Commission based on an enhanced MC. The favoured option was a Commission which would make its own references, carry out research on its own initiative, have additional powers of investigation, and a director general or registrar of competition to organise the research effort. There would be additional full-time members. One controversial question concerned efficiency audits of nationalised industries which, on the whole, officials thought would be helpful.

The paper also talked of the case for reducing the merger threshold from one-third to a 25 per cent market share. In short, the paper 'delivered' Roskill's July vision of an expanded MC with many of the powers and functions which were later to be undertaken by the OFT.

Thus, in under twelve months, the Commission had been faced with two very contrasting proposals. First was submergence in the CIM machinery of intervention and price control. Second was a huge expansion of its traditional role with the emphasis on competition, disengagement and establishing a framework. In the traditions of civil service neutrality officials had worked hard to design and gain acceptance for each of these models. However, the speed, commitment and eloquence with which the second proposal had been formulated raises the suspicion that the ex-BoT officials were far more enthusiastic about the Competition Commission. Indeed, if they had succeeded in having it adopted by Cabinet the country would have seen a momentous move to a liberal and more effective competition regime. Whether it would have worked better than the OFT model is a matter for debate but it would have avoided the disheartening three-year delay before the OFT came into existence. It would also have avoided the odd combination of competition and consumer protection powers in one agency, and it would have allowed liberal-minded officials and ministers to embed the principles and activities of a competition agency in a Government still committed to 'disengagement' before the U-turn to interventionism. The Competition Commission would have rewritten history as the apotheosis of the MC.

The genesis of the OFT

The 'Super Monopolies Commission' was swamped in the tidal wave of change that came with Heath's *Reorganisation of Central Government* White Paper in October 1970. It merged the DEP into the new giant DTI with John Davies as Secretary of State and Nicholas Ridley as the Parliamentary Under-Secretary responsible for competition policy. The competition brief was passed to the new ministers, who were told by officials of the plans for reform and the urgent need for change. Officials from the IC 3 Division noted that:

> Certainly the Chairman of the Commission, and those officials concerned with operating the legislation think that the process has worked very unsatisfactorily indeed: references which were fully justified were not made on grounds quite unconnected with competition policy eg to avoid upsetting friendly, personal relations with the heads of large companies.[46]

Public expectations had also been raised. *The Times* of 13 October had carried a story about a proposed 'new Commission for Competition' and ministers wanted to make progress. The immediate outcome was a Commons statement by John Davies on 17 December in which he declared his intention 'to reshape the Monopolies Commission, to widen its scope and powers and to make it more effective'.[47] At this stage he was envisaging legislation along the lines outlined by the DEP but many of the officials in the new DTI from MinTech were more sceptical of the proposals. While internal debate proceeded, Davies determined to make more use of existing powers. For instance, he invited proposals for references from the Commission and, in the only such case of own-initiative references, the Commission belatedly came up with primary batteries in November 1971. Internally the Department persevered with the difficult job of persuading its colleagues to make references. An internal memo went at the most senior level to Deputy Secretaries noting that:

> I know very well that Industry Divisions find references of the industries which they sponsor to the Monopolies Commission very unattractive. At the same time the Secretary of State is determined to make references in the near future and I should be most grateful for your co-operation in putting forward, say, four possibilities which you would regard as least unattractive.[48]

Breakfast cereals, sugar, plasterboard and cables were all mentioned. Of these, breakfast cereals (a MAFF responsibility) was one of a series of important references made in the spring and summer which *The Times* approvingly said showed 'refreshing simplicity and intelligent conservation', and the *Economist* felt indicated that the Government was taking competition seriously.[49]

Davies's statement in December was a holding operation. Throughout the early months of 1971 the DTI engaged in internal debate over the strengthening of competition policy. It consulted with the CBI, with other business interests, with individuals and with consumer bodies. Its real concern was with the machinery of policy, not the substance. In this process one event stands out. Late in December Ridley proposed a meeting between ministers and the MC. A date was set for 12 March 1971, and some trouble was taken by officials in IC 3 and the Commission to set up an agenda and agree ground rules. It was a high powered event involving a morning meeting at ten o'clock at the DTI which included fourteen members of the Commission, the Secretary of State (John Davies), the Parliamentary Under-Secretary of State (Nicholas Ridley) and nine DTI officials headed by the Permanent Secretary (Jack Rampton) and by Cyril

Coffin (the Under-Secretary heading IC 3). In the course of the meeting ministers were encouraging and stressed the importance of competition. Ashton Roskill pressed for incremental adaptation of existing legislation and a series of topics was covered, from references to procedures; and from the concept of competition to the evolution of the EEC competition rules. Some important general points were made but also some opinionated, marginal and detailed observations which were at best tangential to questions of policy development. The Commission seemed to speak as it existed, as a group of independent individuals. Few consistent or coordinated themes seemed to emerge. This extended debate, in which virtually all members of the Commission spoke, was followed by the arrival of a fleet of taxis which took the participants to a congenial lunch at the Criterion Hotel.

Set piece meetings of this magnitude have been exceptional in the history of the Commission. Ashton Roskill was not in favour of allowing members to come together to form a collective view. This meeting persuaded the DTI that the Commission should be more collegiate, that more use should be made of Deputy Chairmen, and that Ashton Roskill should be replaced (he wanted to stay on but was replaced in 1975[50]). As regards new legislation, the meeting confirmed the view that it would be difficult to build a new competition body on the foundation of the existing Commission, with its existing membership. Officials brought this experience together with debate and consultation, and the various strands met in IC 3 in April 1971.

Quite independently of direct ministerial guidance, officials in IC 3 drew up proposals to integrate the Office of the Registrar of Restrictive Trade Agreements, some staff from the DTI and some staff from the MC, into a new body called (at that time) the Office of Business Practices. It would be headed by a person of public stature with an arm's-length relationship with the Secretary of State. The Office would operate with extensive administrative discretion but both the MC and the Restrictive Practices Court would be retained. As far as the Commission was concerned, 'the Commission would revert to the role of an administrative tribunal for which, as a rather unwieldy body of part-time laymen, it is best fitted'. Officials envisaged that the new Office would do much of the inquiry and investigatory work on behalf of the Commission.[51] The key paper, described as 'a cockshy outline', was written by Cyril Coffin.[52] It brought these ideas together in a concise four-page summary which can be identified as the origins of the OFT. The paper was written in the knowledge of CBI proposals but was influenced as much by the views of young barristers[53] as by those of the CBI or TUC. It responded to the long-standing criticisms of the MMC acting as 'prosecutor and judge' by shifting the prosecuting function to the new Office – although this initial clarity was fudged in the eventual legislation. Above all it represented an intelligent pragmatism. It did not adopt new principles or new theories. It rejected the prohibition approach of European legislation in favour of the prevailing British approach already in existence. The blueprint for the OFT thus emerges as a synthesis by officials and underlines a consistent feature of the evolution of British competition policy – the importance and power of imaginative officials to mould policy and shape legislation. The pivotal actor in this case was Cyril Coffin, who had begun his career in Agriculture. He had moved into the Competition Division at the end of 1970 to replace Frank Glaves-Smith as Under-Secretary. He recalls little briefing on the problems and little overlap with his predecessor.[54] It seems that a new mind was helpful. Within four months the DTI had made a major shift of direction and was set on the path of creating a new competition agency.

The influence of the DTI officials is further illustrated by a contrast with the main outside source of policy initiative – the CBI. The interpretative balance to be struck between this episode as an example of bureaucratic power, or alternatively as an example of business power, depends on how one reads the actions of the DTI officials. Were they pursuing their own agenda, or were they anticipating the CBI's views? They did, after all, know that the CBI was in favour of a new Competition Commission, but their own version did differ materially from the CBI ideal. The CBI's Trade Policy Committee had also laboured during early 1971 to produce a substantial nine-page paper on new legislation. It argued for:

• the abolition of the Restrictive Practices Court
• a new Commission for Competition to combine the MC and the residue of restrictive practices control
• a Director of Investigation and Research for monopolies and mergers – to reach agreement on a voluntary basis or to recommend reference
• no control over mergers (or failing that raise the threshold)
• registration of restrictive agreements.

It also wanted the public interest test to be abolished in favour of a European-style 'abuse of dominant position' criterion, and it relayed the standard list of complaints against the procedures of the MC. As regards Europe and the attack on restrictive practices legislation, the paper was in a direct line of descent from Methven's drafts in 1966–67, and the proposal for a single 'Commission for Competition' followed up

Methven's initial preferences (and was described in the press as 'immaculate'[55]).

The paper was approved by the CBI Council in May and sent to John Davies at the DTI with a summary for the press. In June the full text of the paper was released and CBI leaders visited Davies to make their case. There is little indication that Davies was sympathetic to his former colleagues at the CBI, who were, in any case, two months too late. The DTI simply noted the areas of agreement and disagreement. It recognised that on the monopolies and mergers front there was substantial agreement, but that in respect of restrictive practices the DTI was in complete disagreement. Later, in August, the DTI team of Davies, Ridley, Rampton and Coffin met the CBI team of Partridge, Campbell-Adamson, Gray (Director of Legal Affairs) and Carr (Acting Chair of the Trade Practices Committee) at the House. Officials had advised Davies that 'he might give the CBI representatives in strict confidence a broad outline of his ideas, particularly about the appropriate institutional framework for competition policy'.[56] Ridley also revealed the proposal to reduce the market share threshold from one-third to 25 per cent. At this meeting and in subsequent correspondence the CBI expressed disappointment about restrictive practices but welcomed the monopolies and mergers proposals. In September the DTI sent a confidential summary of the proposed legislation to the usual tripartite partners and in October the proposals, unchanged by CBI lobbying, were announced as prospective legislation in the Queen's Speech.[57]

The response of Roskill and the Commission is not recorded. In May officials noted that the proposals might come as a shock to the Commission but by August 1971 Roskill had been informed. His feelings seem to have been of pleasure rather than betrayal. The experiment of the Commission proposing references had not worked well and a note on that subject observes 'Sir Ashton Roskill's evident relief that the Commission is not after all to be given an initiation function'.[58] From September 1971 onwards DTI officials began putting together the draft Bill. Eric Phillips at the MC was closely involved, and the process of working through the details and gaining agreement from other departments was prolonged. But the work in drafting the Bill was in vain. Yet again the pressure of parliamentary time pushed competition legislation down the pecking order. Priority was given to the European Communities Bill to take the UK into the EEC on 1 January 1973, and it became apparent by March that there would be no room for the DTI's Bill. Thus the Monopolies, Mergers and Restrictive Practices Bill was delayed for another year and eventually introduced into a very different industrial policy climate.

Moreover, it had by then collected the consumer policy brief and become a Bill for 'Fair Trading' rather than 'Competition'.

Shotgun marriage: competition and consumerism

It has been the fate of competition legislation to suffer extended parliamentary delays and, in this case, the delay of over a year meant that legislation came after the legendary 'U turns' of 1972 and therefore after the abandonment of the neo-liberal policy of 'disengagement' from industry. Indeed, disengagement was replaced by radical engagement. While DTI civil servants were finalising the monopolies Bill a team under Sir William Armstrong in the Cabinet Office was conducting a review of industrial policy which led to the 1972 Industry Act.

The Industry Act in sections 7 and 8 contained some of the most interventionist powers to direct and subsidise industry ever taken outside wartime. They constituted a rejection of the liberal individualism expressed in the early days of the Heath Government which has, rightly, been seen as the precursor to the Thatcherite revolution of the 1980s. The creation of the Industry Act displayed the extent of prime ministerial power. It was undertaken in secret, deliberately without involving the DTI or its ministers. By now Heath had become disillusioned with the lacklustre John Davies and had become exasperated by Nicholas Ridley and his constant press leaks. He felt (quite correctly) that Ridley would have fought the Act. The Industry Act was premised on the need to bring coherence to policies of industrial support but also on the belief that industry still desperately needed to be rationalised and modernised in anticipation of joining the EEC. For Heath this required a partnership of a far more technocratic nature funded by the state and with the objective of comprehensive renewal of the British industrial base. When the Bill was revealed to the DTI in April 1972 the junior ministers – Frederick Corfield, John Eden and Nicholas Ridley – all protested and all were removed. This was a bitter episode, especially for Ridley, whose claims to have resigned were subsequently belittled by Heath – 'I had made it clear to him that he was no longer wanted at the DTI.'[59] John Davies stayed to see the Industry Act through Parliament but he, like the industries he had been obliged to support, was a 'lame duck', to be replaced by Peter Walker.

Thus the 1972 Act removed the genuinely 'pro-competition' ministers from the DTI and spelled the end of the Government's commitment to a tough competition policy. The interventionists and planners came back into favour, together with a set of arguments about industry which again stressed the utility of co-operation, agreements, scale and national champions. In this setting the MC and its reform fell again into the category of possible mechanisms for price control and as one more weapon in the complex field of anti-inflation and industrial relations.[60] In this light it is perhaps less surprising that the monopolies Bill was taken to the altar as part of a shotgun marriage, with Sir Geoffrey Howe's finger on the trigger.

By the autumn of 1972 the delay in monopolies legislation was becoming a *cause célèbre*. Among the other items jockeying for consideration was a Bill designed to introduce measures for consumer protection. This had its origins in public dissatisfaction about the abolition of the Consumer Council and in concern expressed by ministers (especially John Davies) and by the Conservative Research Department.[61] Heath had been sufficiently persuaded of the case to establish an inter-departmental committee in 1971 and to commission a report from the Central Policy Review Staff (CPRS). The committee had produced a blueprint for legislation by June 1972, including a proposal for a Minister for Consumer Affairs with Cabinet rank. This was strictly a consumer protection package. It advocated a network of local advice centres and also envisaged a body that would be capable of entering the market, perhaps using the courts, and which would react quickly to new abuses. The agenda was very much to do with fair trading, including advertising, warranties, access to credit, misleading statements, and so on.

At this point the maverick element of parliamentary time again entered the picture. The Cabinet's future legislation committee could find no time for a consumer protection Bill and CPRS officials became very concerned. With a paternal eye on the consumer legislation they suggested that it be combined with the monopolies Bill. In this it was aided by major developments in prices and incomes policy. In June and July of 1972 the pressure was mounting, inside and outside Whitehall, for statutory incomes policy. Heath invested immense energies in trying to create a voluntary agreement, and in so doing directed his attention to prices and price control as one ingredient in the wages bargain. This gave impetus to the consumer Bill and persuaded Heath to take Sir Geoffrey Howe from his post as Solicitor General to appoint him as Minister for Trade and Consumer Affairs at the DTI, with a cherished seat at the Cabinet table. The appointment took effect on 5 November, just after the Downing Street talks had broken down, and the day before the Government was compelled to announce a statutory prices and incomes policy. Thus, although Howe was appointed as a consumer minister, and took enthusiastically to that role, the mission which put him into the DTI was price control. His appointment was 'in Ted Heath's eyes as the "Minister for Keeping Prices Down"'.[62] The legislation on competition policy was thus overshadowed by the re-launch of consumer protection policy, and by a preoccupation with anti-inflation measures.

As Howe jovially conceded, he was the midwife of the Fair Trading Act, not the parent. All the same, he did introduce some last minute changes and he also agreed to allow a film crew to follow through the legislation for a 'fly on the wall' TV documentary. The film makes interesting viewing and made minor celebrities of some of the officials.[63] Howe greatly expanded section 2 of the Act which gives the Director General a duty 'to keep under review' commercial activities. This was much wider than officials had planned. In the very last meeting to approve the draft Bill he also inserted 'and Mergers' into the title of the Monopolies Commission. No one felt bold enough to stand out against this change, which discomposed the typists and caused some surprise for the Commission.[64] The two pieces of draft legislation – on competition and on consumer protection – were hastily stapled together, there was no time for a White Paper, and the draft Bill was published at the beginning of December 1972. It was long and complex; in Cunningham's words, 'the Act itself is not a model of clarity, it is more an example of what legislation should not be'.[65] The consumer protection sections came in Part II, which created the Consumer Protection Advisory Committee. The statutory consumer protection powers have barely been used but, as we see below, Directors General have given at least equal weight to that side of their responsibilities.

The press greeted the draft Bill enthusiastically, calling it 'the biggest shake up of competition policy since the war'. A lot of attention was given to the reduction in the market share criterion to 25 per cent, which had been stressed by Howe in his first speech on the proposals.[66] This was not, of course, an innovation. We have seen that officials had planned this reduction as long ago as 1970 and the CBI had certainly been informed in the autumn of 1971. The CBI was considerably less enthusiastic and sent Howe a four-page letter complaining that 'we find the Bill tortuous and involved in its layout in much of its drafting (sic)'.[67] Their Trade Practices Policy Committee had been meeting twice a week to analyse the Bill, and Trevor Skeet MP had agreed to talk on its behalf to ministers and to voice the concerns of the CBI in the House and in Committee. The CBI noted 'much in the Bill which we welcome and support' but it had two big worries and two smaller ones. The first big issue was lowering the market share threshold to 25 per cent which had 'no adequate explanation'. The other was Europe. In an interesting, and almost visionary, exposition Campbell Adamson argued that 'the Government has the opportunity by this Bill to bring British law and practice into accord with what for brevity I can call the Rules of Competition in the European Communities. If this opportunity were taken, the benefits to British industry could be immense.'[68] On the smaller issues the CBI asked for block exemptions for some categories of restrictive practice, and pressed for a Director General with practical experience of industry and with a staff appointed by the DTI rather than on his or her own initiative. Howe's reply gave no ground. Regarding Europe he said that, 'I have considered the CBI's arguments to the effect that the time has come to abandon the basic principles of the UK legislation and to move towards a national law based on principles similar to those of Articles 85 and 86 of the EEC Treaty. I am afraid I am not persuaded by them.'[69]

More detailed issues were raised in Committee between January and April during which the faithful Trevor Skeet tabled fifty-five amendments, mainly on behalf of the CBI. On the whole changes were minimal. Labour tried to get the burden of proof on mergers shifted, Conservatives tried to get the thresholds lifted. All familiar and unsuccessful, although a certain piquancy was injected into the debate on the thresholds by the revelation that the DTI had a list of 114 industries in which the leading firm had between 25 and 34 per cent of the market. It included sausages, toothpaste and bread, and formed a potential feast for the OFT and the MMC. Quite a lot of energy was expended on topical issues such as pyramid selling and the vexing new powers of reference of restrictive labour practices (only one reference has ever been made, of *Labour Practices in TV and Film Making*, published in 1989). The position on nationalised industries was interesting. References to the MMC were made possible but, in the case of total national monopolies, they could only be made by a minister. Further, the DTI intended to require the DGFT to agree a confidential protocol covering any proposed referrals of any of the non-excluded activities of nationalised industries.[70] Coverage of the nationalised industries was therefore controlled entirely by ministerial discretion until the 1980 Competition Act (see chapter 8).

The Fair Trading Act had a fairly smooth passage and received Royal Assent in July. The final touch was the appointment of the all-important Director General. Not only should it be a person of standing and experience, it should be someone able and inclined to negotiate and to intervene in the consumer and the competition fields. The CBI, in its May 1971 paper, had envisaged an official 'of such calibre that they would be capable of maintaining a continued dialogue with industry', who would engage in 'consultation with a company found to engage in monopolistic practices with a view to securing termination or amendment of the practice'.[71] The DTI shared this view of a DGFT who

'would often be able to negotiate the modification of specific objectionable practices'.[72] The DGFT was therefore conceived of as both independent and possessed of extensive discretion. Ramsey implies that the
concept followed from the abolition of the Registrar of Restrictive Practices, but its genesis was rather different.[73] It could be traced back to the
Poole Committee report of 1963 with its recommendation of 'an independent officer of the Crown responsible for referring cases to the
Monopolies Commission'.[74] The proposal had been picked up in the 1964
White Paper, kept alive by the CBI and borrowed by DTI officials.

The Director General model was momentous. It provided the
model of the 'single person' regulator which became such a distinctive
feature of the British system of utility regulation. It should be noted,
however, that the DTI watered down the Poole Committee's concept,
which was to take the reference process entirely out of the hands of the
DTI. The reflex of retaining ministerial discretion was too strong. First,
the Director General was appointed by the Secretary of State, not the
Crown. Second, he or she was appointed for only five years and the Act
specifically provided for compensation for loss of office just in case the
Minister and the Director General did not 'hit it off'. Third, the reference process was hedged with safeguards. Not only were merger references to be made by the Secretary of State but the minister also had a veto
over monopoly references in the under-emphasised (and never used) section 50(6) of the Act. When the legislation was being drawn up the DTI
had exchanged notes with the Civil Service Department on the question
of independence. The exchange was revealing, if not exactly surprising
for seasoned observers of Whitehall. A senior official in the Civil Service
Department had observed:

> *Should the Director be Completely Independent?* The arguments point two
> ways. You want to give him the appearance of considerable independence.
> In part this is to avoid any suspicion that the Department's 'sponsorship
> role' puts it in the pocket of the industries sponsored, and makes it more
> reluctant to embark on investigations. On the other hand you want to
> retain ministerial control over the making of References … Given this
> degree of control my own view – and I think you agreed when we discussed
> it – is that the appearance of independence can be adequately ensured by
> setting up a separate Office and there is no need to strengthen it unduly.[75]

The 'unduly' is a particularly nice touch.

It did not prove easy to fill the post. After an extensive search, the
DTI produced a rather remarkable name, that of John Methven. He was
relatively young, at forty-seven, and was introduced as 'a former ICI

executive who shops regularly with his wife, likes touring in his caravan and is concerned about the non-availability of raisins and bananas in Cheshire'.[76] Of far more interest than his shopping habits was his former membership of the CBI's Trade Practices Policy Committee. We have seen the role he played in defining the CBI's policy position; he was now in the privileged position of putting his ideas into effect, but was also experiencing the delicious irony of being responsible for the restrictive practices legislation that he had been so keen to abolish.

There are two ways of looking at Methven's appointment. It could be seen as a supreme act of regulatory capture in which the lobbyist becomes the regulator. Alternatively, it could be regarded as a shrewd role reversal in which the poacher becomes a vigorous gamekeeper. There is evidence for both views although Methven was already, in any case, a member of the MC. His Office opened on 1 November but he did not make his first reference until July 1974 (of cables which took nearly five years to publication in March 1979). He also stressed, especially in his second annual report, his commitment 'to securing improvements by negotiations whenever possible'.[77] On the other hand he did make important references of frozen foods, copying, petrol, and so on. He admitted to spending much of his early time on the new consumer side of his Office and, of course, completed the circle by moving back to the CBI as Director General in May 1976, to be replaced by Gordon Borrie.

This brief review of the origins of the Act underlines the modesty of the substantive changes. There were significant elements. Some small, such as article 72(2), which required merger reports to specify 'particular effects, adverse to the public interest' – and thus significantly tightened the burden of proof on the Commission. Others were more substantial, such as the public interest section 84 (see Appendix), which gave prominence to 'effective competition' and generally implied a greater stress on competition,[78] although it might be noted that a strong strain of opinion within the DTI had wanted a far stiffer and pro-competition public interest clause. The extraordinary aspect of the legislation, however, was the last minute marriage of consumerism and competition. Was this, as many arranged marriages are said to be, a functional success?

Successive DGFTs have repeated John Methven's initial assertion that the consumer/competition combination was a great advantage. Geoffrey Howe also made a great virtue of this necessity both during the debates on the Bill and in his retrospective assessments. In practice, however, the two activities have been administered in substantial separation from one another and it is not very clear that there are great benefits. Consumer protection policy is concerned with developing and applying quite detailed rules about commercial behaviour. There is no obvious or logical link with market structure or competitive conditions, and the clients tend to be the public, consumer groups and local authorities through their trading standards offices. In contrast, competition policy is about business structure and strategy, and the clients tend to be businesses, lawyers and economists. Clearly 'the consumer' should be the ultimate beneficiary but that statement verges on pious moralising. The downside of the marriage has been the diversion of energies, the consumer preoccupation of Directors General, and the diffusion of attention away from the competition brief.

Conclusion

The detailed analysis of the first twenty-five years of UK competition policy is conducted against an intellectual background that is critical of policy. The early years are typically regarded as a 'failure'.[79] After 1956 the area of restrictive practices was more successful but the control of monopolies continued to be weak. This picture is perhaps overly influenced by the thinking of the 1990s. In comparison with Europe and Japan, British policy was far more significant, although it would be difficult to claim much direct economic impact. The nature of monopoly policy was moulded by the relationship between government and industry. A respectable case can be made for the argument that industry was the dominant influence over the development of policy but that it was often uncertain of its collective interests and was not always able to articulate them adequately. Moreover, although the BoT repeatedly made concessions it did so as part of a continuing bargaining process and as part of the voluntaristic relationship which underpinned the post-war settlement.

Rather than business exerting dominant influence it was accorded a privileged position by officials who recognised the importance of sustaining co-operative relationships. At some points, indeed, officials were willing to ignore or reject business preferences. The key actors were the BoT Under-Secretaries and, in terms of our six opening models of the policy-making process, the one that most closely approximates to the politics of this policy area is that of administrative dominance. Recent econometric research suggests that in the immediate post-war period the country paid a substantial price for its weak competition policy, in the shape of lower productivity and economic growth.[80] If this is the case then the easy explanation would be to 'blame' the officials in the BoT. This would be too easy. Officials had no particular gift of economic wisdom, economists were divided on the question of competition and, in any case, significant initiatives required the support of ministers and the political parties.

One really striking feature of this account is therefore the lack of policy leadership from the parties and the bi-partisan character of the development of policy. Since the political parties did not develop strong views on competition, this policy area escaped the doctrinal inter-party conflict that dogged so much of supply-side policy, but it fell by default under the control of the civil service. In turn this brought into play the civil service norms analysed in chapter 1 and allowed the unchallenged consolidation of the prevailing regime, thus enhancing the forces of path dependence. The officials' instincts were to respect company autonomy, to privilege property rights and to conform to the 'weak state' attitude that was part of the post-war settlement. The officials were not trapped by corporatist bargains or captured by an influential policy network, but they chose to build on existing arrangements and to use their power very hesitantly.

What of the MC? Up to 1956 it did its job with sincerity, dedication and some distinction. To brand it a 'failure' would be to criticise the policy, not the organisation, and is in any case unfair. After 1956, however, it became too circumspect. The 'wilderness years' up to 1965 seemed to cast a shadow into the later 1960s. The Commission was independent and performed its tasks with integrity but it was unimaginative, reactive and introverted. That is the clear message conveyed by the press and by contemporary accounts.[81] Its Chairmen, Levy and Roskill, conceived the Commission in a reactive, quasi-judicial role. Not political, not even particularly economic, but a creature of legal impartiality. Hence when the great opportunity came in 1970–71 to expand and redefine the role of the Commission its leadership backed away. Perhaps, historically, this was a benign outcome and the economy needed something like the OFT. But it is curiously counter-intuitive to see an organisation apparently so sceptical about the opportunities for expansion.

The chapter ends with the remarkable story of the creation of the Fair Trading Act. It was a piece of legislation driven by officials, with some novel and creative aspects. On the whole, however, it codified and rationalised the pre-existing regime and projected it forward for another twenty-five years. We come back to the second half of the story in chapter 9, after considering the two growth areas of merger control and utility regulation.

Notes

1 Detailed references are not offered for the theoretical material squeezed in here.
  General surveys can be found in P. John, *Analysing Public Policy* (London, Pinter,
  1998) and W. Parsons, *Public Policy* (Aldershot, Edward Elgar, 1995).

2 K. Middlemas, *Power, Competition and the State Volume 1: Britain in Search of Balance, 1940–61* (London, Macmillan, 1986), p. 1.

3 See C. Lindblom, *Politics and Markets: The World's Political-Economic Systems*
  (New York, Basic Books, 1977).

4 C. Lindblom, 'The science of "muddling through"', *Public Administration Review*,
  19 (1959).

5 PRO, BT64/318, The Control of Monopoly (17 July 1943), p. 49.

6 H. Mercer, *Constructing a Competitive Order: The Hidden History of British
  Antitrust Policies* (Cambridge University Press, 1995), ch. 4, pp. 5, 71.

7 *Ibid.*, p. 105.

8 PRO, BT64/4158, IM 1, 'The problem of operating the Monopolies Act' (1950),
  undated and unsigned.

9 PRO, BT64/508, 'Monopolies and Restrictive Practices Commission, discussion
  with Chairman, programme for the first year' (October 1948).

10 Barbara Castle, *The Castle Diaries 1964–70* (London, Weidenfeld and Nicolson,
   1974), pp. 783, 792. See also Richard Crossman, *The Diaries of a Cabinet Minister:
   Secretary of State for Social Services*, vol. III (London, Book Club Associates,
   1976), p. 511; when the issue came to Cabinet he calls it 'a delicious old fashioned
   talk' and puts it down to Harold Wilson's desire to keep an institution which he
   created.

11 *The Times*, 'Minister lists Britain's monopolies' (7 April 1970).

12 See Mercer, *Constructing a Competitive Order*, pp. 106–7, 120; also H. Mercer,
   'The Monopolies and Restrictive Practices Commission, 1949–56: a study in reg-
   ulatory failure', in G. Jones and M. Kirby (eds), *Competitiveness and the State*
   (Manchester University Press, 1991).

13 PRO, BT258/923, 'Membership of the Monopolies Commission, meeting with
   President and Parliamentary Secretary' (3 August 1956).

14 PRO, BT258/1982, 'Monopolies and restrictive practices', George Brown, First
   Secretary, DEA, letter to Douglas Jay, President of the BoT (26 October 1965).

15 *Ibid.*, memo by G. Parker (IM 2) to the Permanent Secretary, Mr Serpell, 'Consultation with DEA about references to the Monopolies Commission' (9 August
   1965).

16 Mercer, *Constructing a Competitive Order*, p. 115. Petrol distribution was eventually referred in 1977; it got a relatively clean bill of health in the 1979 MMC report.

17 For further discussion of these important reports see chapter 7.

18 See N. Harris, *Competition and the Corporate Society: British Conservatives, the
   State and Industry 1945–1964* (London, Methuen, 1972), ch. 13.

19 J. K. Galbraith, quoted in *The Times* (28 November 1966).

20 R. Stevens and B. Yamey, *The Restrictive Practices Court: A Study of the Judicial
   Process and Economic Policy* (London, Weidenfeld and Nicolson, 1965), pp. 136,
   143.

21 G. C. Allen, *The Structure of Industry in Britain* (London, Longman, 1961, second
   edn, 1966), p. 185.

22 See T. Crosland, *The Future of Socialism* (London, Jonathan Cape, 1956). He argued that questions of managerial accountability were uppermost in what was essentially no longer a capitalist state; see, for instance, K. Hoover and R. Plant, *Conservative Capitalism in Britain and the United States* (London, Routledge, 1989), p. 144.

23 PRO, BT258/923, 'Future membership of the Monopolies Commission', minute by Sir Frank Lee (2 July 1956).

24 *Ibid.*, note by Sir Frank Lee (25 October 1956).

25 J. Jewkes, 'British monopoly policy 1944–56', *Journal of Law and Economics*, 1:1 (October 1958), p. 2.

26 *Ibid.*, p. 8.

27 MRO, MSS.200C/1/14/1, 'Working Committee on Restrictive Practices', minutes of meetings, 7 May and 18 June 1957 (4 February 1958).

28 See Stevens and Yamey, *The Restrictive Practices Court*, p. 135.

29 MRO, MSS.200/C/1/14/1, 'Minutes of the Meeting of the Working Party of the Trade Practices Committee' (8 August 1966).

30 J. Boswell and J. Peters, *Capitalism in Contention: Business Leaders and Political Economy in Modern Britain* (Cambridge University Press, 1997), pp. 15–19.

31 See N. Kipping, *Summing Up* (London, Hutchinson, 1972).

32 Boswell and Peters, *Capitalism in Contention*, pp. 15–19.

33 See W. Grant and J. Sargent, *Business and Politics in Britain* (London, Macmillan, second edn, 1993), p. 104; W. Grant and D. Marsh, *The CBI* (London, Hodder and Stoughton, 1977).

34 Castle, *Diaries*, pp. 427, 442–3.

35 MRO, MSS.200/C/1/14/1, 'Minutes of Trade Practices Policy Committee meeting' (23 June 1966).

36 See *The Times*, 'Monopolies Board likely to be given new powers' (quote in picture caption) (23 December 1968).

37 MRO, MSS.200/C/1/14/1, 'Minutes of the working party' (8 August 1966). Methven had consulted Mr Cairns and Mr Fisher at the DEA.

38 A. Sutherland, *The Monopolies Commission in Action* (Cambridge University Press, 1969).

39 See *The Times* (20 February 1968).

40 Maurice Corina, 'Anxiety over role of MC', *The Times* (16 September 1968).

41 *The Times* (5 November and 23 December 1968).

42 Castle, *Diaries*, pp. 753–4; earlier references, pp. 698, 708–9.

43 F. W. S. Craig (ed.), *British General Election Manifestos 1900–1974* (London, Macmillan, second edn, 1975), p. 332.

44 PRO, FV 56/15, MMP197/1970, 'Monopolies: future of the Monopolies Commission legislation'. Note of a meeting.

45 PRO, FV 56/15, MMP/197/1970, 'Official Committee on Competition and Incomes', minutes of a meeting (11 September 1970).

46 PRO, FV 56/16, MMP206/1970, 'Monopolies: future of the monopoly legislation'. Submission to the Secretary of State (30 October 1970).

47 Statement by the Secretary of State for Trade and Industry cited in *Monopolies and Mergers Acts 1948 and 1965. Annual report by the Department of Trade and Industry, year ended 31 December 1970*, HC, 291 (London, HMSO, 1971), p. 9.

48 PRO, FV 56/19, 1/MMP239/1970, 'Future of the monopolies legislation', covering note (late November 1970).

49 *The Times* (19 May 1971); *Economist* (22 May 1971).
50 See Sir Ashton's obituary, *The Times* (29 June 1991), written by a former senior civil servant.
51 PRO, FV 56/19, 1/MMP239/1970, future of the monopolies legislation. 'Draft. Competition policy: a new institutional framework?' (21 April 1971).
52 Interview with Cyril Coffin (February 1999).
53 Specifically John Swift and James Cunningham. The latter wrote the standard study of the Act, *The Fair Trading Act 1973: Consumer Protection and Competition Law* (London, Sweet and Maxwell, 1974).
54 Interview with Cyril Coffin (February 1999).
55 *The Times* (27 May 1971).
56 PRO, FV 60/40, IC3/396, 'Restrictive trade practices, competition policy and the CBI … and TUC', steering brief (28 July 1971).
57 See *The Times*, 'Drastic reform of merger and monopoly laws in next Parliamentary session' (27 October 1971).
58 PRO, FV 60/48, IC3/418, 'Monopolies – contact with the Monopolies Commission on suggestions for references', file note (19 August 1971).
59 E. Heath, *The Course of My Life* (London, Hodder and Stoughton, 1998), p. 400. For these developments see also J. Campbell, *Edward Heath: A Biography* (London, Pimlico, 1994), ch. 23.
60 A point endorsed by Campbell, *Edward Heath*, pp. 331, 448.
61 This section draws on W. D. B. Roberts, 'The formation of consumer protection policy in Britain – 1945–73', PhD thesis, University of Kent at Canterbury (June 1976), ch. 7, Fair Trading Act; and on I. Ramsey, 'The Office of Fair Trading: policing the consumer marketplace', in R. Baldwin and C. McCrudden (eds), *Regulation and Public Law* (London, Wiedenfeld and Nicolson, 1987), who similarly leans on Roberts.
62 G. Howe (Lord Howe of Aberavon), 'The birth of an office: a midwife's view', paper presented at the 'Fair Trading: Past and Future' conference organised by the OFT, May 1992. See also E. Heath, *The Course of My Life*, p. 416.
63 The film was broadcast in 'The State of the Nation' series in 1973 and produced by Brian Lapping. It is available as a video from Granada Learning, Manchester.
64 Correspondence with Cyril Coffin (1999).
65 Cunningham, *The Fair Trading Act*, p. ix.
66 *The Times* (1 December and 23 November 1972).
67 MRO, MSS.200/C/3/COM/21/3, letter from Campbell Adamson, Director General of the CBI, to Sir Geoffrey Howe, Minister for Trade and Consumer Affairs (19 January 1973).
68 *Ibid.*
69 MRO, MSS.200/C/3/COM/21/4, letter, Howe to Campbell Adamson (31 January 1973).
70 PRO, BT281/115 Fair Trading Act, Volume 2, 'Brief for the second reading' (1973).
71 MRO, MSS.200/C/3/COM/21/3, 'Monopolies, mergers and restrictive practices legislation', paper approved by Council (May 1971).
72 PRO, BT281/115, Fair Trading Act, Volume 2, 'Brief for the second reading' (1973).
73 Ramsey, 'The Office of Fair Trading', p. 182.
74 Poole Committee, *Monopoly and the Public Interest* (London, Conservative Political Centre, 1963), p. 18.

75 PRO, FV 60/57, IC3.460 Pt1, 'Monopolies and Restrictive Practices Bill: instructions to parliamentary counsel', exchange of correspondence with Civil Service Department (10 September 1971).

76 *The Times* (14 August 1973).

77 *Annual Report of the Director General of Fair Trading, 1975* (London, HMSO, 1976), p. 13.

78 Cunningham argues that section 84 is very different from the 1949 Act in stressing value judgements rather than economic benefits. To this extent it broadens the test; see *The Fair Trading Act*, pp. 148–9.

79 To borrow the verdict of Mercer's 1991 chapter; Mercer, 'The Monopolies and Restrictive Practices Commission', p. 78.

80 S. N. Broadberry and N. Crafts, 'The post-war settlement: not such a good bargain after all', *Business History*, 40:2 (April 1998).

81 See C. Rowley, *The British Monopolies Commission* (London, Allen and Unwin, 1966); Sutherland, *The Monopolies Commission in Action*; and M. Peston, 'A new look at monopoly policy', *Political Quarterly*, 41 (1970).

7

The control of mergers

Merger control is the most visible face of competition policy and excites the most interest from the press and the academic community. The MMC has produced more merger reports than any other single type of report, and mergers have provoked some of the procedural changes and many of the analytical changes in the work of the MMC. Thus the emphasis on 'speed-up' and the shift to a more explicitly 'effect on competition' criterion were both catalysed by concern over mergers. Many individual reports have been headline news and constitute landmarks in contemporary politics as well as competition policy. The first merger to be turned down was *Ross Group/Associated Fisheries* in 1966 which created a mild furore. Later dramatic cases included *Lonhro/House of Fraser* in 1981; *The Government of Kuwait/British Petroleum* in 1988; *National Power/Southern Electric* in 1995; and *British Sky Broadcasting Group/Manchester United* in 1999. In all these cases mergers were blocked but prevention of mergers is the quite exceptional side of merger control. The vast majority of cases proceed unhindered in a process that nowadays is sophisticated and relatively predictable. It was not always so.

As context for the chapter the record of merger referrals is presented in table 15. From the hundreds of merger cases each year the OFT identifies those that qualify for scrutiny under the legislation. A proportion are referred by the Secretary of State to the MMC, which reports back to the Minister. Between 1965 and 1997 table 15 indicates that the OFT considered 6,220 qualifying cases (and it reviewed far more than that). Of those a mere 211 were referred to the MMC and of those the Commission found only 81 to be against the public interest and recommended that only 48 of those should not be allowed. In terms of direct control, then, the MMC impact has been extremely modest. Less than 1 per cent of mergers are prevented (about 1.5 per cent if you count those abandoned). But, as with all regulation, a low level of infringements can be a sign of failure or a sign of success. The figures are silent on mergers

Table 15 *Merger cases considered, referred and reported, 1965–97*

	No.	%
Qualifying cases	6220	100.0
Referred to the MMC	211	3.4
Not against the public interest (allowed)	82	1.3
Against the public interest, allowed with conditions	33	0.5
Against the public interest, blocked	48	0.8
Abandoned	48	0.8

Sources: BoT and OFT annual reports, MMC database.
Notes: The qualifying cases are those above the assets threshold or above 25 per cent share of supply.
The categories are the recommendations by the MMC, not the eventual outcomes.

designed to avoid provoking a referral, on those not pursued after confidential discussions, those not referred because suitable undertakings were given, and those simply not proposed because of the likelihood of referral. The MMC can therefore be seen as a deterrent, a 'speed bump' that makes people drive sensibly, or simply as the cornerstone of a regulatory structure. As such, of course, it cannot be treated in isolation. The merger control system is tripartite and the reference practices of the OFT and the DTI are central. In 1990 the European Merger Regulation had also begun to operate and was becoming more effective by the mid 1990s. This removed the larger cases from UK jurisdiction. The Labour Government chose not to reform the merger regime in 1998 which created a nice historical curiosity. Merger control was not conceived of in 1948 but it became grafted on to the British model in the 1960s. In 1998 that British model was reduced to a minor part of the new system. But the old regime of the MMC investigation and the public interest test lived on in the system of merger control for which it was never intended.

This chapter reviews the origins of merger control, studies the definition and adaptation of the guiding principles, and evaluates the role of the MMC. The second half of the chapter goes into the record of referrals and reports, and assesses the respective roles of the MMC, the DTI and the OFT in the tripartite system. It ends in offering an evaluation of the system. It does not deal with the interesting but specialised area of control of newspaper mergers.

The origins of merger control

Almost as soon as the 1956 Restrictive Trade Practices Act had come into force the BoT appears to have realised that a mistake had been made in neutering the MC (see chapter 6). When Peter Thorneycroft had talked of abolishing it entirely the officials had succeeded in saving this 'old and tried horse' although they did not avoid a reduction in size, powers and jurisdiction.[1] By January 1957 Thorneycroft had been replaced by Sir David Eccles, merger activity was starting to take off, and it was becoming clear how little work the reduced MC could undertake. The issue had reached the Cabinet by 1960, so that in July the Economic Policy Committee was asking the President of the BoT (now Maudling) to 'arrange for a general review during 1961 of the effects on industry of existing legislation concerning monopolies and restrictive practices'.[2] As in the early 1990s the review of policy and legislation was glacially slow. The year 1962 was something of a turning point. In February there were two parliamentary debates infused with passion and outrage by the contested bid by ICI for Courtaulds. This, the biggest proposed merger in Britain up to that time, raised many of the issues which were later to excite merger analysts. The treatment of shareholders, the interests of the Boards, the effect on efficiency, on technology, on exports. To all the questions raised over the merger in Parliament the Government front bench had to sit shuffling uncomfortably and admitting there was nothing they could do. Barbara Castle observed that, 'I have never seen a more crestfallen bunch … I heard some of them muttering, "this is terrible", as the right hon. Gentleman was limping from one lame excuse to another as to why the Government could do nothing at all.'[3] All the President of the BoT (by then Frederick Erroll) could manage was to announce a government review of the legislation; a review that was already under way and which reported in December 1962 to the Cabinet's Economic Steering Committee. To keep an eye on ministers Rab Butler, the Conservative Party Chairman, also set up a high powered committee under the Chairmanship of Oliver Poole (Lord Poole), a former Chairman of the Party. At much the same time the Bow Group established a discussion group of young businessmen.

The BoT's December paper proposed a system of merger control operated by an MC which would need to be strengthened to escape current criticism, summarised in the paper as follows: 'the Commission take too long to report: their investigations are unnecessarily wide and go into too much detail; they act as both judge and prosecutor. (The two latter points are made particularly by industry.)' The paper advanced several novel features, including the idea that the tribunal (Commission) would select its own cases. It covered the views of the FBI saying, 'As might be expected, they are opposed to the introduction of any provision for inquiry into mergers.'[4] The FBI argued that since no other government in Europe operated merger controls British industry would be disadvantaged. But, sensing the inevitable, it also argued that if a system were put in place it should be administrative not legal; and should operate after mergers had taken place, not before. This meant that 'since the most usual situation for which a merger might require investigation is monopoly, examination after it has taken place would enable the machinery of the Monopolies Commission to be used'.[5]

In a laborious process the Economic Steering Committee referred the paper to the Economic Policy Committee of Cabinet, which in March 1963 created a Sub-committee on Monopolies.[6] This was a small Committee composed of Erroll (President of the BoT); Edward Du Cann (Economic Secretary, Treasury); Sir John Hobson (Attorney General) and the Minister of Transport, represented by John Hughes-Hallett. They reviewed a series of areas for possible change, including the introduction of public hearings. The 'judge and prosecutor' chestnut came up again and they considered the possibility of a self-contained investigation branch within the Commission. Oddly, they commented that 'it would be useful to have a better idea of how the Commission worked at present, but this would be difficult to obtain' – a testament to the limited communication between the BoT and the MC.[7] Of more import was that 'Miss Dennehy said that the President had himself suggested that the conditions for the investigation of mergers should be brought into line with those for monopolies – that the buyer either before or after the merger should control at least one-third or more of the market'.[8] The minutes convey a faint surprise that a minister should have had an idea, and quite a radical one. Previously officials had envisaged a test of 'a significant reduction of competition' but the market test was broader and, in the event, momentous. The whole tone of these discussions was that mergers were on the whole desirable and not to be discouraged, ministers and officials simply wanted to pick out the few bad apples. But at this point the Treasury was even more hesitant and, if not resisting, at least dragging its collective feet. The paper notes that:

> The Chancellor and the Economic Secretary were anxious not to discourage mergers which would bring about desirable economies of scale or which were necessary in order to enable British firms to compete on equal terms with large foreign firms. They seemed to be suggesting that such mergers should be free even from investigation.[9]

Indeed, Maudling had expressed this view in a personal note to Erroll, where he says that early Sub-committee papers are too negative and

'while we no doubt need more competition we also need more consolidation'.[10] The main points from the Sub-committee's report, sent to the
Economic Policy Committee on 3 July 1963, were:

- the Commission should initiate monopoly inquiries
- powers should be increased to allow break-up of monopolies
- Commission procedures should be 'streamlined'
- mergers should be controlled and the Commission should take the
  initiative in investigating
- mergers should not be held up while investigation takes place
  although subsequent 'undoing' of a merger should be permitted
- services should be considered for inclusion.

Review of these efforts within government in the early 1960s to 'mod-
ernise' competition policy serve to underline the Conservatives' awareness of the need to respond; but equally the uncertainty and reluctance
to innovate. The constituency for change did not exist. The FBI was
opposed to new legislation, consumer pressure was inarticulate, the
Unions held no brief for competition, and within government the Treasury was sceptical. Moreover, the Party was locked into a nightmare of
successive crises. 1963 was the year of the de Gaulle veto on British
membership of the EEC, of the Profumo scandal in June, Macmillan's
resignation in October, and the 'emergence' of Lord Home as leader. If
Erroll and his officials found difficulty in making progress it is understandable, and difficulty they had. Having prevaricated for over three
years the Economic Policy Committee continued in its stance of masterly
inactivity until shocked out of it by the arrival of Edward Heath as the
bright, determined and powerful President of the BoT in the Douglas-
Home Cabinet. Heath hi-jacked the policy debate and bent it towards his
own preoccupation with the highly controversial issue of resale price
maintenance. Strictly speaking this is a sub-set of restrictive practices but
Heath gave it a huge salience. His Bill to outlaw individual resale price
maintenance aroused extraordinary opposition within and outside
Whitehall. Heath threatened resignation and in the second reading
debate, in March 1964, twenty-one Conservatives voted against it and
twenty-five deliberately abstained, making a revolt substantially bigger
even than that over Suez.

The resale price maintenance debate put into the shade the more
important but, at that time, less glamorous question of reform of the MC
and the creation of merger control. But it also broke the Cabinet logjam
and allowed Heath to publish the 1964 White Paper which anticipated the
legislation of 1965 and 1973. Thus his memorandum and presentation to

the Economic Policy Committee rehearsed the case for action and emphasised the Government's present lack of powers to implement MC recommendations (at that time in reports on motor electrical components and wallpaper). He recognised weaknesses in the Commission and 'proposed that a refurbished Monopolies Commission should be enabled to investigate mergers'.[11] Heath got his approval for resale price maintenance legislation but the discussion on mergers was guarded. Ministers were worried about the impact on shareholders of 'undoing' mergers and the possibility that adverse findings might open the door to nationalisation. In summing up, the Chairman (the Chancellor, still Reginald Maudling) nonetheless approved proposals for merger control to go to Cabinet and for Heath to announce the intention to produce a White Paper.

The seven modest paragraphs on mergers in the 1964 White Paper are seminal for UK merger control. What they say in themselves is important, but even more important is the endorsement they give to the official BoT approach and the symbolism of Conservative Party commitment. The White Paper, published in March 1964,[12] thus anticipates the MC investigating mergers at the direction of the BoT and with a direct link to the traditional monopoly approach. The one-third market share test is given as the threshold and the Commission would report to the BoT, treating a completed merger as a monopoly case and leaving the government to act; in other words, mergers grafted on to the existing Commission approach and operating on the same public interest criteria (although the White Paper 'contemplated' a more efficiency-driven specification of the public interest). Here the regime is fully anticipated – administrative, permissive, investigatory and entirely subject to political discretion.

It is possible to see a division in the Conservative Party on this issue between, on the one hand, the 'old guard' (social democrats/one-nation Tories) trustful of industry, respectful of property rights, seeing an organic link between industry and the Party; and, on the other hand, the pro-competition neo-liberals, irritated by the restrictive practices, the inefficiency and the cosiness of existing government–industry relations. This old division could be re-conceived as a contrast between the corporatists who were in the ascendant in 1964 with the pro-planning, pro-intervention stance following the 1960 FBI Conference and expressed in the NEDC; and, on the other hand, the free marketeers who distrusted intervention, wanted to liberalise the market and who had a brief outing with 'Selsdon Man' in 1970.[13] The White Paper was firmly in the 'old guard, new corporatist' camp, as was the Bow Group paper of February

1963. The Bow Group team of young businessmen and financiers asserted the benefits of mergers and boldly argued that 'in many industries a position of dominance or even monopoly may be needed to secure the full benefits of large scale operation'. They maintained that 'a merger is a simple transaction of buying and selling shares, it is a normal exercise of basic property rights ... the onus is on the critic to establish beyond reasonable doubt his case for restricting these basic rights upon which our way of life is founded'. This provides a good representation of the business case and the group went on to approve of the MC and the public interest test. In contrast they disliked the American system, which was regarded as too doctrinaire and legalistic, and they advocated a self-regulatory, compliance-based approach 'in which industrialists themselves should be led to consider the public interest'.[14] This stance was quite consistent with the modernisers' adaptation of the post-war settlement.

The Poole Committee report from the Party's policy-making machinery was far more rigorous and competition orientated. This paper reads like a precursor to the later neo-liberal activism of the Thatcher years and, had it been implemented, would have created a far more stringent system of control. It clearly had an impact but in the rather demoralised Conservative Party of 1963–64, at the fag-end of government, it appeared difficult to create radical initiatives. The Poole Group was composed of nine legislators (two Lords, seven MPs) serviced by the Conservative Political Centre. It was keen to increase competition and criticised the existing machinery of monopoly control – described as 'inadequate', and the 1956 reduction in the number and powers of the Commission – labelled 'a mistake'. Its suggested model of control involved:

- a balance of proof against a merger – 'companies ... should have a duty to convince an independent authority that the likely benefits to the public interest ... are sufficient'
- compulsory notification of mergers of over £1 mn in assets
- prevention of merger pending investigation
- an enlarged MC
- expansion of coverage to include services.

Officials had analysed the proposals from both groups and were dismissive. But one major recommendation from the Poole Committee did enter the White Paper, very late in the day; namely the proposal for a 'Registrar of Monopolies'. The Registrar would undertake an investigation of the facts both for monopoly and for merger references. He or she would be independent, would consult with industry and would refer cases to the Commission 'on objective criteria based on known princi-ples'.[15] The Registrar was clearly modelled on the Registrar of Restrictive Trade Agreements and the Poole Committee would have excluded the BoT from the referral process (a point which the White Paper did not concede). As we saw in chapter 6, this was the precursor of the DGFT.

The parliamentary debate on the White Paper in July 1964 was overshadowed by election fever but the chances of legislation were increased by the inclusion of commitments in the manifestos of both major parties. The October election brought Harold Wilson's Govern-ment with its wafer-thin majority of four, and it brought Douglas Jay as the new President of the BoT.

Despite his early involvement with the Commission, Wilson dis-played little interest in it, or in monopolies and mergers; neither, more peculiarly, did Jay. They had far bigger fish to fry in the fields of indus-trial, economic and trade policy. Monopolies and mergers are barely mentioned in Wilson's account of the Government.[16] Jay's stance is a lit-tle more puzzling given his economic background, his interest in compe-tition and markets, and his close association with Gaitskell. His particular love was distribution of industry and development area policy. When offered the BoT he had explicitly pressed Wilson to confirm that distri-bution of industry would be included. As a staunch Gaitskellite, not a Wilson supporter, Jay was a moderate on industrial policy, prepared to be pragmatic but caught up in the interventionary fervour of the times. At any rate, he devotes very little space to the Monopolies and Mergers Bill in his memoirs, noting only that he had originated the clauses on news-paper mergers and that he found the Standing Committee on the Bill exceedingly tedious.[17] Government was in this period engaging, interven-ing and innovating in its dealings with industry in so many ways that monopolies and mergers were regarded as rather a backwater.

Jay could afford to invest relatively limited energy in the new Monopolies and Mergers Bill because policy was largely agreed, the draft was available, and there was little opposition from the Conservatives. The parallels with 1997–98 are striking. As we have seen, this highly bi-partisan evolution of policy is typical of the history of British competi-tion policy and it places the initiative to an unusual degree with officials. The officials were not really thinking of merger control as a major new competence; their posture could be summed up in a line from the White Paper which concluded that, in respect of merger inquiries by the Com-mission, 'it is expected that in practice an inquiry would seldom be nec-essary'.[18] They wanted reserve powers. There was little sense that they were applying economic principles systematically in pursuit of productivity gains through competition. Hence both the trigger for the inquiry and the criteria by which it would be judged would be the 'political' arguments about the circumstances of the case and the public interest. In a beguilingly frank minute Elizabeth Llewellyn-Smith discussed the tests that should be applied and the possibility of refining the public interest test for merger cases:

> I am doubtful about the suggestion that the first thing to consider in assessing merger or monopoly is the effect on competition. I do not think this would be consistent with the proposition, to which the Government are committed, that monopoly cannot be regarded as bad in itself ... there may well be circumstances in which the existence of little or no competition is fully compatible with the public interest ... and further ... The public interest might in certain circumstances mean ignoring the direct interests of consumers and users.[19]

She was expressing both the logic of the position adopted in 1949 and the civil service preference for pragmatic decision making. Her views of monopoly, which seem slightly shocking in 1999, were quite conventional for the period and certainly congenial to the incoming Labour Government. What is more noteworthy is the continuity, in principles, in administrative machinery and in the pre-eminence of ministerial control, which civil service dominance of policy making produced. Merger control was grafted on to an administrative and investigatory procedure which gave it a low priority, low profile and low impact.

The grafting process was rapid and Labour moved quickly on its manifesto commitment. Having been offered the BoT on Saturday 17 October Douglas Jay had, by 22 October, already talked to Miss Dennehy about the merger proposals. Three important changes arose out of the discussions: Jay proposed mandatory notification of mergers; he prompted officials to review powers to 'freeze' a merger; and he wanted a quick Bill so there would be no room for the Registrar proposals. The standstill powers were eventually incorporated into the Act and were one of the two main aspects which the Opposition attacked. The other aspect was the failure to create a Registrar, which was confirmed in Cabinet due to the pressure on parliamentary time; Cabinet wanted a short Bill of about ten clauses.[20]

In his note of the meeting held by officials to discuss Jay's first thoughts, M. Fessey reveals that officials were concerned about how to define mergers to be notified. 'I said that, if the problem is one of regulating the concentration of financial control, rather than the "Monopoly" problem relating to market shares, the value of assets ... might be the best basis of definition.'[21] Thus the assets test, later criticised as economically illiterate, was initially thought of more logically in terms of size and concentration – not competition. Officials were required to defend the proposals in the draft Bill, and in discussion with ministers had to respond to requests for an assessment of US antitrust (from Jay – which yielded a very perfunctory response); to the suggestion that monopolies created by merger should be nationalised; and to concern about 'non-economic' effects. This last issue provoked an excellent paper to the Steering Group on the Policy Review Chaired by the Permanent Secretary. The paper noted that 'the pressures for mergers to be investigated are not solely economic – there is a whole range of considerations which may be advanced, from the probable effects on employment ... to factors of an ethical or quasi-political nature'. The paper went on to note that the benefits of merger were uncertain and anticipated later debates by observing that mergers might damage efficiency. It then raised a fascinating point about corporate governance which deserves recitation:

> The greater the constraints upon large companies to give the public a full account of their stewardship, and to provide a basis for the assessment of the efficiency of their operations, the less necessary would be control through merger regulation. It is therefore relevant that in new Companies legislation it is proposed to implement the Jenkins Committee recommendations that more information should be made available [the outcome might be a change of] emphasis from the rights of proprietors to the social obligations of company ownership.[22]

It is regrettable that such imaginative official thinking should have been submerged since precisely these points were again high on the agenda in the 1990s. The Steering Committee (not unsurprisingly) did not pursue the idea of non-economic criteria (subsumed in the public interest test) or the idea of bolstering corporate governance. It did, however, note that an assets criterion would mean the potential referral of non-monopolistic mergers to the Commission. This would be a profound step, 'it would suggest that single firms ought to be susceptible to investigation when they become large enough. The meeting noted that if monopolies legislation evolved in this way it would be a most significant and far-reaching departure in policy.' The MC would be investigating *the firm* rather than the industry. The minute noted with astonishment that 'the Department had never given consideration to this possibility'.[23] In fact the precedent of investigating individual large firms simply by virtue of their size did not spill over (at least directly) into the monopoly arena but the official reaction is interesting. Indeed, these official papers are fertile with new ideas and re-appraisals. It is unfortunate that ministers' interests lay elsewhere and that the outcome was a short and tortuously drafted Act which, though important, missed several opportunities.

Thus the assets threshold entered the legislation through the backdoor and was retained, even though Jay's preference for notification of mergers was dropped. As later observers pointed out, the value of assets criteria is virtually irrelevant to assessing competition but it was, and still is, extraordinarily convenient for screening cases. The perceptive November paper had observed that 'a test based on size-of-assets would be much easier to administer, and we should be likely to use it wherever possible'.[24] The accuracy of this prediction was impressive. Nearly twenty years later Godfray Le Quesne was telling a conference that 'every merger reference in my experience has been made on the basis of value of assets … in practice the formal reason for making a reference is not normally based on any likely effect on competition, it is based simply on the size of the merger'.[25] As Pope remarked, sometimes 'what'ere is best administered is best'.

The Monopolies and Mergers Act was passed in August 1965 as a short, twelve-clause Act. In addition to the merger powers it expanded the Commission, extended monopoly jurisdiction to services, and greatly extended BoT powers to remedy monopoly abuses identified by the Commission. It is interesting to speculate on whether the Act would have been passed without the merger priority. Was the refurbishment of the Commission riding on the back of its extension of powers? It is probable that it was. Without the stimulus of merger control the Commission might well have continued to languish, with these powers it was regenerated. On 1 December 1965 Ashton Roskill replaced Richard Levy, who was in poor health, and Moira Dennehy moved on secondment from the BoT to become the new Secretary.

Guiding principles

The debates over the introduction of merger control in the UK were largely about detail and emphasis, they were not marked by fundamental disagreements and were bi-partisan (indeed, tri-partisan, with Liberal support). This allowed an incremental development of policy with much of the running being made by officials in the BoT. It follows that the principles and the core arguments about merger control were not fully exposed and debated. The outcome was, first, that merger control squeezed into competition policy largely unannounced; and second, that the model of control adopted was based on the methods of monopoly control. Charles Rowley was able to observe that 'perhaps the most important post-war extension of the power of the executive in the affairs of the private sector was legislated with scarce a suspicion of public anxiety'.[26] Rowley's view seems initially to smack of hyperbole but, in historical perspective, the interventionist preoccupations of the Labour Government have melted like early morning mist, leaving intact an apparatus of merger control that has become a more and more dominant feature of the regulatory landscape.

This low key series of policy innovations incorporated a series of principles which have continued to influence merger policy. There are six principles to be emphasised:

- mergers are regarded with favour
- merger control is administrative, not judicial
- the American model of prohibition is rejected
- the economic impact of mergers is subject to a 'monopoly' test
- the procedures and the ultimate criteria are politically controlled
- the main discipline is business self-regulation.

These principles are explored later in the chapter and surface regularly throughout the book. Nevertheless, they deserve a little further elaboration here. They emerged in the 1960s, form part of the genetic code of British merger control, and have exerted continued influence over the thirty plus years of merger experience.

Mergers are regarded with favour

A slightly surreal tone is imparted to the debate over merger control by the repeated protestations that mergers are desirable. This surfaces again and again in official papers, in parliamentary debates and in lobbying. In his opening of the second reading debate, Jay observed that 'greater size and further amalgamations may be desirable in the public interest; and the Government may be justified in actually promoting amalgamations'.[27] The official papers are even more adamant. In their response to the Cabinet Economic Development Committee's approval of the Bill, which defined the planned contents, the BoT officials note the need to avoid 'putting obstacles in the way of the larger number of desirable or neutral mergers. Mergers ... may be positively beneficial.'[28] This position echoes down the decades. In 1983 the Deputy Director of Fair Trading (herself one of the originators of the Act) can be found observing to a business audience that, 'We frequently point out to firms that British law is basically *favourable* to mergers.'[29] This encouraging stance rested on an unholy alliance of Labour rationalisers who wanted strategic mergers; industrialists who wanted freedom; early libertarians defending property rights; and the City in pursuit of freedom to transact. Even the TUC General Council expressed concern to the BoT in July 1965 that 'the Government's proposals may "discourage desirable mergers"'.[30] Merger control was therefore created as a system of exceptional intervention to pick up cases of extraordinary harm. It was not seen as a policy systematically pursuing economic or social goals.

Merger control is administrative, not judicial

It is striking that the courts have been kept out of merger control. The choice of an administrative procedure, emphasising discretion and based on a broad public interest test, has moulded the development of policy. This may have been a choice congenial to officials but it also accorded well with the views of industry. As we have seen, the FBI had come to detest the workings of the Restrictive Practices Court. It had proved severe, the burden of proof was against the practice, and appearances before the Court could be quite terrifying.[31] Hence, in their summary of the FBI submission to the BoT, officials noted that, 'if there is to be machinery for inquiry into mergers, the F.B.I. consider that this should be administrative not legal, because the principal matter for consideration in the field of mergers, namely the economic effect of monopoly, cannot in their view be subjected to the rules of judicial procedure'.[32] It therefore proved very convenient to turn to the administrative procedures of the MC and to the case-by-case approach. Later debates about the lack of precedents and guidelines generate criticisms which simply follow logically from this early choice.

Rejection of the American model

At this point the only operational merger regime was to be found in the United States (the German system required reporting of mergers but no control until 1973). Officials spent relatively little energy studying American practice and there is little evidence of US lobbying, although during the passage of the Bill the Foreign Office became agitated about extra-territoriality. Both the Poole and the Bow Group reports examined American experience more systematically but could see little merit in the Clayton Act approach, which involved a prohibition based upon the effect on competition. They and the BoT also reviewed the embryonic mechanisms of EEC competition policy but noted the absence of any system of merger control. The preference was for an indigenous regime and was deep seated. The Bow Group observed, disapprovingly, that competition 'is taken as part of the American way of life and it is almost true to say that competition would be preferred to efficiency'[33] – shades of Keith Joseph! Ellis also saw a basic philosophical divide between an American 'structural' approach concerned to apply general principles, and a British 'performance' approach concerned with a carefully pragmatic analysis of individual cases.[34]

The application of a 'monopoly' test

The stimulus to the creation of merger control was a popular and political concern with industrial giganticism, with the tactics of hostile takeovers, and with foreign takeovers of major British companies. But the policy and the administrative response was to place merger control in the context of monopoly control and in the hands of the MC. The test for judging a merger was therefore, 'is it likely to create a monopoly that would operate against the public interest?', *not* whether it restricted competition, whether the takeover was fair, or whether politically undesirable economic concentration would result.

These early choices meant that the long and elaborate MMC investigation process was also applied to mergers. It also meant that the MMC did not concern itself with the fairness and the dynamics of the merger process itself (that was sub-contracted to the Takeover Panel). It was concerned with predicted outcomes, not mechanisms, although it did become concerned with the managerial aspects of what became known in the 1980s as 'the market for corporate control'. The calibre and likely strategy of management teams featured quite prominently in several early reports and were factors which seemed to incline MMC groups to be more sceptical of hostile takeovers.[35] The logic of linking the merger criteria to prospective monopoly abuses was that size and industrial structure were important in the MMC evaluation. Franks and Harris pointed out that the average value of a rejected bid (1965–85) was five times higher than that of an accepted bid;[36] and observers have consistently pointed out a rough correlation between post-merger market share and rejection. This would have lent itself to a structural guideline as used by the Department of Justice in the US except that the MMC doctrine of case-by-case examination, and the DTI's affection for the public interest test, made such a regularisation of policy impossible. The 1965 Act, therefore, arguably set up a structural test for merger control; but then set up administrative machinery unable to codify structural rules.

The maintenance of ultimate political control

Built into the merger control mechanism is the classic pragmatism of the British civil service. References and the choice of remedies were placed under ministerial control. The only exception (and it is a substantial one) is that if the MMC finds no public interest detriment the matter ends there and the merger is allowed. Later observers stressed the extraordinary politicisation of the process of merger control and, as we have seen with monopolies, the referral process is of central importance. The MMC can only investigate what is referred to it, and it is interesting that the 1963 Cabinet Sub-committee on Monopolies had recommended that 'the initiative for making an investigation into a merger would rest with the Commission'.[37] The White Paper had transferred the initiative to the Registrar and, when that idea was shelved, the referral process was kept within the BoT. Some guidance on the public interest had been canvassed in the White Paper. This stressed 'efficiency, technical and technological advance, industrial growth and competitive power in international trade',[38] which were essentially industrial policy criteria and would have changed the nature of merger control. But the attempt to define the public interest in mergers was abandoned and the 1965 Act defined the public interest in merger cases even more widely than for monopolies (it was aligned to the monopolies definition in the 1973 Act). This emphasis on executive discretion was always built into the system but O'Brien actually identified the resort to administrative and discretionary solutions as growing throughout the 1970s.[39]

Control through business self-regulation

The record of merger control exhibits a tolerant attitude towards industry and a basic belief that industry will behave reasonably. This is in the tradition of the post-war settlement and the 1948 Act but it contrasts with the prohibition approach of the 1956 Restrictive Practices Act and the resale price maintenance prohibitions. This posture reflects, of course, the essentially benign view of mergers, but it also reflects two strong traditions in relations between government and industry (see chapter 1). The first is the respect for property rights, the second a faith in industry's ability to police itself. The respect for property rights is second nature. It rests partly on the fact that the pre-eminent legal responsibility of the company director is to the shareholders and on the norm that companies should have the freedom to contract in pursuit of shareholder interests.[40] This position was re-stated in the DTI's 1988

Consultation Paper, which affirms that 'intervention by public authorities in lawful commercial transactions should be kept to a minimum' and that 'a decision to prevent a merger entails a considerable limitation of property owners' ordinary rights to sell their assets as they choose, and should not be taken lightly'.[41] From this perspective mergers are mainly a concern for shareholders, not a matter of public policy. And even then, both the shareholder interests and the public interest can be defended by self-regulation. The resort to self-regulation, supported by reasonable administrative action rather than legal powers, is entirely characteristic of British relations with industry. In this arena it is seen graphically in the City Panel on Takeovers and Mergers and its associated Code, created in 1967 and so much a part of merger scrutiny that in its evidence to the TIC in 1991 the DTI observes that takeovers 'are subject to both the merger control system and Takeover Code, the two systems running in parallel'.[42]

The idea of working co-operatively and reasonably with the subject community is basic to any system of successful regulation and is equally important in competition policy. Nonetheless, the emphasis on property rights and shareholders, on trust in self-regulation, and trust in the candour and good faith of companies has sometimes been the subject of criticism. As we saw in chapter 4, trust is very much part of the culture of the MMC.

Self-regulation, the City Code and corporate governance

The long-standing British prejudice in favour of business self-regulation has inserted two distinctive expectations into UK merger control. First, that intervention is exceptional and that companies will structure transactions so as to avoid harming the public interest. Second, that the financial transactions of transferring control are immune from intervention and are regulated by commercial law and self-policing. We start with the second of these.

The Fair Trading Act and MMC reports say very little about the conduct of merger and takeover transactions. Although the Commission is very concerned about the creation of monopoly power and the likelihood that power will be abused, it has only exceptionally concerned itself with the financial transactions whereby a takeover is executed. This is the province of the City Code on Takeovers and Mergers, which is operated by the Panel on Takeovers and Mergers. The Code and the Panel date back to 1967 and were stimulated by the same sort of extraordinary disputes that had acted as a catalyst for the 1965 Act. In 1967 there were a number of contested takeovers where secret purchases of shares, deceptive profit forecasts, emergency share issues and so on had aroused great criticism and appeared to disadvantage the small shareholder. In response the Chairman of the Stock Exchange and the Governor of the Bank of England (Sir Leslie O'Brien) set up a Takeover Panel to be Chaired by a former Deputy Governor of the Bank and with a Secretariat from the Bank.[43] The Panel and the Code had limited success and by November 1968 Crosland (President of the BoT) and Wilson were hinting at legislation along the lines of the American Securities and Exchange Commission. In response the Code was strengthened, a new Chairman was appointed (Lord Shawcross) and a new Panel took office in May 1969. The sanctions were reinforced and at the extreme allowed the Stock Exchange and associated bodies to expel members in flagrant breach of the Code. The Panel came to work through its Executive and also set up an appeals mechanism.

The City Code is important symbolically in that it underlines the rights of companies to regulate their own affairs within the law. It is important substantively in that the MMC is at least partially insulated from the more feverish pressures of stock market speculation. Since 1974 the Code has provided that a bid will lapse on referral to the MMC and can be reactivated when (and if) the merger is allowed.[44] This is a rule that is now quite taken for granted. The Code was drafted primarily to ensure fair and equitable treatment of all shareholders in relation to takeovers. It consists of a series of general principles, a substantial list of specific rules, and technical appendices. It is by now elaborate and well entrenched. It has no statutory force but it can give rise to civil litigation and has developed a body of 'soft' case law. The Code is exceedingly narrow in purpose. It does not consider commercial advantage or disadvantage, does not consider competition policy issues, questions to do with ethics and social responsibility, or the character of the parties. The Code operates within the legal and normative framework of company law and commercial practice, which has been well described by Parkinson as 'profit maximisation within the law',[45] in the ultimate and exclusive interest of shareholders.

The City Code therefore sustains independence for large companies and City institutions in defining the rules which create the market for corporate control and creating acceptable principles of corporate governance. Paradoxically, the vigorous application of the Code makes the work of the MMC more rather than less necessary. The system requires and expects that Boards of Directors will calculate the value of certain courses of action for their shareholders. This is their primary fiduciary duty. They are effectively prohibited by current company law and by the Code from considering the range of alternative social or economic criteria, which the Commission would consider within the concept of the public interest. Directors do not (or should not) consider issues varying from international competitiveness to regional prosperity, employment or exports. If the system of corporate governance involved the consideration of such wider factors then perhaps government merger control would be less essential. Indeed, if systems of corporate governance were more effective, then perhaps takeovers would be less necessary. The TIC shared this view and remarked that, 'the Committee sees force in the argument that the takeover process is often a costly and disruptive means for allowing improved corporate efficiency'.[46]

The MMC has not entirely avoided consideration of some aspects of corporate governance and takeover tactics. The Commission had to consider the merits of leveraged bids, which were becoming more common in the 1980s and reached heights of ambition in the *Elders IXL/Allied Lyons* bid of 1986. Here the financial issue was specified in the reference, an unusual feature. The Commission found itself considering the technicalities of bid prices, debt ratios and financial projections. While it recognised a fragile financial structure it did not prohibit the merger (in the event Elders bought Courage and did not renew its bid). Such issues continue to arise. Financial gearing was the main issue in the 1997 *PacifiCorp/Energy Group* reference and, in *Stora/Swedish Match/Gillette* in 1991, concerns about high gearing contributed to an adverse finding. Some overlap is also seen in direct personal contacts. Thus Sir Alexander Johnston went from being Deputy Chairman of the MMC in 1976 to become Deputy Chairman of the City Panel (a Bank of England appointment). Ashton Roskill became Chairman of the Panel's Appeal Committee. In the reverse direction David Richards, MMC Deputy Chairman from 1983, had served on the City Panel. But the activities of the two bodies are seen as quite distinct and the criticism aimed at the City Panel tends to stress its lack of independence[47] (as opposed to the marked independence of the MMC). The TIC considered the arguments over the non-statutory basis of the Panel and endorsed the voluntary principle but it did note several of the criticisms. BAT Industries, for instance, argued that, 'the Code itself and the rulings of the Panel show a strong bias towards offers coming before shareholders rather than not, towards market activity, enabling exchange of control ... and towards shareholders, alone, deciding whether or not control of their company should change'.[48] There was repeated criticism that the

Panel process was dominated by, and encouraged, a 'deal-driven mentality'. This is a not implausible position and it would be hard to find a more clear-cut case of regulatory capture. The Panel is drawn from those with huge vested interests in the takeover market so that self-regulation in this area has taken on the nature of regulation by the finance sector mainly in the interests of the finance sector. The important point, however, is that the City Code is representative of a faith in self-regulation and reasonable business behaviour which also informs the merger control regime.

The first facet of self-regulation mentioned above was the stress on the exceptional nature of merger intervention. The best form of regulation is regulation that is never invoked because the clientele freely comply. The promotion of self-regulation embodied in codes of conduct is very much a part of the consumer policy side of the OFT and is encouraged by the Fair Trading Act. It has an even more ancient lineage in merger control. Ellis suggests that the first call for merger control came in the Colwyn Report of 1918 on bank mergers. It argued that there should be no further mergers. No legislation was passed but, says Ellis, 'in typical British fashion the banks undertook voluntarily to be bound by ... [the recommendation]'.[49] The encouragement of compliance with merger control does require that companies know what is expected of them. Historically, the breadth of the public interest test made it difficult to predict referrals and findings. This is, of course, why so much emphasis has been put upon precedents and guidelines; they can convey enough certainty to allow companies and their advisers to avoid reference.

It would accordingly seem advisable to give companies as much information as possible about merger control. But oddly, it was not until 1969 that the BoT issued its first booklet on mergers (which revealed the existence of the Mergers Panel). Equally oddly, the OFT did not issue a successor booklet until 1978 and was obliged to concede in it that, 'it is not possible to publish a few simple rules from which it can be readily determined whether or not a particular merger is likely to be referred'.[50] This revelation was followed by ten pages outlining the sorts of factor which might be considered. In the 1980s the procedure became more open (at least as far as the OFT and the MMC were concerned). In 1988 the new MMC emphasis on transparency saw the publication of the MMC *Annual Review*, followed by a booklet on *Assessing Competition*;[51] the OFT intensified its provision of confidential guidance; and the expertise within the legal profession steadily increased. The certainties evolving from the Tebbit Doctrine helped but it was not until 1995 that a comprehensive legal text dealing exclusively with UK merger control became available.[52] Certainly developments such as the stress on competition from the mid 1980s, the essentially permissive attitude to conglomerate mergers and the accumulation of experience made merger control at the beginning of the 1990s a far less haphazard process. Thus Swift[53] and Soames[54] could talk of predictability and a good record of consistency, and hence enhanced opportunity for self-regulation.

A 'refurbished' MC

The Commission emerged from the 1965 Act far stronger and far more secure than in the dog-days of 1963. A new Chairman was in place and popular with an important group of members. The new Secretary, Moira Dennehy, had piloted the legislation through and, like Alix Kilroy in 1949, moved over to supervise the growth of the Commission, to which twelve new members were appointed in 1965–66 (including Dame Alix herself). The main focus was still on monopolies but the new merger powers were to have far-reaching significance for the status of the Commission as well as for its workload.

Merger powers are the glamorous area of competition policy. They are the shop window, the bright lights, and for good reason. Not only are the big takeover battles infused with drama – empires built, reputations lost – they have a massive financial impact. Mergers and takeovers dominate the financial press, they are the subject of Hollywood films, melodramatic books and intense speculative fever. The prose can be purple. The military metaphors prove irresistible:

> Vast pools of leveraged capital under the command of corporate war lords, in every respect as brave and cunning as their military counterparts, are thrown into takeover battles where, once a company is 'in play', the fighting will go on to the bitter end. Armies of consultants, bankers, lawyers, accountants, PR experts and other advisers will, like modern day soldiers of fortune, serve the master that amasses the most power and pays the richest price. Regulators seek to keep the warring parties under control but are constantly frustrated by their manoeuvring and ever changing strategies.[55]

This is not the atmosphere which one associates with the MMC, but it would be naïve not to recognise the pressures that exist in this major area of City activity. Moreover, in this area the MMC has real power. Since the 1973 Act a merger approved by the Commission cannot be blocked, here the Commission is making the final decision. Equally, since Commission advice is nearly always accepted, the rejection of a bid will have substantial financial consequences. Common sense would suggest that referral to the MMC and rejection of a bid would depress share prices and market values and, indeed, this is what happens. Franks and Harris confirm that, 'The evidence thus indicates a cost to shareholders of MMC deliberation and rejection – a cost that falls upon target shareholders'; they calculate the cost over a fourteen-month period before and after an MMC report as shown in table 16. Crudely, therefore, capitalisation of target companies was nearly a third lower, and of bidders a tenth lower, as a result of an MMC rejection. These can be figures in the billions of pounds and the financial muscle which the MMC is therefore exerting has made it a player of key importance.

Table 16 *The impact of MMC findings on market values*

	Average market value change from report date (– 12 months to + 1 month)	
	Target company	Bidder company
MMC accepted	38%	6%
MMC rejected	9%	– 6%

Source: J. Franks and R. Harris, 'The role of the Mergers and Monopolies Commission [sic] in merger policy: costs and alternatives', Oxford Review of Economic Policy, 2:4 (1986), p. 67.

This influence became more pervasive through the routine nature of merger control. Monopoly references are episodic. They depend on the incidence of complaints and the discretion of the OFT. Mergers, on the other hand, are all scrutinised (if they exceed the threshold) and must therefore all be considered in the light of regulatory risk. Every executive, merchant banker and lawyer will have to form a judgement about a possible MMC response. A practitioner-orientated text observes that, 'one of the first matters that the parties to a takeover will need to address is whether the takeover falls within the statutory framework for possible reference to the MMC'.[56] This underlines the role of the MMC as a standard component of the regulatory framework. Not exceptional, not idiosyncratic, but a routine element and part of the stock in trade of specialist lawyers and financiers.

After the 1965 Act merger control got off to a slow and unsatisfactory start. The first case was the proposed merger of *BMC and Pressed Steel*, referred in August and signed in November 1965 (only three months) but not published until the end of January 1966. The merger was allowed (subject to voluntary undertakings) but the nineteen-page report was superficial by today's standards, and the quality of the analysis and the argument in this and other early reports was extensively criticised.

Some of the fiercest criticism came from the MC's self-appointed biographer, Charles Rowley, who roasted the Commission in a substantial academic article. He pointed to the low referral rate and the pragmatic, permissive approach to mergers, but directed his main vitriol at the competence and attitudes of the Commission. After analysing three reports in depth he accused the Commission of analytical errors, of interpretative errors and of ignoring dynamic economic theory, and concluded that 'the Monopolies Commission has failed to measure up to the considerable responsibility imposed upon it'. He conceded the difficulty of anticipating future behaviour and pointed to 'a very real danger of the Monopolies Commission being pressed into reliance upon intuition and presentiment as a substitute for scientific analysis in its assessment of the future consequences of mergers'. This risk might seem real to members of current merger panels but they would undoubtedly not accept the barbed and damaging view that 'the Commission has set about its task in a positive – some would say a cavalier – fashion'.[57] Later analysts were less strident but also critical. In a study commissioned by the BoT Sutherland produced a report critical in tone in which he remarks that 'it is not easy to see ... the underlying logic of the MC's approach'.[58] The serious press tended to focus rather more on the cautious referral practices of the BoT and on its reception of the reports. In reviewing referrals Ellis observed that the Act had made little impact and that the MMC was being marginalised, especially by the BoT practice of securing informal assurances in lieu of referral.[59] The first five years of merger control are therefore marked by a Government unpersuaded of the need to control mergers, and a Commission uncertain as to how to. Merger control required the Commission to anticipate the future behaviour of a new company – a much more uncertain business than the monopoly investigations, which could draw on a concrete, researchable record. So concerned was the Commission that, uniquely, it published an *obiter dictum* in the 1969 *Unilever/Allied Breweries* and the *Rank Organisation/De La Rue* merger reports. It pointed to the growth in company size, the novel financing techniques and the necessity for greater disclosure of information. This was a significant attempt to use the Commission's reports to contribute to the wider debate.

From the Labour Government's viewpoint the emphasis was very much on desirable, rationalising mergers, often encouraged directly through the IRC.[60] None of the mergers promoted by the IRC, such as BMC/Leyland and GEC/AEI/EE, were referred, despite a clear eligibility. Members of the Commission complained publicly[61] but Ellis rather scathingly calls the conflict a 'self-inflicted wound. Surely the failure of the MC to develop and commit itself to a clear and coherent body of policy principles contributed to the weakness of its position vis-à-vis the IRC.'[62] The Commission remained, however, firmly shackled to the monopolies-type public interest criteria. It did not seek to develop a more theoretically stringent approach which would have had to have come from economic theory. At this time Williamson was just publishing his influential work on the trade-off between efficiency effects of horizontal mergers (through economies of scale) against price costs (increases in price due to additional monopoly power). Equally the first work on the 'market for corporate control' was beginning to emerge.[63] But although there were economists on the Commission there were none on the staff. One of the first to join, in 1973, was Martin Howe, who in a 1972 article had noted the criticisms and explored the utility of the United States' Department of Justice approach.[64] Howe went on to head the Competition Policy Division at the OFT from 1986, personifying the increased influence of economics and economists.

The new Conservative Government of June 1970 was embroiled in the comprehensive re-appraisal of competition legislation analysed in chapter 6. This was a Government committed initially to disengagement, to freeing the market and to mobilising the creative forces of competition. All the same, there was only one merger reference in 1971 (later abandoned) and only two in 1972. Mergers continued at a high level but referrals did not pick up until after the DTI junior minister, Anthony Grant, announced in November 1972 that the Government intended to refer far more mergers, including conglomerate proposals.[65] Perhaps the DTI was preoccupied with its U-turn, perhaps it was biding its time before passing the 1973 Fair Trading Act, but the fact remains that merger control was even more relaxed in the early years of the Heath Government than it had been under Labour.

The tripartite structure which emerged from the Fair Trading Act produced a more regularised system for appraising and referring mergers with a far greater continuity in the OFT than among Industry ministers. Before looking at the pattern of referral, decision and action we should expand on some of the principles of merger control outlined above. There are four particularly salient aspects of control which, if handled differently, could have produced a very different and a more rigorous merger regime. These aspects are 'extra-legal', within the scope of discretion, and it bears repetition that the administration of competition policy plays an extremely important part in defining the effectiveness of policy. This truism is arguably more applicable to mergers than to any other area of policy, a point made elsewhere in discussion of European merger control.[66] Merger control is administrative, discretionary, almost unavoidably political, and subject to the most intense pressure of lobbying and publicity. The powers that have been granted can be used proactively and rigorously or reactively and passively; the way they operate is influenced by political calculation, by administrative entrepreneurship, and by the legacies of established practices. The four key aspects that became embedded in the early days were the balance of proof; the arcane referrals system; the lack of precedent; and the definition of the public interest.

Balance of proof

As reviewed above, the balance of proof in merger cases is that the Commission should establish that a merger 'operates or may be expected to operate against the public interest' (Fair Trading Act 1973, Section 72(2). Thus the onus is on the Commission to establish damage. A frequently cited authority is from the *S & W Berisford/ British Sugar Corporation* merger report of 1981, which explained that:

> The question we have to consider is not merely whether there is a possibility that the merger will operate against the public interest ... The question is whether the evidence creates an expectation that the merger will operate against the public interest. To put the matter colloquially, the required conclusion is not, 'This may happen', but 'We expect that this will happen'.[67]

This is a high threshold of proof. In contrast the Poole Committee in 1963 thought that companies 'should have a duty to convince an independent authority that the likely benefits to the public interest ... are sufficient'.[68] Sutherland thought that for big mergers 'the parties [should] ... show how the public interest would be likely to be advanced' and in 1972 Howe proposed 'a requirement that a merger should show a net benefit to society'.[69] But the 1973 Act actually increased the bias by requiring that 'the Commission shall specify in their report the particular effects, adverse to the public interest' (clauses 54(3) and 72(2)). One former Deputy Chairman observed that 'The 1973 obligations are important in the conduct of investigations – the need to specify adverse effects is unquestionably a real discipline for MMC groups.'[70] The degree to which the burden of proof is biased towards allowing mergers to proceed has been a central source of debate up to the present. The first Liesner review in 1978 made this the centrepiece of its recommendations. It proposed shifting the proof to a 'neutral' stance and recommended policy declarations and guidance to the Mergers Panel as well as amendment of the Fair Trading Act.[71] There was widespread disappointment, at least among economists, when this proposal fell with the Labour Government in 1979. The issue was considered again in the second Liesner review in 1988, although this time no change was suggested.[72] When the TIC came to look at the issue it established that there remained concern about the bias (especially, and predictably, from target companies in hostile bids) and received evidence from the DGFT and the MMC itself, tending to favour a shift towards a more demanding criterion. Eventually, however, it endorsed the status quo.[73] The debate simmers on and the Labour Party again proposed a shift in the burden of proof before the 1997 election. After the election Margaret Beckett decided not to pursue the idea and the regime retains its traditional pro-merger bias.

The referrals system

A second persistent issue is reference policy. This has raised constant interest and complaints, and was termed in 1971 'the most important and the most mysterious aspect of British merger control'.[74] Nowadays it is perhaps a little less mysterious but no less important. This puts many controversial mergers beyond the reach of the MMC and it should be remembered that both the Poole Committee and the 1963 Cabinet Sub-committee on Monopolies recommended that the Commission should have the power to initiate inquiries. The Fair Trading Act provides for the Secretary of State, not the DGFT, to make references; all the relevant powers are expressed in his or her name and the DGFT makes 'recommendations' to the Minister. In practice the Minister nearly always accepts the DGFT's recommendations but the tripartite system elevates the separation of powers to a position that is not only confusing but is inconsistent with typical patterns of British administration. The existence of three distinct sources of administrative discretion makes it difficult to establish general principles and makes procedures opaque, but does have the same effect as the separation of powers in the American constitution – it prevents the development of arbitrary (or determined) policy by any one branch of government. This is why industry likes the present arrangements – they may be clumsy but they are not threatening.

The key issue with referral policy is how it is administered. Fairburn puts the question provocatively when he points to apparent anomalies in the reference process and asks, 'do the Director General and the Secretary of State sometimes differ, but essentially pursue the "correct" policy, or do they and the system conspire to neglect dozens of mergers which are harmful to competition?'[75] The answer is embedded in characteristic British administrative processes of judgement, accommodation and compromise, but the central vehicle is the Merger Panel. The Panel was created in 1965 and is a standing inter-departmental committee. It used to be Chaired by the DGFT but nowadays is normally Chaired by the Director of Competition Policy at the OFT, in 1999 Margaret Bloom. In fact John Bridgeman has hardly ever Chaired the Panel. It considers only the larger or difficult cases, about 10 per cent of the total, and has a variable composition according to the cases under consideration. The standard members are from the DTI and the Treasury (and in the past from Employment). There may well be additional participants from the Scottish Office, Transport, Agriculture, Defence and the Foreign Office, and a new group of occasional members is the utility regulators. Representatives of the MMC also attend.

Merger Panel deliberations are based on a short Panel Paper, introduced nowadays by the case officer, which summarises the OFT's investigations and initial conclusions on the case. The Panel is only advisory and Gordon Borrie's practice in the late 1980s was to introduce the case and to invite the views of all the Panel members. He would then sum up but would not necessarily come to a conclusion and the DTI members might return to Victoria Street with no certain view of what the DGFT intended to recommend.[76] Nowadays the outcome of the discussion is reported to the Director General, who will decide on the advice to be given to the Secretary of State.[77] If reference is recommended and accepted the Panel Paper will (at least since the late 1980s) provide the springboard for the MMC investigation. Recent practice also provides for the MMC staff to visit the OFT and review its papers on the case. Earlier practice, up to the mid 1980s, did not involve such substantial sharing of material, so that the parties often had to duplicate their submissions. This caused sustained complaint although it was partly the fault of the companies, which would understandably provide slightly different, and probably less, material to the OFT in the expectation of avoiding a reference. The merger reference process is driven by relatively technical arguments about the nature of competition in the industry, market share, entry barriers and so on, but these are weighed up in a process of discretionary judgement. It is therefore impractical for the OFT to provide clear rules or guidelines but it has always encouraged informal discussion through a system of 'confidential guidance'. Since

1990 a system of statutory pre-notification under the 1989 Companies Act has also been put into operation. This requires the DGFT and the Minister to give a decision within twenty working days (with one possible fifteen-day extension). This method has become more widely used although it has not proved as popular as some expected – practitioners suspect that obliging the authorities to make a decision may in fact prompt an early reference. The process is therefore subject to the subtle interplay of arguments, trade-offs and political preferences through the Merger Panel which has the potential to introduce the whole complexity of Whitehall inter-departmental horse trading into the process. This constitutes a system that was opaque and uncertain in the 1960s and is only slightly more transparent, if noticeably more certain, in the 1990s.

Precedent

The third aspect is the question of precedents. This is a general issue running through all MMC cases and is discussed in chapter 5. It has been a constant source of criticism in merger cases and has been a matter of sustained concern for the Commission. From Sutherland's study in 1969 to the TIC investigation in 1991, analysts have searched for consistency across the various merger cases and complained that it was not to be found. Different critics stress different aspects of consistency. Certainly the procedures are consistent but what about the reasoning, the economic analysis and the findings? Fairburn's influential discussion is fairly typical. He concludes that 'it is hard to trace the Commission's reasoning from report to report, or even to perceive that it regards such continuity as an important matter'.[78] This may reflect a difference of perception between economists and lawyers. While lawyers are concerned with regularity and precedent they are less concerned with universal economic principles. They tend to understand that legally precedent does not bind the Commission and that each case is different. Economists might accept that the cases are different but insist that the principles are the same. Curiously it has therefore been the economists who have been most agitated about precedent, lawyers have been more forgiving.

The Commission's concern about precedent in the late 1980s was fuelled by Peter Lilley's speech in June 1991 in which he declared, 'I welcome the emphasis Sir Sydney Lipworth ... has given to maintaining consistency and developing the greater use of precedent in the MMC's work.'[79] A *Precedents Handbook* was prepared in 1988 and is regularly updated and circulated to team managers and Chairmen. Similarly when Graeme Odgers was appointed in 1993 his creation of the

Deputy Chairman's group was explicitly orientated towards maintaining consistency over time and between cases. Every meeting included briefings on current cases. But, despite all this attention, the fact remains that each case is different; the public interest test cannot be reduced to a formula. Moreover, each group is different. Chairmen have different mixes of skills and priorities and a group considering a particular precedent might well feel that it would not have come to the same conclusion. In honesty most members would concede this reality. One recently retired member observed in his valedictory note to the Chairman that, 'I am suspicious of resort to precedents in looking at cases. The facts of every case are different, and the application of similar principles might well lead to different conclusions in cases which might look similar on superficial investigation ... I look upon the MMC very much as an economic jury, making individual judgements.'[80] The precedents issue also has a temporal dimension. A case from 1976 may provide poor precedent in 1999, where industrial context, the stress on competition and evolution of economic theory would all bring new perspectives to bear. With the Commission constituted on its present basis it has put its emphasis on consistency of approach. Not only would binding precedents be of doubtful legality, they would contradict the whole essence of the Commission concept.

The public interest

The fourth and final aspect is the public interest. In the original design of the 1948 Act officials had noted the almost complete inability to define 'the public interest'. There was no definition in the original Bill and the public interest clause was added as an amendment in the House.[81] Since neither the 1965 nor the 1973 Acts took the bold step of redefining the test to stress a more operational definition such as competition, so the merger regime was saddled with the vagaries of a test devised twenty years earlier to deal in a far broader and more leisurely way with restrictive practices. The definition of the public interest, and especially the balance between the various criteria specified in section 84, have been meat and drink to analysts of merger reports. In one early review John Pickering examines the public interest under nine headings, of which competition is only one.[82] By the early 1980s Fairburn and Kay were suggesting that a crisis had developed in merger policy.[83] The Commission was extensively criticised for being influenced in coming to the public interest judgement by management competence, regional issues and foreign ownership. The Anderson Strathclyde case in 1982 was particularly symbolic. Here a majority of 4:2 found against the merger, mainly on grounds of potential harm to the Scottish economy, but the merger was allowed with the help of a minority report. The target company obtained judicial review but the courts provided an important authority when they firmly held that the Minister was absolutely in the right and that the report from the MMC was strictly advisory (see chapter 5). The Commission was considering a wide range of factors in coming to the public interest judgements. For their part ministers were making some idiosyncratic references. The two Sotheby's references in 1983, for instance, excited much comment. Sotheby's successfully lobbied Lord Cockfield for a reference to fend off an American takeover while it found a 'white knight'. There were no competition issues.

In this atmosphere Norman Tebbit sought to reintroduce stringency through the Tebbit Guidelines, which have subsequently come to dominate reference policy. The Guidelines were the result of a departmental review of policy, which also raised the assets threshold to £30 mn. Strictly speaking, they are not 'guidelines', they are expressions of current policy, and state that 'my policy has been and will continue to be to make references primarily on competition grounds'.[84] A whole panoply of expectations has been raised on this narrow base which, as Swift has pointed out, is far from unambiguous (what is 'competition'?) and which left section 84 unchanged.[85] MMC insiders have been surprised at the weight given to the Tebbit Guidelines. Although they have been explicitly endorsed by most of his successors,[86] they were not the first such statement (John Nott said something similar in 1979)[87] and they have no statutory effect. The TIC criticised Sir Gordon Borrie very pointedly for accepting the Tebbit Guidelines so completely and commented that he was 'both limiting his independence and compromising the integrity of the advice he gives'.[88] When similarly pressed by the Committee Sir Sydney Lipworth gave a response grounded in statute. Asked if the 'Tebbit rules' operated as directives, Sir Sydney responded, 'Sorry, but I am not bound by any direction of the Secretary of State; I am bound by section 84 of the Fair Trading Act.'[89] Certainly it is evident in the conduct of MMC investigations that the full breadth of the public interest criteria is addressed and neither members nor staff feel that 'competition' is absolutely dominant.[90] On the other hand, the effect on competition has become the main element in merger inquiries. In part this is because only competition cases are referred nowadays, in part it reflects a shift in the Commission's normative framework which would now identify 'competition' more closely with the public interest itself. This does not necessarily ensure harmony across the tripartite system, as we see in chapter 9. There is plenty of room for the agencies to hold widely varying views about how much competition exists and how competition can best be encouraged.

The record

Qualifying mergers

The OFT now provides a full statistical picture of merger activity falling under the Fair Trading Act. The pattern shows a cyclical but substantial level of merger activity – never less than 100 qualifying cases per annum since 1971 and peaks of activity in 1979, 1988 and 1995. It should be borne in mind that many mergers will fall outside the coverage of the Act. Thus in 1986 there were over 1,500 mergers and only 18 per cent qualified by the assets or market share tests for consideration under the Fair Trading Act. Since 1979 the OFT has given statistics of cases actually reviewed as potentially qualifying mergers under the Act. These reached a peak of 533 in 1996 – 10 mergers a week for the OFT Mergers Secretariat to examine in some detail – a Secretariat in 1995 of only 18 people with a massive workload. Of these cases a very small proportion are recommended for referral. The number of cases actually referred only went into double figures in 1982, when ten cases were passed to the MMC (these figures exclude water and newspaper cases). The peak year was 1990, when an extraordinary twenty-five cases were referred, 9.6 per cent of the qualifying cases (and 10.5 per cent if confidential guidance cases are excluded from the calculation on the grounds that they have been considered separately). Although the market share criterion for referral has stayed at 25 per cent of market share since 1973 the all-important assets threshold has been raised three times, from £5 mn to £15 mn in 1980; to £30 mn in 1984; to £70 mn in 1994. The OFT responsibilities have been broadened to include liaison with the European Merger Task Force, so that in 1996 an additional 131 European notifications were considered (and 2 were 'repatriated' to the UK under section 9 of the Merger Regulation for consideration by the UK authorities – both were referred to the MMC). This underlines the very significant shift in competition casework to the European Commission and the OFT's necessary preoccupation with European developments.[91]

The process of making merger references

Reference policy is central to merger control and to the work of the

MMC for three reasons. First, and most obviously, it dictates the nature and intensity of the merger caseload. Second, the initial sifting and definition of the issues by the OFT sets an opening agenda for the MMC inquiry. Third, the reference policy establishes an agenda and therefore represents implicit direction given by a minister to the Commission.

Formal references are only the tip of a large iceberg of OFT merger activity. Most parties contemplating a merger will be likely to discuss their plans with the OFT, either directly or through one of the several firms of solicitors who have come to specialise in the field. Consultation has been strongly encouraged by government and is now formalised as 'confidential guidance'. It can be fairly clear when structural changes (such as divestment) or behavioural undertakings (such as codes of conduct) would eliminate any harm to competition and would be very likely to avoid referral. Formally, of course, guidance cannot provide an absolute guarantee and mergers have been referred despite conforming to official advice. This was alleged (inaccurately) in the *Ladbroke Group/Coral Betting Business* case in 1998, which provides an example of the possibilities for misunderstanding. The companies may have misinterpreted the signals they were receiving informally from the OFT.[92] Informal contacts provide the 'hidden face' of merger control and place emphasis on the commitment, competence and judgement of the small group of officials in the OFT's Merger Secretariat who are headed by an Assistant Director (grade 5). The figures on confidential guidance, notifications and references are given in table 17. They cover the period since 1979, when the information began to be released, and show a much higher intensity of activity than reference rates indicate.

This picture of OFT activism reflects deliberate government policy to increase certainty and speed by avoiding referral to the MMC where possible. Thus the 1989 Companies Act followed the 1988 Liesner report proposals for statutory undertakings in lieu of reference, to some extent formalising previously informal arrangements, and targeted at potential divestment. This trend was reinforced by the 1994 Deregulation and Contracting Out Act, which extended the principle of statutory undertakings to areas other than divestment and which, for the first time, included monopolies as well as mergers. The extension of discretion in this way diverted work from the MMC so that, for instance, in 1996 Granada agreed to divest its twenty-one 'Welcome Break' motorway service stations as a condition for being allowed to take over Forte without reference to the MMC.[93] This decision was based on a modest OFT investigation and not a full-scale MMC review.

The discussion thus far has mainly been confined to the OFT. A

Table 17 *Merger cases considered and referred, 1965–97*

Year	Qualifying cases	Confidential guidance	Prenotified	Undertakings in lieu	DGFT advice rejected	Actual references	% of qualifying cases
1965	48					1	2.1
1966	63					4	6.3
1967	96					1	1.0
1968	133					2	1.5
1969	126					3	2.4
1970	80					2	2.5
1971	110					1	0.9
1972	114					2	1.8
1973	150					8	5.3
1974	124					5	4.0
1975	157					4	2.5
1976	171					4	2.3
1977	187					8	4.3
1978	229					2	0.9
1979	257	26			2	3	1.2
1980	182	21				5	2.7
1981	164	15				8	4.9
1982	190	32			1	10	5.3
1983	192	37			3	9	4.7
1984	259	43			1	4	1.5
1985	192	34				6	3.1
1986	313	55			2	13	4.2
1987	321	40				6	1.9
1988	306	45				11	3.6
1989	281	32				14	5.0
1990	261	22	51	2	4	25	9.6
1991	183	15	38	3	1	7	3.8
1992	125	21	12	3		10	8.0
1993	197	46	13		2	3	1.5
1994	231	76	7	3		8	3.5
1995	275	72	12	2	2	9	3.3
1996	274	74	30	4	1	11	5.1
1997	229	41	51	1	4	10	4.3
Total	6220	747	214	18	23	219	

Sources: BoT and OFT annual reports.
Notes: Excludes newspaper and water cases.
Thresholds for qualifying cases: 1965 £5 mn; 1980 £15 mn; 1984 £30 mn; 1994 £70 mn.
Confidential guidance is guidance actually given.

more political and controversial element is introduced by the Secretary of State's indication of policy, willingness to refer and, on occasion, rejection of the advice of the DGFT. There is absolutely no doubt that some Secretaries of State have been 'softer' on merger control, and equally little doubt that legal practitioners have drawn the appropriate conclusions and advised their clients accordingly. Michael Heseltine's period at the DTI would be an example of a more relaxed application of the law, with a stress on 'competitiveness' rather than 'competition'.[94] Hence occasions when the Secretary of State openly disagrees with either the DGFT or the MMC take on a considerable symbolic significance. In the area of reference policy, disagreements have been rare and all the more noteworthy.

In total up to 1997 the Secretary of State rejected the advice of the DGFT in twenty-three cases. In fourteen he refused to refer cases and in nine cases he referred them in spite of advice not to. Three of these incidents were prior to 1979, and fourteen have come since 1990.[95] In some cases a refusal to refer appeared part of a systematic policy relaxation, as with Heseltine's rejection of advice to refer GEC/Philips and Airtours/Owners Abroad (both in February 1993). In others the initiation of references was a deliberate refocusing of policy, as with Peter Lilley's opposition to bids by foreign state-controlled companies. He regarded such bids as nationalisation by the back door. The so-called 'Lilley Doctrine' (or perhaps the Lilley/Redwood Doctrine) was announced in January 1990[96] and resulted in a spate of five references, three made against the advice of the DGFT.[97] Four of the Lilley references were cleared by the Commission and the fifth, *Kemira Oy/ICI*, was found against the public interest on conventional competition analysis.[98] This effectively spelled the end of the policy and is rightly taken as proof of MMC independence (see chapter 3).

Analysis of merger references by government does not indicate any striking party-political pattern. Labour is slightly less likely to refer than the Conservatives but both the highest and the lowest reference rates occurred during the 1979–97 Conservative period of office. Reference rates peaked during 1987–92. Neither does the record show any particular pattern in MMC decisions, although table 15 indicates that there has been a recent increase in the proportion of cases allowed by virtue either of not being found against the public interest, or found against the public interest but with a recommendation for the acceptance of various conditions.

More definite patterns emerge if an analysis is undertaken by minister rather than by government. Table 18 indicates outcomes since 1979 and shows considerable variation by minister. The more enthusiastic referrers were Young, Ridley, Lilley and Lang; the hesitant ones Nott, Tebbit and Heseltine. Ridley's resort to the MMC is particularly striking. His panegyric on Margaret Thatcher reasserted his commitment to competition and his suspicion of the monopolistic instincts of British business. It was he who wrote the compulsory referral of mergers into the Water Act 1991 and he was openly critical of the MMC decisions to allow the takeover of Plessey by GEC/Siemens and of British Caledonian by BA; 'both these decisions were wrong'.[99] The conclusion is therefore that the personal attitude of the Secretary of State to competition and mergers might be more important than party divisions. This should hold despite the acknowledged influence of Directors General and despite the volume of qualifying mergers. Sir Gordon Borrie served as Director General for the whole of the period up to June 1992; and there is no clear correlation between the number of mergers taking place and the incidence of references.

Table 18 *Merger references by Secretary of State, 1979–98*

Secretary of State	Period	No. referred	References p.a.
John Nott	5/79–12/80	5	3
John Biffen	1/81–3/82	9	7
Lord Cockfield	4/82–6/83	10	9
Cecil Parkinson	6/83–10/83	3	7
Norman Tebbit	10/83–9/85	8	4
Leon Brittan	9/85–1/86	3	9
Paul Channon	2/86–6/87	10	7
Lord Young	6/87–7/89	22	11
Nicholas Ridley	7/89–7/90	23	23
Peter Lilley	7/90–4/92	23	13
Michael Heseltine	4/92–7/95	19	6
Ian Lang	7/95–5/97	20	11
Margaret Beckett	5/97–7/98	13	11
Peter Mandelson	7/98–12/98	3	7
Stephen Byers	12/98–	1	

Sources: MMC database and OFT annual reports.
Notes The 'references p.a.' is the annualised rate of referral.
The figures exclude newspaper mergers.

Reference policy is only the most public manifestation of ministers' attitudes. Their known stance has a pervasive and quite proper effect on the administration of policy both within the DTI and in the OFT. Thus table 17 indicated the high incidence of confidential guidance cases. Often they result in adverse advice, sometimes they still result in referrals, sometimes the cases are too finely balanced for any advice to be given. The experience here is quite volatile. Thus in 1991 the OFT advised against the merger in one confidential guidance case but against fifteen in 1993. In these cases OFT officials follow the normal Merger Panel process and clear their advice with DTI officials and the Parliamentary Under-Secretary of State – the Competition Junior Minister – because formally it is the Secretary of State's decision. This process is entirely confidential. We have little idea of how ministers will strike a balance and when they will choose to advise that a merger would be likely to be referred. This is a hidden face of ministerial discretion and the room for the exercise of political preferences is substantial.[100]

MMC handling of cases

The MMC now has far more experience of mergers than any other type of case. The procedure to be followed, the nature of the examination and the contents of the reports are all recognisably descendants of the investigatory procedures set in place in 1949. In this respect merger cases are no different from any other of the Commission's group procedures discussed in chapter 5. The procedures are extremely important. They can make a real difference to outcomes and are studied intensively by lawyers, who are extremely concerned with such issues as confidentiality, access to the file, cross-examinations, rebuttal, exchange of evidence, and so on (for a flavour of the procedural concerns see the 1993 House of Lords report[101]). The MMC has managed to avoid much of this legal minefield by virtue of its status as an administrative body.

The nature of the investigations has changed over the years and is now dominated by time pressures, by the threat of judicial review, by the dynamics of smaller groups, and by a greater concentration on economic analysis. The Commission originally reported within six months but is now required by the BoT to report on most mergers in three months and on newspapers in two months (with a possible three-month extension). This is extremely tight for a subject that may be new and complex, and for which the procedures impose rigorous demands. Third-party views have to be solicited, hearings arranged, material 'put back' to respondents, and the part-time group has adequately to debate its findings. Sir Godfray Le Quesne felt that any further compression of time would require cutting out parts of the procedure. He was not sure that business would approve and commented that, 'what is certain ... is that any party, faced with a choice between a longer inquiry with full opportunity to present its case and meet its opponents' arguments and a shorter inquiry with a less adequate opportunity would unhesitatingly choose the longer'.[102] Unless the MMC moves to a short summary along European Commission lines it has probably reduced the time to the minimum practicable. There is always the danger that analysis could suffer and that the range of possibilities to be considered might be narrowed. The volume of work has also led to a reduction in the number of members in a merger group from a typical six or seven up to the late 1980s to a typical five nowadays. In fact the minimum was reduced to three in 1989, which would still allow a dissenting voice with the requisite two-thirds majority. Clearly a group of four or five limits the range of specialisms that can be included. It may make it impossible to include (say) a lawyer or an economist, and might provoke some concern that the traditional concept of a multi-talented group can barely be sustained (certainly many members regret the reduction in group size).

Merger inquiries are said to be a bit easier than others since the parties are usually eager to have the procedures completed and tend to be prompt and co-operative. The early work is done by the staff and then proceeds through the cycle of site visit, factual hearings, issue hearings and perhaps a remedies hearing. Since 1989 relations with the OFT have been closer. Generally relations are improved by occasional movement of staff between the Offices and the nature of the meetings between the MMC and the OFT is seen as more constructive. Traditionally the early meetings between the OFT and the Commission were rather severe, almost adversarial. In the 1990s, however, they have come to involve a presentation by the OFT which is more informal and often leads to a lively discussion. Similarly, at the end of the process, if a remedies meeting is required, the OFT is often given a good idea of the MMC's thinking.[103] The OFT dislikes behavioural remedies, partly because they are difficult to police and make demands on resources; and partly because structural remedies are felt to be more suitable for structural problems. Throughout this process price sensitivity accentuates the native confidentiality of merger inquiries. Close attention is paid to press clippings, which can provide wry amusement at how wrong they can be, but they also underline the danger of leaks. Sometimes such leaks can be extremely destructive, as in the case of the generator mergers mentioned below in which the findings were leaked to the *Economist*.

The recommendations in a merger report must be carefully balanced. Chairmen and members are adamant that they are not remotely influenced by any sense of what the DTI or the OFT would like to hear but they must be tactically concerned with the courses of action available once the report is delivered. If the conclusion is 'not against the public interest' then the merger proceeds and the DTI has no option but to acquiesce. But the MMC may have reservations about all or part of the outcome, in which case a partial finding against the public interest can open the door for the DTI and the OFT to negotiate undertakings. Negotiations have been a feature of the merger process since the first case, where BMC gave assurances about continuity of supply of car body pressings, although in that case they were non-enforceable and given to the Commission itself. Table 15 indicates the growth of 'conditional' against the public interest judgements since 1980. Such reports specify the conditions which, in the view of the group, would offset the public interest detriments. This allows the OFT to negotiate on behalf of the DTI although the eventual conditions may be very different from those suggested by the MMC. Conditional reports have become much more usual in the 1990s. In twenty-one of the ninety cases referred between 1990 and 1997 the Commission found the merger to be against the public interest but stipulated conditions that would make it acceptable. The conditions most often involve structural remedies, usually divestment, but behavioural remedies such as reporting and price control may also be recommended. This raises a rather interesting question: for whom are the merger reports written?

Reports are addressed to the Secretary of State and are public documents. It would be expected that they would also be read avidly by the parties, others within the industry, lawyers and competition specialists, and academics. The 'real' audience, however, is the officials in the DTI (and the OFT). When reports are 'delivered' (usually by a junior member of the staff, by taxi to Victoria Street) the umbilical cord is cut and the MMC (to mix a metaphor) washes its hands of them. There is no subsequent discussion, no meeting with the officials or ministers; the MMC group is dissolved and all the DTI has to go on is the report. It is the report alone which defines the problem, advances the reasoning and suggests any remedies. As Sir Godfray Le Quesne remarked, 'the Secretary of State receives the report and nothing more ... The report ... contains all that the Commission wishes to say.'[104] To this extent reports are major administrative documents on which momentous decisions are based. This is curious. The MMC and OFT officials meet during the inquiry and 'bright line' distinctions are most unusual in British government. But on this score all parties are agreed, the procedure, the culture and the instincts of propriety forbid even informal contact. There does not appear to be any statutory requirement to ensure this level of formal independence, beyond the risk of judicial review – a weak sanction that certainly does not inhibit informal exchanges elsewhere in Whitehall. No, this is a powerful tradition and an effective 'Chinese Wall' that is both procedurally impressive and probably functionally harmful.

Having received, read and digested the report, officials and the Secretary of State almost always accept it in principle. Nevertheless, the Minister will take advice from the DGFT and, in some dramatic instances, the MMC's recommendations have been rejected; for instance:

- In 1982 the Commission rejected the Charter Consolidated bid for Anderson Strathclyde with a 4:2 majority (the Chairman was in the minority). The Trade Minister, Peter Rees, nonetheless allowed the bid to proceed, which prompted a judicial review and the resignation of one of the members, Professor Andrew Bain.
- In 1995 the Commission considered competing bids by GEC and BAe for the warship builder VSEL. The Commission found one of the bids, by GEC, to be against the public interest, but Michael Heseltine decided to allow it (against the advice of the DGFT). In this case there had again been a two-person minority report.
- In 1996 came another painful case where the group approved the takeovers by National Power and Powergen of the regional electricity companies, Southern and Midland. Here there was a dissenting minority report from Patricia Hodgson. Because the group had identified some minor public interest conditions for approval, Ian Lang was able to go with the minority report and he blocked both bids. In this case the Director General had also advised blocking.
- In 1997 the Commission recommended allowing the Bass, Carlsberg, Tetley merger with conditions. Margaret Beckett, however, endorsed the minority report and, in accordance with the advice of the DGFT, and a minority report, prohibited the merger.

Divergencies of view of this nature are perhaps becoming less exceptional. It is becoming more helpful not to view reports in black and white terms of approving or blocking but to see them as often setting an agenda for subsequent negotiation. Nonetheless, the potential for political input has continued to cause concern. In 1998 Peter Mandelson raised the prospect of reform of the merger regime (see p. 237).

Evaluation of merger control

A rather crude historical perspective on UK merger control would identify a policy that was weak and peripheral when introduced but which gradually gained in salience and status during the late 1970s. It only came into its own in the mid 1980s, when the shift away from intervention gave it further legitimacy and the level of cases decided gave merger policy greater exposure and greater impact. By 1990 UK merger control, and the MMC's central role, had been sanctified by tradition and UK policy was at the height of its influence. In this many factors conspired: the increased influence of economics; the competence of the Commission; the pro-competition policies of ministers; the need to control ever-higher merger waves; and the fresh responsibilities created by privatisation and utility regulation. But by 1992 confidence was being deflated. The scepticism of Michael Heseltine was the proximate cause but the longer-term 'threat' to UK merger control was the European regime, legislated in 1989, initiated in 1990 and by 1992 well established and popular with business. In the second half of the 1990s the European Merger Task Force was receiving around 170 notifications a year. Of these several involved large British mergers. Thus the massive and important Glaxo/Wellcome merger was considered by the Task Force in 1995 and not opposed. With mergers of this magnitude considered in Brussels it was inevitable that attention would move away from the MMC and towards the OFT, which could make an input into the European deliberations. Thus from 1991 UK merger references, while important for the parties concerned, tended to be minor in their economic impact. The referrals were dominated by buses, utilities and rather narrow retailing mergers. The bigger cases (VSEL and power generation) created conflict with the DTI and it had become clear that the 'action' (and the fees – and therefore the lawyers) had shifted to Brussels.

Despite this, or perhaps because of it, when Margaret Beckett announced law reform she noted that: 'I have considered carefully the case for widening the scope of the Competition Bill to include reform of the merger regime ... I see value in the investigatory approach of the Monopolies and Mergers Commission, and I intend that the current framework for considering mergers should continue, essentially unchanged, within the new Competition Commission.' She went on to reaffirm the stance of her Conservative predecessors to note that, 'References to the Commission should be made primarily on competition grounds' and that, 'I see no need to change the burden of proof in assessing the public interest.'[105] This represented something of a vote of confidence in the established regime and meant that in this area analysis of historical development had a continued purchase in interpreting future changes.

A less crude analysis of merger control would evaluate it in terms of the goals and effectiveness of policy, and in terms of its relationship to other policies and to the system which it seeks to regulate. There is little point in lawyers bemoaning its lack of predictability; economists complaining that it does not achieve efficiency; or businesspeople saying it does not defend Boards – if it is designed to do none of those things. We need, therefore, to ask four questions:

- Is the policy technically competent (efficiency)?
- Does the policy secure its goals (effectiveness)?
- Are the goals of policy 'right' (objectives)?
- Does merger control enhance British capitalism (competitiveness)?

Taking these questions in reverse order, the 'fit' between merger control and the main features of British capitalism is close. Indeed, merger control can be seen as an important part of a sympathetic regulatory environment. British capitalism is 'stock market' capitalism characterised by an emphasis on the free market – in goods and in shares – and by a respect for freedom to contract and the autonomy of the individual company. While the formal emphasis is on shareholder interests, the practical effect is to allow immense independence to managers. Much lip service is paid to competition but high levels of market closure have always been tolerated. Merger control facilitates this system through limited intervention and respect for company autonomy. The two key elements are the self-restraint of merger control where financial markets are concerned, with deference to self-regulation and the Takeover Panel; and the MMC's role in creating trust in the system by being there – aloof and incorruptible – to pick up the more far-fetched excesses of takeover practice.

As regards the third question, the goals of policy, ministers have been driven from the early 1960s by three goals: competition, pragmatism and permissiveness. The goal of competition has clearly and sincerely been important – perhaps more important to ministers than to officials – it was definitely an important part of the ideological make-up of pivotal ministers such as Heath, Jay, Howe, Nott and Tebbit. But if the encouragement of competition provided the background, the foreground was occupied by 'informed' public opinion which was concerned over the years by a variety of issues from the manipulative profit forecasts of the ICI/Courtaulds takeover battle to issues of excessive market concentration, foreign takeovers, leveraged bids, the extinction of regionally important companies, or simple bare-faced monopolists or asset strippers. The instinct of British officials, aware of the probability of such problems and of their unpredictability, has been to cleave to the ancient pragmatism of ministerial responsibility. Wary of general rules, equipped with a very hesitant judiciary which is uncomfortable with economic judgements, officials (and ministers) have kept an ultimate political hand on the tiller. Even under the new legislation the last resort Fair Trading Act powers of political intervention have been protected.

Other analysts, and particularly Mercer, have downplayed public opinion in favour of the influence of business opinion. This is indeed important and provides the third goal. Ministers have wanted a 'business friendly' system which finds expression in the imperatives of not deterring 'good' mergers. This is despite repeated concern that mergers encourage short-term financial opportunism and fail to deliver economic efficiency. From Maudling to Heseltine, via the IRC and the NEB, ministers have had various motives for encouraging mergers and have applied the test of 'will the system prevent benign mergers?' As the key operational norm the permissive regime has consistently favoured acquisitive companies and financial interests. These three goals of policy help to explain why the system has evolved in its present form. The priority has shifted, there is nowadays more emphasis on competition and less whole-hearted belief in the virtues of mergers, but the system continues to serve all three goals. We might criticise the goals, regard them as inefficient, unfair or inadequate, but it would be illogical to accuse the institutions of failing to deliver goals which they were never designed to deliver.

The second question concerns the effectiveness of the system, the extent to which the agencies of merger control deliver the goals outlined above. Here there is more room for debate and this is the level at which most controversy is pitched. Has the regime encouraged competition? Not nearly enough would be the conclusion of many economists, consumer activists and backbench MPs. Over the years economists have tended to be critical of this aspect of policy, although it does depend on what is meant by 'competition'. Thus the big debate on industrial concentration during the 1970s ended with the widely shared conclusion that mergers did not necessarily produce concentration,[106] although it is accepted that in earlier periods they were a major cause of concentration.[107] Neither was there necessarily agreement that concentration reduced competition. Equally, the dynamic view of competition held by the Chicago School and the Austrians would, in its more extreme forms, suggest the abolition of merger control altogether.[108] Just as the pursuit of competition has periodically been inadequate (especially prior to 1979), so critics have concluded that at times policy has been overly pragmatic.

The debate about the 'crisis' of merger control in the early 1980s was cen-tred on the accusation that the policy had lost all sight of general princi-ples. Ministers were concerning themselves with conglomerate mergers, with regional factors, with foreign bids, with state-owned companies; where was the consistency?

Similarly the third goal, of permitting most mergers, has come in for consistent criticism. The debate about the burden of proof simmers on and has occasionally come to the boil. Mergers were justified in the 1960s by arguments about the benefits of rationalisation and the need for national champions. In the 1970s and 1980s the arguments had shifted to the strengths of dynamic management teams and the need to allow them to inject efficiencies into target companies. But such arguments have been superseded by awareness that many mergers appear to be unsuccessful in improving efficiency or profitability and that they impose great frictional costs.[109] Mergers have always aroused criticism. They are said to be short-termist, they preoccupy and enrich senior management, yield little value, stifle competition, and generate huge fees and windfall gains for merger-driven City institutions. These argu-ments had a particular impact in the early 1990s but they have not over-turned the accumulated weight of past policy. Neither the OFT nor the MMC has been inclined to stand against the presumptions of decades. The OFT is under constant pressure and scrutiny from big market play-ers and their legal advisers. A shift to a more sceptical policy would require ministerial initiatives. The MMC is more comfortable with analysis of market structure than with analysis of potential efficiencies and managerial motivation; moreover, it does not see it as any part of its role to agitate in a debate on new policy. In these three areas, therefore, of competition, pragmatism and permissiveness, the system as a whole can certainly be criticised for failure to clarify options, refine practices and respond to changing perceptions of market efficiency. It sometimes seems as if the independence of the DGFT and the MMC is interpreted too negatively, as freedom from constraint; and not sufficiently posi-tively, as licence to speak out.

The final evaluative question concerns efficiency. Do the various agencies of merger policy discharge their functions with technical and financial efficiency? It is here that the MMC would feel that criticism would be unjustified. The technical and financial questions have already been considered in chapters 3 and 5. The nature of merger inquiries does put the system under particular stress. The industry-wide analysis, involving a search for the whole range of public interest issues, has been borrowed from the monopoly investigation model but it demands a very high level of expertise and commitment from staff and members. The study has to be conducted from scratch, under punishing time limits, with the onerous requirements of fairness and natural justice, in the glare of publicity, and with the knowledge that the outcome will generate substantial financial gains or losses. Several of these features could be questioned, including the need to undertake such a wide background study and the pressure of a three-month time limit. A policy which panders to the eagerness of the City to complete deals, carries the danger of superficial or orthodox analysis. Even the EU Merger Task Force has four months to complete second-stage investigations with the added advantage of having undertaken the first stage and without the need to publish a full and persuasive report.

Given these pressures the MMC has developed a system, which, by the late 1980s, had won widespread respect. Merger reports nowadays are far less vulnerable to the damaging criticisms levelled by Rowley at the first reports. Rowley talked of inadequate research, poor technical analysis, incompetent economics and an 'anti-profit' mentality among the Commissioners. By 1980 Pickering's review of merger reports contained few of these sorts of procedural criticism; and the thorough collection by Fairburn and Kay contained almost no criticism of the MMC's efficiency (although there is plenty of criticism at the 'effectiveness' level). Thus the conclusion to be drawn is of a system in which the MMC is regarded with confidence and respect, and in which its recommendations are seen to be well grounded in research and considered judgement. A critic might suggest that here we have a poor policy well administered.

Conclusion

In historical context merger control in the UK appears as a triumph of administration over legislation. It is remarkable how little extended debate went into the original design of policy, which was adopted so cautiously and tacked on to the prevailing monopolies machinery. The policy was devised in 1964–65 and provided with a more adequate administrative machinery in 1973. The Liesner consultative reports on mergers, in 1978 and 1988, were important stocktakings but the 1978 report in particular did not succeed in changing the system. Even in 1998 the merger regime was retained. Whether it can be operated along traditional lines when the rest of the competition regime has been so radically altered is doubtful. It is likely that the precedents and the legal arguments offered by ten years of the operation of the European Merger Task Force will have an increasing influence. More speculatively, as the UK and European systems become more closely aligned, a pattern of closer working, reflecting real subsidiarity, is likely to emerge. In any event the reform process is not yet complete and in November 1998 Peter Mandelson promised a consultation document on reform. His review was prompted by the controversy over the BSkyB bid for Manchester United. He was inclined to reduce the political input into the reference process but, in a very familiar manner, he expressed the view that when 'there are aspects of the public interest the public is going to expect their interests to be represented by someone who is elected'.[110] The allure of the public interest is perennially seductive.

UK merger control has become elaborate, sophisticated and, in its own terms, successful. Regulation of merger activity is immensely important in a country where the national and international market for corporate control is so well developed, and where mergers and takeovers have such a profound effect on economic life. The literature on takeovers, mergers and industrial structure is substantial. It has not been possible in this long chapter adequately to consider the context of industrial concentration or of the growth of international trade. Neither has it been possible to review the scope and the arguments of MMC merger reports, which provide such a rich insight into so many companies and markets. It is appropriate to conclude with three thoughts, which are returned to in the final chapter. First, the MMC is applying a rule of reasonableness in its merger reports. The mix of MMC groups and the public interest test militates in practice towards a standard of reasonable business behaviour. This will evolve as business practices evolve but it is a test that in some ways is very familiar to lawyers. Second, the MMC investigation is earnestly to be avoided. Reference of takeovers to the MMC is rare. When it happens the demands of an MMC inquiry are very intense, especially for senior management, and it is no accident that over 20 per cent of cases referred are subsequently abandoned. The fearsome prospect of an MMC reference acts as a substantial deterrent and provides the OFT with a very potent bargaining position in its discussions and negotiations. Third, the Commission is aware of precedent in its merger analysis and does develop doctrine about criteria by which to judge a merger. But each case is different and the Commission is willing to be unpredictable and even iconoclastic in following the logic of the analysis. It has the ability and the inclination to take each case from first principles and it undertakes a fresh competition analysis. This is a precious competence which is constantly generating new insights and of which welfare economists should approve.

The motif of current welfare economics is 'it all depends'. The MMC report allows a full and fascinating examination of what the case depends on.

Notes

1 H. Mercer, *Constructing a Competitive Order* (Cambridge University Press, 1995), p. 129, citing BT64/4838, minutes from J. K. Rees (Assistant Secretary, BoT) to Elizabeth Ackroyd (Under-Secretary, BoT) (10 and 11 October 1955).
2 See PRO, EW2715, BoT report, 'Review of policy and legislation on monopolies and restrictive practices' (1 November 1962).
3 Debate on mergers, *Hansard* (16 February 1962), col. 1684.
4 See PRO, EW2715, review of policy, para. 14c.
5 See *ibid.*, BoT summary of FBI views, para. 15.
6 For references on this Committee see PRO, CAB 134/1708.
7 PRO, BT258/1653, note of a meeting on 30 May 1963 to discuss future policy on monopolies, mergers and resale price maintenance.
8 *Ibid.*
9 *Ibid.*
10 PRO, BT258/1653, letter from Reginald Maudling to Frederick Errol (6 May 1963).
11 PRO, CAB134/1805, Economic Policy Committee, E.P.(64), minute 2 (8 January 1964).
12 BoT, *Monopolies, Mergers and Restrictive Practices*, Cmnd 2299 (London, HMSO, March 1964), 8 pp.
13 The Selsdon Park Hotel conference in January 1970 produced a temporary commitment to a new brand of free-market ideological conservatism which became known as 'Selsdon Man'.
14 Bow Group, *Monopolies and Mergers* (London, Conservative Political Centre, February 1963), report of a group convened by Henry Bosch, pp. 18, 29, 62, 82.
15 Conservative Political Centre, *Monopoly and the Public Interest* (London, CPC, March 1963), report of a Committee Chaired by Lord Poole, p. 18; earlier references, pp. 11, 27, 15.
16 H. Wilson, *The Labour Government, 1964–70* (London, Weidenfeld and Nicolson and Michael Joseph, 1971).
17 D. Jay, *Change and Fortune* (London, Hutchinson, 1980), pp. 318, 297.
18 Cmnd 2299, para. 23.
19 PRO, BT258/1954, 'Review of legislation, minute 10, E. Llewellyn-Smith to Miss Dennehy (29 July 1964).
20 See PRO, 'Cabinet Economic Development Committee', E.D.(64) (14 December 1964).
21 PRO, BT258/1956, 'Preparation of legislation', note of meeting, by M. C. Fessey (23 October 1964).
22 PRO, BT258/1957, 'Preparation of legislation', MRPR(64), supplementary consideration on mergers, IM2(4) (27 November 1964).

23 PRO, BT258/1957, note of the 24th meeting of the Steering Group (30 November 1964), para. 7.

24 *Ibid.*, paper by IM2(4) (27 November 1964), para. 22.

25 Godfray Le Quesne, 'The role of the MMC', *Financial Times* Conference, collected papers (20/21 October 1983), p. 4. Note that by the 1990s the share-of-supply test was being used with some regularity.

26 C. K. Rowley, 'Mergers and public policy in Great Britain', *Journal of Law and Economics*, 11 (1968), p. 83.

27 D. Jay, President of the BoT, *Hansard* (29 March 1965), col. 1208.

28 PRO, BT258/1958, 'Preparation of legislation, the Monopolies Commission', note by officials (16 December 1964), para .14.

29 E. Llewellyn-Smith, 'The role of the OFT', *Financial Times* Conference (20/21 October 1983), p. 8.

30 PRO, BT258/2146, 'Progress through Parliament', meeting with the TUC (30 July 1965).

31 See D. P. O'Brien, 'Competition policy in Britain: the silent revolution', *The Antitrust Bulletin* (Spring 1982), p. 234.

32 PRO, EW 2715, BoT report, 'Review of policy and legislation on monopolies and restrictive practices, first report to the President of the BoT by officials' (1 November 1962), para. 59.

33 Bow Group, *Monopolies and Mergers*, p. 61.

34 T. S. Ellis, 'A survey of the Government control of mergers in the United Kingdom – part I', *Northern Ireland Legal Quarterly*, 22:3 (Autumn 1971), p. 256.

35 Analysis of hostile bids referred indicates a high proportion pre-July 1984 with a high rate of adverse findings against hostile bids. I am indebted to Hans Liesner for these observations.

36 J. Franks and R. Harris, 'The role of the Mergers and Monopolies [*sic*] Commission in merger policy: costs and alternatives', *Oxford Review of Economic Policy*, 2:4 (1986), p. 62.

37 PRO, CAB134/1708, Cabinet Economic Policy Committee, Sub-Committee on Monopolies, 'Final Report' (4 July 1963), para. 10.

38 Cmnd 2299, p. 4.

39 O'Brien, 'Competition Policy in Britain'.

40 The influence of this feature of company law is nicely explored in J. E. Parkinson, *Corporate Power and Responsibility: Issues in the Theory of Company Law* (Oxford, Clarendon, 1993).

41 DTI, *Mergers Policy: A DTI Paper on the Policy and Procedures of Merger Control* (London, DTI, 1988), pp. 6, 19.

42 TIC, *Takeovers and Mergers, Memoranda of Evidence*, 1990–91, HC226–I (February 1991), DTI Memorandum, p. 5.

43 See Sir Alexander Johnston, *The City Take-Over Code* (Oxford University Press, 1980).

44 For a detailed treatment of the rules see G. Stedman, *Takeovers* (London, Longman, 1993).

45 Parkinson, *Corporate Power and Responsibility*, p. 42.

46 TIC, First Report, *Takeovers and Mergers*, 1991–92, HC 90 (London, HMSO, 1991), p. xlviii.

47　See M. Wright, 'City rules OK? Policy community, policy network and takeover bids', *Public Administration*, 66:4 (Winter 1988), p. 407.

48　TIC, *Memoranda of Evidence*, Memorandum by BAT Industries, p. 51.

49　Ellis, 'A survey', p. 278.

50　OFT, *Mergers: A Guide to the Procedures under the Fair Trading Act 1973* (London, HMSO, 1978), 45 pp.

51　MMC, *Assessing Competition* (London, MMC, revised edn, 1993). This eight-page booklet reviews approaches to competition and gives prominence to Michael Porter's approach.

52　R. Finbow and N. Parr, *UK Merger Control: Law and Practice* (London, Sweet and Maxwell, 1995).

53　J. Swift, 'Merger policy: certainty or lottery?', in J. A. Fairburn and J. A. Kay (eds), *Mergers and Merger Policy* (Oxford University Press, 1989), p. 279.

54　T. Soames, 'Merger policy: as clear as mud?', *ECLR*, 2 (1991), p. 70.

55　Martin Waldenstrom (President, Booz Allen Acquisition Services), 'Foreword', in S. Gray and M. McDermott, *Mega-Merger Mayhem* (London, Mandarin, 1990).

56　Stedman, *Takeovers*, p. 435.

57　Rowley, 'Mergers and public policy', pp. 130, 86, 84.

58　A. Sutherland, *The Monopolies Commission in Action* (Cambridge University Press, 1969), p. 69.

59　Ellis, 'A survey', pp. 228, 297.

60　For analysis of the IRC see S. Young with A. Lowe, *Intervention in the Mixed Economy: The Evolution of British Industrial Policy 1964–72* (London, Croom Helm, 1974).

61　See *The Times* (16 September 1968), p. 17.

62　Ellis, 'A survey', pp. 290–1.

63　O. Williamson, 'Economies as an anti-trust defense: the welfare trade-offs', *American Economic Review*, 58 (1968); H. G. Manne, 'Mergers and the market for corporate control', *Journal of Political Economy*, 73 (1965).

64　M. Howe, 'Rethinking British merger policy', *The Antitrust Bulletin*, 17 (1972).

65　See DTI, *Monopolies and Mergers Acts 1948 and 1965*, annual report by the DTI, year ended 31 December 1972 (London, HMSO, 1973), p. 5.

66　S. Wilks, 'Competition policy in the EU: creating a federal agency?', in B. Doern and S.Wilks (eds), *Comparative Competition Policy* (Oxford, Clarendon, 1996), p. 230.

67　*S & W Berisford and British Sugar Corporation: A Reort on the Proposed Merger 1980–81*, HC 241 (London, HMSO, 1981), para. 9.40.

68　Poole Committee, *Monopoly and the Public Interest*, p. 15.

69　Sutherland, *The Monopolies Commission*, p. 77; and Howe, 'Rethinking British merger policy', p. 305.

70　Private correspondence.

71　DPCP, *A Review of Monopolies and Mergers Policy: A Consultative Document*, Cmnd 7198 (London, HMSO, May 1978), p. 3.

72　DTI, *Mergers Policy*, p. 5.

73　TIC, *Takeovers and Mergers*, pp. lx, lxi.

74　Ellis, 'A survey', p. 286.

75　J. Fairburn, 'The evolution of merger policy in Britain', in Fairburn and Kay (eds), *Mergers and Merger Policy*, p. 212.

76　Interview with former Panel member.

77 Interviews and correspondence with OFT officials.
78 Fairburn, 'The evolution of merger policy', p. 66.
79 Peter Lilley, speech to a Combined Law Society lunch (12 June 1991) p. 5.
80 Private correspondence with recently retired member.
81 Dame Alix Kilroy, 'The task and methods of the Monopolies Commission', paper delivered at a Seminar on Problems in Industrial Administration, London School of Economics (December 1952), p. 16.
82 J. Pickering, 'The implementation of British competition policy on mergers', *ECLR* (1980).
83 J. Fairburn and J. Kay, 'Introduction', in Fairburn and Kay, *Mergers and Merger Policy*, p. 7.
84 DTI Press Release (5 July 1984).
85 Swift, 'Merger Policy', p. 267.
86 Details in Finbow and Parr, *UK Merger Control*, pp. 99–101.
87 Interview with a former official of the OFT.
88 TIC, *Takeovers and Mergers*, p. lvii.
89 TIC, *Takeovers ad Mergers, Minutes of Evidence*, MMC, 1990–91, HC 226–v, (London, HMSO, 1991), p. 196.
90 Interview with MMC team manager.
91 The interaction of the two regimes is examined by Sebastian Eyre in 'The politics of merger control in the EU and the UK', PhD Thesis, University of Exeter (1999).
92 See *The Times* (1 April 1998), p. 25, and the comments by Ladbroke about its contacts with the OFT in *Ladbroke Group PLC and the Coral Betting Business*, Cm 4030 (London, The Stationery Office, September 1998), p. 144.
93 OFT, *Annual Report of the Director General of Fair Trading*, 1996, 1997–98, HC 104 (London, Stationery Office, 1997), p. 41.
94 S. Wilks, 'The prolonged reform of United Kingdom competition policy', in Doern and Wilks (eds), *Comparative Competition Policy*, pp. 175–6.
95 For details see Fairburn, 'The evolution of merger policy', p. 212, fn. 15; Finbow and Parr, *UK Merger Control*, p. 80, fn. 74; OFT annual reports.
96 DTI Press Notice (26 July 1990).
97 See the useful discussion in Soames, 'Merger policy', pp. 64–5.
98 See Finbow and Parr, *UK Merger Control*, pp. 109–10.
99 N. Ridley, *'My Style of Government'* (London, Hutchinson, 1992), p. 56.
100 Interview with former senior DTI official.
101 Select Committee on the European Communities, *Enforcement of Community Competition Rules*, 1993–94, HLP 7 (London, HMSO, 1993).
102 Sir Godfray Le Quesne, 'The Monopolies and Mergers Commission at work', in K. George (ed.), *Macmillan's Merger and Acquisitions Yearbook* (London, Macmillan, 1988), p. xiii.
103 Interviews and correspondence with OFT staff, August 1998.
104 Le Quesne, 'The Monopolies and Mergers Commission', p. xiii.
105 Margaret Beckett, Foreword to *A Prohibition Approach to Anti-competitive Agreements and Abuse of Dominant Position: Draft Bill* (London, DTI, August 1997), p. 3.
106 A. Hughes, 'The impact of merger: a survey of empirical evidence for the UK', in Fairburn and Kay (eds), *Mergers and Merger Policy*, pp. 56–7.

107 See the summary in D. J. Hay and D. J. Morris, *Industrial Economics and Organization* (Oxford University Press, 1991), pp. 553–4.

108 For the Chicago version see the admirably clear statement in R. Bork, *The Antitrust Paradox: A Policy at War with Itself* (New York, The Free Press, expanded edn, 1993), p. 406.

109 The efficiency point is conceded quite explicitly in the 1988 Liesner consultative paper; DTI, *Mergers Policy*, p. 38.

110 Peter Mandelson (Secretary of State for Trade and Industry) quoted in the *Financial Times* (30 November 1998). A consultation paper on mergers policy was promised in DTI, *Our Competitive Future: Building the Knowledge Driven Economy*, Cm 4176 (London, Stationery Office, December 1998), p. 51.

8

Regulation of the privatised industries: a new role for the MMC

It is remarkable that such a vigorously pro-competition Conservative Government so signally failed to reform competition policy after 1980. On the other hand, the extent to which competition was introduced into hitherto protected parts of the economy was if anything more remarkable. The promotion of competition became a principle of economic and industrial policy although the relationship between competition and privatisation was far from simple. The programme of privatisation produced a quite astonishing restructuring of the British economy from 1984, when British Telecom was privatised, to 1992, when the bulk of the privatisations was complete. Privatisation of itself was a highly experimental and uncertain process in which the raw power placed by the British system in the hands of a determined Prime Minister was amply demonstrated. As has regularly been pointed out, privatisation did not necessarily create a free market. To convert huge public monopolies such as British Telecom and British Gas (BG) into huge private sector monopolies was hardly likely to promote competition. In later privatisations, especially electricity, more determined structural measures were taken but in this and the other industries the job of introducing competition was bequeathed to the new utility regulators and the competition agencies.

Post-privatisation regulation was an even more uncertain process. The creation of the regulatory offices and the appeal function given to the MMC were the product of extemporisation and opportunism. The new system of utility regulation experienced some serious crises but has come to work more effectively than any of its architects had any right to expect. Another victory of administration over legislation. In 1999 further utility reform was planned but, as seen later in the chapter, the plans promised only limited change.

This chapter reviews the involvement of the MMC, first with the nationalised industries, and then with their privatised successors. The system of utility regulation has been relatively volatile and is affected by the growth of competition and by the reform of the competition laws. The 1998 Competition Act attaches extensive new competencies to the utility regulators, who have concurrent powers to apply the competition prohibitions. They retain their licensing powers and it is in the operation of the licence, rather more than in the application of Fair Trading Act powers, that the MMC has become central to the regime of utility regulation. The way in which it has discharged its major new role may have influenced the Government towards retaining the Commission in its traditional form. At the same time we can see a potential shift in the balance of the MMC's work towards utility regulation. In this regard it is significant that the DTI indicated a re-orientation by appointing as Chairman of the Commission in 1998 Derek Morris, a distinguished economist who was also a noted specialist in the economics of regulation.

The cycles of history provide an ironic contrast between the 1940s and the 1980s. In 1948, when the MRPC was being created, free-market economists and the Conservative Opposition were pointing to the inconsistencies of nationalisation. On the one hand Labour had the MRPC, on the other hand it was creating massive public sector monopolies in coal, electricity, transport, railways and (most controversially) steel. In the spirit of the times, and consistent with the Morrisonian model, the nationalised industries were concerned with co-ordination and planning, not competition. Their efficiency was the responsibility of their Boards, which were stubbornly resistant to external efficiency audits in the 1940s and continued to resist audit up to the 1980s.[1] In the 1980s the boot was on the other foot – not only were the monopolies being privatised, they were coming under the influence of the Commission.

Prior to 1980 the nationalised industries had largely kept the competition authorities off their patch. Their statutory monopoly effectively made them immune from restrictive practices legislation and it would have been illogical for ministers to refer a nationalised industry to the Commission. Section 50 of the Fair Trading Act provided exclusions for a range of nationalised and other industries (mainly in transport and agriculture) which prevented reference by the DGFT. In addition ministers ensured that the DGFT would not refer the non-statutory elements of the industries (see p. 185). In respect of efficiency audits, the nationalised industries had managed to avoid statutory audit in favour of parliamentary scrutiny by the Select Committee for Nationalised Industries created in 1957. As the industries fell into deficit, concerns about efficiency became more intense, and efficiency audits were undertaken by the NBPI from 1967–70[2] and again by the Price Commission from 1977–80. By the end of the 1970s the efficiency of the nationalised industries was high on the political agenda. It was a key concern of the Treasury,[3] which was being pressed by industry in general and parliamentary committees in particular to devise a more effective efficiency regime. Yet the Conservatives were determined to abolish the Price Commission.

The 1980 Competition Act is best remembered for introducing the anti-competitive practices provisions which had been advocated by the first Liesner report. But at the time, and in political debate, it was seen primarily as 'the abolition of the Price Commission Bill'.[4] The Conservatives were under heavy fire and so, in addition to the anti-competive prices powers given to the Director General, sections 11–13 gave the Secretary of State power to refer nationalised industries to the MMC, and price rises to the DGFT, for investigation. Section 11 covers references of 'public bodies' to the MMC, which was required to apply a 'public interest' test but was explicitly prohibited from considering 'the appropriateness of financial objectives given by ministers'. The Act (section 11, 8a) actually required the MMC to 'exclude from their investigations and report' such matters, but the Commission put the emphasis on 'appropriateness' and felt free to discuss financial objectives but not to evaluate them.[5]

It does not appear that section 11 of the 1980 Act was given extensive thought, or that it was part of a systematic approach to imposing discipline on the nationalised industries. It was something of a face-saver to head off criticism. The involvement of the MMC also proved a useful excuse for not bowing to pressure to allow the Comptroller and Auditor General (CAG) and his or her Department (which became the NAO in 1983) to audit the nationalised industries. The Treasury was keen to keep the CAG out of the nationalised sector – for reasons which aroused cynical criticism from the Expenditure, Procedures and Public Accounts Committees of the Commons. In its March 1980 paper on audit in the public sector[6] the Treasury defended its position and stressed the role to be played by the MMC. By this time the MMC was producing its first reports – on the *Inner London Letter Post* in March 1980 (actually a Fair Trading Act reference), the *British Railways Board* in October and the *Central Electricity Generating Board* (CEGB) in March 1981. The reports were thorough, the arguments authoritative; ministers were impressed and became more committed to the MMC avenue. Thus, in November 1981, Nicholas Ridley announced in a debate on the CAG that 'the Government have therefore decided on a number of steps to strengthen and supplement the role of the Commission', specifically:

- increase nationalised industry references to six per annum
- each industry to be referred at least every four years
- an annual programme of references
- strengthen membership and staffing of the Commission
- more effective follow-up with timetabled responses from the industries at four and twelve months after the report.

'Thus, the Monopolies and Mergers Commission in its strengthened form will remain the main instrument for the external scrutiny of these industries.'[7] Of course, Labour saw this as part of an attack on the nationalised industries but others, more concerned with their efficiency and accountability, rather regretted the substitution of the MMC for the NAO. Their criticism was of the system, and the extension of ministerial prerogative, rather than of the Commission. Thus Garner is complimentary, saying that 'the MMC has handled its initial assignments with distinction', but he finds it 'incongruous' that the MMC should have taken on this role. The Commission was dependent on ministers for references (unlike the NAO) and had no power of access to papers and premises (also unlike the NAO). Hence, he argued, 'the Government has given the responsibility to an organisation "cabin'd, cribb'd, confin'd, bound in" to the Government's interests on timing and direction of inquiries'; therefore, 'efficiency auditing has been introduced in a manner that considerably strengthens ministerial control whilst making only incidental and indirect contributions to accountability to Parliament'.[8] This line of criticism is considered further below but, as far as the MMC was concerned, section 11 and the ensuing programme of inquiries constituted a major new area of activity. This period, 1979–84, was, of course, one of the periods of MMC growth, one of the 'weddings' introduced in chapter 2. Section 11 was one element in the Conservatives' dowry to the Commission.

Efficiency audits of the nationalised industries

Contrary to early expectations, the MMC spent far more time on section 11 reports under the Competition Act than on the controversial anticompetitive practices provisions. The programme of inquiries never achieved the target of six reports per year, but five were signed in 1985 and in total thirty-five reports were produced between 1980 and 1993. Here we briefly review the areas covered and the intensity of the work before picking up some of the common features of the reports.

The efficiency audits covered the range of nationalised industries shown in table 19. They became a particularly important element of MMC activity from 1982 to 1988, when twenty-five of the reports were signed – 27 per cent of all the MMC reports signed over this seven-year period. It is striking that neither telecommunications nor gas were referred. Partly this was due to early privatisation, but partly also due to their profitability. Industries that made no demands on public funds were simply less of a problem for their sponsoring departments, which, in any case, were predictably reluctant to encourage scrutiny. Foster points out that British Telecom, even when part of the Post Office, was never subject to a Select Committee or MMC report.[9] In addition agricultural bodies such as marketing boards were not reviewed despite provisions in section 11 allowing scrutiny. This bears testament to the consistent way in which the MAFF managed to defend agriculture from review by the competition authorities. Of the industries reviewed in table 19 some had repeated MMC inquiries which allowed the Commission to review progress. The 1981 statement had envisaged a four-year cycle but in the event only three industries had follow-up reports on the same terms as the original – the CEGB (1981 and 1987), the Civil Aviation Authority (CAA) (1983 and 1990), and the British Waterways Board (1987 and 1994). On the other hand, both British Rail and the Post Office enjoyed four investigations into various aspects of their activities.

The nationalised industry inquiries were overtaken by privatisation and the programme effectively came to an end in 1993. Some of the later reports were also some of the more weighty. Thus the *London Underground Limited* report of 1991 brought some startling facts and criticism to the surface. This was sufficient to persuade some members of the MMC group that an adverse public interest finding would have been justified. The *United Kingdom Atomic Energy Authority* inquiry of 1992 extended the critical evaluation of the economics of nuclear power generation which had already been critically reviewed in the earlier CEGB reports.

Section 11 allowed the DTI to refer specific questions to the MMC provided they related to a) efficiency and costs, b) services provided, or c) possible abuse of a monopoly situation. In practice most references dealt with efficiency and costs, and therefore required a very different approach from that applied in conventional monopoly cases. While the monopoly inquiries were concerned with the strategy, the performance and sometimes the organisation and financing of large companies, the analysis was framed in terms of the relevant market. For efficiency studies, however, the emphasis was reversed. While the market was important it was usually a domestic monopoly and the basic focus was on the internal operation of the undertaking, which led into

Table 19 *Efficiency reports on the nationalised industries, 1980–94*

Year	No. reports published	Industry
1980	2	Inner London Letter Post (FTA reference)
		British Railways; London & South East Commuter
1981	2	CEGB
		Severn Trent Water
1982	2	Five bus companies
		Two water authorities, sewerage functions
1983	4	Caledonian MacBrayne Shipping
		National Coal Board
		Yorkshire Electricity
		CAA
1984	4	London Transport, maintenance
		South Wales Electricity
		Post Office, letter post
		Yorkshire Water
1985	4	Four electricity boards, revenue collection systems
		British Rail, property activities
		North Scotland Hydro-Electric
		BAA
1986	3	Seven water companies
		South of Scotland Electricity
		Post Office, procurement activities
1987	3	British Waterways Board
		CEGB, transmission
		British Rail, Network South East
1988	3	Welsh Water Authority
		Post Office, counter services
		British Steel Corporation
1989	3	British Coal Corporation
		British Rail, Provincial Division
		Two northern Ireland bus companies
1990	2	CAA, navigation and air traffic control
		Northern Ireland Railways
1991	1	London Underground
1992	2	United Kingdom Atomic Energy Authority
		Commonwealth Development Corporation
1993	0	
1994	1	British Waterways Board
Total	36	

Sources: MMC database and reports.
Notes: – Analysed by date of publication; abbreviated titles.
– All reports under section 11 of the Competition Act 1980 except the first, which was under the Fair Trading Act.

questions of managerial competence, industrial relations and investment appraisal that were, at first, relatively unfamiliar to the Commission and its staff. The problem was alleviated by the absorption of some experienced staff from the Price Commission, in particular industrial advisers under Maurice Shutler, and two officials, Alan Blair and Bernard Gravatt, who became team managers on section 11 (and other) inquiries. The nature of the inquiries gave rather more prominence to staff work and, since staff were also dealing more systematically with colleagues elsewhere in Whitehall, some members felt that the critical edge of inquiries was sometimes blunted.

Reports were required within six months but in practice most of the bigger inquiries were extended to nine months. The Commission operated in its normal fashion with inquiry groups and the usual limited recourse to outside consultants. The outcome was substantial, thorough and detailed reports, which had many of the hallmarks of a management consultancy report. The MMC invited evidence from all interested parties, absorbed massive amounts of information from the undertakings, and analysed what it found intelligently and in the light of the experience of the members. To some extent such inquiries must be reactive to the information supplied but the staff and members appear to have had some stimulation from arranging detailed investigations. Thus in the *CEGB* inquiry, 'officials made detailed inquiries at a number of power stations' and for the *British Railways Board Commuter Services* inquiry, 'members ... visited a number of London termini, signal boxes, train control offices and regional maintenance and cleaning depots'.[10] One imagines stalwart members of the Commission, clad in Winston Churchill-style boiler suits, manfully gleaning telling evidence from the less accessible crannies of the British Rail empire. The reports were not spectacular or revolutionary but they were voluminous, in contrast to the much briefer reports from the NBPI and the Price Commission. They delivered a sound audit of efficiency with extensive supporting information. For instance, in the National Coal Board case they analysed and published the operating results for each pit and for the first time publicised the problem of high cost pits. This was an important innovation which had a marked effect on Coal Board management and may have had a demonstration effect elsewhere in the nationalised industries. Where the Commission found shortcomings it was quite clear and critical. Areas such as investment planning, use and remuneration of staff, Board structure, absence of marginal cost pricing and so on featured regularly in reports. On a more critical note, however, the investigations were constrained by prevailing norms. One member who worked on several water inquiries noted that the groups had no idea what extraordinary scope for greater efficiency would later be flushed out as a result of privatisation.[11]

Section 11 catered to the MMC's customary ways of working by including a public interest test, which in this context appears rather clumsy and inappropriate. Reports typically found a wide variety of shortcomings and made many recommendations (twenty-six in the first *CEGB* report; forty-eight for the *British Steel Corporation* in 1988). Whether shortcomings were sufficient to 'operate against the public interest' was a moot point and mainly relevant only if radical follow-up action was required. Thus the first *CEGB* report did find that 'there are serious weaknesses in investment appraisal' such that in this area (but not others) the Board had operated against the public interest.[12] There was some reluctance among staff to find 'against the public interest' and among members what might be called a philosophical problem. Since the organisations under inquiry were already publicly owned was it contradictory to conclude that they acted contrary to the public interest? The public interest test was therefore not terribly helpful and was sometimes ignored. Thus the later *British Steel Corporation* report does not mention the public interest but instead congratulates the Company: 'BSC is right to be proud of the efforts of its workforce and management.'[13]

The section 11 reports acted as a catalyst and one member of staff observed that 'the superb work done on these references by the MMC laid the groundwork for the subsequent privatisations'.[14] Not all assessments have been quite so positive and the reports had some less predictable consequences. Thus the early 1981 report on the *Severn Trent Water Authority* criticised the size and composition of the membership of its Board. It argued that it was unwieldy, expensive, and gave too much representation to local authorities and not enough to consumers. The report led to the Water Industry Act of 1983, which abolished the statutory link between the local authorities and the regional water authorities. Thus the MMC's observations provoked a major shift in the governance of the sector.[15] Certain members of the Commission were at ease with the idea of reports disturbing the complacency of the nationalised industries. Baillieu notes, mischievously, that 'it was thought at the Commission that the test of a good section 11 report was the amount of industrial unrest that it caused in the workplace and upset in the relevant ministry'. He takes the catalytic viewpoint to an extreme, noting that the recommendation in the 1983 National Coal Board report that the profitability of individual coal mines should be calculated 'led to the McGregor reforms and the miners' strike'[16] – perhaps an unduly large charge to lay at the door of the Commission.

Despite the views of individual members the Commission collectively was cautious in its reporting. There was therefore some criticism of the limited impact of the reports and the Commission's reluctance to publicise them. A contemporary survey noted that reports were quickly forgotten, that MPs had clearly only read them superficially, and often unfairly attacked the Commission. These commentators felt strongly that the Commission should have been less cautious, less ambiguous in its recommendations, and willing to lobby for change.[17] Wider criticism of the system of efficiency audits by the MMC centred on four concerns, and echoed Garner's perceptive early observations noted above. First, that the MMC could not choose the industries to be examined, or the terms of reference. Second, that the Government's financial framework for the industry was immune from investigation. Third, that the MMC's powers of investigation were inadequate. Fourth, that follow-up was erratic and implementation patchy.

In each of these four respects the MMC system was compared unfavourably with the NAO arrangements. Indeed, there was force in these criticisms, but the DTI saw audit as the tool of the executive rather than the legislature, and stolidly defended the retention of discretion by the Secretary of State. Thus Sir Brian Hayes (DTI Permanent Secretary) and Sir Godfray Le Quesne put up a united front to the PAC. In a (probably rather annoying) double act, Sir Brian opined that 'the present system does provide an ideal way of scrutinising these bodies' by a Commission which has 'a collective background of relevant experience which is unique to themselves'. Sir Godfray gave no ground. He asserted that the MMC had no wish to choose references, that it was not handicapped by inability to review the financial framework, that it had no trouble getting information, and that he was happy to leave follow-up to the DTI. On information he rather magisterially informed the Committee that 'the members of the Commission represent a very considerable quantity of very varied experience and that enables them to have, if I may say so, a good nose to start with'. The wine-tasting approach to investigation prompted the rather acidic comment from Sir Gordon Downey, the CAG, that 'Personally I do not see it as comparable to the rights we have of direct access to documents and records ... indeed, the rights to direct access are regarded as fundamental to our ability to undertake value-for-money inquiries, as they would be so regarded by external auditors of every other country I know'. On reference policy he went on to observe, 'It is conceivable to think that government would have areas that they would prefer not to have inquired into.'[18] These exchanges perhaps say more about the contrasting views of executive and legislative accountability. The DTI undoubtedly felt that the MMC was a more congenial and constructive reviewer than the NAO but the PAC registered serious criticisms. In response the DTI declared that in future the MMC would be consulted more deliberately on references, and that there would be more systematic follow-up through reports from the industry. In fact these commitments were rather empty since, by 1987, it was clear that the 'solution' to the problem of nationalised industry efficiency would be through privatisation instead of audit.

As a result of section 11 the Commission was well placed to contribute to the privatisation and regulation process. Indeed, this work represented something of a triumph of the MMC over competitor agencies. The NBPI and the Price Commission had both undertaken nationalised industry audits but focused rather more on incomes policy and price control than on efficiency *per se*. Both bodies had fallen under the steamroller of adversary politics leaving the MMC to step in. As a result the allocation of responsibility to the MMC may have raised its salience and expertise to a sufficient level to commend it to officials and ministers as the appeal body when the regulatory clauses of the 1984 Telecommunications Act were being drawn up. Thus the MMC made the transition from evaluating the efficiency of the nationalised industries to regulating their post-privatisation pricing regimes. From efficiency through audit, to efficiency through regulation, and eventually through competition.

A 'powerful ghost': the MMC and the regulation of the privatised utilities

The British system of utility regulation grew up in an almost unbelievably haphazard manner from 1982 as Margaret Thatcher's first Government began to plan for the privatisation of British Telecom. The British state stepped almost absent-mindedly through the door from an interventionist mixed economy to a regulated private sector economy. The regulatory state has grown up in a peculiarly 'British' fashion. It has evolved incrementally and pragmatically, with principles and agencies growing from practice, rather than from programmes of regulatory reform. It presents a classic case of the victory of means over ends in the design of policy.

This is not to suggest that ministers did not have a definite set of priorities in embarking on privatisation. They had a clear sense of the benefits of markets with their consequent virtues of freedom, choice, and productive and allocative efficiency. But this was in the realm of 'high politics' and studies of privatisation are unanimous in indicating that the successive Thatcher Governments stumbled doggedly but experimentally towards suitable arrangements for the big privatisations.[19] Thus the question of how to secure the benefits of markets despite the absence of competition remained unresolved until late in the day and the DTI frantically sought appropriate practical mechanisms. The saviour came in the seminal paper by Stephen Littlechild, written for the DTI in 1983, which advocated the system of 'incentive regulation' manifest in the ubiquitous retail price index (RPI) $-X$ price control formula. This formula, Lawson recalls, 'was originally envisaged as a rough-and-ready short term solution',[20] thus illustrating the way in which the expedients of the moment have become enshrined in the regulatory system. It was consistent with this experimental approach (analogous to the Austrian School liking for 'discovery' in markets) that Littlechild also argued the case for competition as an eventual substitute for continued regulation. In one of his most cited observations he suggests that, 'regulation is essentially a means of preventing the worst excesses of monopoly; it is not a substitute for competition. It is a means of "holding the fort" until competition arrives. Consequently, the main focus of attention has to be on securing the most promising conditions for competition to emerge.'[21] The effect of this posture was to downgrade questions of regulatory design. If regulation was to be transient then less attention needed to be given to the agencies and processes through which it could be implemented. This again militated towards grafting the job on to the existing agencies. Thus when the DTI considered how best to administer the regulation of British Telecom following privatisation in 1984 it turned to the OFT. Gordon Borrie was most reluctant to take on this new duty, partly for the prosaic reason that he strongly doubted that he would be given sufficient extra staffing.[22] A new Office, a 'mini-OFT', was created in the shape of the Office of Telecommunications (OFTEL), with Bryan Carsberg as the first Director General of Telecommunications (DGT). The design borrowed from the OFT model of a single-person regulator with extensive discretionary power, and the new regulator was given concurrent powers under competition law to refer monopolies and anti-competitive practices to the MMC and to advise on merger references. The major innovation came in OFTEL's main function, which was to administer licences for telecommunications operators. Technically the Secretary of State granted new licences on advice from the DGT and the Director General undertook modifications. Licences were modified in the light of the DGT's primary and secondary duties and it is interesting to note that the duty 'to maintain and promote effective competition' is only a secondary duty within the 1984 Act, although by the early 1990s it had become dominant.

The creation of OFTEL proved extraordinarily influential. It operated as a blueprint for the subsequent regulatory offices and acted as a model for their goals, methods and accountability. Procedurally the regulators were free to devise their own systems. There were no legal requirements beyond the residual risk of judicial review, certainly nothing as systematic as the American Administrative Procedures Act of 1946 with its requirements for consultation, hearings and appeal.[23] The powers of the utility regulators, like those of the DGFT, were vested in the individual, not their Offices, and they chose to be quite open by British standards. Unlike civil servants, they were free to speak out on the issues that concerned them. They became significant public figures, tending to be more outspoken than the DGFT and certainly more than the Chairman of the MMC. Their level of administrative discretion was substantial and relatively unusual. Traditionally departments have been reluctant to give such extensive discretionary powers to bodies detached from direct control by the Secretary of State. The regulators have used their discretion to prioritise their objectives (for instance, balancing economic efficiency against environmental protection); to express preferences on the structure of their industries; to define acceptable price levels, and therefore RPI − X; and to define quality and service standards. These views find their way into regulatory decisions in a manner that prompted criticism of the 'personalisation' of regulation. In conducting its regulatory inquiries the MMC has therefore found itself dealing with regulators unafraid to express their views and light years away from the studied neutrality of the Secretary of State, or even the DGFT. When taking evidence from such regulators, members are inevitably aware of the public profiles and the established positions which they have declared. This presents the dilemma of the MMC either defending or undermining a known preference, not a position it has traditionally relished.

The resort to administrative discretion was quite deliberate. Just as with the early monopolies legislation, Foster records that 'the Government and its civil service advisers who drafted the 1984 Telecommunications Bill and the British Telecom licence were determined to avoid creating a legalistic system, one that would employ lawyers to present cases and which could lead to endless delays in hearings and on appeal'.[24] This determination was in part a reaction against American legalism, and the resulting level of discretion has been exploited to an extent that has raised astonishment among foreign observers, especially Americans. The corollary of regulatory discretion was some sort of appeal mechanism. If the courts were not to be used then the obvious recourse was to the same mechanism used by the OFT, the MMC. Hence a vital element in the privatisation Acts provides for a method of changing the licence to implement changes in price controls or other issues such as changes in the basket of regulated activities. Licence amendments will be proposed by the regulator and the regulated companies have the choice of accepting the amendments, in which case they become binding. If, however, they reject the amendments the regulator will refer the proposals to the MMC for an investigation that is part adjudication and part recommendation. At this point the MMC's brief is wide. It is again applying a public interest test but one that differs from section 84. The MMC must 'have regard' to the duties placed upon the regulator in the appropriate legislation. Confusingly, these vary slightly from industry to industry. The group is not obliged simply to 'arbitrate' between the regulator and the company. If it finds the existing licence to be against the public interest (which will be necessary for a change to be made) then it will also suggest specific modifications. The regulator will take account of the MMC's suggestions but is not bound by them, and the regulator will go on to make revised licence modifications. The company will be bound by these new modifications, which might differ materially from those recommended by the MMC. This feature of the process excited some disquiet and was addressed by Labour's *Response to consultation* paper which proposed that the MMC should have a statutory duty to approve the regulator's revised proposals (see below).

The creation of these arrangements was momentous. In opting for the MMC as a method of appeal the Government was relying on its acknowledged independence and status. But it was also drawing on a level of expertise that would be impossible to find in a court of law. Indeed, the courts have been consistently reluctant to adjudicate on competing economic and accounting arguments which are often thought to be 'non-justiciable'. In contrast the MMC could draw upon specialist staff and members. It was probably a coincidence, but it is nonetheless symbolic, that Stephen Littlechild had himself joined the Commission in 1983. The role allocated to the MMC in the system of utility regulation is therefore complex, both in itself and in its impact on the behaviour of the other actors. The MMC is applying a version of its time-honoured 'public interest' test which may imply the same priorities as the regulator, but equally well may not. The MMC's stress on competition in the 1980s made consistency of approach more likely but far from guaranteed. Thus neither the regulator nor the regulated company find it easy to predict how the MMC group will react. For the company there is the risk that the

MMC will side with the regulator, and something of a risk that it may actually go further. Additional disincentives for going to appeal are the demand on senior management time, the amount of information to be provided and published, the delays, and the impact on the share price of the attendant uncertainty. These procedural disincentives are a familiar aspect of any MMC inquiry and were explored in chapter 5. The regulatory inquiries have been large and protracted, comparable to monopoly investigations. For example, one of the early airport references involved a six-month inquiry which involved 490 papers from the main party, 100 submissions from third parties, 20 minor hearings and 3 main hearings, at a cost to the MMC of 900 'man days' and £420,000.[25] Quite what this may have cost the main party is unknown but it was reported in 1993 that BG had spent £6.5 mn alone 'on advertising, PR and political lobbying against the MMC inquiry'.[26] The 1993 gas inquiry took thirteen months from reference to publication, but that included the Fair Trading Act references. The 1995 water disputed determinations took ten months but the electricity licence modifications were nearer six months.

Apprehensiveness about an MMC reference has become part of the structure of the system. Dieter Helm has observed that 'the role of the MMC in encouraging compliance to regulators... is crucial. It is the lynch-pin of the system. If utilities face uncertainty about the outcome of an MMC inquiry, together with its costs, then the powers of the regulator to exercise discretion are increased.'[27] Regulators do indeed appear to have used the Commission as a 'threat' in bargaining, comparable to the threat to go to law. Two significant examples were, first, the explicit threat by the Office of Electricity Regulation (OFFER) in 1993 to refer the duopoly of the two big fuel generators to the MMC unless they divested 6,000 MW of generating capacity (this was also encouraged by the Select Committee on Energy). Second was the threat by OFTEL to refer the 1996 price control to the MMC unless British Telecom also accepted the controversial proposals to incorporate a fair trading condition into the licence (in some quarters this appeared close to blackmail).[28] Of course, the arguments about transaction costs apply to the regulators as well as to the companies. A major MMC investigation will impose very extensive demands on the regulator to submit evidence, attend hearings, discuss remedies and respond to requests for elaboration. The pressures to negotiate apply to both sides and might even lead into a 'capture'-type dynamic where the regulator and the company have a mutual interest in avoiding referral.

Thus the MMC appeal mechanism is sufficiently intimidating to bolster the power of the regulators. It enhances their ability to secure concessions and provides incentives to reach an agreement. In the case of electricity, it has been observed that 'while the MMC has only been involved directly in the regulation of the [electricity supply industry] to a limited extent so far, it is a powerful ghost'.[29] This 'ghostlike' effect means that the MMC is a fleetingly visible, spectral presence in all serious negotiations between the regulators and the companies. To this extent it is like a court of appeal in that its judgements have a pervasive precedent value. One important resolution will allow the parties to form views about how the MMC would settle their own dispute and therefore will have an effect that ripples through the regulatory system. MMC reports therefore need to be evaluated according to their wider impact as well as in terms of the specific case. In this respect the Commission is returning to its original investigatory function. In its early days investigations into monopolies were genuinely exploratory; nowadays monopoly and merger references have become more routine. In utility cases, however, genuine resolution of previously unresolved issues can be achieved. For this reason some of the most influential and interesting MMC reports of recent years have arisen from utility inquiries. We can go on to review some of them in more detail.

The MMC privatised sector cases

As outlined in chapter 2, the proliferation of regulatory Acts and the growth of regulatory agencies after 1984 confronted the Commission with a bewildering array of new sector-specific obligations. There are some subtle and puzzling differences between several of the Acts as regards grounds for referral, the tests to be applied and the way in which reports are treated. In particular:

- Referral of designated airports was mandatory (up to 1998), on a five-year rolling programme. The role of the MMC was strictly to give advice, the CAA decided on the basis of the MMC report.
- In contrast, on water industry appointment (licence) price determination references, (as opposed to adjudication references), the MMC's decision is binding on both parties.
- In other cases the regulator is bound to comply with a public interest finding on a licence dispute but can vary the MMC's proposed recommendations (this has provoked judicial review and practice is being changed; see below).
- The broadcasting provisions allow regional Channel 3 TV licence

holders or the Independent Television Commission to refer to the MMC disputes on the competition provisions of licences. The MMC applies a test which includes a provision similar to article 85(3) of the Rome Treaty (i.e. an economic efficiency test) and it may also specify the modifications required.

- In the electricity sector the Secretary of State can prevent a referral of a licence dispute to the MMC (it has never happened) but in the other sectors he or she has no such power.

In addition to references under the privatisation Acts, the MMC can also be asked to consider these sectors under the general competition legislation. The sectoral regulators (except for airports) were given concurrent powers with the OFT to make references. The concurrent powers were also included in the Competition Act (against considerable opposition) so that the European-type prohibitions and fines can be applied by the utility regulators (see chapter 10). Thus there have been some important references under the Fair Trading Act and some key merger references which were made by the Secretary of State in the usual way following advice from the DGFT. For these purposes the sectoral regulator will provide written advice and will become a member of the OFT's Merger Panel.

In the fourteen years up to March 1999 this rash of legislative provisions produced thirty-five inquiries. Examination of the pattern of cases confirms a reluctance to resort to the MMC. Table 20 shows four cases under the Fair Trading Act, five mandatory airport references, seven mandatory water merger references, eight other mergers, one broadcasting inquiry, and a rump of only ten licence modification or price determination reports. The licence adjudications are at the heart of the Commission's 'new' utility role and in turn break down into two gas, two electricity, four various aspects of telecommunications, and two water. Going a step further, it can be seen that the water inquiries concerned price determinations and were binding on the two sides. The telecoms references were rather specialised, as, too, were the electricity references, which had a strong regional dimension. It is mainly in gas that the MMC has been at the heart of the regulatory relationship and it is the gas references that have attracted most attention and most influence as precedents. We come back to them below.

The airports inquiries have been extremely significant for Britain's largest airports. They cover the British Airports Authority airports (BAA) (of its several airports Heathrow, Gatwick and Stansted are 'designated') and Manchester. The first quinquennial review of Manchester,

Table 20 *MMC reports on regulated companies, 1985–99*

Year	No.	Type	Subject
1985	1	merger	British Telecom and MITEL
1986	0		
1987	1	airport	Manchester Airport
1988	1	monopoly	Gas, supply of gas to non-tariff customers
1989	1	telecom	Chatline and message service
1990	3	water merger	General Utilities, Colne Valley and Rickmansworth Water
		water merger	Southern Water and Mid-Sussex
		water merger	General Utilities and Mid-Kent
1991	1	airport	BAA, economic regulation of the south-east airports (Heathrow, Gatwick and Stansted)
1992	2	airport	Manchester Airport
		monopoly	TV broadcasting services: report on publicising the goods of the broadcaster
1993	3	broadcasting	Channel 3 networking arrangements
		monopoly	Gas, two references, supply of gas and conveyance, and storage of gas
		gas	BG, two references, conveyance and gas tariffs
1994	0		
1995	7	electricity	Scottish Hydro-Electric
		water merger	Lyonnaise des Eaux and Northumbria
		water	Portsmouth Water, price determination
		water	South West Water, price determination
		telecoms	Telephone number portability
		merger	Belfast International Airport and Belfast City Airport
		monopoly	Classified directory advertising service
1996	7	merger	National Power and Southern Electric
		merger	PowerGen and Midlands
		airports	BAA
		water merger	Severn Trent and South West Water
		water merger	Wessex Water and South West Water
		merger[a]	National Express and Midland Mainline
		water merger	Mid Kent and General Utilities, and SAUR Water
1997	6	electricity	Northern Ireland Electricity
		gas	Gas, restriction of prices for transportation and service
		airports	Manchester Airport
		merger[a]	National Express and Scot Rail
		merger[a]	National Express and Central Trains
		merger[a]	Pacificorp and the Energy Group
1998	0		
1999	2	telecoms	Cellnet and Vodafone, charges
		telecoms	BT, charges for Cellnet and Vodaphone connections
Total	35		

Sources: MMC report listing and reports.
Notes: [a] For these mergers only one of the parties was a regulated company.
The reports are analysed by date of signature; abbreviated titles.

in 1987, was also the first privatised sector report (although, technically, of course, Manchester is public – being owned by the local authority). The Commission was asked to recommend a price control formula, but in the knowledge that the government had already opted for RPI – X for the BAA airports. All the same, the team provided an endorsement of RPI – X and rehearsed the advantages in its report. It might not be entirely irrelevant that the MMC team included Stephen Littlechild. The two subsequent quinquennial reports on Manchester have been quite stringent in setting 'X' and have been critical of Manchester's efficiency. The Airport appears rather to have resented the MMC's investigations and in 1997 asked the Government to abolish the quinquennial review,[30] which it duly promised to do in the 1998 *Response to Consultation* paper. The airports regime was anomalous in giving the MMC a regular partnership role.

Of the fifteen merger references within the utilities a distinction should be made between the seven water mergers and the remainder. Referral of substantial water mergers is mandatory and the principle of 'yardstick competition' is built into the process. This is based on the recognition that true competition is technically impractical in a network industry such as water supply and therefore that one reasonable alternative is to compare the performance of as large a group of companies as possible. Thus the MMC is required to evaluate the public interest in the light of 'the principle that the Director's [Director General of Water Services'; DGWS'] ability ... to make comparisons between different water companies should not be prejudiced'.[31] The commitment to yardstick regulation has also involved the accounting ring fencing of regulated activities and the regulator has pressed for separate stock market listing of appointed businesses (so far unsuccessfully), even when a utility becomes part of a larger group. Given this stress on comparison it is not perhaps surprising that the Commission has found six of the seven mergers to be against the public interest. In one early case (*General Utilities/Colne Valley Water Company/Rickmansworth Water Company*), the Secretary of State, Nicholas Ridley, allowed the bid in exchange for price cuts, and subsequently both the DGWS and the MMC have tended to look for price reductions as a condition for allowing bids. All the same, the MMC has been stringent. It recommended against the competing bids by Wessex and by Severn Trent for South West Water in 1996, even though the DGWS had advised that they should be allowed if price cuts could be secured.[32] The bids were blocked. In the case of water, therefore, the post-privatisation structure of the industry has largely been maintained by unusually demanding legislation policed with vigour by the

MMC. Here we see again the legacy of Nicholas Ridley, who was the Environment Secretary responsible for the hugely unpopular privatisation of water in 1989. As indicated in chapter 7, he was the most activist Secretary of State for Industry when it came to merger referrals and had an evangelical belief in the virtues of competition. In water, however, xenophobia also played a part. Lawson recalls the embarrassment caused when French water companies (some partly publicly owned) began buying up their smaller British counterparts. 'Nick eventually decided to halt the traffic, making it clear he would refer any bid worth more than £30 million to the Monopolies and Mergers Commission'.[33] Thus the water regime owes something to hostility to foreign ownership of such a basic resource, as well as to approval of yardstick regulation.

As regards licence modifications, as late as 1992 the Commission was regarding itself as 'an unfired gun', and not sure whether to bemoan such pacifism or be concerned about an impending fusillade. Sydney Lipworth pointed to the possibility of the Commission receiving thirty-three water references simultaneously if the companies disputed their 1994–95 price reviews. Similarly there would have been the prospect of ten simultaneous electricity references if the companies had disputed the 1994–95 distribution price review (which was, of course, controversially revised by Stephen Littlechild in May 1995). But to prepare for such an influx the Commission had only the examples of the Chatline and the airport inquiries on which to draw. The picture changed in July 1992 when the Commission received four gas references.

The privatisation of BG is cited as a textbook example of how not to privatise a state monopoly. The creation of a huge, arrogant, inefficient and exploitative private sector monopoly was a serious misjudgement on the part of a Government committed to competition. The prime reason for not privatising the gas industry on a competitive basis was the opposition of its directors, and especially Denis Rooke. Lawson describes him as 'my most formidable opponent'. 'He dominated British Gas and regarded the Energy Department as the principal obstacle to his plans ... treating ministers and officials alike with a mixture of distrust, dislike and contempt.'[34] Lawson charts his difficulties with introducing competition and blames his successor as Energy Secretary, Peter Walker, for caving in to Rooke and to his desire to create 'a powerful British company' rather than a competitive industry. Eventually, says Lawson, he accepted the plans but recognised that 'I would have to rely on the regulatory authority, after privatisation, to introduce competition.'[35] Thus was created one of the most problematic and controversial regulatory relationships in recent history.

The passage from the 1986 monopoly to the 1996 introduction of retail competition in gas is extraordinary. The MMC's 1997 Transco report observed that 'we are aware of no other country in which the gas market has experienced the development of competition, particularly to supply domestic users, of this scale'.[36] While the Office of Gas Regulation (OFGAS) has clearly been the dominant architect of change, the process has been punctuated by three highly significant MMC inquiries. The MMC has helped to shape the gas industry to a remarkable extent, thus bracketing it with the small number of industries for which MMC reports have had a constitutive role – examples such as glass, beer, contraceptive sheaths and the professions come to mind.

As noted above, the BG Board had avoided a section 11 inquiry although there had been a rather confrontational Fair Trading Act report on *Domestic Gas Appliances* in 1980. The MMC made contact again in November 1987, when the DGFT referred the supply of gas to non-tariff customers under the Fair Trading Act. This was the non-regulated side of BG's business and the referral was prompted by bitter complaints from industrial customers, some of whom wanted BG split up. In one sense the MMC was therefore performing a classic role of adjudicating between industrial interests. The scale of the adverse effects found was gross and damaging. The six-person MMC group was Chaired by Holman Hunt. It found extensive price discrimination, refusal to supply, unfair contract terms, inadequate information and undue purchasing power. Clearly there was a monopoly and clearly it was against the public interest. The recommendations were adopted by the Government and included a limit on purchasing more than 90 per cent of the output from new gas fields as well as an end to price discrimination. The report changed the industry's competitive conditions and spelled out the scale of the monopoly problem.[37]

The next reference came in July 1992 in an atmosphere of acute and sometimes vitriolic disputation between the gas regulator, James MacKinnon, and the BG Board under Chairman Robert Evans. Following an OFT review in 1991, which had proposed that BG should plan a reduction in its share of the domestic market to 40 per cent, James MacKinnon proposed a stringent transportation price cap. In July failure to agree the transportation pricing methodology caused the regulator to refer transport and tariffs to the Commission and, in response, BG argued that the whole context should be considered and asked Michael Heseltine to make a parallel but wider Fair Trading Act reference. He agreed, thus extending coverage to the non-tariff market. The report was thorough and radical. It was produced in four volumes over twelve months by a group

Chaired by Dan Goyder and comprising Ian Barter (industrialist), Roger Davies (businessman), David Thomson (banker), Michael Beesley (economist) and Geoffrey Whittington (academic accountant). Their report performed 'one of the functions at which the MMC is particularly good – prompting the powers-that-be to think about the future of the market and forcing them to face up to issues which they would prefer not to confront'.[38] The recommendations, published in August 1993, were extensive and included:

- the dramatic proposal that BG be legally divested into separate transport and trading arms
- a reduction in the threshold for tariff monopoly, and accompanying increase in the allowed tariff price from RPI – 5 to RPI – 4
- cautious recommendations for an end to the tariff monopoly.

The proposals for separating the transport and trading activities had already been put forward in the 1991 OFT report and BG had agreed to organisational separation. In March 1993 OFGAS infuriated BG by publishing its evidence to the MMC, which canvassed several divestiture options including creation of twelve autonomous gas regional supply companies. BG's Chairman attacked both the unconventional publication of MMC evidence (legal but unusual) and the proposals themselves. In fact, when Heseltine announced his response in December he rejected the MMC proposals for legal divestiture while confirming the organisational and physical separation of trading and transport within BG. Observers were unsurprised, pointing out that this was consistent with the DTI's evidence to the Commission and also that MacKinnon had himself changed his mind a few weeks before his retirement.[39]

Whatever the DTI's formal response, the MMC report put immense quantities of invaluable information into the public domain. It aired and gave weight to the pro-competition suggestions and marked a milestone towards a competitive market. It was also, of course, subsequently vindicated by BG's demerger into BG plc (Transco and BG International) and Centrica (production, sales and trading) in February 1997. Further, the report produced important methodological conclusions which became influential in respect of appropriate rate of return on capital and the calculation of the regulated asset base.

The third gas inquiry came in October 1996 in more conventional circumstances. The gas regulator, Clare Spottiswoode, had proposed price caps for BG's supply business and for the Transco pipeline business. BG accepted the supply proposals but rejected the pipeline calculations, arguing that they were too stringent and would starve the company of capital investment and create huge job losses. Accordingly, the dispute was referred to the Commission as a specific licence modification. The referral itself included a technical appendix of fifteen pages, illustrating the increased complexity of price cap calculations. The report explored the relationship between the public interest criteria and the duty 'to have regard to' the duties of the Director General. It confirmed that the Commission was not simply arbitrating, its public interest net was cast wide so that the Director General's proposals 'represent a useful starting point, but we are not confined to considering the adverse effects specified by the Director-General, or her proposed remedies, nor to examining points of difference between the Director-General and BG'.[40] The public interest definition under the Gas Act does seem more limited than the very wide terminology under the Fair Trading Act, but the 1993 Gas report had noted that, 'In practice, we have not found any conflict in public interest criteria between the two Acts.'[41] Thus the MMC group considered the balance of interest between consumers and shareholders, although it focused primarily on financial performance and the components of the price regulation formula – such as capital and operating expenditure, gearing, dividends and profitability. This group was the most streamlined yet for a utility inquiry. It had four experienced members, with Graeme Odgers in the Chair, Stanley Metcalfe (economist), Gill Owen (utility consumer specialist) and Graham Stacy (accountant). Stacy had served with Geoffrey Whittington on the 1996 BAA inquiry, which provided vital accounting continuity, and, between them, the group had served on fourteen previous utility references.

The report provided a fairly straightforward adjudication but one which confirmed a number of key elements in what had become a convergent methodology for price control. It settled the transportation price control very near the OFGAS proposals, calling for an initial price cut of 21 per cent in 1997–98 followed by RPI – 2. This was marginally more lenient than OFGAS but observers were able to argue both that 'it appears that OFGAS won the battles' and that 'Transco was right to take its price control to the MMC ... it ... won a number of important concessions'.[42] The MMC recommendations were based on projections of allowable revenue, which in turn was derived from a cost of capital of 7 per cent and a regulatory asset base of £11.6 billion. At this point we are entering an arcane world of utility regulation where the incantations are familiar for the practitioners but exotic to the lay observer. It is, however, important to lift the veil a little to demonstrate the new role that the MMC was playing in this field. Certainly it was resolving individual

cases, but it was also establishing principles that were influential throughout the regulated industries.

The price regulation formula of RPI − X, operated through periodic reviews (typically every five years), has a built-in incentive to cut
costs. If companies can exceed the performance set by the regulator they
retain the additional profit. It is a method chosen in preference to the
American 'rate of return' regulation in which companies are allowed a
given rate of return on their capital assets. This gives them no incentive
to increase efficiency and every incentive to engage in wasteful capital
spending. But in the British system, at each periodic review, when the
regulator has to reset 'X', he or she must come to some judgement as to
what revenues and profits are reasonable. They should minimise costs to
consumers, while giving a fair return to shareholders, and allow the managers to finance the ongoing activities (this last point is one of the regulator's primary duties for all the utilities). At this point rate-of-return
regulation and price cap regulation are based on similar data because esti-
mation of a reasonable revenue is in practice derived from the assets
invested in the business which have to be valued on an equitable basis.
This has become known as the regulatory assets base. Allowable capital
and operating expenditures are added in, then a return on capital per-
centage is applied to that base to give a figure for reasonable revenues. In
this sense it could be argued that RPI − X and rate of return are con-
verging as methods of regulation and that they differ in degree rather
than in kind.[43] In practice, however, RPI − X continues to operate as an
incentive system designed to cut costs, increase efficiency and generate
rewards. It is operated in this light as a dynamic system and is regarded
by economists as very different from the static operation of rate-of-
return regulation. The periodic recalculation of 'X' has moved away from
the original Beesley/Littlechild bargaining model to become a complex
and subtle calculation with immense implications for profits and share
prices, but it is still an incentive system.

The calculation of the asset base poses a number of dilemmas about
historic versus current cost accounting, but also raised a huge question
of fairness in that the assets were sold at privatisation at a substantial discount. It would be intolerable to give the shareholders assets at a reduced
price, and then to allow them returns on the full value. Thus, in the 1993
gas report, the MMC developed the concept of the market to asset ratio
(MAR) – the ratio of stock market value to asset value. This expresses the
discount from the current cost of capital valuation at which the shares
were sold. For gas it was 41 per cent at the date of privatisation in 1986
(and for water it was even lower!) In other words, the assets were sold at

41 per cent of their true value. The 1993 report posed the dilemma that, 'if there was no allowance made for the MAR, shareholders would enjoy significant and continuing gains at the expense of BG's customers'.[44] The solution offered was to calculate the MAR five years after privatisation, in 1991, based on the share price immediately before the events leading up to the MMC investigation. This was an heroic exercise in judgement. There is no technically correct way of producing these figures and the group concluded that, 'on balance, an MAR of about sixty per cent would seem reasonable'. Geoffrey Whittington observes that the judgement was made 'on the ground that gains up to that time represented the initial discount on privatisation and subsequent efficiency improvements obtained by the company which could reasonably be expected to benefit shareholders'.[45] Thus BG's huge inventory of assets at the time of privatisation was reduced for this calculation to 60 per cent of their current cost value and a cost-of-capital figure was applied to the resultant total of £11.6 billion.

Judgement of a reasonable rate of return on capital (the 'cost of capital') has been an essential concern of the MMC ever since the early monopoly reports. Comparison of a rate of return on assets compared with the norm across the sector, or across industry at large, provides a rough index of excessive monopoly profits and early reports maintained a sequence of comparisons. In recent decades return on capital employed for industrial companies (excluding North Sea) has fluctuated around 6 to 9 per cent.[46] For BG the Commission concluded in 1993 that 'a real rate of return of between 6.5 and 7.5 per cent on new investment would be reasonable under current conditions to attract capital to the industry'.[47] This judgement provides one of the other key elements of the RPI − X equation.

The MMC proposals were accepted by Clare Spottiswoode, who adopted the 7 per cent figure for the 1997 Transco price review. In that inquiry the MMC was offered cost-of-capital figures of between 6.01 per cent (shippers group) and 9.1 per cent (BG). It stayed with the 7 per cent figure, thus confirming a general convergence within the regulatory system of setting a cost of capital around 6–8 per cent. Whittington notes a range in MMC reports around 6.4–8.3 per cent (*BAA*, 1996) and 6–8 per cent (*South West Water Services* and *Portsmouth Water*, 1995).[48] The convergence across the regulated industries towards 7 per cent has been criticised for the lack of rigour on which the calculation is based, for the lack of discrimination between very different industries, and for its relative generosity. It is argued that the risk premium for the regulated industries should be low and should indicate a cost of capital lower on the scale. This is an endless and tendentious debate in which someone has to adjudicate. This task has fallen to the MMC, which has performed the essential service of providing some certainty. Grout observes that the MMC has brought consistency and consensus and that 'the treatment of the cost of capital has been dominated by the views held by the MMC'.[49]

The part played by the MMC in defining best practice is also seen in the furore over the treatment of depreciation in the BG cases. In 1993 the Commission applied the MAR to the asset base at privatisation but allowed full depreciation to be built into the calculation for allowable revenue. This could be justified as allowing BG to fund the replacement of assets but it was relatively generous and conceptually inconsistent. Several witnesses pointed to the anomaly during the 1993 inquiry and at least one member of the group was unhappy with the eventual resolution.[50] With the passage of time, the calming down of the OFGAS/BG relationship and the arguments of senior OFGAS staff (especially Dr Eileen Marshall, OFGAS's respected Chief Economic Adviser) the MMC changed its approach in 1997. It concluded in the 1997 report that the depreciation charge on assets existing in 1986 should be reduced to the MAR (to 60 per cent), thus having the effect of inflating the profit used for the regulatory judgement. This was widely remarked upon and justified in the report itself with the words that 'The 1993 MMC report was produced at a relatively early stage in the development of utility regulatory thinking in the UK'.[51] Again, this was an important technical adaptation but it did not feed mechanically into the judgement. Whittington agrees that the 1993 treatment of depreciation was 'unfortunate' but notes that it 'did not affect the overall judgement made about the price cap in 1993'.[52] It was widely felt that the MMC had got the treatment of depreciation right in 1997, and this episode illustrates both the flexibility of the MMC, which is able to respond pragmatically to the current environment, and the uncertainty of UK utility regulation, which has had to 'invent itself' as it has developed. The 1997 MMC report was accepted by OFGAS, which announced, with just a hint of triumphalism, that the 'MMC has endorsed Ofgas's position on key financial issues'.[53] In fact the regulator then went on to make some changes to the MMC recommendations in revising the price cap proposals. BG regarded the MMC report as 'tough' but was prepared to accept it. What it complained about was the regulator's changes. This raised again the problem of the regulator's right to amend MMC recommendations which we return to below.

The abbreviated discussion of the sequence of gas inquiries illustrates the profound impact that the MMC has had on the structure and conduct of the industry. In the process it has consolidated its role as the pivotal regulator in the utility sector and established, or confirmed, a series of regulatory practices that have become norms of utility regulation. Derek Morris suggested, early in 1999, that the creation of principles of economic regulation had 'crystallised into a distinctive regime' as a result of the MMC reports published from 1995 to 1997 and the debates they generated.[54] As a significant contributor to those debates Morris went on to delineate some of the most pressing issues to do with asset valuation and calculation of the rate of return. The issues are passing into a second generation of complexity. To take one potentially explosive example. The utility companies are allowed only efficiently incurred operating expenditure in calculating their regulated profits. If an equivalent logic were applied to their financial structure it would emphasise that the companies are massively under-geared and could afford to raise huge amounts of debt. If they were required to operate using an 'efficient' financial structure, which would require them to increase their debt to approach the optimum debt/equity ratio, then it is estimated that they could release at least £15 billion of value. Should regulators insist upon this? And who would benefit? Shareholders or consumers?[55] This technically complex issue had been hovering in the wings for some time but it was anticipated that it would begin to feature large in the debate. It will fall eventually to the Commission to define an acceptable approach.

Through its gas, electricity and water reports the MMC has therefore enhanced its reputation for expertise, independence and sound judgement. The reports have followed a careful path through the quicksands of regulatory uncertainty. Again we see a quintessentially British institution adapting and working sympathetically within a very British process of policy innovation. We also see the Commission balancing a series of logics. In these reports it is arbitrating between antagonistic parties; it is adjudicating in a quasi-judicial fashion as to the fairness of the processes and the proposals; it is applying technical expertise in economics and accounting; and it is weighing the arguments advanced by the range of interested parties. This is an extraordinarily subtle task for which the idea of the 'public interest' remains a suitable concept. There is, however, a public interest in the particular case and a wider public interest in producing a rational, acceptable and stable regime of utility regulation. The MMC's stature as a well-established, serious and disinterested body lent valuable ballast to a potentially unstable vessel. Before moving on to assess the place of the Commission in relation to the system as a whole, we should consider three further aspects of its influence. First, the design of the RPI – X price cap; second, the application of the Commission's distinctive investigatory tests; and third, its resources and competence.

The design and operation of the RPI $-X$ price cap has been a dominant feature of the regulatory regime. The method is attributed to Michael Beesley and Stephen Littlechild, and its adoption arose from Littlechild's 1983 report to the DTI in which he was asked to comment on alternative systems of profit control for British Telecom. He advocated a 'local tariff reduction scheme' incorporating RPI $-X$, for a number of reasons, including its incentive properties and the minimal level of intrusive intervention which it required. (He also recommended automatic reference to the MMC after five years.) RPI $-X$ did not materialise out of thin air. Price controls had been recommended by the MMC in a number of private monopoly inquiries such as *Breakfast Cereals* (1973). However, the most influential case was the second report on *Contraceptive Sheaths* published in November 1982. Stephen Littlechild had joined the Commission in 1983 and gained familiarity with its recent reports. The sheaths report advocated shifting from the rate-of-return price control imposed on LRC by the 1974 report, to a control based on a 'compound index' of its costs less an efficiency reduction. Thus, for a five-year period, LRC was required to limit its price rises to the compound index less 1.5 per cent. This, it was argued, 'would remove the disincentive to increase efficiency'.[56] Littlechild was influenced by this report and cites it approvingly, with the comment that 'such controls are easy to understand, relatively cheap and simple to monitor, they preserve the incentive to efficiency, and they can be focused precisely on the areas of concern so as not to restrict the operation of the business in other respects'.[57] Perhaps, therefore, the members of this inquiry group should share some of the credit for RPI $-X$ (they were John Eccles, Chairman, an industrialist; Bernard Owens, industrialist; John Sadler, civil servant and industrialist; Richard Smethurst, economist; and J. Wallis, industrialist).

The MMC could be expected to continue to endorse a methodology that came out of the MMC stable, particularly when it had a distinguished in-house evangelist. Stephen Littlechild served on fourteen inquiries, including the first airports inquiry and the first gas inquiry. It seems, therefore, that the MMC is partly responsible for the design of RPI $-X$, for its introduction, for the uniform use of the formula across the privatised industries, and for its subsequent refinement. In all of this the formula has never been rigid. It has been adapted to circumstances and has formed a basis for negotiation. From the beginning Beesley and Littlechild accepted that RPI $-X$ lends itself to bargaining[58] and is therefore consistent with considerable discretion on the part of the regulators. They did not anticipate the towering superstructure of accounting and economic data that has grown up around it. In his defence of the 'accidental' utility regime that has grown up in Britain, Foster celebrates this continuing discretion and adaptation and approves of appeal to the MMC, suggesting that 'there is much sense in this arrangement which means that appeal lies from one discretionary regulatory body to another'.[59] But the appeal rests on a common regulatory methodology and the development of shared norms across the regulatory system.

A second general aspect concerns the MMC's methods and tests. Once again, new legislation adopted the MMC's time-honoured methods of a full investigation and a public interest test. One rather startling development was the virtual exclusion of the Secretary of State from the process. There is no equivalent to the Minister's ability to over-ride an adverse public interest finding in a merger reference. It might be thought that the public interest test is too artificial for licence inquiries where there will normally be an adverse conclusion in order to allow the discussion of changes. The public interest test is also, however, important in allowing the MMC to expand the breadth of the inquiry. Thus a reference to the MMC opens up Pandora's Box. A wide range of matters can be considered, including quality of service, coverage of regulated activities, entry barriers, and so on. Conceivably the Commission could also involve itself in the social and environmental considerations that also form part of the regulator's duties. Thus it considered environmental aspects in the *South West Water* price determination and considered the environment and low income consumers in the 1997 BG inquiry. In the main, however, it has avoided those minefields and restricted itself to economic regulation. But even in the economic field there is no question of the Commission limiting the inquiry to the resolution of 'X'. As noted above, this unpredictability helps to explain the reluctance on the part of both the regulator and the companies to opt for an MMC reference; it also explains the reaction of the stock market, which will invariably mark down utility share prices following a reference.

The MMC's role is therefore wider than adjudication – although that is the noun conventionally used. This causes concern to many in the regulatory community, and especially lawyers, who value predictability and precedent. On the other hand, it could be seen to increase the accountability of the regulators. They know that a reference may well expose the whole range of regulatory requirements. Related to this feature of the relationship is the MMC practice that reports apply only to the company being referred. The group may well consider wider implications but it is unable to make wider recommendations. Thus in the *Scottish Hydro-Electric* case the MMC effectively found in favour of the company in a way that had implications for a second regulated company,

Scottish Power. This second company had originally accepted the supply price-control determination but now argued that it should benefit from the amendments made in the *Scottish Hydro-Electric* case. It had to go to judicial review, which it eventually won against the regulator in the Court of Appeal. Thus, in the utility cases, the question of precedent takes on an increased salience. If a regulator is to treat a group of companies consistently a successful appeal may have an unavoidable knock-on effect through the natural justice requirements of judicial review. Here it seems more difficult than with most inquiries to sustain the insulation of the case-by-case principle. The MMC's impact on utility sectors is more systemic.

A third intriguing question concerns the competence of the MMC in privatised industry inquiries. Thus far the Commission has produced reports to high standards of technical excellence but by 1998 the 'regulatory community' was becoming steadily more sophisticated and the technical questions steadily more complex. The licences themselves were becoming so complicated that they were thoroughly understood only by a very small band of specialists. The practice of utility regulation had become an area of recognised expertise, with its own practitioners, its academic specialists, think tanks, management consultants, and its own specialist journals (such as *Utilities Law Review* and *Utilities Weekly*). The law was becoming steadily more complex and the European dimension was becoming intrusive. Furthermore, the financial and the political weight attached to these considerations was formidable. For major regulated companies the ability to operate within the regulatory environment is as important as the ability to operate within the commercial environment. The regulated firms have substantial regulatory departments managed at a senior level. It was not altogether fanciful to imagine that the American companies which entered the electricity industry through acquisition of the regional electricity companies were motivated partly by the belief that they could 'work' the UK regulatory system. There are huge financial gains to be made from accurate analysis of regulatory developments, and influential City players have added to the political salience of regulatory policy.

In this light the MMC's resources could be stretched. First we can consider the membership. Analysis of the thirty privatised industry reports published up to the end of 1997 indicates that a broad cross-section of members were involved both in Chairing and in serving on groups. There was some limited specialisation, shown in tables 21 and 22, but it was rather transient. The experience accumulated by members such as Graeme Odgers, Dan Goyder, Stanley Metcalfe and Geoffrey

Table 21 *MMC members serving on regulated industry inquiries, 1987–97*

Chairman	No. of cases chaired
Sir Godfray Le Quesne	1
Holman Hunt	1
Richard Smethurst	1
Sir Sydney Lipworth	3
Hans Liesner	3
Dan Goyder	6
Sir Graeme Odgers	8
Peter Dean	3
Derek Morris	4
Total	30

Source: MMC published reports.
Note: Data taken from thirty of the cases listed in table 20, excluding the MITEL merger case, the Broadcasting cases and the cases in 1999.

Whittington was dissipated by retirement. Further, the majority of members served on a limited number of cases. Among the fifty-one members who served in these groups only seven had been drawn from the specialist panels on water, electricity or telecommunications. These members were only eligible for the licence modification inquiries (and there was no panel for gas). Their expertise was valuable although there is an implied inconsistency between the strict conflict-of-interest rules

Table 22 *Members who have served on one or more utility inquiries*

No. of cases undertaken	No. of members[a]
1 case	17
2 cases	18
3	5
4	6
5	2 (S. Metcalfe and J. Pickering)
6	1 (D. Thomson)
7	1 (G. Whittington)
10	1 (D. Jenkins)
Total	51

Source: MMC published reports.
Note: [a]Excluding Chairmen

applied to normal members and the declared specialism of Utility Panel members. One possibility would be to use specialist members as 'assessors' rather than as full group members but Labour's *Response to Consultation* paper instead proposed the creation of a single Utilities Panel to replace the three industry-specific panels. The weight of utility inquiries thus rests on normal MMC members. It is asking a lot of new members to require them to acquire a full grasp of regulatory developments, as well as corporate activities, in industries as complex as telecommunications or water. This places additional pressures on the staff. There are extremely able team managers and specialist economists and accountants, some of whom have built up extensive expertise in utilities work. But they are limited in number and availability. There may be only half a dozen truly qualified and experienced senior staff and the Commission does not follow any formal practice of creating expertise in respect of a given industry or set of issues. In the case of unpredictable monopoly and merger references this is perhaps inescapable, but there might be a case for investing in regulatory expertise on a more systematic basis. Curiously, the level of regulatory work fell away sharply in 1998 but, especially when compared with the resources on which the companies can draw, the MMC would be stretched if several inquiries arrived at once. As part of the debate on regulatory reform Labour proposed more extensive and structured exchanges between regulators on matters of common interest, including questions of methodology and best practice. They settled on 'a duty on the regulators to give collective consideration to matters of common interest'.[60] If the MMC were involved in this process it would allow members and staff to keep abreast of developments.

A long-term role? Managed competition and 'a truly modern regulatory framework'[61]

The MMC stepped into its role as utility regulator of last resort with the aplomb that a mature actor brings to a new role. It was prepared by virtue of its section 11 nationalised industry studies and was in good heart in the late 1980s, confident and effectively led. There was also a sense in which the tide was flowing in a congenial direction and the Commission itself was happy to put a shoulder to the Thatcherite wheel. The whole emphasis of post-privatisation economic regulation was consistent with the refocusing of the mission of the MMC around the promotion of competition. Further, as discussed in chapter 5, many of the members appointed by the DTI in the 1980s tended to be instinctive liberalisers and the Commission embraced many fervent supporters of the privatisation project. Members such as Stephen Littlechild, Patrick Minford, Michael Beesley, Colin Baillieu, Catherine Blight, Graham Mather and Ann Robinson were all active in the pro-privatisation camp.

Despite the almost accidental incorporation of the Commission into the system of utility regulation it took on four roles which made it a pillar of an edifice which at times seemed distinctly wobbly. First, the Commission reinforced the accountability of the regulators; it was, second, available as a sort of consultancy to resolve particularly intractable problems through references; third, it played a part in establishing best practice and providing a centre of gravity for the system; and fourth, it supplied credibility. At times after 1986 every major element of the system was the subject of powerful criticism. The companies were seen as rapacious, inefficient and dishonest; Government ministers were seen as simultaneously theoretically doctrinaire and financially opportunist; and the regulators were seen as over-personalised with a tendency to pursue personal obsessions. There was also a longer-term danger of regulatory capture in which regulators became too dependent on the industry for ideas, information and support. This was hardly a problem with gas but was an issue raised with water and electricity. In contrast it is striking in reading over the substantial literature from the period how relatively little criticism was aimed at the systemic role of the MMC. There was some criticism, especially from consumer bodies, but even here the MMC was acknowledged to be disinterested and independent. Thus the TIC, which had called for the merger of the MMC into the OFT in 1991 (see chapter 9), took a very different line in its report on *Energy Regulation*. It observed that:

> many witnesses agreed that the MMC had a valuable role to play in arbitration of major disputes ... Scottish Hydro-Electric told us that their overall experience with the MMC was constructive and that they found the MMC to be businesslike and practical ... *We recommend that the Government ensure that the MMC be adequately resourced to allow appeals ... to be dealt with more speedily.*[62]

Criticism of the overall system of utility regulation had become so intense by 1995 that serious observers were talking of a 'crisis' in the system.[63] The debate included reports by the NAO,[64] by parliamentary committees[65] and by a rapidly growing band of think tanks.[66] Much of the debate was nicely brought together in the Hansard Society's 1996 report, which was well thought out and aimed at reforms to strengthen the existing system. It stressed issues of legitimacy and transparency and in important respects it anticipated the DTI's later Green Paper.[67] Clearly this was an important issue for Labour's 1997 election manifesto but it was handled in very general terms. The manifesto simply promised that 'in the utility industries we will pursue competition' and went on to talk of 'tough, efficient' and 'open and predictable' regulation.[68]

After the election Margaret Beckett, as the new Trade and Industry Secretary, took the heat out of the issue with a moderate statement on 30 June that announced a further review of utility regulation, rather than immediate reform. It became clear that the DTI was putting the prime emphasis on reform of the competition law, and here the concurrent powers for regulators to apply the competition prohibitions promised to be equally as momentous as the outcome of the utilities review (see chapter 9). The review was leisurely and the Green Paper did not emerge until March 1998, by which time all the radical proposals for the sharing of excess profits and reform of corporate governance within the utilities had been firmly laid to rest.[69] Nonetheless, the really rather moderate set of possible reforms was seen as potentially interventionist and the *Economist* observed that 'the reaction of the current regulators to these proposals ranges from mild scepticism to outright hostility'.[70] In consultation the proposals became even more incremental and the DTI's *Response to Consultation* largely consolidated the existing system, although one major change was the proposal to replace individual regulators with three-person regulatory boards. In addition the DTI announced that it intended to:

- give the regulators new statutory guidance
- merge the gas and electricity regulators
- legislate to define 'a new primary duty on the regulators to protect the interests of consumers, wherever possible and appropriate through promoting competition'
- keep the $RPI - X$ price control formula
- place new statutory duties on regulators to consult, to explain and to publish decision criteria.[71]

The Government did not hide the fact that legislation would be slow to arrive in an over-burdened legislative programme. In addition some of the more knotty problems (as over directors' pay and publication of company information) were delayed for yet further consultation. The general impression was that the Government had been responsive to the lobbying of business and that Margaret Beckett's more interventionist instincts had been reined in by Gordon Brown. This perspective evoked the older criticism that, although the sectoral regulators had not been 'captured' by their industries, that capture had taken place before they were appointed and had been built into the system. Certainly the companies had an interest in minimising change and appeared to have been rather successful. The consultation response focused much more on the regulators than the companies. The pervasive emphasis on 'transparency' was to have far more impact on regulators' Offices than on company Boardrooms. This was a bi-partisan exercise, building on the Conservative legacy.

Curiously, however, the Green Paper said more about the MMC than many of the earlier reformist studies. The DTI officials who drafted it, led by Catherine Bell, clearly had a better idea of the pivotal role of the Commission and of some of the associated problems which they intended to resolve. There was some questioning of whether the MMC was the right forum in which to settle complex technical issues such as monitoring of capital expenditure or access pricing, but these were set to one side and the three MMC issues emphasised were MMC procedures on licence modification, the regulators' discretion following MMC licence modification reports, and the MMC utility panels.

The consultation response concluded that:

- The MMC should 'push ahead with further experiments in the use of open hearings' (see p. 59) and should try for greater disclosure of written evidence.
- 'The Government intends to introduce legislation to require regulators to seek final endorsement from the MMC that any licence modifications developed following a reference to the MMC are required to remedy or prevent the adverse effects identified by the MMC.'
- Government will replace existing Utility Panels with a single cross-utilities panel.[72]

These proposals were well received by the Commission, especially the requirement for the MMC to give subsequent approval to licence modifications proposed by regulators after reports. This would deal with the issue of regulators' adaptations noted above but it would require the Commission to 'come back to' an inquiry. This would be novel. The practical effect, of course, might be to make regulators even more unwilling to see cases go to the Commission and could therefore strengthen the pressure for bargaining and compromise even further – an outcome probably quite congenial to the DTI.

In the small print there were further significant proposals. The

Government intended to leave the MMC with the final say in disputed water price determinations, but it proposed to end mandatory referral of quinquennial designated airport price reviews. In the interests of consistency the CAA was to be treated like the other regulators, with referral to the Commission only in the event of a dispute over the licence modification. Of course, these changes required legislation which, in 1999, was still pending.

By early 1999 the Commission was emerging from the New Labour reforms with its position in utilities regulation clarified and bolstered. It had been in a good position to influence the policy review thanks to its knowledge of the field and established links. Penny Boys, for instance, had served as Deputy Director General of OFFER before joining the Commission as Secretary and was well placed to engage in the reform dialogue between the regulators, the OFT and the DTI. Perhaps the most significant conclusion in relation to the privatised industries, sixteen years after Stephen Littlechild's seminal paper, was that government had reconciled itself to continuing long-term regulation of the utilities. The Littlechild vision of a withering away of regulation had proved a mirage. It has become accepted that the residual natural monopoly characteristics of network industries, especially water, necessitate continued regulation. RPI – X was still in place and being used extensively; competition was being pursued, partly through retail competition, but also through regulation rather than instead of regulation. Thus the structures of the gas, water, electricity, telecommunications and railway industries were being manipulated to facilitate competition by continuing intervention of the regulators. Burton termed this 'organised competition'; it could equally be called 'managed competition'.[73] Burton drew pessimistic Hayekian conclusions from this stalling of free and open competition. He anticipated a likelihood of increased lobbying, increased chances of regulatory capture and a diversion of entrepreneurial energy into wasteful regulatory games.

A more positive interpretation of organised competition would be to accept the social constructionist view that all competition is organised (crudely, no state, no competition). Left to themselves businesspeople would happily eliminate all competition – that is, indeed, why we have competition policy. Moving on from there, a widespread acceptance that regulation is inevitable should focus attention on improving regulatory agencies and regulatory performance. Thus the DTI's *Response to Consultation* paper concluded that for water, and for gas and electricity distribution, there is a continued need for 'tough and effective sectoral regulation'.[74] The MMC will be part of that regulatory framework with a role that extends into the longer term. It may have an increasingly important role in checking any tendency towards regulatory capture but here will be inhibited by its inability to initiate references. More uncertainty will be created by the extent to which the sectoral regulators choose to use their concurrent powers under the Competition Act and how appeals to the new appeal tribunals arm of the Commission will be handled (see chapter 10). But however these issues develop, the Commission and the regulated utilities look set for a continued close relationship.

Notes

1 See C. Foster, *Privatization, Public Ownership and the Regulation of Natural Monopoly* (Oxford, Blackwell, 1992), pp. 80–1; and Sir Godfray Le Quesne, evidence to the Public Accounts Committee (PAC), *Efficiency of Nationalised Industries: References to the Monopolies and Mergers Commission*, 1986–87, HC 26 (London, HMSO, 1987), p. 4.

2 A. Fels, *The British Prices and Incomes Board* (Cambridge University Press, 1972), p. 40.

3 See the third White Paper, Cmnd 7151, *The Nationalised Industries* (London, HMSO, 1978).

4 John Smith, *Hansard* (23 July 1979), col. 114.

5 See Le Quesne, evidence to the PAC, p. 5.

6 Cmnd 7845, *The Role of the CAG* (London, HMSO, 1980).

7 Nicholas Ridley, *Hansard* (30 November 1981) vol. 14, cols 48–9.

8 M. Garner, 'Auditing the efficiency of the nationalised industries: enter the Monopolies and Mergers Commission', *Public Administration*, 60:4 (Winter 1982), pp. 428, 420, 425.

9 Foster, *Privatization*, p. 81.

10 MMC reports, *Central Electricity Generating Board*, HC 315 (May 1981), p. 2; *British Railways Board: London and South East Commuter Services*, Cmnd 8046 (October 1980), p. 4.

11 Interview with a former member of the Commission.

12 *CEGB*, HC 315, pp. 292–3.

13 MMC, *British Steel Corporation: A Report on the Efficiency and Costs in Discharging its Functions of the British Steel Corporation*, Cm 437 (London, HMSO, 1988), p. 157.

14 Correspondence with a former MMC staff economist.

15 W. Maloney and J. Richardson, *Managing Policy Change in Britain: The Politics of Water* (Edinburgh University Press, 1995), pp. 43–4, who also review criticism of the MMC report.

16 C. Baillieu, *The Lion and the Lamb* (London, Wilfred Street Conferences for the Conservative 2000 Foundation, 1996), p. 12.

17 B. Collins and R. Wharton, 'External reviews of nationalised industries and the work of the Monopolies and Mergers Commission', paper presented to the PAC Conference, University of York, September 1984; the authors worked for Peat,

Marwick Management Consultants, quotes, pp. 25, 27.

18 Evidence, PAC, *Efficiency of Nationalised Industries*, pp. 1, 4, 5.

19 See, for instance, C. Graham and T. Prosser, *Privatizing Public Enterprises: Constitutions, the State and Regulation in Comparative Perspective* (Oxford, Clarendon, 1991), pp. 185–6; Foster, *Privatization*, p. 205.

20 N. Lawson, *The View From No. 11* (London, Transworld, 1992), p. 223.

21 S. Littlechild, *Regulation of British Telecommunications' Profitability* (London, DTI, February 1983), p. 7.

22 See Foster, *Privatization*, p. 125.

23 Some specialists suggest that the American procedures offer useful lessons; see T. Prosser, *Law and the Regulators* (Oxford, Clarendon, 1997), p. 286.

24 Foster, *Privatization*, p. 267.

25 MMC, internal seminar papers, May 1993.

26 R. Bruce, 'Pressure turned on gas', *Certified Accountant Magazine* (10 May 1993), p. 10.

27 D. Helm, 'British utility regulation: theory, practice and reform', *Oxford Review of Economic Policy*, 10:3 (1994), p. 26.

28 See P. Strickland, 'Telecommunications regulation in 1996–97', in P. Vass (ed.), *Regulatory Review 1997* (London, CIPFA, 1997), pp. 77–9; C. Graham, 'The Office of Telecommunications: a new competition authority?', in B. Doern and S. Wilks (eds), *Changing Regulatory Institutions in Britain and North America* (University of Toronto Press, 1998).

29 G. MacKerron and I. Biora-Segarra, 'Regulation', in J. Surrey (ed.), *The British Electricity Experiment: Privatization: The Record, the Issues, the Lessons* (London, Earthscan, 1996), p. 99.

30 T. Bass, 'Airport Regulation 1996–97', in Vass (ed.), *Regulatory Review*, p. 18.

31 Water Industry Act, 1991, section 34.

32 B. Baker, 'Water and wastewater regulation 1996–97', in Vass (ed.), *Regulatory Review*, p. 104.

33 Lawson, *The View from No. 11*, p. 233.

34 *Ibid.*, pp. 213–14.

35 *Ibid.*, p. 216.

36 MMC, *BG plc: A Report under the Gas Act 1986 on the Restriction of Prices for Gas Transportation and Storage Services* (London, Stationery Office, May 1997), p. 9.

37 See MMC, *Gas. A Report on the Matter of the Existence or Possible Existence of a Monopoly Situation in Relation to the Supply in Great Britain of gas through Pipes to Persons other than Tariff Customers*, Cm 500 (London, HMSO, 1988), pp. 112–23; C. Price, 'Gas regulation and competition: substitutes or complements?', in M. Bishop *et al.* (eds), *Privatization and Economic Performance* (Oxford University Press, 1994), p. 148.

38 C. Robinson, 'Gas: what to do after the MMC verdict', in M. Beesley (ed.), *Regulating Utilities: The Way Forward* (London, IEA, 1994), p.11.

39 J. Stern, 'Gas – regulation and the MMC review 1993', in P. Vass (ed.), *Regulatory Review 1994* (London, CIPFA, 1994), p. 25.

40 MMC, *BG plc: A Report*, p. 7.

41 MMC, *British Gas plc Volume 1 of Reports under the Gas Act 1986 on the Conveyance and Storage of Gas and the Fixing of Tariffs for the Supply of Gas by British Gas plc*, Cm 2315 (London, HMSO, 1993), p. 6.

42 *Energy Utilities* (July 1997), p. 5 'News Analysis'; p. 16 'Transco MMC report'.
43 Prosser, *Law and the Regulators*, p. 300.
44 MMC, *British Gas plc Volume 1*, p. 37.
45 *Ibid.*, p. 37; G. Whittington, 'Regulatory asset value and the cost of capital', in M. Beesley (ed), *Regulating Utilities: Understanding the Issues* (London, IEA, 1998), p. 93.
46 Central Statistical Office, summarised for MMC Seminar, May 1993, unpublished paper.
47 MMC, *British Gas plc Volume 1*, p. 3.
48 Whittington, 'Regulatory asset value', appendix 1.
49 P. Grout, 'The cost of capital and asset valuation', in Vass (ed.), *Regulatory Review*, p. 199.
50 Interview with a former member of the Commission.
51 MMC, *British Gas, Volume 1*, p. 41.
52 Whittington, 'Regulatory asset value', pp. 95, 96.
53 OFGAS, Press Release (18 June 1997).
54 D. Morris, 'New challenges in regulation', speech to Hertford Seminar on Regulation (29 January 1999), para. 6.
55 *Ibid.*, para. 31.
56 MMC, *Contraceptive Sheaths*, Cmnd 8689 (London, HMSO, November 1982), p. 50.
57 Littlechild, *Regulation*, p. 37.
58 A point made strongly in M. Beesley and S. Littlechild, 'The regulation of privatised monopolies in the United Kingdom', *RAND Journal of Economics*, 20:3 (Autumn 1989), pp. 454–72; reprinted in M. E. Beesley, *Privatisation, Regulation and Deregulation* (London, Routledge, 1992).
59 Foster, *Privatization*, p. 284.
60 DTI, *A Fair Deal for Consumers: Modernising the Framework for Utility Regulation – The Response to Consultation* (London, DTI, undated but July 1998), p. 28, conclusion 7.8.
61 The quote is from the DTI utility paper, *ibid.*, p. 33.
62 TIC, *Energy Regulation*, 1996–97, HC 50–1 (London, Stationery Office, 1977), p. lix.
63 See S. Wilks, 'The amoral corporation and British utility regulation', *New Political Economy*, 2:2 (1997).
64 NAO, *The Work of the Directors General of Telecommunications, Gas Supply, Water Services and Electricity Supply*, 1995–96, HC 645 (London, HMSO, July 1996); this is huge at 360 pp. and was followed up by the PAC report, HC 89 of 1995–96. It says little about the MMC as such.
65 See, for instance, PAC, *The Work of the Directors General of Telecommunications, Gas Supply, Water Services and Electricity Supply*, 1995–96, HC 89 (London, HMSO, 1996); TIC, *Liberalisation of the Electricity Market*, 1996–97, HC 279 I (London, Stationery Office, 1997).
66 The OXERA consltancy headed by Dieter Helm was a vocal critic, partly through its journal *Energy Utilities*. The Institute of Economic Affairs was a very active participant in the debate, as were bodies such as the European Policy Forum. The Labour-associated Institute for Public Policy Research (IPPR) also produced a stream of reform-orientated papers.
67 The Hansard Society and the European Policy Forum, *The Report of the Commis-*

sion on the Regulation of Privatised Utilities, Chairman, John Flemming (London, Hansard Society, December 1996).

68 The Labour Party, *New Labour: Because Britain Deserves Better* (London, The Labour Party, 1997), pp. 15–16.

69 DTI, *A Fair Deal for Consumers: Modernising the Framework for Utility Regulation*, Cm 3898 (London, Stationery Office, March 1998).

70 *Economist* (28 March 1998), p. 34.

71 DTI, *A Fair Deal ... Response to Consultation*, p. 8 and elsewhere.

72 DTI, *A Fair Deal for Consumers*, pp. 30–3.

73 J. Burton, 'The competitive order or ordered competition?: the "UK model" of utility regulation in theory and practice', *Public Administration*, 75:2 (Summer 1997).

74 DTI, *A Fair Deal ... Response to Consultation*, p. 17.

9

The tripartite system, the European challenge and the new Competition Commission

Compared with the MMC the OFT is a mere stripling but, even so, it has survived rather successfully and was able to celebrate its twenty-fifth birthday in 1998, along with that of the tripartite structure of British competition authorities. In 1995 the DTI affirmed that 'the tripartite structure is designed to provide for effective action against damaging monopolies, and at the same time to provide checks and balances to the exercise of power by the authorities ... The Government are content with this broad structure, which they believe has shown its worth over a period of more than 20 years.'[1] The tripartite structure, with its checks and balances, has proved attractive enough to be retained for merger control and for some aspects of monopoly control. Under the 1998 Competition Act, however, the 'operational' aspects of the tripartite structure have been abolished. The prohibition will be operated by the DGFT who will become a more important, and a more controversial, figure. The 'structural' aspects of the tripartite system are, however, being retained and the system will continue to rely on co-operative relations between the OFT, the new Competition Commission and the DTI.

This chapter begins with a review of the OFT as the post-1973 partner of the MMC. It reviews its organisation, its pattern of activity and its relations with the DTI and the MMC. It then goes on to chart the steadily increasing influence of 'Europe' and the European competition rules which culminated in the passage of the 1998 Competition Act. The chapter assesses the dynamics which gave rise to the Act and chapter 10 outlines the initial creation of the Competition Commission.

The OFT

It is remarkable that the OFT as an agency has received even less attention than the MMC. Many lawyers, economists and consumer specialists have dealt with various aspects of its work but there is, as yet, no book-length study of it as a body in its own right.[2] The OFT is a non-ministerial government department, which says very little about its powers or the general rationale for its creation in this form. The early 1970s saw a prolific growth in non-departmental agencies – some tripartite (the Manpower Services Commission, 1973; the Health and Safety Commission, 1974); some regulatory (the CAA, 1972); some functional or specialised (the National Consumers' Council, 1975; the NEB, 1975). Arguments about expertise and continuity were used to justify their creation but in fact the justifications and patterns were virtually immune from logical analysis. The OFT was seen as a device for winning client support through consumer incorporation in the Consumer Protection Advisory Committee. Equally it could have been regarded as a 'hiving off' of routine activities as advocated in the Fulton report or, alternatively, as what Hood calls the 'Pontius Pilate effect' of shifting hot issues to intermediary organisations to avoid political controversy (applicable here especially to merger references).[3] If, therefore, the OFT is not one of a recognisable general type, then we need to look at its particularities.

The OFT has become a very considerable actor with powers to police the market place, to speak for consumers and materially to affect competitive conditions within the economy. Its annual reports cover a bewildering array of activities, ranging from financial services to estate agents to anti-competitive practices and high profile mergers. The OFT has acquired a portfolio of activities growing in scope and importance. In 1991 Gordon Borrie observed that, 'I did not know what a fascinating range of activities I would be engaged in nor how many new powers and duties would be given to the Office of Fair Trading, tempting me to undertake further terms of Office.'[4] The tortuous creation of Borrie's empire (as it steadily became) was reviewed in chapter 6. The design embodied an almost revolutionary change for policy on consumer protection but, as regards competition, it embraced two very different dynamics – for continuity and for change. The pressures for change were represented by the radical and imaginative idea of an independent DGFT. It is a curiosity of the Act (repeated in the 1998 Act) that all the powers are vested in the Director General and there is no mention of the OFT. He or she is empowered to delegate to staff but the OFT operates to give expression to the Director General's decisions and acts in his or her name. In this respect administration is 'personalised' and, in the case of the cloned utility regulators, we see the dangerous implications of that degree of personal prominence (which the DTI declared in 1998 was to be ended; see chapter 8). As we saw in chapter 6 the level of independence of the DGFT was rather less than was publicly declared but, nonetheless, this well-resourced, legislatively empowered individual had very extensive room to define and pursue a competition policy and consumer brief. He or she was potentially a prophet, an evangelist, equipped with a licence to speak out and with considerable influence over the policy agenda. There were also strong forces for continuity which were more obvious to insiders and to academic commentators. For competition the changes were evolutionary, there was no great principled shift and really rather little change in staffing. The burden of proof was unchanged, particularly on mergers, which struck many economists as a lost opportunity. Similarly the investigatory powers and resources were barely strengthened, and the penalties for infringement continued to be minimal. The MMC was to continue in substantially its traditional fashion and the restrictive practices machinery was submerged in the larger Office.

Assessing the changes from a position of bureaucratic expediency, the creation of the OFT could be seen as very convenient for the officials in the DTI's Fair Trading Division. A small group of these officials transferred to the OFT, taking with them the controversial process of merger review and the problematic process of generating monopoly references. The officials remaining in the DTI competition division could henceforth disclaim responsibility for both processes, thus allowing them to sustain co-operative relationships with industrialists and their colleagues in the production departments. In fact, taking the reference process out of Whitehall may, as suggested in chapter 6, actually have weakened it. The ability of the OFT – outside the Whitehall magic circle and with few bargaining counters – to persuade production departments to suggest monopoly references was no greater than that of the DTI. Officials thus sloughed off much of the routine reference work but retained control over policy through the retention of ministerial discretion. They also, of course, maintained a degree of control over the OFT through the appointment of the DGFT and by the despatch of their own officials. This interpretation would square with Dunleavy's 'bureau shaping' approach, which argues that officials seek to maximise their job satisfaction by seeking policy work and a congenial collegiate atmosphere.[5] Consciously or not, the creation of the OFT would seem to have reduced the routine work of those officials remaining in the DTI.

In this context it is noteworthy that the OFT had always appointed a DTI senior official as the Deputy Director General of the OFT – until 1997 when the post was abolished. At that point a DTI official had become Director of Competition Policy (Margaret Bloom, who succeeded

Martin Howe after an open competition). Over the twenty-five-year period five senior officials have served as Deputy Director General, providing great DTI continuity. The pattern was set in 1973 when Frank Glaves-Smith, who had been involved with the design of the 1973 Act, joined the OFT as Deputy Director General and simultaneously held the post of Director, Monopolies and Mergers, until the Competition Policy Division was formed to include restrictive practices in 1977. He served until 1979 at the rank of grade 2 (Deputy Secretary), to be succeeded by Ernest Warne (1979–82), Elizabeth Llewellyn-Smith (1982–87), Tony Lane (1987–90) and Jeffrey Preston (1990–96). It was clearly advantageous to have senior management who understood how Whitehall worked. As civil servants such officials would work to the OFT brief and might actually have relished the chance to apply the competition principles. At the same time they were naturally attuned to BoT/DTI thinking, and Ramsey is clear that there was early opposition to the appointment of non-civil servants.[6] In the late 1990s posts associated with the expansion of the OFT were openly advertised and it may be that specialist outsiders will be brought into the Office, as was originally envisaged.

In assessing the history of the OFT the period can be broken up in several significant ways. Referring mainly to consumer issues Ramsey identifies a 'crusading' phase from 1973–78 and a later transitional or 'reflective' phase. Another obvious dividing point is 1979, with the Conservative victory and the passage of the Competition Act in 1980. Examination of staffing, budgeting and references suggests a further transition in 1989–92. In 1989 OFT staffing was at 315, its budget £11.6 mn. By 1992 staffing had soared to 420 and the budget to £19.3 mn – increases of 33 per cent and 66 per cent, respectively. This is in contrast to a general trend of stable funding and it is not easy to see any new responsibilities, initiatives or technical factors which would justify increases of this magnitude. Rather than dramatic new responsibilities the increases appear to reflect the steady growth in the OFT's responsibilities, including consumer regulation, new liaison with the utility regulators, financial services and broadcasting. Rather than take political or budgetary periods, however, it is useful to look at the OFT from the point of view of successive Directors General. This is especially appropriate because Gordon Borrie dominated the history of the OFT, and his period of office, 1976–92, over sixteen years, can almost be taken as a policy period in its own right. Borrie's period of office spanned the shift from an 'industrial policy' linkage to competition policy under Labour, to encompass the successive competition, disengagement and re-regulation experiences under the Conservatives.

The story starts with the first Director General, John Methven. As we saw in chapter 6, Methven was a lawyer formerly with ICI and active in the CBI's Trade Policy Committee. His qualifications were further enhanced by membership of the MC where he had served on two monopoly inquiries in 1972–73 (*Plasterboard* – against the public interest; *Cross-Channel Car Ferries* – not against the public interest, the latter Chaired by Ashton Roskill). His was not an easy job. The consumer powers were brand new and staff serving in the OFT at that time recall the consumer side of the Office as 'a bit of a farce' with staff uncertain as to how to proceed.[7] Methven thus conceded in his first annual report that he had concentrated his energies on the consumer side and left the competition matters largely to the pre-existing administrative staff from the DTI and the Office of the Registrar of Restrictive Trade Practices (ORRTP). Thus he made no monopoly references until *Frozen Foodstuffs* (July 1974) under the minority Labour Government elected (in the wake of the miners' strike) in February 1974. This was a terrible time to take up any post dealing with industry and the economy. It was a time of crisis, for Middlemas almost an industrial earthquake in which familiar planes slide to produce an alien landscape such that 'individuals who lived through it recall a dangerous, disorientating time when what counted most was to survive'.[8] Labour's February manifesto had said nothing about competition policy but had promised an Industry Act, planning agreements and a programme of socialist intervention. The October Manifesto stressed the creation of a Consumer Agency (to become the National Consumers' Council) and the intended NEB. The liberal conception of competition which underpinned the work of the MMC and the OFT was at such odds with the industrial policy debate that it was virtually invisible. Perhaps in these circumstances it is not so surprising that John Methven should have chosen to leave the OFT in June 1976 to join the embattled CBI as Director General.

Methven's approach had displayed a positive commitment towards negotiation in monopoly and mergers cases, with a view to avoiding a reference to the MMC where possible. He also insisted on strengthening the application of the restrictive trade practices law. Although he was strongly sceptical about the whole design of the law (see p. 174) he warned against failure to register agreements and pointed up the potential to discover unregistered agreements as a by product of MMC investigations. He was bullish about the potential for the Office, of which he said, 'in US terms it combines the functions of the Anti-Trust Department and the Federal Trade Commission. It is a regulatory agency.'[9] Methven was well liked by the competition staff, who remember him as a tough, no-nonsense Director General who was also refreshingly non-hierarchical. He established an office style of informal give and take with decisions discussed around the Director General's table, very unlike the formality of the DTI at that time.[10] There was initially a crusading spirit, especially among the economists, and an enthusiasm to get on and make references. This did not always go down well with the DTI. One staff member recalls undertaking work on parallel pricing in one industrial sector which, they strongly felt, laid the foundations for a monopoly reference. The team were called over to the DTI for a discussion with the Deputy Secretary in charge of the sponsoring division, who told them, in no uncertain terms, that they should keep out of this territory, and they did.[11] Interventions of quite this clarity seem to have been unusual and the Director General was, in principle, in a position to attack monopolies on a wide front. Senior MMC figures were full of praise for Methven and felt that his business credibility and connections were intensely valuable for getting the OFT successfully established.[12] Later, wearing his CBI hat, Methven could be critical of the Deputy General and observed that, 'there is an enormous panoply of powers being invested in one man'.[13] This was perhaps a bit disingenuous but it underlined the potential for exploitation of these powers by his successor, Gordon Borrie.

Like his predecessor, Borrie was a lawyer; unlike Methven he came squarely from the world of consumer protection, where he had made his mark as an activist, academic and author.[14] He was already a member of the ill-fated OFT Consumer Protection Advisory Committee before his appointment by Shirley Williams. He was associated then, and in his later work for Labour's Commission for Social Justice, with a position of social democracy and it was a testament to mutual forbearance and the bi-partisan nature of competition policy that he served a succession of right-wing ministers. In his early days Borrie appeared to give priority to the consumer side of the Office. This reflected not only his particular expertise but the structure of government itself. After the February 1974 surprise election victory Harold Wilson had split the giant DTI between Industry (Tony Benn, then Eric Varley); Trade (Peter Shore); and Prices and Consumer Protection under Shirley Williams. Competition policy was assigned to the DPCP, which at one and the same time separated it from the intense and emotional debate over industrial policy and planning, and associated it again closely with anti-inflation policy, price control and consumer activism. It was not until 1978 that Borrie began to give very much attention to competition policy in his annual reports, and the pattern of monopoly references also seemed to indicate a consumer bias. Methven had referred some significant intermediate product industries to the Commission whose efficiency had a potential impact on industrial productivity – such as petrol, bricks and cables. In contrast the Borrie references during the 1970s tended to be of industries supplying final product markets, with high consumer visibility and potential retail price effects. Thus his first reference was of ice cream, followed by electricity meters, credit cards, domestic gas appliances and tampons in 1979. His main 'industrial' reference in this period was of 'metal fasteners' (nails, rivets, screws, etc.) in 1976. This was an odd example of a reference that was actually abandoned two years later due, apparently, to difficulty in defining the market and assembling data.[15]

There was a slight increase in the rate of monopoly references after the creation of the OFT, to about four a year, but it was not easy to detect a significant shift in policy. From the point of view of the DGFT the prolonged MMC investigations produced what must have been a disquieting disjuncture. Borrie's ice cream reference was not published as an MMC report until August 1979, three years later, when his own thinking must have faded in time and perhaps been overtaken by market developments. The *Petrol* report, which came at the beginning of 1979, Borrie found very disappointing. The Commission did not find against either exclusive distribution arrangements or against the practice of localised price reductions.[16] Very unusually, Borrie went public with his criticisms, prompting commentators to roast the Commission and to compare it unfavourably with the Price Commission.[17] As if to underline the time lags this had not even been Borrie's reference, having been made by Methven.

A similar picture was seen in mergers and restrictive practices. A distinct increase in the tempo of merger references came into play from 1973 although the public interest test produced a motley range of justifications for reference. In his first annual report Borrie noted that, 'particular attention is currently being given to the relationship of the merger under consideration with the Government's industrial strategy and the extent to which the merger might improve the competitiveness of British industry'.[18] As in the late 1960s, merger policy was operating in the shadow of industrial policy and remained subject to political influence. Within months of taking on the job Borrie found himself recommending the reference of important industrial mergers such as *Pilkington/UKO*, *Babcock and Wilcox/Herbert Morris* and *Freuhauf/Crane Freuhauf*. He also became exposed to the worst kind of Cabinet battle over the sugar industry. He and Shirley Williams had both felt that the Tate and Lyle bid for Manbre and Garton should be referred. Their decision was taken to Cabinet and was overturned. Shirley Williams cited effects on employment in support of her reluctant acceptance that the bid should not be referred. The *Economist* was horrified at this 'scandalous' acceptance of an unambiguous and unpopular monopoly.[19] This baptism of political fire over mergers was an introduction to an area of growing attention and controversy as economists and commentators increasingly drew attention to the downside of mergers. But politics as well as economics continued to provoke confrontation. Thus Borrie and his Minister, now Hattersley, were again over-ruled in Cabinet over the takeover of J. B. Eastwood by Imperial Tobacco. In this case John Silkin and the MAFF, as the sponsoring department, again played the employment card. This time Borrie devoted a paragraph of his annual report to the case, making clear his annoyance and observing that 'this was only the third occasion in the history of the OFT that a Director General's recommendation for a reference to the Commission was not acted upon'.[20] The OFT was exhibiting an increased confidence and independence.

The other aspect of the OFT's competition brief was restrictive practices, which began as a headache and steadily grew into a nightmare. The 'oil and water' combination of administrative monopoly and merger control, and judicial restrictive practices control, created a tension both in operating policy and in explaining it to the business community. The OFT inherited a stringent regime through the Restrictive Practices Register and Court that amounted virtually to a *per se* prohibition on price and market-sharing agreements. Although most other agreements could, in practice, be exempted there was a triple worry that worthwhile agreements might be inhibited, that damaging agreements were avoiding registration by ingenious drafting techniques, and that many agreements were not being registered and were going undetected. Criticism of the system dated back to the 1960s but was mounting in the 1970s and, as we see below, had become overwhelming by the 1980s.

The OFT had inherited a register of about 3,000 agreements in 1973. In 1976 the statutory order came into effect which extended coverage to services. The competition policy staff transferred from the ORRTP found themselves stretched in advising on, and processing, this new body of work. By 1979 there were 3,900 manufacturing agreements on the register and 500 service agreements – a total of 4,400 that was to grow remorselessly to total 14,000 by the time the requirement to furnish agreements was removed in 1999 for all agreements except price fixing. But were they the right agreements? As early as 1977 Borrie was making representations to the DPCP for additional powers to investigate restrictive practices – cartels, in fact. The investigatory powers were modest, the procedures slow, there were no interim powers of control, and minimal penalties. As Sir Bryan Carsberg later complained, 'very little behaviour in Britain is illegal. Almost invariably the approach is to investigate, investigate again, report, and investigate some more.'[21] The OFT was particularly handicapped by a 1969 Court of Appeal judgement in the *Daily Mirror Newspapers v Gardner* case that in order to issue a notice requiring parties to furnish details of a suspected agreement the Director General had to have strong grounds (not just suspicions) for believing that an agreement existed. This put the Director General under a classic 'catch 22' – 'you cannot ask for evidence of a cartel – unless you already have evidence of a cartel'. Despite promises of legislation ministers never remedied this inadequacy and Borrie kept up a constant stream of criticism against 'this almost Gilbertian absurdity'.[22]

Whether the fault was all in the legislation or in the administration was a moot point. It does not seem that the restrictive trade practices case load was scrutinised especially stringently. The staff were dominated by the backlog of cases and in the period up to the late 1980s seemed governed by a desire to process them with a minimum of fuss.[23] The 1968 Restrictive Practices Act had introduced the possibility of securing 'directions' from the Secretary of State allowing exemption of agreements with little economic significance. This became section 21(2) of the 1976 Restrictive Practices Act and it was used prolifically, in over 3,000 cases up to 1990 according to Whish, who was critical of the lack of transparency surrounding this procedure.[24] Later cartel cases served to indicate that the provisions could be used constructively if the administrative determination was present, but for much of the 1970s and 1980s the restrictive trade practices legislation was operated permissively. Thus the machinery for restrictive practices proceedings in the Restrictive Practices Court became largely unused but it was not entirely sidelined. Now and again the OFT found a productive use of the Court, most significantly in the case that the Office began in 1979 to assemble against the Stock Exchange. The Stock Exchange case indicated what a determined Director General could achieve, but also indicated the limits of the competition authorities. Confronted with the massive power of the City, ministers took the case out of the OFT by passing legislation to exempt the Stock Exchange from the Restrictive Trade Practices Act. In return, of course, the City agreed the package of reforms that introduced the 'Big Bang' in 1986. Although annoyed by the Government's pre-emption of the action, Borrie engaged in an understandable piece of triumphalism: 'Without the *commencement* of the litigation', he pointed out, 'there would have been no compulsion, no incentive for the Stock Exchange to give up minimum commissions.'[25]

By 1977 the worst of the industrial confrontation was over. Ministers and officials were closely and sincerely involved with the industrial strategy, which was not as empty as later dismissive accounts imply.[26] The industrial strategy involved sectoral debate, the promulgation of best practice, sectoral indicative planning and facilitative actions by the Treasury and the Department of Industry. The NEDO machinery (under the ubiquitous Ronald McIntosh as Director General from December 1973 to late 1977), with its Sector Working Parties, was at the heart of the process. The macro-economic climate had also stabilised after the 1976 sterling crisis and the International Monetary Fund loan. The 'winter of discontent' was still a year away and the minds of ministers turned to the hardy perennial of the reform of competition policy.

The next two years saw yet another appraisal of competition policy which, in many respects, constituted an uncanny re-run of 1968–70. The policy review was prompted by three pressures. First, there was the central role being played by the industrial strategy, the difficulty of co-ordinating competition policy with the industrial strategy and its associated agencies (the NEDC and the NEB in particular), and Roy Hattersley's concern to have his department more closely involved. Second, there was something of a sea change in perceptions of the development of the industrial economy. A series of studies from the late 1960s onwards had underlined the growth in industrial concentration and the dominance of the economy by a limited number of huge enterprises. Indeed, the opportunity to influence, and to manipulate, the dominant companies was the rationale behind the idea of planning agreements.[27] Work by Hannah, Utton and especially by Prais had brought the issues to the forefront and provoked a wide debate.[28] At the same time there was an evolving perception that mergers led to industrial concentration (an idea rather obvious but nonetheless challenged[29]) but that mergers in themselves did not necessarily create greater efficiency. Hence it was felt that these changing economic perspectives needed urgently to be fed into the policy process. A third factor was the desire of officials in the main economic departments to reinforce competition policy and to avoid a complete incorporation of policy into the industrial strategy – thus the advocacy of an inter-departmental committee to conduct the review.

This was the backdrop to the two 'Liesner reports' of 1978 and 1979 on Monopolies and Mergers and on Restrictive Practices. The monopolies report was announced in November 1977 and undertaken under some time pressure. In the spring of 1977 Hattersley had already hinted, in a move identical with Barbara Castle's plans for the PIB/MC combination, that he was pondering a merger of the MMC into the newly expanded Price Commission. Hattersley's plans were contingent on the Liesner report and perhaps delayed by it. Hans Liesner was Chief Economic Adviser to the three ex-DTI departments of Trade, Industry, and Prices and Consumer Protection. He had come into the civil service after holding a Cambridge Fellowship in economics but was known for his work on European trade integration rather than for a specialism in competition policy. His Committee drew its membership from three further departments (MAFF, the Foreign Office and the Treasury) and from the OFT. It was a Committee strongly influenced by economists and its report provided an excellent summary of current economic thinking as well as policy suggestions. We can briefly review its analysis before moving to recommendations and impact.

Broadly the report registered a shift of analytical opinion towards large firms and towards mergers. In the 1960s large firms had been thought to be unproblematic and possibly desirable as far as industrial efficiency was concerned. The 'national champion' concept had considerable attractions.[30] Now the argument was more agnostic. Much attention was given to the increased dominance of large firms and the associated increase in industrial concentration – both aggregate concentration and that within given product markets. The broad trends of increased concentration were examined and accepted. Thus over 40 per cent of industrial activity was now accounted for by the largest one hundred private companies; and the five-firm concentration ratio indicated that in fully a quarter of product markets over 90 per cent of output was accounted for by the top five firms. Thus the report confirmed a picture of a Britain dominated by large firms, operating in oligopolistic markets, and displaying these characteristics to a greater extent than any other major industrial power. The report also gave weight to current research, which was critical of the efficiency effects of mergers and regarded many of them, in the words of Meeks's influential study, as 'disappointing'.[31] Thus 'mergers are often found to be unprofitable by those carrying them out and little in the way of efficiency gains seems to be realised'.[32] This was a major shift of posture. The accumulated weight of analysis confirmed a need to define and apply a more rigorous and sceptical policy on monopolies and mergers. This was something of a victory for the OFT economists and for the head of its economics branch, Martin Howe, who, together with David Elliott, had prepared much of the background analysis.[33]

In developing policy options to reflect the analysis the group drew extensively on the record of MMC reports covering monopolies, mergers and the general references analysed by Denys Gribbin. In this respect the exercise was faithful to the original investigatory origins of the MMC. Just as the *Collective Discrimination* report had drawn together the experience of the first seven years, so now the Liesner group could draw out lessons from the later reports. On monopolies it noted that in only three out of the thirty-two reports published between 1959 and 1976 had the Commission given the industry a complete bill of health (in *Flat Glass*, *Cigarette Filter Rods* and *Dog and Cat Foods*). Nonetheless, the Committee was not prepared to argue that large firms, oligopoly or industrial concentration were in themselves intrinsically undesirable. Instead it analysed the types of practice typically criticised in MMC reports. It identified a set of discriminatory practices which amounted to 'behavioural type entry barriers' and which could be targeted by *per se* prohibitions or by small-scale investigations. This condemnation of practices such as restriction on the sale of competitors' goods, and full line forcing, led to the recommendation that 'consideration should therefore be given to dealing with such practices on a more general basis than can be provided by MMC monopoly investigations'.[34] This was the origin of the anti-competitive practice proposals which were developed further in the 'Liesner 2' Green Paper on Restrictive Trade Practices published in 1979 and which were later incorporated into the 1980 Competition Act.

The Green Paper trod a very careful path between the competition policy and the industrial policy camps. In reality it should be seen as a defence of competition policy and it failed to give ammunition to the interventionists. Thus it argued that competition policy and industrial policy were 'complementary' but that competition policy should be 'flexible'. There was decided tension within the Committee and the industrial policy proponents had pressed hard for this acceptance of 'flexibility'. But the victory was rather empty since the degree of flexibility (shorthand for permitting industrial policy-approved mergers) depended ultimately on the machinery of implementation, and here no change was suggested. The group sat squarely on the fence over Hattersley's preference for merging the Price Commission and the MMC. The Price Commission was seen as 'reinforcing' competition policy and it was felt that there could be 'advantage in bringing the MMC and the Price Commission together in due course'. The most radical proposal actually worked counter to the rationalising tendencies of the industrial strategy and came in the proposal that the balance of evidence in merger cases should be tipped from broadly favourable to 'neutral'. This was a very important proposal explored at some length.[35] A full-scale presumption against merger was rejected, partly on grounds of practicality – it would have implied virtually all mergers going to the MMC. A neutral approach was expected to increase the MMC workload by three to four times. Allied with changing the burden of proof, the group advocated changing the MMC's criteria to analyse whether a merger was likely to prevent, restrict or distort competition, and also to amend the public interest test to stress both competition and international competitiveness. For the Merger Panel it advocated a two-stage process (that actually looks rather like the later European Merger Task Force procedure). The impact of this change of stance would, it accepted, have had a 'marked effect' on the operation of policy.[36] The proposal was not taken up, either then or by the successor Tory Government, a failure that was 'a disappointment to many economists'.[37] One of the authors remarked in retrospect that perhaps the recommendation of neutrality over mergers was just too subtle, attractive to insiders but unlikely to fire the imagination of ministers.[38]

This comprehensive policy review thus reflected and confirmed the traditional British approach. It concluded that 'the present broad pattern of UK monopoly and mergers policy is still best suited to the needs of our economy'.[39] This is particularly noteworthy in that the Committee had looked at a range of other national systems and studied the European regime. Here it concluded that 'no fundamental change is necessary on the UK's part in the light of EEC policy and practice'.[40] Was this a missed opportunity? As reviewed in the next section, British policy spent the next twenty years coming to grips with the European model. At this time, however, European policy was if anything weaker than the British regime. Also the focus of the group was on mergers and article 86. The Liesner 2 Green Paper on Restrictive Practices was rather more revealing on Europe and article 85. Although it argued for retention of the British 'form-based system' it did so unconvincingly and almost, it seemed, against its own logic. Indeed, at one point the report accepts that 'if restrictive practices legislation were now being introduced for the first time, there would be much to be said for adopting a full effects system'.[41] This Green Paper was published in March 1979, two months before the election and eighteen years of Conservative government. The Conservatives proceeded to pass the Competition Act, with its provisions for control of anti-competitive agreements, but the debate over restrictive practices and the European model languished for another ten years.

Where did competition policy stand on the eve of the great neoliberal revolution that came to be known as Thatcherism? The OFT was secure. Gordon Borrie was an effective Director General and the Office had played an important role in the major policy review which had consolidated its mix of responsibilities. Indeed, the debate had become one about the strengthening of competition policy, although the form it was taking was to canvass the merger of the MMC and the Price Commission. For the MMC therefore, the position was far less secure. In the early 1970s it had chalked up some significant victories. Thus the Hoffman La Roche report in 1973 had been regarded as a great breakthrough and yielded very substantial repayments to the Department of Health and Social Security – it asked Roche for £11 mn in 1973.[42] The *Parallel Pricing* general report in 1973 was also well received and helped to mould the OFT's early reference profile, while the *Insulated Electric Wires and Cables* inquiry successfully uncovered a raft of restrictive agreements and also generated repayments, this time of £9 mn to the Post Office. The nine reports on professional services in 1976 constituted a significant and sustained attack on restrictive practices in the professions. At the same time some reports had been poorly received, continuing complaints were heard over procedure, and, as reviewed in chapter 5, the Commission was facing a replay of the 1969–70 problem of a threatened merger with the Price Commission.

In 1979 things had not gone so far as in 1969 and legislation had not been introduced but Godfray Le Quesne (who had become Chairman in 1975) was certainly concerned about the future of the MMC. He recalls that the MMC was treated very openly and he had no complaints about Roy Hattersley's approach to the issues, but the MMC had an utterly different approach to inquiries and an utterly different function from the Price Commission. The MMC was much more independent and, with understatement, Sir Godfray observed that it was 'a good thing that did not happen'.[43] In fact the MMC absorbed some staff from the abolished Price Commission (see p. 249). In the MMC's favour was its current involvement in the policy process through its general inquiry into full-line forcing and tie-in sales which had been made by Hattersley in April 1979 as a direct result of recommendations in Liesner 2. Moreover, here was a Government committed to competition and the market. The OFT and the MMC might have expected a substantial boost to their resources as the duo of Keith Joseph and John Nott took over the reins at Industry and the DPCP.

At this point we can turn to the development of competition policy under the Conservatives after 1979. This was a Party which left office in 1997 in a blaze of Euro-scepticism but whose views about Europe were complex. The Conservatives' natural suspicions of European bureaucracy and state intervention were tempered with an admiration for the concept of a free trade area, deregulation and the single market. This ambiguity about Europe was reflected also in ambiguity about European competition policy and, as an overture to the reform of policy in the late 1990s, we should examine the nature and impact of 'Europe' on British competition policy.

The reluctant suitor: the UK and European competition law

There has been an extraordinary hesitancy in the British approach to European competition rules. At first blush the startling aspect of the 1998 Competition Act is not that it embraces the European approach, but that it has taken twenty five-years after membership of the Community to cross the bridge. British policy makers initially rejected the rigour and dogmatism of American antitrust and latterly rejected the comprehensiveness and economism of the European approach. For the British, it could be argued, American law was too tough on companies, European law was too tough on politicians, and both regimes attached altogether too much importance to competition. Instead the British, as argued in chapter 1, developed a unique and flexible system which catered to the peculiarities of British administration and British capitalism. The long-standing hostility to the European regime reflected a basic tribal incompatibility. The European system embodied elements and assumptions which were (and perhaps still are) quite alien to British practices. In particular the European system sprang from an Austrian–German conception of the role of competition and regulation in a market economy. This conception stressed the importance of an orderly, stable and objective market order detached from politics and existing as an 'economic constitution' of the state. This ordo-liberal vision was to be reinforced by agencies which had an independent legal existence and which sought to meld economic and legal principles in a specialised and superior body of law. The Germans did not wholly succeed in achieving this vision in the BundesKartellamt but the conception was of an autonomous monopoly office, 'the function of the monopoly office was to apply objective criteria. It thus needed career specialists with a high level of economic and legal training, and they had to be largely protected from outside political or pecuniary interests.' Indeed, 'the monopoly office is as indispensable as the highest court'.[44] This almost metaphysical elevation of competition policy into semi-constitutional status meant that it should be virtually immune from political interference (an understandable aim in the light of twentieth-century German history), and it would therefore be applied sometimes in ways that would inconvenience the government of the day. Nothing could be more objectionable to British officials with their instinctive and profound commitment to administrative discretion and ministerial responsibility. The fact that the European competition rules inherited this philosophical approach and, to a limited degree, incorporated these principles of administration, made them a natural object of suspicion.

It would be exceptional for British officials or politicians to express their disquiet about the European competition rules in such a developed or philosophical fashion and there were, in any case, more immediate and obvious sources of rejection. In the early years of the 1960s British policy makers took an interest in the competition rules, even after the de Gaulle veto of British membership in 1963. It was clear that the rules were capable of being applied expansively and effectively after the *Grundig* case of 1964. Briefly, in *Grundig* the European Court of Justice prohibited any system of distribution which conferred absolute territorial protection and confirmed that the 'effect on trade' provisions of Article 85 could be interpreted widely to catch agreements with only an indirect or potential effect on trade between the member states. In addition, Regulation 17 of 1962 ensured that DG IV of the European Commission would be an independent and potentially powerful administrative actor. Accordingly the European rules were seriously analysed both in the internal debates leading up to the 1965 Act and in the CBI's Trade Policy Committee. At this point, however, they were embryonic and, with a Eurosceptic President of the BoT in the shape of Douglas Jay, the European model was not regarded as a serious option.

By the time of the 1973 Fair Trading Act a superficial coincidence of timing would suggest that this was the perfect moment at which to move to a European model, just as Britain was joining the Community. In reality, as we saw in chapter 6, the main assessment of policy was undertaken in 1970 and officials had drawn up a draft Bill by the summer of 1971. It was not until May 1971 that Heath and Pompidou had agreed the principle of British entry, and not until October that Parliament had accepted it.[45] Not only did the impetus of British entry come late in the day, the European Communities Bill had to be fought through the House during 1972. It was the centrepiece of the Parliament (and squeezed out the Fair Trading Bill, as noted in chapter 6[46]). Even so, the DTI's inclination to revisit the question would hardly have been enhanced with the vehemently Eurosceptic Nicholas Ridley as Parliamentary Under-Secretary of State. Further, membership of the Community was still the subject of heated controversy. The bi-partisan basis for the reorientation of a major plank of economic policy simply did not exist. It was also the case that European competition policy was implemented tentatively. DG IV was small and only gradually developing its competence, the principles of European control were emerging but most energy was being expended on vertical agreements. British officials noted that the major objective of European policy was integration of the market and much of that policy seemed almost irrelevant to a British economy preoccupied with concentration and mergers. At this time European control of horizontal agreements was in its infancy with landmark cases such as the *Dyestuffs* price cartel (which featured ICI prominently) decided by the Court in 1972. Monopoly control was virtually non-existent. The concept of dominance under Article 86 was not defined until later in the 1970s with the *United Brands* case in 1978 and *Hoffman La Roche* in 1979,[47] and European control over oligopoly was, and remains, the weakest element in the European competence. Thus the passage of the Fair Trading Act as a purely British approach to competition policy was logical. We have seen that Geoffrey Howe rejected the CBI's advocacy of the European approach (see p. 185) and George and Joll noted in 1975 that 'it is not possible to discern in the Fair Trading Act 1973 any marked impact of Community membership'.[48] For another ten years European policy and UK policy developed in separate spheres.

As noted above, the 1978 and 1979 Liesner Green Papers were far less dismissive of European law and practice. They did not endorse European models but they did concede many of the emerging strengths in the application of Article 85. These pointers were not picked up by the incoming Conservative Government, which instead moved quickly to introduce the 1980 Competition Act which gave effect to the proposals for control of anti-competitive practices recommended in the Green Papers. As we saw in chapter 8, the consideration of policy was superficial and the Act was driven by the political urgency to abolish the Price Commission. The incremental approach was expressed by Sally Oppenheim, who called the Bill 'a natural evolution in competition policy'.[49] Not that ministers were under any particular pressure to take the European road. In a two-stage second reading debate that was often passionate and sometimes perceptive the whole issue was overshadowed by the Price Commission and control of prices. Ministers came under pressure to reinforce policy and to steer additional resources into the MMC but, extraordinarily, there was not a single mention of the European competition rules. The Minister, John Nott, made several references to the avoidance of undue legalism to which American-style *per se* prohibitions could give rise, but made no reference at all to a European alternative.[50] Indeed, in an adjournment debate later in 1980 the Parliamentary Under-Secretary of State, Reginald Eyre, noted that the Liesner review had considered and rejected the European approach to the reform of restrictive practices. He pinned the colours of the Conservative Government to the same mast, noting that 'we accept this general conclusion'.[51] Within five years, however, the Government's view had undergone a radical transformation and by 1985 the DTI was looking very seriously at the utility of Article 85. Thus in June 1986 Paul Channon announced a review of policy on mergers and restrictive practices, to be undertaken, once again, by a man who was by now becoming 'Mr Competition Policy' – Hans Liesner, still Chief Economic Adviser and now also a Deputy Secretary in the DTI. So what had changed, why had the European approach come into favour?

The early 1980s saw one of those seismic shifts in the national psyche which sociologists could express in terms of symbols or cognitive frameworks, but which might better be expressed in Shakespearian language as 'a tide in the affairs of man which, taken at the flood, leads on to fortune'.[52] The tide was the European market, which became the reference point for industry and the new framework for economic policy makers. The idea of 'the market' is one of the most complex in economic thought, but as far as policy makers were concerned the revelation was borne in that the European market was a reality and could be manipulated by British policy makers and companies. This broadening of horizons to embrace a European landscape was accompanied by a reduction of suspicion. Margaret Thatcher's determined pursuit of a British rebate secured a big refund in 1983 and an agreed rebate formula at Fontainebleau in June 1984. Relations with the Community entered something of a honeymoon and the British redefined the European vision in their own minds as a market. Mrs Thatcher later regarded this as a delusion and bitterly regretted her agreement to the Single European Act but, at the time, she felt that 'the first fruits of what would be called the Single European Act were good for Britain. At last, I felt, we were going to get the Community back on course, concentrating on its role as a huge market, with all the opportunities that would bring to our industries.'[53] The single market programme was, of course, a British-inspired initiative based on Arthur Cockfield's 1985 White Paper. It said very little explicitly about competition policy but it greatly boosted the influence of DG IV and tied the European competition authorities firmly into a neo-liberal mission of market creation. This was important in that it diverted suspicions that European competition policy was unduly politicised and too often biased by objectives of industrial policy. Suspicion was also alleviated by the character and performance of the competition commissioners who held robustly free-market views, from 1985 Peter Sutherland and from 1989 the reassuring figure of Leon Brittan.

The combination of the seductive allure of the single market, and better relations between the Government and the Community, increased interest in the European competition rules, which had begun to have a more effective role. It was not until the early 1980s that the European regime began to develop in a serious and effective fashion. At the beginning of the decade it was still a peripheral competence, by the end of the 1980s it had become the most effective antitrust regime in the world.[54] This startling transformation can be illustrated in a number of ways. One could point to the increasing ambition of Article 85 prosecutions, the steps to implement Article 86 (and to apply it to mergers), the moves to attack public monopolies under Article 90, and the creation of the merger regulation after sixteen years of lobbying. In this the remorselessly supportive and teleological judgements of the European Court of Justice were of fundamental importance, but so, too, was the morale of the Commission and its staff, who began to demonstrate a zeal, effectiveness and evangelism which was in marked contrast to the hesitant 1970s. The importance of the competition rules began to be borne in on large European companies by the growing willingness of DG IV to impose fines. In the early days fines were rare and trivial but in 1983 the Court agreed that large and punitive fines, designed to have a deterrent effect, were acceptable and the Commission proceeded to use them.[55] Fines were financially unwelcome but, equally important, provoked damaging and embarrassing publicity. Senior management began to take the European rules far more seriously. More attention was paid to competition lawyers, and big, vulnerable firms such as ICI began to set up compliance programmes (which nevertheless did not prevent later transgressions and fines). The shift of emphasis from a strictly UK to a European focus was nicely symbolised by the dentists. In 1950 dental goods had provided the MRPC with its first case upon which to cut its teeth. In 1985 the British Dental Goods Trade Association was again in trouble, this time with DG IV for excluding overseas competitors from its trade fairs. It was fined ECU 100,000[56] thus suffering a judgement and a penalty that was beyond the powers of the British authorities to impose.

The importance of European competition law to companies, and the maturation of the law itself and of DG IV as an agency, went hand in hand with the growing influence of law and the lawyers. Competition law as an important and lucrative specialism mushroomed in the mid 1980s with tremendous growth in the competition sections of the big City law firms and the creation of substantial offices in Brussels. There was similarly a rapid growth in the legal discourse with the development of principles and doctrines which have hardened into accepted wisdom. Specialised journals such as the *European Competition Law Review* date from 1979 and the standard texts emerged in the mid 1980s.[57] The assumptions and priorities associated with an increasing legal dominance of this policy area have a considerable effect. The 'community' of competition specialists is increasingly made up of lawyers who move from company, to practice, to competition agencies, to the courts, the legislature and to the administration itself, and who lubricate the system. Their views about what is proper and acceptable mould expectations and bias reform proposals.

The reorientation of competition policy in the mid 1980s grew from a positive shift in attitudes to 'Europe' and also from a negative dissatisfaction with the operation of restrictive practices law. A further pressure, which produced a strong sense that policy needed to be reviewed, was the rekindled controversy over merger policy, the merger boom and the adequacy of the British system of control. This was a matter of great interest to ministers, MPs and the public (nicely symbolised by the Nestle hostile takeover of Rowntree in April 1988 which aroused deeply felt sentiments). Although the 'Liesner mark 3' 1988 DTI consultation paper on mergers suggested only incremental improvements, it represented both an official unease and a sense that mergers and competition policy generally had to become sensitive to the European context.[58] It is likely that the DTI decided upon a decisive shift in policy during 1986–87, following an internal review set up by Leon Brittan before he left the DTI in January 1986. The June 1987 election then intervened and the policy was not made public until Lord Young's Enterprise White Paper in January 1988 – and not outlined in detail until a Green Paper in March 1988. Lord Young's memoirs show him to be much more involved in merger policy than with restrictive practices. He talks at some length about merger referrals and about efforts to streamline and explain merger policy, but he does not mention restrictive practices or the Green Paper.[59] This might again reinforce impressions of a policy driven by officials because the Green Paper contains the initial commitment to a major reorientation of policy. The Paper declares that 'the registration system will be scrapped', to be replaced with a prohibition approach based on the principle of 'effects on competition'. It would create an Article 85-type system in Britain which would 'align' British law with EC cartel law. The aim would be to incorporate 'into UK law as much of the principles of Community law as seemed appropriate'.[60] As far as institutions were concerned the DTI opted for an OFT with discretionary power similar to DG IV, although appeal would be to the Restrictive Practices Court (the idea of the Competition Commission Tribunal came with the White Paper in 1989).[61] The new competition policy was thus a child of the 1980s. It was devised in 1986, publicised in 1988 and formalised in the 1989 White Paper. The Conservatives then sat on it for eight long years and accepted the prolonged and infuriating delays summarised in the chronology in table 23. Why the delay? This is examined further below. It was undoubtedly mixed up with the deep divisions opening up within the Conservative Party over Europe. Policy reform was caught in a double bind. The DTI ministers in favour of free competitive markets were virulently anti-European (especially Ridley, Lilley and Redwood) while the pro-Europeans were sceptical about excessive competition (chiefly Heseltine). In the meantime, however, the existing British institutions had to sustain administration of the traditional policy.

Table 23 *The 1998 Competition Act: chronology of reform*

June	1985	Internal market White Paper launched and endorsed at the Milan Summit. Includes the 1992 programme
December	1985	Leon Brittan, Secretary of State for Trade and Industry, initiates internal DTI review of competition policy
February	1986	Signature of the Single European Act
June	1986	Paul Channon announces review of law and policy on mergers and restrictive trade practices. Inter-departmental Committee Chaired by Hans Liesner
June	1987	Conservative election victory. Lord Young becomes Secretary of State for Trade and Industry
October	1987	Young's interim statement on mergers stresses competition
January	1988	*DTI – The Department for Enterprise*, Cm 278, outlines some changes in the merger regime
March	1988	*Mergers Policy, A DTI Paper on the Policy and Procedures of Merger Control* proposes modest changes through statutory pre-notification and undertakings in lieu of reference
March	1988	*Review of Restrictive Trade Practices Policy*, Cm 331, Green Paper. Proposes 'alignment' with EC cartel law but retention of Restrictive Practices Court. Followed by extensive consultation

–	1989	*Companies Act 1989* enacts incremental changes in merger policy
July	1989	*Opening Markets: New Policy on Restrictive Trade Practices*, Cm 727, White Paper. Announces a prohibition approach very similar to Article 85 and with a Competition Tribunal within the MMC
July	1989	Nicholas Ridley replaces Lord Young at the DTI. John Redwood as Minister for Corporate Affairs
November	1989	John Major succeeds Margaret Thatcher as Prime Minister
July	1990	Trade and Industry Sub-committee starts inquiry into mergers and takeovers
October	1990	EC merger regulation comes into effect
December	1991	Trade and Industry Sub-committee report on mergers is published; fails to make significant impact
December	1991	Maastricht Treaty signed and endorsed in Commons debate
January	1992	Appointment of Bryan Carsberg as DGFT announced (from June 1992)
April	1992	Conservative election victory. Michael Heseltine becomes President of the BoT with Neil Hamilton as Parliamentary Under-Secretary of State
November	1992	*Abuse of Market Power: A Consultative Document on Possible Legislative Options*, Cm 2100, Green Paper. Outlines three options of strengthen, prohibition, dual system. Extensive consultation follows
December	1992	Graeme Odgers announced as new Chairman of the MMC
April	1993	Neil Hamilton announces intention to adopt option 1, to strengthen the Fair Trading Act
July	1993	Major finally wins a confidence motion on ratification of the Maastricht Treaty
September	1993	*Consultation Exercise on Possible Changes to Competition Legislation and Procedures to Reduce the Burden on Business*, report by the DTI and the OFT. Results in raised thresholds, speed-up of investigation and extension of statutory undertakings. Derived from

		consultation with business as part of deregulation initiative
January	1994	DTI announces changes to be incorporated in the Deregulation and Contracting Out Act
May	1994	John Smith dies. Tony Blair becomes Labour leader
May	1994	John Watts MP launches the 'Competition Forum' to agitate for law reform
November	1994	Bryan Carsberg announces intention to resign as DGFT
December	1994	TIC announces inquiry into 'the effectiveness of the MMC'
January	1995	Carsberg gives 'stunning' TIC evidence arguing for a unitary authority
May	1995	Carsberg leaves the OFT
May	1995	TIC report, *UK Policy on Monopolies*, critical of MMC, presses for legislation and unitary authority
July	1995	Following leadership election Michael Heseltine becomes Deputy Prime Minister and Ian Lang becomes Secretary of State for Trade and Industry
July	1995	DTI publishes response to the TIC report: 'not persuaded'
August	1995	John Bridgeman announced as next DGFT, from October
March	1996	*Tackling Cartels and the Abuse of Market Power*, consultative document from DTI
August	1996	*Tackling Cartels and the Abuse of Market Power: A Draft Bill*, an explanatory document from the DTI. Embodies the Article 85 prohibition but rejects Article 86 (consistent with the 1993 announcement)
May	1997	Labour election victory, Margaret Beckett becomes Secretary of State for Trade and Industry
August	1997	Graeme Odgers resigns as Chairman of the MMC
August	1997	*A Prohibition Approach to Anti-competitive Agreements and Abuse of Dominant Position: A Draft Bill* accepts Article 86-type prohibition but retains Fair Trading Act powers. No action on mergers. Creation of a new Competition Commission. Further consultation invited

October	1997	*Competition Bill* published for introduction into the House of Lords. Some technical and procedural changes from August draft. but main points retained
November	1998	*Competition Act 1998* receives Royal Assent
April	1999	New Competition Commission replaces the MMC
March	2000	Act comes into effect

Parallel universes: EC and UK competition policy

European competition policy is unusual in that neither the Council nor the national authorities have direct influence over its operation. It escapes all the convoluted implementation through committees that goes under the name of 'comitology'. Instead the Treaty and the key regulations allow DG IV to operate policy with almost complete independence, with the exception that it requires Council approval for new legislation such as regulations to create block exemptions. In practice it liaises with the national 'competent authorities', which in the UK includes the DTI, the OFT and the MMC (for mergers only). The authorities are represented in the Advisory Committee on Restrictive Practices and Monopolies, they have the right to attend hearings and, since 1990, they also attend the Advisory Committee on Concentrations, which deals with mergers. There is procedural law guaranteeing the national authorities access to case material and rights to participate. In these meetings individual cases are discussed and so also are drafts of subordinate legislation such as regulations or block exemptions. This machinery is important. Although the Committees are advisory their reports can be published (at the discretion of the Commission) and Commission officials will think carefully before they act contrary to the unanimous advice of a Committee. The Advisory Committees keep OFT and DTI officials abreast of developments in important cases and give them some influence in the European administrative process over, for instance, negative clearances, exemptions and the level of fines.[62] Since 1973 the OFT has been participating in meetings and hearings, sometimes intensively. In 1984, for instance, it attended fifty-four Brussels engagements, by the late 1990s it would be more like two hundred. This has required the Office to develop a clear view of the principles of European law and their application. It has also been possible to explore the treatment of similar issues under the two regimes.

Cross-fertilisation between the competition authorities has been impeded by the political realities of dealings between Whitehall and Brussels which means that questions of policy development, and participation in significant hearings, were for many years undertaken by DTI officials. For its part the OFT is in constant discussion with DG IV on a daily basis and over multiple issues. Since 1997 it has also begun to take part in the more substantive and delicate discussions with Brussels. For the DTI and ministers, therefore, contact with DG IV was likely to be concerned with protecting British national interests – which means protecting British companies – as well as with a more objective debate over the development of policy. Thus the DTI represented British interests in, for instance, hearings on big cartel cases and may have sought to justify the actions of British companies (and certainly to try to reduce the level of fines). This balance is reflected in Lord Young's experience at the DTI. Although the decisive White Paper on restrictive practices was issued in his name he again makes no mention of it in his memoirs. Instead he was preoccupied with merger policy and references, including the difficult Lonhro case; and with monopoly reports, especially the *Beer* report, which caused him immense political difficulty. In effect the brewers forced him to make substantial concessions, a fascinating use of raw political muscle which hastened his departure from office.[63] His contacts with Brussels and with Peter Sutherland were over state aid rather than competition policy. He had a sequence of difficult meetings during the spring of 1987 to defend the state aid going to lubricate the BAe takeover of Rover. The position was so desperate that he describes his June meeting with Sutherland as 'the single most important meeting of my entire decade in government'.[64] There is little evidence that ministers at the DTI were gaining an appreciation and respect for the European competition regime. Their endorsement of the European approach owed more to their officials, who were, in turn, influenced by informed opinion and by the preferences of large companies which were learning to live with the requirements of DG IV.

At the level of cases and the implementation of policy European questions did not begin to make an impact until the late 1980s. It was not until 1988 that Gordon Borrie even mentioned DG IV in his annual report but, when he retired in 1992, he conceded that 'the European dimension' had constituted 'one of the biggest changes during my period of office'.[65] By then the merger regulation had come into effect, a development which gravely concerned Sydney Lipworth and the DTI as well as Borrie. For the MMC the turning point was the *Beer* report published in March 1989. This was an extraordinary, bold and controversial report. It took the rare step of recommending divestment and, under the subsequent beer orders, brewers owning over 2,000 licensed premises were required to dispose of half the excess. For the Commission and the industry a major factor was the EC block exemption (1984/83) for certain exclusive purchasing agreements. The exemption has special provisions for beer which effectively allowed the tied house system. The brewers argued that the EC exemption took precedence over UK law and negated an MMC inquiry. The beer orders, although appreciably weaker than the MMC recommendations, were nonetheless stronger than the EC regulation. DG IV did not object to them, arguing 'that this was not incompatible with the supremacy of EEC law since it did not strike at the root of the block exemption'.[66] The case left unresolved the question of whether individual or block exemptions under Article 85(3) can legally be overridden by the UK competition authorities. The issue remained undecided up to 1998, mainly because the European Court had backed away from the issue and had avoided giving an unambiguous judgement on the relative status of exemptions under EC law and measures taken under national law.[67]

For the MMC the *Beer* case brought home the importance of EC law and its potential to influence inquiries. Since then an increasing number of MMC inquiries have been affected by European provisions or actions. The European issue can have an indirect effect on the reasoning but its powerful direct effect is on the definition and application of remedies. European influences have been seen in *Petrol* (1990), *Carbonated Drinks* (1991), *New Motor Cars* (1992) and *Fine Fragrances* (1993). It has also had an impact on mergers such as *P&O/Stena* (1997). In some industries the parallel development of UK and EU jurisprudence provided an extraordinary interweaving of thinking and precedent. This is especially true in the case of ice cream, which provides a rather unlikely example of an industry where recent development has been absolutely dominated by a sequence of competition cases. In the UK there were MMC reports in 1994 and 1998, and a new reference in 1999. In Europe the Commission was dealing with similar issues of freezer exclusivity in Germany and Ireland. This retailing method involves ice cream manufacturers providing freezers free of charge on the condition that they are used exclusively for the sale of the manufacturer's products. For many small outlets, with room for only one freezer, this therefore prohibits sale of competitors' products. The MMC report in 1994 was limited by the reference to retail outlets and did not find against this technique but DG IV was more robust. Commentators were very critical of the MMC report and one observed that 'the fact that the MMC once again appears to be manifestly out of line with its senior authority DG IV should hasten the process of a thorough review and reform of UK national competition laws'.[68] The concept of the 'superior authority' is revealing, as is the expectation (not the legal requirement) that the MMC should conform to EU practice.

Accordingly the MMC liases increasingly with Brussels over parallel cases, to verify the parties' accounts of dealings with DG IV and to explore legal interpretation. Where there is comment on specific inquiries the Commission is careful to refer to it explicitly in the report. The importance of European links has been underlined by the new Act, in preparation for which the Commission's senior legal adviser undertook a three-month posting in Brussels during 1998. DG IV is genuinely committed to greater subsidiarity, as demonstrated by its 1997 notice on Co-operation with National Competition Authorities.

The endorsement of an Article 85 prohibition to replace the restrictive trade practices legislation had been relatively easy. The administration of the law itself was in disrepute and the legislation had few friends. Moreover, Article 85 was regarded as simple, comprehensible and increasingly effective. But in the monopolies and mergers area the decisions were much more difficult. As we have seen, the OFT and the MMC were operating British policy successfully. Their encounters with European law were becoming more frequent but they were quite manageable and the two systems were running reasonably in parallel. The pressures for reform were not emerging from the administration of policy.

Biting the European bullet

In retrospect the passage from the 1989 White Paper to the eventual incorporation of the principles of European competition law into the 1998 Competition Act has the stamp of inevitability. There seems little logical alternative. In this light the extraordinary feature of the 1998 Act was not the revolutionary change in British competition law, or the momentous adoption of the *acquis communautaire*, but the cautious and conditional way in which it was done. The resistance to European legal principles had several facets but became dominant through ministerial concern. In this sense party politics did become atypically important in the evolution of legislation, but in the form of intra-party rather than inter-party confrontation.

The prolonged debate over legislation had some important, if subtle, effects. Most importantly, the delays, the indecision and the reluctance even to legislate the half-way house of reform of restrictive practices encouraged the Labour Government to go for 'The Full Monty'[69] with a comprehensive Act. Further, the debate gave time for the regime of utility regulation to settle down and made room for the bold step of allowing the utility regulators concurrent powers under the legislation in respect of their sectors. This area will provide one of the least certain aspects of the new law (see chapter 8). In addition, the ten-year delay saw a maturation of the European regime itself. DG IV lost some of its hubris in the face of enhanced control by the Court of First Instance and it developed an awareness of the necessity for subsidiarity. This opened up the promise of a smoother and more creative partnership with the European authorities.

Throughout this period, 1989–98, several debates were conducted, in parallel and with reciprocal effects. There was a debate, first, on the strength of UK policy and the perennial question of the relationship between competition policy and industrial policy. Second was a debate, on the nature and attraction of the European model and, from the reverse perspective, on the strengths of the British model. Third, there was an important debate about the administration of policy, the involvement of politicians and the relative merits of a tripartite or a unitary system. We go on to review these debates and to trace their influence on the new regime established under the 1998 Act.

The debate on the activism of UK competition policy posed some powerful challenges to the MMC and involved also harsh criticism of the DTI under Heseltine. The strength of the criticism symbolised something of a sea change in the reception of UK competition policy. It was in some ways a compliment to the importance of policy and also expressed an impatience with its traditional pro-industry bias. For the MMC, the turn of the decade saw the Commission sustaining a rugged independence. The extraordinary level of activity over 1988 and 1989 prompted Sydney Lipworth to talk of the Commission 'buzzing' – this was in a complimentary profile following his 1988 *Annual Review*.[70] The first signs of trouble came with the *Beer* report. The DTI found itself unable fully to implement the recommendations on divestiture and backed down in the face of fearsome pressure from the brewers during the summer of 1989. The brewers launched a huge, high profile media campaign against the Commission. Its recommendations were likened to Henry VIII dissolving the monasteries and to the Luftwaffe bombing London. The focus in 1990–91, however, was on mergers. In July 1990 Peter Lilley

announced the 'Lilley Doctrine', which was to resist nationalisation by
the back door through takeover of British companies by state-owned foreign companies. Observers identified this position also with John Redwood, the Parliamentary Under-Secretary of State, and together Lilley
and Redwood referred five foreign takeovers to the Commission, three
against the advice of the DGFT. The Commission found against the
merger in only one case (*Kemira Oy/ICI*) and on the basis of an orthodox competition analysis found no problems with the other four. On this
basis ministers had no option under the Fair Trading Act but to allow the
takeovers and, in a speech in July 1991, Peter Lilley accepted that the
Doctrine could not be sustained. He cited the MMC reports, and the
view that the Commission could not work on a general presumption, and
conceded that 'I too will take account of the findings in the reports so far
published in deciding whether or not to refer any future cases that arise.'[71]
Although the CBI had welcomed the Lilley Doctrine its demise was seen
as evidence of the MMC's independence.

Later in 1991 the storm clouds began to gather. In December the
long-awaited Trade and Industry Sub-committee report on mergers recommended strengthening the Commission (with full-time Deputy
Chairmen, for instance). The Committee, Chaired by Kenneth Warren
MP also, however, recommended that the OFT and MMC be combined
into a unitary Competition and Mergers Authority. Otherwise, most of its
recommendations were modest and in fact generated little change. From
here the attention shifted from mergers to monopolies and the MMC
endured three years of sometimes bitter criticism as conflict surged
around the question of vertical restraints. A distinction is now conventionally made between horizontal and vertical restraints. A vertical
restraint exists when there is some condition or agreement covering
transactions between different levels in the chain of production and sale.
Mainly they deal with distribution and retailing and are far more common
than horizontal restraints. In effect, business runs on vertical restraints.
The question for policy is how harmful they are to efficiency and consumer welfare. The first big battle came over the huge parallel reports on
new motor cars and car parts published in February 1992.

The *New Cars* report was potentially as significant as *Beer* with
great implications for Britain's most important manufacturing industry.
It found a complex monopoly with harmful distortions resulting from
the company car market and the Japanese voluntary export restraint –
which it wanted scrapped. But it did not find exploitative pricing and
did not recommend the abolition of selective distribution. Consumer
bodies, and especially the Consumers' Association, launched a vitriolic

attack. Stephen Locke, the articulate Director of Policy at the Consumers' Association, became a prominent critic of the Commission, attacking its competence, its allegedly pro-industry bias and eventually its very existence.[72] Some observers felt that the Commission had backed away from a confrontation with the EC, others that it had allowed itself to be overwhelmed by industry lobbying which had been provoked by a leak of the Ludvigsen consultancy report on car prices in 1991. Yet others pointed to the currently parlous state of the industry during the 1992 slump.[73] However these factors had played out within the group, it was striking that two members of the five-person group, Patrick Minford and Colin Baillieu, were free marketeers and adherents to the Chicago School permissive approach to vertical restraints.[74] The Chicago School position was, crudely, that 'every vertical restraint should be completely lawful',[75] the reasoning being that the real problem is horizontal restraints and, if entry barriers are low, then vertical restraints are more likely to be welfare generating than not. Whether or not Minford and Baillieu were persuasive within the group (Chaired by Sydney Lipworth), it did appear that the MMC was taking a permissive approach to vertical restraints. This was an approach still controversial among economists,[76] and an approach neither approved of, nor understood, by the mass of consumers.

While reports published at much the same time on contact lenses and gas attracted much praise from consumer bodies, fuel was added to the vertical restraints bonfire by further reports on *Fine Fragrances* (November 1993), *Ice Cream* (March 1994) and *Recorded Music* (June 1994). In each case scale or complex monopolies were found, but they were not felt to be operating against the public interest. With each report the hostility intensified and the conflagration spread from the consumer bodies to Bryan Carsberg (who took over as DGFT in June 1992), to MPs and to the press. Perhaps the most damaging aspect was the rift that opened up with the OFT. Bryan Carsberg put emphasis on 'various kinds of exclusionary practice or vertical restraint'[77] and he was exasperated with the MMC for its failure to share his view. Thus journalists noted that 'Sir Bryan did not try to hide his disagreement with the Monopolies Commission's report on perfume'.[78] Some economists undoubtedly regarded Sir Bryan's views as old fashioned but he and his economic advisers simply disagreed with the Chicago view. They conceded that in the long run there might be merit in the Chicago-type arguments but they were concerned with consumer detriment here and now.[79] Sir Bryan's status and authority lifted the debate on to a higher and more dangerous plane. It did not help that his views held popular and common sense appeal and were further reinforced by the March 1994 *Ice Cream* report, which was very widely, and perhaps more fairly, criticised. Critics saw a pattern developing of a softening of policy in both the MMC and the DTI. Criticism reached a crescendo in the summer, when in major articles journalists took up the OFT cudgels. Thus Robert Rice wrote that 'competition officials [in the OFT] … believe the Department of Trade and Industry and the MMC have relaxed policy to help create strong UK champions capable of competing in European markets'.[80] The idea that the MMC was being directed by the DTI (or by Graeme Odgers) was wide of the mark. The issue was more to do with the adoption and application of economic ideas. Economists within the OFT felt that the MMC approach was influenced too literally by Chicago thinking and the way it had been adopted in American antitrust. They felt that the simplicities of the Bork approach were too detached from the practical conditions. But, if the MMC reports were veering towards the permissive end of the spectrum, it reflected views held widely across the Commission. Each of the controversial reports came from different groups and different Chairs. Graeme Odgers Chaired only the *Recorded Music* team, but each group also contained Chicago (or Austrian) thinkers. For some observers this indicated Conservative free-market Commission appointments coming home to roost. It was unfair, as alleged by some commentators, to lay any permissiveness at the door of Graeme Odgers (who only became Chairman in March 1993). He used the MMC 1994 *Annual Review* to rebut criticism, reasserting the importance of the public interest test and the salience of competition as a process leading to consumer benefits. Carsberg was not won over. In one of the most dramatic of institutional developments in November 1994 he suddenly announced his resignation.

It was natural that commentators should attribute Sir Bryan's resignation to opposition to the DTI and the MMC. The *Financial Times* observed that 'one of the frustrations of Sir Bryan's job has been the MMC's rejection of his views'.[81] He consistently maintained that his resignation was only incidentally a protest and that he was genuinely attracted by his new job as Director General of the International Accounting Standards Authority, which brought financial advantages. This, he maintains, is 'the absolute truth'.[82] At the same time, with a different Secretary of State, and with positive legislative developments, it is likely that he would have stayed. He was appointed by, and had a very good working relationship with, Peter Lilley and the contrast with Michael Heseltine was striking. By all accounts his personal relationship with Graeme Odgers was frosty. They had previously been adversaries under the telecommunications regime when OFTEL was dealing with Odgers as Managing Director of British Telecom, but they worked on the basis of mutual respect. Carsberg recalls that he was the first Director General to meet an MMC panel for free-ranging discussion (in the gas inquiry).[83] Sir Graeme did not share Carsberg's views on the merits of a unitary competition authority and Sir Bryan's resignation led him to be if anything more vocal in his criticism. He was presented with a dream platform by the TIC, which announced on 12 December an investigation into 'UK policy on monopolies' which was provoked by, and focused on, the Commission. The low point of OFT/MMC relations thus came on 22 February 1995 when Sir Bryan Carsberg made his opening statement to the TIC. It was made following evidence from the MMC Chairman and Deputy Chairmen and in their presence. He was not sure, until Richard Caborn MP gave the green light, that the Committee would allow an opening statement but when it did he delivered a direct attack on the British system, saying that 'I would favour the establishment of a unitary authority for the UK'.[84] His views on the subject were already known but to state them quite so bluntly and publicly, and in the formal constitutional setting of the House of Commons, was something of a shock. Not only did he flatly contradict the MMC evidence, he also rejected settled Government policy. As he conceded, 'the civil servants were quite fed up with me at the time'.[85]

The TIC endorsed Carsberg's views on the unitary body. Its report was critical of UK policy; it advanced fairly exhaustive criticism of the MMC and recommended the creation of a single Competition Authority.[86] The TIC provided a vehicle for a whole range of critics. As the *Economist* vividly expressed it, 'they found themselves listening to one long scream of rage. Those testifying before the committee have unleashed a barrage of criticism at the country's competition laws and regulatory bodies'. Some of the criticisms were tendentious and some clearly 'over the top'. Thus 'Sir Paul Nicholson, Chairman of the Brewers' and Licensed Retailers Association told the committee that the MMC's procedures were "grossly flawed". It acted as prosecutor, judge and jury, using part-time lay members. "I wonder", he said "whether some of them were even half awake during the hearings".'[87] The report was undoubtedly damaging although neither the Government nor the Commission gave any ground and the TIC declared itself disappointed with an almost total lack of movement.[88] Although the DTI must have felt embattled over this period, with critical attacks also from the National Consumers' Council and from the Competition Forum,[89] it rode out the storm. Michael Heseltine was not a Minister to be swayed by backbench agitation and the DTI sustained the argument that 'the Government attaches great importance to the separation of powers which provides checks and balances in the regulatory process'.[90] Of perhaps more significance for the MMC was the reaction of the Labour Party. In a speech in March Gordon Brown took up Sir Bryan Carsberg's theme. He promised a more determined competition policy in a speech that was seen as symbolic of New Labour's embrace of market competition.[91] This was a preface to the Party's discussion of an OFT/MMC merger during 1996 which we come back to below.

Criticism of the MMC for its allegedly 'pro-industry' bias was one side of the coin. The other was Michael Heseltine's more permissive stance. This was illustrative of the unholy alliances that competition policy creates. While MMC 'permissiveness' was partly due to developments in antitrust thinking, Heseltine's 'permissiveness' was the result of an old-fashioned industrial policy targeted at international competitiveness. New-fangled Chicago anti-interventionism and old-fangled industrial policy combined apparently to soften the implementation of policy from 1992 onwards. Heseltine's lack of interest in competition policy was well known. His post-Westland resignation tract had reaffirmed his belief in government 'involvement' with industry and in the need for sympathetic dialogue. He believed in international competitiveness and not in competition for its own sake. 'The present criteria for reference to the MMC', he observed, 'are concerned too narrowly with competition. The law provides for a wider reference.'[92] The pragmatic support of industrial interests was open and well thought through. In a keynote speech to the CBI early in 1994 he stressed his commitment to competition policy but observed that, 'the competition authorities ... must be flexible enough to recognise the *realities* of today's business world'. For him there were three realities: the globalisation of industry; the need to create players big enough to take on the foreign competition; and the pace of technological change with its effect of overturning market power.[93] He spoke of a commitment to vigorous UK and EC policy but the context was the Deregulation Initiative, which lifted the merger thresholds and took steps to avoid the need for reference to the Commission.

Heseltine's permissive approach led him into conflict with Bryan Carsberg. He over-ruled the DGFT twice in February 1993, first over the referral of a GEC/Philips merger, second over the Airtours bid for Owners Abroad. The Airtours case was headline news. It was portrayed as a slap in the face for Carsberg and as damaging for competition policy. This episode clearly demonstrated Heseltine's priorities and his willingness to impose them. Later, in May 1994, Neil Hamilton used the reserve power under the Competition Act to instruct the Director General not to proceed with an inquiry into Arran Transport, a bus company on the Isle of Arran. It was felt to be too small a case but this was the first time such a power of direction had been invoked and it indicated a quite unprecedented level of intervention by the BoT. The final, surreal, intervention came in March 1995 when Heseltine again refused to refer a merger, this time the Hasbro/Waddington merger. Waddington was the manufacturer of the 'Monopoly' board game (Hambro, a huge American toy company, ranked Sindy and Action Man among its offerings). This rather unkind decision deprived the MMC of the delights of adjudicating on the monopolisation of Monopoly. Heseltine's motives here were revealing. He hoped 'to achieve greater sales of UK board games overseas'.[94] Much was also made of Heseltine's appointment of 'pro-business' leaders to the MMC and the OFT. Graeme Odgers was certainly seen as a business-friendly appointment and conceded that, 'I felt comfortable with Mr Heseltine's expressed viewpoint about competition when he thought it proper to offer me the job.'[95] Heseltine also selected John Bridgeman deliberately as a business executive for the post of DGFT (although he was a member of the MMC and took office only after Heseltine had moved on).

There is little doubt that there was a shift of emphasis in the implementation of competition policy from the principled enthusiasm of the Ridley/Lilley/Redwood regime prior to 1992 and the Heseltine regime after that date. It is questionable whether a full-scale alignment of British policy with the European model would have been possible with the Eurosceptics being so prominent in the Major Government. In any event, Heseltine did not have sufficient enthusiasm for strengthening policy to want to make the attempt. The constant refrain from the November 1992 Green Paper *Abuse of Market Power* onwards was of a lack of parliamentary time, but in fact Heseltine made only one attempt to secure parliamentary time for a Bill and then shifted his attention to other issues. Within the DTI the team of officials assembled to work on the Bill was disbanded.[96] Things changed in July 1995 when Ian Lang was rewarded with the DTI after playing a prominent part in John Major's re-election campaign. He was persuaded that the Conservative Government should not leave office before undertaking competition legislation. A consultation document released in March 1996 was followed by a draft Bill in August. The Bill did not, of course, incorporate the Article 86-type prohibition; neither did it advocate a Competition Commission, although it proposed a new appeals tribunal. In fact the draft Bill left many factors undecided and the DTI did not win space for it in the last legislative session of the Conservative Government. Instead, in a continued bi-partisan pattern, it was available as a blueprint for the incoming Labour Government.

The debate on the strength of UK competition policy was sometimes superficial, occasionally shrill, but was paralleled by a more sober and technical debate on the contrasting virtues of UK and EC law. Of course, British companies had been exposed to European law since 1973. They recognised that the European regime, centred on DG IV, was far from perfect and there were well-established lines of criticism of its procedures, the culture and attitudes of the staff, the goals of policy, and the design of the law itself. There were reservations about aspects of the adoption of Article 85-type provisions but the broad principles were widely agreed. For Article 86, however, there was much greater uncertainty and the more technical legal and economic debate centred on whether the Article 86 principles constituted a sensible response to the problems of monopoly control in the domestic British setting.

The hesitation over Article 86 owed something to Euroscepticism and something to industry's preference for British pragmatism. In the main, however, it was prompted by the manifest inadequacy of the European provisions. The 1992 Green Paper pointed out the shortcomings of Article 86. The provisions did not deal effectively with oligopoly or duopoly, they were weak in dealing with exploitative behaviour, and they did not allow structural remedies, only fines and a prohibition on the abusive conduct. Generally Article 86 only came into play in respect of undertakings with over a 40 per cent market share; the general view of lawyers and economists was that it had significant flaws. The lawyers were concerned at the difficulty of defining 'abuse' of a dominant position. 'Abuse' is far more ambiguous than in cartel cases, the case law is relatively sparse and some of the cases had been subject to telling criticism. The Commission had shown some partiality towards smaller firms and commentators worried that ambiguity might actually chill or discourage genuine competition.[97] Economists were concerned about the efficiency implications of Article 86. There are no efficiency-based exemption clauses and Hay, for instance, observed that 'it is not evident that the switch to a policy modelled on Article 86 is in all respects an improvement ... In terms of economic efficiency alone, a general prohibition is simply not supported in the same way that a general prohibition on cartels, for instance, is supported.'[98] The CBI stressed these drawbacks and in April 1993 persuaded the Conservative Government to choose 'option 1' from the Green Paper, strengthening the British law, rather than options 2 or 3, which would have meant adopting an Article 86 prohibition. The TIC responded more positively and advocated an Article 86 prohibition. It pointed out that in consultation the majority of views were actually in favour of Article 86, including those of lawyers, consumers and smaller businesses.[99] By this time the DTI was coming under pressure from the Treasury, both ministers and officials, to toughen policy by including Article 86-type provisions. Ian Lang's consultation exercise in 1996 did not propose an Article 86-type prohibition but it was far more agnostic and, at Treasury insistence, argued that 'the options merit further discussion'.[100] The incoming Labour Government bit the bullet and incorporated the prohibition into chapter II of the 1998 Act. It dealt with the drawbacks of Article 86 by implementing 'option 3' so that the issues of market share, oligopoly and structural remedies were dealt with by the retention of the Fair Trading Act scale and complex monopoly provisions. The OFT regarded the complex monopoly provisions as essential but was agnostic about the scale monopoly powers. The MMC, on the other hand, felt that it was important to retain the scale monopoly provisions. One curiosity is that ministers have declared that a reference under the scale monopoly powers will only be made if the undertaking has already been proceeded against and fined under the chapter II provisions. This has not been incorporated in legislation, and does not apply to the sectoral regulators, but constitutes a significant obeisance to the business lobby.

The drawbacks with Article 86 are only the worst of the problems with EC competition law. Legal practitioners will take comfort from the fact that the OFT is likely to be rather more efficient than DG IV and has taken pains to avoid the 'notification overload' which has been the bane of the Commission. The time taken to process many Article 85 notifications puts criticism of the UK regime nicely in context. In comparison to the many years which DG IV can routinely take to deal with cases the UK authorities are paragons of rapidity. Other substantive problems of European law are more likely to appear in British law. The European preoccupation with integrating the internal market has historically given it a fixation with measures of market segmentation and therefore with vertical agreements. The wide and all-embracing scope that DG IV and the Court have attached to Article 85 prompted Whish and Bishop to observe that, 'EC competition law would have developed in a fundamentally different – and many would argue in a far better way – if the Court in *Constan and Grundig* had accepted the idea that vertical agreements could not be caught by Article 85(1) at all'.[101] DG IV has been re-appraising vertical agreements and has drafted guidelines and exemptions. The UK approach will be to design a statutory order to supplement the Act and to exclude vertical agreements from the operation of the Act. Similarly the block exemptions pose problems. The exemptions have been developed to overcome the notification overload but they convey the danger of forcing all agreements into an orthodox mould using a formula that might be less appropriate to the competitive conditions.[102] In applying Article 85 exemptions there has also been criticism of an undue legalism with insufficient attention being given to economic arguments and to an assessment of economic efficiency.[103]

In short, the design of European competition law and its implementation, as incorporated into accepted practice and into case law, reveal a less than perfect system. Concerns with Article 86 generated quite wide sympathy for the CBI's reaction to the Bill that 'it is wrong to base the UK prohibition of abuse of a dominant position on the wording of Article 86 ... [a] much more tightly defined prohibition is required'.[104] But by then it was too late. The CBI had made a serious mistake in the late summer of 1996 when it indicated that it would support an Article 86-type prohibition. This went back on its earlier opposition and entirely disconcerted the DTI, which had based its proposals in the draft Bill on the earlier CBI view. Officials found this CBI U-turn quite baffling and it reduced the Government's inclination to give time to Lang's Bill. By 1997 the CBI had returned to its earlier opposition and in its comments on the 1997 Bill it proposed a prohibition based on Canadian competition law. At this stage, however, the gravitational pull of the European model and the powerful arguments of logic and consistency had committed the Labour Party to Article 86. Optimists hoped that an intelligent adaptation of the European model by the British authorities would overcome the problems seen in DG IV and might catalyse the overdue reform of the European law. The CBI thus observed that 'we hope that a successful new competition regime might serve as a model for reform of the EU system'[105] – a thought that reminds us that policy borrowing within Europe is not all one way.

The CBI's reservations might remind us of the potential strengths of the new Act. With increased investigation powers and far greater consistency the restrictive practices and monopolies provisions will constitute a real deterrence. This will be supplemented by the Fair Trading Act approach. The complex monopoly provisions allow oligopolies with only an aggregate 25 per cent market share to be investigated, and open up areas such as parallel pricing. The virtues of the scale monopoly provisions included the option of structural remedies.[106] The logic of retaining them was increased by the retention of British-style merger control. The combination of the European prohibition, the Fair Trading Act provisions and well-resourced competition agencies therefore gave Britain in 1998–99 a powerful competition regime. In 1995 Sir Bryan Carsberg had complained that Britain had fallen badly behind other countries in the application of competition policy.[107] Now Ian McCartney was able to say in the second reading debate that 'the Bill brings United Kingdom competition laws up to date after years of indecision on the part of the previous administration'.[108] Ministers called the Bill 'strong' and 'tough'. They did not claim that it was stronger than elsewhere, but the CBI did. Rather plaintively it observed that the proposals 'will impose a more extensive regime for regulating the competitive behaviour of firms than presently exists in the UK or anywhere in Europe or North America, and possibly anywhere else in the world. We see no pressing need for such heavy regulation.'[109] If the CBI did not see this need who did? Perhaps lawyers, certainly the consumer lobby, but most decidedly DTI officials. As Opposition spokesman, John Redwood had revealed that 'I never supported the proposal to rebase our competition laws in such a fundamental manner. Officials proposed this sort of Bill when I was competition Minister, and I shall tell the right hon. Lady that I turned it down. I refused to introduce it to the House.'[110] Arguably we see yet again in this legislative process DTI officials playing a patient waiting game. They consulted widely but both devised and desired 'option 3' in the 1992 Green Paper. Eventually they secured this outcome, six years later and under a very different Government.

A third debate that developed over the early 1990s concerned the competing merits of the tripartite system and a unitary authority. The debate sometimes appeared superficial, and occasionally bitter, but it was based on the serious and important issue of regulatory compliance. One thoughtful exponent of the view that the OFT and the MMC should be merged into a unitary authority was Robin Aaronson. He was a competition specialist with Coopers and Lybrand but had served as Senior Economic Adviser at the MMC and as specialist adviser to the TIC investigation of takeovers and mergers. He put his finger on the key to an effective competition policy – willing compliance by companies, based on a good working knowledge of clear legal requirements which are reasonable and acceptable. His argument was that British companies had a poor understanding of British law. They made minimal efforts to comply, with the effect that many harmful practices were not deterred, and some constructive practices were. In this sense policy was failing because the policy outcomes were either ineffective or perverse.[111] He argued that it was imperative to increase clarity, consistency and trust in the competition authorities, and that one way to do that would be to merge them. The TIC accepted this line of argument and endorsed the idea of a new

Competition and Merger Authority which would combine the MMC with the monopolies and mergers sections of the OFT.[112] It was not a very well thought through proposal (presumably restrictive practices would have been left with a rump OFT) and, in response to the concerns about fairness and accountability, the Committee proposed a division of functions within the new Authority.

The stick of a unitary authority was used to beat an increasingly unpopular MMC by the consumer lobby, by MPs and eventually, as we have seen, by Sir Bryan Carsberg. The DTI gave no encouragement to this line of argument and the issue was well aired in the TIC inquiry on monopolies. Again a unitary authority was endorsed but this time in a more thorough proposal. The Committee cited the example of the Italian competition authority (a favourite of Bryan Carsberg's). It advocated including all the MMC functions in a new authority, including utility adjudication, and rejected the idea of an appeal to the courts on matters of substance. The new Competition Authority would have the last word, except in exceptional cases where the Secretary of State would retain powers. Both the CBI and the MMC argued against the combination. The MMC's evidence is worth quoting at length; it argued that a unitary authority would be 'prosecutor, judge and jury' and that:

> The separation of functions between the MMC and the OFT ensures maximum fairness of investigation and objectivity of judgement. It is important that any body charged with investigation, whatever its institutional form, should be as independent as possible. It should be, and seen to be, totally objective and detached, and free from both pre-conceived views and extraneous pressure. The benefit of the separation of powers that is inherent in the present system is that it removes the potential conflicts of interest that arise if the body responsible for the detailed investigation of a possible monopoly situation (currently the MMC) were also the body that initiated the proceedings (currently the OFT).[113]

After publication Graeme Odgers publicly reiterated this position. He pointed to weaknesses in the European regime and argued that, 'the proposed integration of the OFT and the MMC would in my view be a retrograde step ... The MMC's functions are judicial: to come to judgements on the public interest.'[114] Indeed, the proposal for a unitary authority had two flaws: first, it was based on a dubious model; second, business did not want it.

On the first question, the model of DG IV has been the subject of perennial criticism over its combination of functions (policeman, prosecutor, judge, jury and probation officer – or executioner – to give the whole criminal metaphor). At this time it was coming under increasing criticism from the Germans over its alleged politicisation, with the Germans pressing for a 'European cartel office'.[115] Moreover, DG IV enjoyed some degree of insulation from national lobbies due to its supranational status and was in any case subject to oversight by the European Court of Justice and by the new and stringent Court of First Instance. The idea of reproducing DG IV within the domestic polity was intriguing but far from compelling.

The position of industry was interesting. Aaronson had derived inspiration for his unitary authority proposals from surveys of industrial opinion during 1991 which were critical of the British regime and of the MMC. A survey of twenty-five companies involved in MMC inquiries by Ernst and Young in 1993 generated similar criticisms but also some support for the MMC. Although 62 per cent of respondents endorsed a unitary system for monopoly cases (but only 42 per cent for mergers) still the criticism was as much of the arbitrary OFT as of the cumbersome MMC. Indeed, the MMC reports were described as 'first rate' and 'very professionally done'. One correspondent relayed a view that industry had held since the late 1950s, that 'I prefer a system where you do have separate bodies because there is less chance of the MMC being captured by the parties. It's very easy for the body involved in the investigation to have political interest in a given matter and not to present it in an impartial light.'[116] This was eloquent of a schizophrenic attitude in industry. Companies were quick to complain of the time, the effort, the uncertainty and the procedures surrounding an MMC report but they were even more unhappy with a short, sharp inquiry conducted in secret; and even more unhappy if it was combined with the power of a 'prohibition and fine' system. The MMC might be bad but a unitary authority would be worse.

The tripartite system earned reputable approval by providing the certainty of a thorough, impartial inquiry. It also earned disreputable approval by providing a multiplicity of 'veto points' at which companies and their well-resourced advisers could bring their arguments to bear. At the extreme the tripartite system and the separation of powers opened up a potential to 'divide and conquer', to play the agencies off against one another. This was not an advantage that industry wished to surrender. Thus the CBI argued strongly in favour of the tripartite system to the TIC and greeted Labour's draft Bill with the comment that, 'we are pleased that the Government has taken into account the suggestions put forward last year by the CBI and has chosen to preserve an independent body with the power to conduct a full review of the DGFT's decisions'.[117]

Labour had in fact thought carefully about the idea of a unitary authority. Its 'business manifesto' published in 1996 treated a combined authority as a serious possibility and Robin Aaronson prepared a paper for the IPPR Commission on Public Policy and British Business which repeated the proposal.[118] Aaronson worked at the IPPR with Dan Corry, who became a special adviser to Margaret Beckett at the DTI. Of perhaps more weight, however, was Gordon Borrie's view. He also advised Labour and had commented that:

> I am not too keen on joining the OFT and MMC together because they have different cultures and the more questioning, partisan, activities of the OFT are not naturally combined with the necessarily more cautious, impartial and judicious approach of the MMC. Yes, you can combine in one body the roles of investigator, prosecutor and judge but justice does need to be seen to be done.[119]

Another threat to the continued existence of the MMC, which would have catered to the need for checks and balances, was the possibility of the creation of a court. All systems must embody a mechanism to hear appeals and adjudicate disputes. In several other systems the courts provide that role. The Competition Act does indeed create a legal tribunal but it has been created as a second arm of the Commission and leaves its reporting functions intact.

The Competition Act 1998

With an elegant accident of symmetry the Act comes exactly fifty years after the Monopolies and Restrictive Practices Act 1948. It is potentially a revolutionary piece of legislation which has considerable implications for the institutions of British capitalism. As explored in the concluding chapter, the 1948 Act catered to the voluntarism, the self-regulation and the accommodative arm's-length relationship between government and industry which permeated the political economy of the 1940s. The 1998 Act creates a more formal and legally objective framework for industry. It provides didactic guidance rather than the co-operative exploration which underlay its 1948 predecessor. The formal provisions of the Act are briefly reviewed in chapter 10.

Despite its European provenance, the new Act is a piece of British legislation although it builds in novel provisions to employ European jurisprudence. It is designed to dovetail with the European regime and doubtless many hope that this new, more effective, Act will increase the element of real subsidiarity. It represents something of a compromise, as can be seen if it is considered in the context of the debates reviewed above. In respect of the first debate it almost certainly represents a more active British competition policy, and one that stresses 'competition' as a principle rather than 'the public interest'. In respect of the second debate it adopts the European stance of prohibition and an effects doctrine, and does so for monopolies as well as restrictive practices. But the monopolies element is enacted with due caution and the mergers regime remains unaltered. In respect of the third debate the institutions have changed in their relationships with one another and in the abolition of one court and the creation of a new tribunal. These changes have been the product of wide consultation. The Government has pursued a neo-pluralist path of involvement of the policy network through a proliferation of Green and White Papers and by giving every indication of listening to the responses. There is nothing impetuous or dogmatic about this legislation. Government has sought advice, built consensus and moved with judicious caution. This is indicative of a neo-pluralist policy stance which seeks to build consensus but which also requires technical support. The Government was genuinely uncertain about the potential effects of new legislation and in true civil service style (and very unlike the sweeping Thatcherite policy initiatives) it enrolled the views and the advice of business, lawyers and other specialists. It is indicative of this caution that the new model has perhaps embraced the European certainties too emphatically. After years of being reproached as not being European enough, some lawyers are now suggesting that the Government has become too European.[120] The European blueprint does indeed involve some major shifts in the regime of monopoly control. In order to evaluate the extent of change consider the following:

- the shift from agnostic investigation to prohibition
- the replacement of the 'public interest' test by an 'effect on competition' test
- the exclusion of the Secretary of State from the administrative process as regards actions and remedies
- the incorporation of the principles of European competition law jurisprudence into British administration
- hence the likely growth of legal involvement through defence, appeal and third-party action
- the empowerment of third parties through rights of appeal and the potential to pursue damages in the courts
- the imposition of substantial penalties.

Change of this magnitude is potentially of extraordinary significance and it is curious that press coverage of the Act was relatively subdued. What really matters, however, is the fashion in which the new procedures will be administered and it is here that civil service caution has come into its own. There is a sense in which the UK Competition Act is an expression of 'beating them at their own game'. The European law is accepted but it is brought firmly under national control by British institutions.

The influence of the old British institution of competition policy on the operation of the new law is difficult to anticipate but the key factor is the continuity in the agencies. The DTI will retain some influence on the OFT and the Competition Commission, if only over their personnel. The OFT will operate the law according to the prohibition and European jurisprudence, but the context will be reasonable business behaviour in the British economy. Business will have to make the adjustment to the new regime, so will the officials who implement it and, in this respect, path dependence would lead us to expect a distinctively British use of discretion in pursuing cases, fixing penalties and hearing appeals. The cross-fertilisation between the two sides of the Commission will be particularly fascinating. The tribunals may be influenced by the public interest tradition of the reporting arm but, in turn, the reporting groups may well find themselves infused with a new legal rigour.

Conclusion

This chapter has reviewed, rather breathlessly, twenty-five years in which British competition policy remained resistant to change, only to change almost beyond recognition at the very end of the period. The legislative process displayed familiar features. The 1998 Act, like every earlier competition Act, was long delayed and was bi-partisan in its design and passage. The influences on the Act were also familiar. For recent legislation it is difficult to disentangle the decisive influences but a good case can be made for continued civil service influence over the development of policy. Ministers were influential in delaying legislation but the pattern of a tenacious pursuit of a particular model of policy design is indicative of a persistent line taken by civil servants in the DTI. Consistent with this interpretation is a lower level of business influence on the design of policy – not because business is any less influential in the 1990s or under New Labour, but because business did not know what it wanted. An instinctive business response was to argue for a permissive policy administered in the traditional pattern by familiar institutions. This reflex dominated the public CBI input into the policy debate. But a more realistic response from individual companies and executives was to recognise that companies were in any case subject to the European regime and that it made good sense to align the British system with the European model. DTI civil servants found themselves closer to the business realists and, as has again been the case over the years, were willing to reject quite dogmatically much of the public face of CBI protests.

The DTI and the CBI were closer on the subject of agencies. This chapter began with the question of why the Government had proved so loyal to the tripartite system. A variety of partial explanations were offered. There was the 'Pontius Pilate' principle of distancing the DTI from uncomfortable decisions; the 'bureau shaping' hypothesis, that the DTI wished to retain only the interesting policy-making work; and the 'business influence' suggestion, that the DTI was creating a system that was susceptible to business pressure and unlikely to attack deeply embedded business practices. In a rather less cynical vein, the DTI also had a very real concern to support successful businesses, to sustain business morale and to use competition to increase efficiency and competitiveness. Officials as well as ministers had adopted the Michael Porter perspective that a strong domestic competition policy was important for international competitiveness. As Sir Bryan Carsberg observed, 'I think it is actually very unusual for efficiency overseas to be combined with inefficiency at home',[121] and there was a genuine commitment to strengthening policy. But a new and stronger policy could only be entrusted to sensible British agencies that would implement it intelligently and pragmatically. The DTI shares business apprehension at the ambiguity and potentially destructive nature of a prohibition on abuse of monopoly power. Restrictive agreements are inevitable, monopoly is inevitable, sometimes both are benign. The fifty-year experience of the MMC, and the twenty-five years of the OFT, provided reassurance that policy would be applied reasonably. We can expect a British-style doctrine of a 'rule of reason' to emerge from the OFT.

Notes

1 DTI, Memorandum, TIC, *UK Policy on Monopolies: Minutes of Evidence*, 1994–95, HC 249–iv (14 March 1995), para. 2.
2 But see I. Ramsey, 'The Office of Fair Trading: policing the consumer marketplace', in R. Baldwin and C. McCrudden (eds), *Regulation and Public Law* (London,

Weidenfeld and Nicolson, 1987); S. Wilks, *The Office of Fair Trading in Administrative Context*, CRI, Discussion Paper 5 (London, CIPFA, 1994).

3 C. Hood, 'Keeping the centre small: explanations of agency type', *Political Studies*, 26 (1978), p. 41.

4 Sir Gordon Borrie, 'Reflections of a retiring Director General', OFT, *Annual Report of the Director General of Fair Trading, 1991* (London, HMSO, 1992), p. 7.

5 P. Dunleavy, *Democracy, Bureaucracy and Public Choice* (Hemel Hempstead, Harvester Wheatsheaf, 1991), p. 207.

6 Ramsey, 'The Office of Fair Trading', pp. 181–2.

7 Interview with a former OFT staff member.

8 K. Middlemas, *Power, Competition and the State, Volume 3: The End of the Postwar Era: Britain since 1974* (London, Macmillan, 1991), p. 3.

9 J. Methven, 'Keynote address', in K. George and C. Joll (eds), *Competition Policy in the UK and EEC* (Cambridge University Press, 1975), p. 3.

10 Interview with a former official of the OFT.

11 Interview with a former official of the OFT and correspondence with a former senior official of the OFT.

12 Interview with Sir Godfray Le Quesne (February 1999).

13 *The Times* (2 April 1980), quoted criticising the Competition Act.

14 See G. Borrie and A. Diamond, *The Consumer, Society and the Law* (Harmondsworth, Penguin, fourth edn 1981, first published 1964).

15 See OFT, *Annual Report, 1978* (London, HMSO, 1979).

16 For discussion see R. Clarke, S. Davies and N. Driffield, *Monopoly Policy in the UK* (Cheltenham, Edward Elgar, 1998), pp. 151–2.

17 For instance, the *Economist*, 'Sleeping Cerberus' (13 January 1979).

18 *Annual Report of the Director General of Fair Trading, 1976* (London, HMSO, 1977), p. 8.

19 See the *Economist* (19 September 1976 and 3 December 1976).

20 *Annual Report of the Director General of Fair Trading, 1978* (London, HMSO, 1979), p. 10.

21 Sir Bryan Carsberg, *Competition Regulation the British Way: Jaguar or Dinosaur?*, Wincott Memorial Lecture (London, IEA, 1996), p. 16.

22 Sir Gordon Borrie, *Annual Report of the Director General of Fair Trading, 1986* (London, HMSO, 1987), p. 13.

23 This section draws on interviews with a former OFT official and a lawyer.

24 R. Whish, *Competition Law* (London, Butterworths, third edn, 1993), pp. 158–61.

25 Sir Gordon Borrie, 'Restrictive practices control in the United Kingdom: big bangs and lesser detonations', The Travers Memorial Lecture, City of London Polytechnic (11 March 1986), reprinted in the *Journal of Business Law* (September 1986), p. 359.

26 For a sympathetic treatment see T. Buxton, P. Chapman and P. Temple (eds), *Britain's Economic Performance* (London, Routledge, 1984); see also K. Middlemas, *Industry, Unions and Government: Twenty-One Years of NEDC* (London, Macmillan, 1983).

27 S. Wilks, *Industrial Policy and the Motor Industry* (Manchester University Press, expanded edn, 1986), p. 48.

28 S. Prais, *The Evolution of Giant Firms in Britain* (Cambridge University Press, 1976); see also M. Utton, 'On measuring the effects of industrial mergers', *Scottish*

Journal of Political Economy, 21 (1974); and L. Hannah, *The Rise of the Corporate Economy* (London, Methuen, 1976, second edn, 1983).

29 The concentration hypothesis is challenged by Stephen Littlechild, 'Myths and merger policy', in J. Fairburn and J. Kay (eds), *Mergers and Merger Policy* (Oxford University Press, 1989), pp. 303–5.

30 For a productive review see J. Hayward (ed.), *Industrial Enterprise and European Integration: From National to International Champions in Western Europe* (Oxford University Press, 1995).

31 G. Meeks, *Disappointing Marriage: A Study of the Gains from Merger* (Cambridge University Press, 1977).

32 DPCP, *A Review of Monopolies and Mergers Policy: A Consultative Document*, Cmnd 7198 (London, HMSO, May 1978), p. 104.

33 Which formed the basis of D. Gribbin, *The Post-War Revival of Competition as Industrial Policy*, Government Economic Service Working Paper 19 (London, Price Commission, 1978).

34 DPCP, *A Review of Monopolies and Mergers Policy*, pp. 75, 3.

35 *Ibid.*, pp. 34–5, 3.

36 *Ibid.*, p. 38.

37 J. F. Pickering, 'The implementation of British competition policy on mergers', *ECLR* (1980), p. 196; see also chapter 7 of this volume.

38 Interview with a Committee staff member.

39 *A Review of Monopolies and Mergers Policy*, p. 2.

40 *Ibid.*

41 DPCP, *A Review of Restrictive Trade Practices Policy: A Consultative Document*, Cmnd 7512 (London, HMSO, March 1979), p. 61.

42 The report was *Chlordiazepoxide and Diazepam* (librium and valium), HC 197 (London, HMSO, 1973). PRO, BT281/118, Documents on Passage of the Bill. Second reading, confidential note.

43 Interview with Sir Godfray Le Quesne (February 1999).

44 D. Gerber, *Law and Competition in Twentieth Century Europe* (Oxford, Clarendon, 1998), pp. 255, 254; the second quote is from Walter Eucken.

45 For Heath's account see E. Heath, *The Course of My Life* (London, Hodder and Stoughton, 1998), ch. 13.

46 See J. W. Young, 'The Heath government and British entry into the European Community', in S. Ball and A. Seldon (eds), *The Heath Government 1970–1974: A Reappraisal* (London, Longman, 1996), p. 277.

47 See D. G. Goyder, *EC Competition Law* (Oxford, Clarendon, third edn, 1998), pp. 320–1.

48 George and Joll (eds), *Competition Policy*, p. 211.

49 S. Oppenheim (Minister for Consumer Affairs) second reading debate, *Hansard, HCD* (23 October 1979), col. 265.

50 See the second reading debate in *Hansard, HCD* (23 July 1979) (23 October 1979).

51 *Hansard, HCD* (6 August 1980), col. 1065.

52 Julius Caesar, act iv, scene iii, 217; the speech is by Brutus.

53 Margaret Thatcher, *The Downing Street Years* (London, Harper Collins, 1993), p. 556, referring to the Luxembourg Council of December 1985.

54 See S. Wilks with L. McGowan, 'Competition policy in the European Union:

creating a federal agency?', in G. B. Doern and S. Wilks (eds), *Comparative Competition Policy* (Oxford, Clarendon, 1996).

55 See Whish, *Competition Law*, pp. 307–8.

56 *Ibid.*, p. 425.

57 The prime examples are R. Merkin and K. Williams, *Competition Law: Antitrust Policy in the UK and EEC* (London, Sweet and Maxwell, 1984); Whish, *Competition Law* (first edn, 1985); Goyder, *EC Competition Law* (first edn, 1988); and C. S. Kerse, *EEC Antitrust Procedure* (London, European Law Centre, first edn, 1988).

58 I am indebted to Hans Liesner for this emphasis.

59 DTI, *Review of Restrictive Practices Policy: A Consultative Document*, Cm 331 (London, HMSO, March 1988).

60 *Ibid.*, p. 8.

61 *Ibid.*, pp. 2, 22; DTI, *Opening Markets: New Policy on Restrictive Trade Practices*, Cm 727 (London, HMSO, July 1989).

62 For details see Kerse, *EC Antitrust Procedure* (third edn, 1994), ch. 5.

63 Lord Young, *The Enterprise Years* (London, Headline, 1990), p. 319.

64 *Ibid.*, p. 298.

65 Borrie, 'Reflections of a retiring Director General', p. 12.

66 Whish, *Competition Law*, p. 577.

67 See Goyder, *EC Competition Law*, pp. 507–8.

68 Julian Maitland-Walker, 'Ice cream wars', editorial in *ECLR*, 8 (December 1995), p. 453.

69 The title of a popular film of the period – meaning 'going all the way'.

70 Nikki Tait, 'Busy year unleashed on monopolies watchdog', *Financial Times* (29 March 1989).

71 Peter Lilley, Speech to the Combined Law Society Lunch (12 June 1991).

72 See S. Locke and K. Scribbins, 'Cars and the MMC report: a fair deal for consumers?', *Consumer Policy Review*, 2:3 (July 1992), pp. 156–60; and S. Locke, 'A new approach to competition policy', *Consumer Policy Review*, 4:3 (July 1994) pp. 159–68.

73 See, for instance, the *Independent* and the *Financial Times* (6 February 1992).

74 See Colin Baillieu, *The Lion and the Lamb* (London, Wilfred Street Publications, 1996) with an Introduction by Patrick Minford. The cars issue is discussed on pp. 26–7.

75 From R. H. Bork, *The Antitrust Paradox: A Policy at War with Itself* (New York, The Free Press 1978), quoted in M. Waterson, 'Vertical integration and vertical restraints', *Oxford Review of Economic Policy*, 9:2 (Summer 1993), p. 41.

76 Clarke, Davies and Driffield, *Monopoly Policy in the UK*, ch. 8.

77 Sir Bryan Carsberg, 'Reflections of an incoming Director General', *Annual Report of the Director General of Fair Trading, 1992* (London, HMSO, June 1993), p. 7.

78 H. Dixon, 'Carsberg investigates food prices', *Financial Times* (25 November 1993).

79 Interview with Sir Bryan Carsberg (February 1999).

80 R. Rice, 'Watchdog barks but the MMC moves on', *Financial Times* (17 May 1994).

81 Leader article (30 November 1994).

82 Interview with Sir Bryan Carsberg (February 1999).

83 *Ibid.*

84 Transcript of evidence, para. 67, published as TIC, *UK Policy on Monopolies; Minutes of Evidence*, 1994–95, HC 249.

85 Interview with Sir Bryan Carsberg (February 1999).
86 TIC, *UK Policy on Monopolies*, 1994–95, HC 249–I (London, HMSO, May 1995),
    p. v.
87 *Economist*, 'Screaming at the umpire' (1 April 1995), p. 27.
88 TIC, *Government Observations on the Fifth Report from the Trade and Industry Com-
    mittee (Session 1994–95) on UK Policy on Monopolies*, 1994–95, HC 748 (London,
    HMSO, July 1995).
89 See National Consumers' Council, *Competition and Consumers* (London, NCC,
    May 1995), which also backed a unitary authority. The Competition Forum was set
    up as a lobby group by John Watt MP and Dafydd Wigley MP in March 1994 and
    it kept up a stream of criticism during 1994–95.
90 TIC, *Government Observations*, para. ix.
91 'Gordon Brown outlines Labour commitment to pro-competition, pro-consumer
    … policy for dynamic market economy', Labour Press Release (17 March 1995),
    speech at the Royal Society of Arts.
92 M. Heseltine, *Where There's a Will* (London, Hutchinson, 1987), pp. 125–6.
93 M. Heseltine, Speech to the CBI conference (1 February 1994), transcript.
94 *Financial Times* (1 March 1995).
95 *Independent* (22 March 1994).
96 Interviews with present and past DTI civil servants.
97 See, for instance, F. Fishwick, *Making Sense of Competition Policy* (London, Kogan
    Page, 1993), pp. 193–4; Whish, *Competition Law*, pp. 279, 737.
98 D. Hay, 'More like Europe? An economic evaluation of recent changes in UK com-
    petition policy', paper to a Conference on the Europeanisation of UK Competi-
    tion Law, UCL (September 1998), p. 65.
99 See TIC, *UK Policy on Monopolies*, paras 103–5.
100 DTI, *Tackling Cartels and the Abuse of Market Power: A Draft Bill: An Explanatory
    Document* (London, DTI, August 1996), p. 128; see also DTI, *Tackling Cartels and
    Abuse of Market Power: A Consultation Document* (London, DTI, March 1996).
101 R. Whish and W. Bishop, 'The treatment of vertical agreements under the Com-
    petition Bill: a report for the Competition Bill Team of the DTI', copy (February
    1998), 33 pp.
102 Goyder, *EC Competition Law*, p. 568.
103 D. Neven, P. Papandropoulos and P. Seabright, *Trawling for Minnows: European
    Competition Policy and Agreements Between Firms* (London, CEPR, 1998), p. 166.
104 CBI response to the draft Bill, copy (September 1997), para. 32.
105 *Ibid.*, para. 3.
106 See Fishwick, *Making Sense*, ch. 5, for additional strengths of the British system.
107 'UK has lost competitive edge says Carsberg', Mary Fagan interview, *Independent*
    (6 February 1995).
108 Ian McCartney (Minister of State, DTI), *Hansard*, HCD (11 May 1998), col. 117.
109 CBI response, para. 44.
110 *Hansard*, HCD (11 May 1998), col. 43.
111 See his subtle article, R. Aaronson, 'Do companies take any notice of competition
    policy?', *Consumer Policy Review*, 2:3 (July 1992), pp. 140–5.
112 TIC, *Takeovers and Mergers*, 1991–92, HC 90 (London, HMSO, November 1991),
    para. 290.
113 MMC Memorandum, quoted in TIC, *UK Policy on Monopolies*, para. 136.

114 G. Odgers, personal view, 'The future of competition policy', *Financial Times* (18 May 1995).

115 S. Wilks and L. McGowan, 'Disarming the Commission: the debate over a European cartel office', *Journal of Common Market Studies*, 33:2 (June 1995); A. Riley, 'The European Cartel Office: a guardian without weapons', *ECLR*, 18:1 (1997), editorial.

116 Ernst and Young, 'Competition inquiries: a new approach', copy, p. 13; reported in the press (1 and 2 March 1993), for instance, R. Rice, 'Companies call for merger inquiry reform', *Financial Times* (2 March 1993).

117 CBI response, para. 57.

118 Labour Party, *Vision for Growth: A New Industrial Strategy for Britain*, foreword by Margaret Beckett (London, Labour Party, undated but September 1996); R. Aaronson, *The Future of Competition Policy* (London, IPPR, 1996).

119 Lord Borrie, 'Discussant's comments', in Aaronson, *Future of Competition Policy*, p. 18.

120 F. Barr, 'Has the UK gone European: is the European approach of the Competition Bill more than an illusion?', *ECLR*, 19:3 (1998), p. 144.

121 Sir Bryan Carsberg, TIC, *UK Policy on Monopolies*, minutes of evidence, para. 78.

10

Conclusion: organisational survival and a new settlement

It is not easy to draw conclusions about the operation of fifty years of competition policy. The goals of policy are generalised and it is almost impossible to measure the economic contribution made by the competition rules. The policy itself is intangible and poses the problems posed by all programmes of regulation. How do we evaluate the impact on behaviour? How can we evaluate the force of deterrence and the extent of compliance? In this respect competition policy presents a more elusive target than policies such as education or health care. In these areas there are huge spending programmes, quantified objectives, ministerial statements of intent and measurable outcomes: do children pass exams; do people live longer? For competition the equivalent questions – is the economy more efficient; can entrepreneurs exploit their ideas; are consumers better off? – are questions related to the operation of the market economy as a whole. The relative contribution of competition policy cannot be disentangled.

The conclusions offered below are not therefore centred on economic performance. They are written from a standpoint of political science and public administration, and they attempt to draw together some of the historical patterns and the arguments initiated in the earlier chapters. Perspectives based on law or economics would stress different features of the record and, to some extent, readers must draw their own conclusions from the material presented above. A small amount of new material is also introduced in the final section. It seemed sensible to present at least the bare bones of the new system of competition policy that will come into effect in 2000 as a result of the Competition Act 1998. Strictly speaking this is outside the remit of the history but the shape of the new legislation does bear on the argument about the place of competition policy in the post-war settlement and it would be perverse not to provide the reader with a signpost to future developments.

The material and the arguments of the earlier chapters can be evaluated at several different levels. Accordingly the Conclusion offers four approaches to the drawing of historical conclusions. First we tackle the question of the MMC itself. How has it survived? Is its survival due to its success and, if so, in which respects has it been successful? This perspective stresses issues of organisational longevity. Second, we look more broadly at competition policy as a regime. The perspective here is the question of whether competition policy has taken on the coherence, authority and influence of an institution within the market economy. Third, we consider the relationship between competition policy and economic policy more broadly. Competition policy is one element within supply-side policy but it is based on an entirely different philosophy from that of industrial policy. We therefore consider the degree to which competition policy has been operated actively, and make some tentative comments on its contribution to enhanced economic performance. Fourth, we come back to the big questions of industrial politics explored in chapter 1. There it was suggested that competition policy reflected the main features of the 'post-war settlement'. The settlement itself disintegrated in the 1970s. We therefore speculate on whether a new settlement was established in the 1990s and whether the reformed competition regime can similarly be seen as the reflection of that new settlement.

Organisational survival: the genius of the MMC

The MMC reached its legislative fiftieth birthday on 30 July 1998; and its administrative birthday on 1 January 1999, fifty years after the first members were appointed. It is not exceptional for regulatory agencies and government corporations to enjoy a long life but it is unusual for administrative tribunals and for Royal Commissions.[1] A 'commission of inquiry' which is still inquiring after fifty years sounds like an oddity, especially, as noted in chapter 1, when it has survived in the jungle of British supply-side policy where life for creatures such as MinTech and the Price Commission has been short. Moreover, since the MMC became the Competition Commission on 1 April 1999 its life will be prolonged, although it will lose the word 'monopoly' from its title. Perhaps it is the association with monopoly that explains some of the MMC's staying power. Like the poor we have monopoly always with us. The evils of monopoly were eloquently attacked by Adam Smith in 1776[2] and have been a constant source of concern. Once having established a body to combat this evil, government could hardly abolish it without putting something in its place. This ratchet effect is apparent across all the world's market economies. Competition agencies are created and grow, their abolition is unusual.

At a less rarified level the Commission has always behaved with propriety and dignity. It gave government no grounds to criticise its conscientiousness and it is striking how often criticism has been prefaced with compliments about the sincerity, thoroughness and fairness of the Commission as an investigatory body. As seen in chapter 4, the members have been hard working and committed, often remarkably so, and have behaved with a public-spirited integrity which has placed them beyond reproach. To this extent the Commission is an excellent example of traditional British administration. From its own perspective the Commission would no doubt like to attribute its longevity to the importance and quality of its work. Members of the Commission will defend and elaborate on the reports with feeling. In historical perspective this is a less convincing argument.

MMC reports are remarkable documents for which economists and academics are, or should be, extremely grateful. Since competition problems are reproduced across market economies they also find a specialised audience abroad, and foreign antitrust practitioners marvel at the luxury of being able to explore problems in such depth. But the reports themselves, and the procedures by which they are produced, have been the subject of periodic, and sometimes well merited, criticism. In this study it has not been practicable to analyse the reports systematically but each chapter, and especially chapters 6, 8 and 9, has relayed criticism. Sometimes the reports were flimsy; sometimes the technical accounting or economic arguments were poorly developed; sometimes the Commission seemed guided by an impressionistic approach or an over-literal regard to the evidence. Such criticisms were particularly marked in the 1960s and 1970s. At this time the criticism levelled against the civil service at large by the Fulton report and the 'modernisers' could equally well have been levelled against the Commission. Sir Ashton Roskill's preference for 'a good investigating mind' (see p. 144) was really no excuse for the hesitancy in using economists and attuning inquiries to current research. Equally, the Commission's procedures were evidently less than satisfactory. Criticism again from the 1960s and 1970s speaks of a laborious, pedantic, slow-moving organisation which appeared complacent to the companies under investigation and suffered in comparison to the alternative investigatory agencies (see chapter 5). The time taken over some of the reports from this era was quite indefensible and in fact some of the Commission's procedures are still hard to defend. The Commission pays a price for the all-encompassing reach of its inquiry process, for the level of detail and the gradual development of thinking through hearings.

As argued in chapters 2 and 5, the procedures of the Commission do serve a separate purpose of securing objectivity and natural justice. Very recent experiments with joint hearings and the publication of issues letters indicate a recognition that things could be improved, but at the heart of the procedural issue is the question of the part-time principle. Time and again, from Sir Archibald Carter in 1952, to the TIC in 1995, there has been exploration of the merits of a greater proportion of full-time Commission members. The idea has been resisted by the DTI, probably rightly. The Commission would lose something of its character, something of its objectivity and a lot of its raw expertise if full-time members predominated. But it should be recognised that the benefits of this constitutional principle are dependent on an ability to retain room for manoeuvre in something like the public interest test. Here, and in other respects, the Commission itself is in the hands of the DTI and the legislation.

As chapter 5 emphasised, the repeated inclination of the BoT/DTI at every legislative juncture has been to leave procedures well alone. It would undoubtedly have been possible to restrict the breadth of the Commission's investigation but in each case, and with the complicity of the Commission, the procedural box was left unopened. This is path dependency exemplified. The original motive for the wide investigation and the elaborate procedures was a genuine uncertainty about the extent and effect of monopoly and restrictive practices. But the world, and economic theory, has moved on. Inquiries could be conducted with greater focus but the DTI has left it up to the Commission to pursue reform. The Commission has managed to get increased performance out of a rather ancient machine, as seen in the 'speed-up' of inquiries in the late 1980s, which was a considerable achievement. The procedures allow extensive participation, yield valuable information and provide welcome reassurance, but it is doubtful that they are the most effective way to discharge the Commission's functions or that a modern day organisational architect would design them in this way. The new Competition Act may provide a useful catalyst for change.

The substantive and procedural criticisms left the Commission vulnerable to abolition. In 1956 and again in 1969, 1979 and 1995–97 there was a real likelihood that the Commission would be wound up or merged with another body. In 1970 the Bill was actually in a committee of the House and the Commission was saved by a general election. In 1995–97 the threat was probably less acute but the proposals for a unitary authority or an alternative court procedure were certainly taken seriously by the DTI and the Labour Party. How, then, is survival to be explained? One approach is to examine incentives to support the Commission.

In rough order of importance, lawyers, economists, business and the civil service have all had, at various times, good reason to support the Commission. British lawyers have consistently been sceptical about the justiciability of disputes over competition issues. The arguments are often finely balanced and there is typically insufficient certainty in policy, legislation or economic theory upon which to base a legal judgement. Lord Kilmuir, as Lord Chancellor, had to read the riot act to the judiciary in order to persuade them to accept the Restrictive Practices Court in 1956. Subsequent experience with the Court did not endear court procedures to the profession or its clients and it has been the development of European jurisprudence that has finally persuaded the legal establishment of the virtues of a legalistic approach. Moreover, the legal principles of natural justice, the need for a machinery of appeal and the advisability of maintaining a separation of powers inclined lawyers inside the DTI in the early 1970s to argue for retaining the Commission as an appeal body. Exactly the same arguments were made by Lord Borrie, and by the Commission itself in the 1990s, as seen in chapter 9. Although it was most emphatically not a court, the quasi-judicial aspects of the Commission made it a familiar creature for the practising legal profession. That it was headed by lawyers for forty of its fifty years must also have helped and, on a less idealistic note, the length and unpredictability of inquiries gave lawyers plenty of material upon which to base advice to their clients and their fees.

The most systematic examination of the Commission and its reports has naturally come from economists. We return to their evaluations below but here we can point out a convergence between the prescriptions of economists and the operation of the Commission. Economists have been critical of the politicisation of competition policy, the diverse criteria allowed by the public interest test, the apparent incompatibility of the reasoning on different reports, and the divergencies from the prescriptions of welfare economics. In important respects the Commission has become less objectionable on all these counts. The appointment of economists as members in the 1960s and as staff in the 1970s was followed by a major shift to competition as a criterion in the 1980s and the appointment of an economist as Chairman in the 1990s. Moreover, as economics as a discipline has become more discriminating in its approach to competition, and more alert to the particularities of every case, so the 'rule of reason' approach embodied in the Commission's procedures has appeared more rather than less suitable.

What of business? The initial business hostility to the Commission was intense. It was argued in chapters 2 and 6 that business crippled the workings of the early Commission but it found the Restrictive Practices Court even less tolerable. By the early 1960s the CBI in particular had become an emphatic supporter of the Commission and its way of working. Individual companies exposed to MMC inquiries were far less happy with the practical operation of the system, and Sir Arthur Knight's account of the experience of Courtaulds with the Commission in the 1960s would persuade any senior executive to keep as far away from the Commission as possible.[3] Nonetheless, business as a collectivity regarded the Commission as significantly preferable to the alternative. As chapters 6 and 9 pointed out, the CBI does not always speak as a disciplined or collective voice for industry. Some companies, and some CBI Directors General have been more in favour of a European approach and, in many respects, this had become an inevitability by the 1990s. The general view of industry, however, has been in favour of maintaining the Commission and its Fair Trading Act base. Quite how important business membership of the Commission has been in this it is hard to say. It could be expected to introduce a 'business friendly' element into reports and it must have had an important symbolic impact. The support of business has been crucial. In earlier years this might have generated the cynical reaction that if a regulatory programme meets with business approval it must be ineffectual or captured. Nowadays that reaction is probably less justified. It bears repeating that business response to competition and competition policy is diverse. Many companies (and not just foreign market entrants) will favour a strong competition policy which allows them to compete evenly and to enter new markets. What they fear is dogmatism, rigidity, and the perverse side effects of legal precedent and bureaucratic rules. The MMC has been mercifully free from these.

The fourth group with reason to support the Commission is the civil service itself, or rather the BoT and the DTI. Naturally the DTI could be expected to defend the agencies and tribunals under its control but its consistent support for the MMC has been exceptional. When ministers toyed with the idea of abolition officials advanced the defence. There are several possible reasons for this. The Commission is responsible, it is controllable, it does a useful job and it is culturally attuned to the civil service. The Commission displays its responsible disposition in the way that it is cautious, does not court publicity and is scrupulously careful not to criticise the other competition agencies. Neither the Chairman nor individual members complain when reports are rejected or ignored. In this respect it is a reliable partner. To say the Commission is 'controllable' should not be misunderstood. As noted in chapter 2, it has taken its independence very seriously and its complete freedom to investigate is respected by the DTI. But the DTI appoints the members and the Chairman, it makes the references (directly on mergers, with indirect influence on monopolies) and it dictates action on reports. In these respects, therefore, the DTI has sufficient influence to maintain a 'responsible' Commission. The job which the Commission does is lengthy, demanding and sometimes tedious. It could not be done in Whitehall and the Commission makes minimal demands on the time of DTI officials. This leaves them to concentrate on 'policy' work. This is an argument that rests on the idea that British government officials prefer policy and political work to management and implementation. Accordingly they shape their organisational approaches appropriately (this 'bureau shaping' argument is rehearsed on p. 71). From this perspective the Commission takes a problem, offers a judgement and suggests solutions. For officials this is perfect. It is convenient and effective. Finally, the civil service might be expected to approve of the cultural predisposition of the Commission and therefore find it easy to understand and to work with. As argued again in chapter 5, the Commission is very like the traditional civil service in its organisation, its pursuit of fairness and its concept of the public interest. This affinity has been enhanced by the appointment of BoT/DTI Under-Secretaries as Secretaries of the Commission. They share the assumptions of their DTI counterparts and are part of the Whitehall village.

This view of the Commission as a favoured vehicle of the civil service does re-emphasise the question of independence. It is a quality which was explored in chapter 3 and it bears repetition that the MMC's operative independence is unquestioned and its freedom of thought is beyond doubt. In respect of individual inquiries there is no hint that any improper influence is brought to bear by ministers or by officials in the OFT or the DTI. The dependence of the Commission is structural and cultural. Its members are appointed by ministers and it works within a normative framework that is institutionalised as part of the competition regime. In this respect it is not so dissimilar from other agencies and tribunals in British government. Independence is never absolute. All such agencies are part of 'the state' and subject to the ultimate political control that the British constitution places in the hands of ministers. Thus, making a general point, Farmer asks, 'do tribunals enable government ministers to have it both ways – to exercise crucial and subtle influence over supposedly independent decision making bodies while denying responsibility for the decisions that are taken?"[4] The answer is yes – of course, but the MMC shares this administrative condition with many other bodies.

The mention of ministers raises the final component in evaluating the survival of the MMC: politics and the political parties. None of the sources of support reviewed above would have been decisive if political parties had concluded that the MMC should go. The forces of administrative continuity and path dependence are modest in the face of a political party which enters government determined on a doctrinal course of action, enshrined in its manifesto. As noted in chapter 1, these doctrinal commitments have been immensely powerful in the area of government and industry. Labour Party interventionism and Conservative Party free marketeering have been expressions of the fundamental political confrontation between class-based parties. In this light the MMC's huge advantage has been its bi-partisan political support and its ability to keep itself out of the ideological firing line. As an agency which 'intervenes in defence of the market' the MMC has paradoxically played to the prejudices of both of the governing parties.

The original Commission was the design of the wartime coalition Government. Since that time it is a remarkable historical fact that three of the key pieces of legislation were substantively designed by one Government and passed by a succeeding Government from the other party. This applies to the 1965 Monopolies and Mergers Act, to the 1980 Competition Act and to the 1998 Competition Act. The 1973 Fair Trading Act was a Conservative statute although, as pointed out in chapter 6, it did not change the substantive provisions of the law, or the MMC. This essential bi-partisan endorsement of the British model of competition policy illustrates the difficulty of locating it on the Left–Right spectrum. Preserving competition is a right-wing principle, but attacking monopoly is a key principle of the Left. At the practical level the Commission's traditionally introverted stance appears wise. The Commission has kept out of political disputation, it has voiced its concerns quietly and privately. Even when confronted with direct attacks from the agencies of selective intervention in the 1960s the members voices were rarely heard (but see p. 174). The Commission has therefore retained its cross-section of support while managing to avoid antagonising the industrial policy makers in the main political parties. Threats to its existence came therefore at the end of the lives of governments, not at their beginning, and the Commission has twice been saved by general elections. It is therefore the relationship between the Commission and the political parties, or rather the lack of a relationship, that has been so important for its survival.

Institutional genesis: the competition policy regime

A second concluding perspective turns from an exclusive focus on the MMC to consider the competition policy regime in the round. Post-war competition policy has moved from a posture of experimental investigation of potential problems to a concern with the overall balance of competitive forces within the economy. The theoretical underpinnings of policy were virtually absent in the 1940s and competition was regarded with scepticism or even hostility. In the 1990s economic theory was host to several schools of thought about competition and there was a widely shared commitment to free competition in an open economy. The theoretical and economic environment had been transformed. In the 1990s competition policy had become a constituent of the British market economy and a defining feature of the new, post-Thatcher, form of British capitalism.

One way of analysing this transition is to regard competition policy (or perhaps competition policy and law) as an 'institution' within the market economy. The concept of the institution and institutional dynamics was introduced in chapter 1 and proposed as one of several models in chapter 6. The theoretical propositions have not been used to structure the chapters, which are instead organised either chronologically or thematically, but the ideas underlie much of the analysis. It was suggested that institutions have regulative, normative and cognitive dimensions (see p. 2). There are a variety of institutional approaches[5] and definition of institutions is not straightforward. An institution has a long term, systematic and predictable effect on human behaviour. Thus the institution of American antitrust has an effect on American corporate behaviour, on the pattern of mergers and acquisitions, and on the acceptable forms of inter-corporate co-operation. Indeed, some critics of American antitrust will argue that it is crippling the competitive potential of the American economy. It was suggested in chapter 6 that there has developed a distinctive British model of competition policy which, by the 1980s, if not earlier, had become an economic institution within the British industrial economy. The evidence for this would be seen in corporate strategy and in the application of competition criteria to industrial restructuring, hence the acceptance of foreign takeovers which increase competition and the tolerance of conglomerate mergers which at least do not reduce it. If, indeed, such an institution has emerged it can be analysed through two main approaches. First, we can explore the origins of the institution and the way in which the key features were created. This provides the 'genetic code' for the institution. Second, we can look at how those key features have been reproduced over time in a pattern of path dependency (see p. 159). This sets the scene for the real challenge, that of explaining adaptation and change. If institutional analysis is to be anything more than descriptive and fatalistic history it needs to embody a concept of change and be capable of explaining those junctures where a novel path was chosen and the institution was transformed.

The origin of the British model in the 1940s provides the 'genetic code' which is, admittedly, an impressionistic metaphor. The human genome has millions of components, competition policy far fewer and, of these, for the sake of manageability, only five are selected:

- The bi-partisan origins. Competition policy is not 'owned' by any political party.
- A civil service design which retains political (and hence administrative) discretion.
- An agnostic position on monopoly (and restrictive practices and mergers) and its economic effects.
- A voluntaristic principle based on co-operation and excluding the courts, legal tests or third-party actions.
- A resort to 'the public interest' as a way of evaluating economic behaviour.

Each of these features has been extensively analysed in earlier chapters. Each of them was still recognisable in the regime prevailing in 1997, but each of them had undergone change. Hence the question: how do we explain continuity and how do we explain the changes?

Explaining continuity is relatively easy. For the first thirty years of its life the policy more or less did what it was intended to do. It allowed government to address episodic problems, it provided a façade of control and it allowed industry, on the whole, freedom to operate in a context of reasonable self-regulation. It did not deliver economic efficiency or consumer welfare, but then it was never intended to. There was little constituency for change within government. The position post-1979 is more difficult to explain. Here we should stress the weight of tradition and the power of the normative framework that had become established by the early 1970s. Broad acceptance had been created for the independence of the MMC, the flexibility of the public interest test and the realities of bargaining with the BoT/DTI/OFT over the process of reference and the negotiation of remedies. At a more detailed level features such as the width of the MMC investigation and the detailed content of reports had become part of the routine of the system. The influence of organisational and bureaucratic inertia is not to be underestimated.

Continuity was also, to a surprising extent, dictated by the law. For instance, as we saw in chapter 5, section 7 of the 1948 Act and section 54(2) of the 1973 Act contain injunctions as to the inclusion of 'a survey of the general position' in MMC reports. These injunctions have been religiously observed, where other provisions have produced less stringent conformity. The creation of procedures and expectations designed to fulfil legal obligations increases their resistance to change, and the role of the law and law making is a striking source of continuity.

This study has emphasised a mundane and easily overlooked aspect of government, the sheer difficulty of passing legislation. For senior civil servants the Sisyphean task of incorporating change into legislation is familiar. It is a process measured in years. For critics of public policy these realities are too easily forgotten. Study from the public record of the passage of the 1948, 1965 and 1973 Acts reinforces an appreciation of the complexity of the legislative process. It involves ground clearing in Whitehall, extensive consultation with colleagues and affected interests (especially business), getting an agreed paper through Cabinet, securing parliamentary time from the future legislation committee, and then taking the Bill through the two Houses. Along the way there are so many obstacles that there is a great pressure to compromise and to skirt round difficulties in order to get the legislation on to the statute book. The passage of the legislation itself is managed by a 'Bill team' of specialised officials whose priority is to pass the legislation and who may advise against holding out for every principle. Genuine innovation becomes more difficult for prosaic and tactical reasons. Thus the Government chose not to include additional powers of investigation in the 1948 Act, a registrar of monopolies in the 1965 Act, and reformed merger control in the 1998 Act. In each case, after 1948, the inclination was to facilitate ease of passage by leaving broadly untouched the provisions concerning the MMC. Hence we see continuity reinforced by the legislative constraints on the introduction of change. This was not the only reason for the legislative delay in the 1990s, but it was certainly a factor.

Explaining change in the institution of the competition rules is less easy. Change can take the form of a gradual and pragmatic adaptation to changing problems and perceptions, or it may involve fundamental redesign of the institution incorporating new principles. Radical change has come at three points: in 1956 with the Restrictive Trade Practices Act, in 1973 with the Fair Trading Act, and in 1988 with the Competition Act. There are a number of other significant turning points, including the treatment of the nationalised industries in 1980, the reinforcement of competition as a principle in 1984, and the application of competition law to the utilities after 1984, but it is the three Acts that

embody a change of principle. In each case change required the engagement of political parties and ministers, so the question can then be refor-
mulated in terms of the motives of the parties. Each of these cases shows
a political party reacting to industrial lobbying and civil service advice
but influenced also by ideas – by changes in the intellectual climate. In
each instance the events, the lobbying and the arguments are complex
and it is wrong to over-simplify.[6] In each case, however, ministers
appeared to be reacting to perceived problems in the industrial economy.
In 1956 Peter Thorneycroft's personal involvement was central, as was
his own commitment to a market economy. In 1973 the whole legislative
process had been initiated by concerns over inflation and productivity. In
1998 'Europe' was important but so, too, was a genuine concern to mod-
ernise the economy, to reinforce competitive forces in the home market as
an aid to competing abroad. In 1956, in 1973 and in 1998 we see a breaking down of aspects of the genetic code and a shift to a path which is revolutionary rather than evolutionary. Indeed, in 1998 virtually every
aspect of the genetic code had collapsed, leading to a reconfiguration of
competition policy to align with what is termed, below, a new settlement.

Competition policy and economic policy

A third perspective on the history is to assess it as a component of post-
war economic policy. This book has not attempted to analyse the success
of competition policy in economic terms although it has reflected upon
the mix of influences that constitute the policy-making process. This section therefore reviews the difficulty of establishing the economic effectiveness of competition policy. It goes on to comment on the
policy-making process and on the changing prominence of competition
policy as one element within the overall mix of economic policies.

      As noted in chapter 6, economic historians tend to be dismissive of
competition policy. The post-war histories tend almost to ignore competition policy as one rather ineffectual facet of industrial policy.[7] The main
exception is restrictive practices and the 1956 Act, which is typically
regarded as a major and successful development that materially altered
competitive conditions. The sting in the tail is that the Act is felt to have
caused a merger boom which limited competition by other means. The
areas given most prominence in this book, monopolies and mergers, are
typically felt to have had little impact. It is certainly arguable that time
lags in historical scholarship will revise this position for the 1980s and
1990s. Over recent decades policy has been enforced more systematically

and the competition agencies have been almost hyper-active. In the two years 1989–90 alone the MMC signed as many reports as in the first twenty-one years of its existence, from 1949 to 1970. This correction will be particularly necessary for the extraordinary innovations surrounding the introduction of competition into the privatised industries.

Merger policy has been the subject of sustained academic attention. Again this book has not attempted to weigh up the contending arguments. There is a sceptical character to much of the analysis of merger policy and some of the briefer textbook treatments tend to give prominence to the 'headline figures' of how few mergers are referred to the MMC and how few are blocked. As chapter 7 illustrated, however, this has been the tip of a very substantial iceberg. Merger policy as currently operated is a very different creature from the feeble 1960s or the febrile 1970s. The time is well overdue for a serious study of the OFT in the 1980s and 1990s which would evaluate the range of screening and advice that it operates, its effect as a deterrent, and its relationship with the 'mergers and acquisitions community' in banks and law firms. Such a study might well delineate a more systematic and effective regime than conventional opinion usually assumes.

This leaves monopoly control as the longest-standing element of policy, and arguably the least effective. The extent of monopoly power in Britain is great, so also is the potential for its abuse. The problem of industrial concentration was high on the industrial policy agenda in the 1970s as studies confirmed that Britain had one of the most highly concentrated manufacturing sectors in the world (see p. 291). Concern on this front fell away in the 1980s as the exposure of Britain to the world economy increased competitive pressures, but this is not a wholly reassuring factor. International competition cannot always counter domestic monopoly. The great impediment to monopoly control, encountered again and again in the earlier chapters, has been the reluctance of government departments to refer potential problems to the MMC. Where references have taken place studies of the content of MMC reports and the subsequent remedial action has diagnosed limited effectiveness. The often quoted studies by Shaw and Simpson of the period 1959–73 indicated that 'the Monopolies Commission had only a minor impact on the competitive process'.[8] The excellent follow-up study by Clarke, Davies and Driffield came to 'a broadly similar conclusion for 1973–95'.[9] The verdict is echoed by former members of the MMC such as Kenneth George.[10] Hay and Morris accept that 'it is very difficult to judge how effective this policy has been' although they add the important caveat that 'it is impossible to judge the possibility that the very existence of the

MMC acted as a deterrent to other firms which would otherwise have been tempted to exploit a dominant position'.[11]

It would be wrong to attempt to summarise a diverse economic debate in a few paragraphs. Some good summaries are available.[12] What can be concluded is that, on the whole, economists do not claim that monopoly policy has significantly increased competitive forces within the economy at large or that, as a result, there has been a significant increase in economic welfare. This is not to deny an effect on individual industrial sectors or on areas such as professional services where successive MMC reports undeniably had a material impact. In the round, however, monopoly control has not, in economic terms, been hailed as a success.

At various points in the earlier chapters we have encountered the groups and bodies which have had an influence on the design and implementation of competition policy. Within government they have included the agencies of the tripartite system with the periodic involvement of the Treasury and other sponsoring departments. Outside government they include lawyers at the small competition bar and the large law firms, and economists, both in Universities and increasingly in consulting firms. Backbench MPs have periodically been involved, especially through Select Committee inquiries. The serious press is important. MMC reports and merger battles are eminently newsworthy but there has also been reasonable coverage of the nature of policy itself. Public opinion is not a particularly significant force but consumers are. Then there is business. Organised business, in the shape of the CBI and forceful executives of leading companies who often have forthright views on policy and the merits of agencies. This book has concentrated on the central agencies and has not attempted to plot the creation or operation of a 'policy network'. It is doubtful that very much of a policy network existed outside government before the 1980s but over the past twenty years a network of interested and involved groups has become more influential. It is a professionalised network of lawyers and economists in the competition agencies, in law firms and in the private sector. It is a network of mutual interest and reciprocal exchange operating within the institutional framework discussed in the previous section.

The development of the 1998 Act, as analysed in chapter 9, was leisurely and subject to wide consultation. The policy network could be seen at work with exchange of information, technical analysis and regular meetings between officials and interested groups, especially the CBI. The CBI was regarded by officials as most constructive. This process centred on officials who stage managed the evolution of the legislation. In earlier decades policy making for competition policy involved a narrower group of participants, it was less technical and the argument of earlier chapters is that is was dominated by officials in the BoT/DTI. The balance of influence between ministers and officials is a matter of constant dispute in the academic study of public administration (and in popular comedy – where Sir Humphrey's ironic 'Yes Minister' is usually a seal of his victory). Similarly, the ability of business to influence government is a constant theme in policy making. The business lobby is one of the most powerful in Britain. While conceding that ministers and business have both been important actors, the emphasis of this book has been placed on the role of the civil service in devising, enacting and implementing competition policy. Mercer noted the remarkable influence of civil servants in the 1940s[13] and this study has found similarly remarkable influence both in the routine administration of policy and, more surprisingly, in the passage of each of the main pieces of legislation. The names that emerge from detailed investigation are certainly the more public figures such as Hans Liesner and Martin Howe, but also the BoT Under-Secretaries at key points such as Alix Kilroy (in the 1940s) Moira Dennehy (in the 1960s) Ronald McIntosh and Cyril Coffin (in the 1960s and 1970s) and, if the pattern held true, the public records might attribute similar roles to Margaret Bloom, Catherine Bell and Arthur Pryor in the 1990s. It has seemed a natural extension of this role and the associated expertise that the management posts of Deputy Director General at the OFT and Secretary at the MMC should be taken by officials. The story of competition policy making is a story of the pre-eminence of civil servants.

The profile of competition policy has undergone some marked fluctuations over the fifty-year period. The issue of cartels and restrictive practices generally was prominent in debate over economic policy from about 1952 through the passage of the 1956 Act up to the controversial Resale Price Maintenance Act in 1964. Policy on monopoly, and even on mergers, was, however, virtually submerged until the 1980s. Throughout the 1960s and 1970s economic policy was dominated by concerns with planning, selective intervention, and prices and incomes policy. Competition policy was the poor relation of industrial policy. By the 1990s the position was reversed. Industrial policy was *passé*, competition policy was central to the economic policy debate. In the next section we consider whether competition policy was being redefined as part of a new neo-liberal settlement at the end of the 1990s. For the earlier history of the policy the relative lack of enthusiasm with which it was implemented raises the question of whether it was seriously regarded as an instrument of economic policy.

In chapters 1 and 2 it was pointed out that competition policy has pursued multiple goals and that in some states policy has been regarded as a component of the 'economic constitution' of the state. It has represented a commitment to a free, fair and open market and its symbolic presence has been as important as its practical implementation.[14] It would be hard to sustain this argument for competition policy in Britain. The market system has not been under threat as in Germany, or in doubt as in Japan. There has not been the public discontent with rapacious capitalists as in the United States, or rather such discontent was channelled into party politics and support for a socialist programme rather than into measures to reform capitalism on its own terms. British competition policy has had a political dimension but it has been directed more at picking up some of the more obvious dysfunctions in the behaviour of firms rather than in the creation of constitutional bulwarks. This is the 'regulation' goal outlines in chapter 2. When designing and operating policy officials have been concerned to cater to the demands of powerful or voluble interests. This can be seen clearly in the introduction of merger control generally and for newspapers in 1965, in the provisions against pyramid selling in the 1973 Act, and in the use of the MMC to defuse potential embarrassments, from *Kuwait/BP* in 1988 to *BSkyB/Manchester United* in 1999.

In a thought-provoking aside on the 1973 Act James Cunningham noted, 'it is possible that the true argument for competition policy, and competition law, may lie, not in the economic sphere, but in political and social considerations. Political and social freedom does not appear to survive where economic freedom is lost.'[15] This is an important observation, in the vein of George Allen's comments in planning the original legislation in 1944 (see p. 13) and in Charles Lindblom's masterful study of 'this great historical fact – the dependence of polyarchies on market and private enterprise' (by polyarchy he means democracy).[16] This perspective can be seen as a counter to the more negative treatment of competition policy by economic historians and by economists. Competition policy has made a minor contribution to the efficiency of the economy, but a major contribution to the legitimacy of the market. The protection of market freedoms, both materially and symbolically, is a crucially important aspect of public policy. This is a value built into the design of the OFT and was always intrinsic to the functions performed by the MMC. The Commission and its reports can certainly be reproached for some examples of inadequate economic analysis, or a modest material impact, but they provide a different, and perhaps more important, role as a political safeguard. The idea of an 'economic jury', although criticised above (see p. 17), may therefore not be too far from the mark. Just as the jury in law symbolises the ultimate sovereignty of the public, the social citizen; so the MMC jury symbolises the sovereignty of the economic citizen.

Beyond the post-war settlement

Chapter 1 introduced the idea of the 'post-war settlement' as an expression of a broad agreement between the main producing interests as to the ground rules of post-war industrial politics. This seems an intangible and grandiose basis upon which to draw conclusions about competition policy but the basic ideas of the settlement help to explain what are otherwise exceedingly puzzling features of the operation of policy. The insights offered by the idea of the post-war settlement help to explain four striking features of 'British antitrust'. These are the voluntaristic relationship between business and the competition agencies; the resort to bargaining and discretion by the BoT; the desire by the BoT to insulate itself from the application of policy; and the flexibility of the public interest test.

The voluntaristic relationship with the MMC, and later with the OFT, reflects the acceptance of a proper sphere of autonomy for business and the company, and a faith that it would behave responsibly. Hence the MMC and the OFT were equipped with quite absurdly modest powers of search and investigation which, in the case of the MMC, they virtually never used. The penalties suffered by companies which repeated unacceptable behaviour were similarly risible. For its part, business tended to co-operate with the Commission and was encouraged in its co-operation by the CBI. Both firms and the CBI regarded the Commission's procedures as acceptable and came to regard the Commission as a preferable mode of control. This mutual respect and accommodation were very much a part of the settlement. Second, the resort to bargaining and the use of discretion by the BoT were again based on the expectation of reaching a reasonable compromise between parties both concerned, ultimately, with the national interest. The extent of BoT discretion, exploited by officials in the name of ministers and sometimes by ministers themselves, was extremely wide. Official papers note with regularity the inclination to reason with companies rather than to make a reference (see p. 163) and the need to cater to industrial preferences (p. 168). Action following reports similarly gave the BoT wide room for manoeuvre, although this was constrained after 1973 by the involvement of the OFT. The third factor was the desire of the BoT to insulate itself from direct resolution of intractable industrial problems. The internal bureaucratic politics of 'bureau shaping' was mentioned above (p. 71) but equally important was officials' desire to retain good working relations with their industrial counterparts. A subsidiary reason for the BoT's support of the 1956 Restrictive Trade Practices Act was the difficulty and embarrassment faced by officials who saw the need to dismantle the apparatus of trade associations which they had been a party to creating in the 1930s and 1940s. It would be far preferable for the courts to do the deed and for the judiciary to bear the opprobrium. BoT officials were typically unwilling to use the power which they undoubtedly possessed. This would have breached the understanding of mutual toleration on which the settlement was based and it exemplifies the hesitancy, noted in chapter 1, of officials to deploy public power.

The fourth feature which is partially explained by the post-war settlement is the public interest test itself. The public interest was conceived of as a judgement arrived at by people who understood and would further a reasonable policy which, it could be suggested, meant maintaining stability and sustaining the settlement. Public interest judgements were therefore expected to endorse reasonable business behaviour, company autonomy and common economic goals. At times they therefore encompassed a respect for the integrity of the Scottish economy, a concern about foreign takeovers of leading British companies and, of course, a concern with the employment implications of cases examined. Clearly Kuwait should not control BP. This did not require an analysis of 'competition'. A telling case was the *Flat Glass* report in 1968. Here Pilkington's complete dominance of the domestic market was found to be in the public interest. The report referred to the socially responsible family management of this private company. In his review of the incomprehensible economic logic of this report Sutherland was almost lost for words,[17] but that was not the point. The public interest did not demand the condemnation of a responsible family company which was an important regional employer and an exemplary exporter. The logic was that of the post-war settlement, not welfare economics.

Middlemas sees the post-war settlement breaking down from 1974 onwards. The commitment to full employment was abandoned in 1976 and the events of 1974–75 marked the end of reasoned bargaining in a collective national interest. The 'governing institutions' ceased to govern and in the dismal decade from 1976 to 1985 there was a crisis of governance that brought depression and despair, from the winter of discontent and the imposition of monetarism to the horrors of the miners' strike. For Middlemas, writing in 1991, there was no new settlement to replace the old, 'only a proliferation of haphazard bilateral treaties or bargains

between the state and particular groups'.[18] Other shrewd observers studied the way in which the state was strengthened in order to dismantle
alternative centres of power and hence to free the economy and bring to
bear the disciplines of competition.[19]

The view from 1999 is of a coalescing of trends into a new settlement under New Labour. The abandonment by the Labour Government
of the old class politics is a development of paradigmatic importance for
economic policy. The shape of the new settlement is still unclear. The
debate over the 'third way' is neither complete nor, sometimes, comprehensible, but it is clear that competition and the market are at the heart of
the New Labour project. It is equally clear that the tendency under the
Conservatives to give even greater recognition to the autonomy of the
firm has been sustained under Labour.[20] The privileged position of business is even more marked in the reconstructed British economy where
the relationship between business and government has shifted from bargaining and reasoned exchange to regulation through sectoral regulators
or through the market. This gives a whole new centrality and importance
to competition policy, especially since proposals to develop an alternative
way of controlling the firm through 'stakeholder' reforms have apparently been abandoned. Labour proponents of the stakeholder approach,
such as Will Hutton, envisaged a comprehensive reform of company law
and the injection of social responsibility into companies through the
enfranchising of workers, of commercial partners and of local communities.[21] These ideas, prominent in Labour thinking before the 1997 election, are not being pursued, which places even more emphasis on market
disciplines.

Viewed in its wider political context antitrust in Japan and Germany has been important in symbolising the protection of the free market from encroachment by the state. In the United States the market was
to be protected from dominant companies, rather than from the state, and
this is the emphasis to be put on the regenerated British competition
laws. On this bold interpretation it can be suggested that British competition policy is taking on a constitutional significance which it did not
previously enjoy. The role of the competition regime in the new settlement is to ensure that the excesses of the market are curbed, while allowing the market to create competitiveness – in other words a genuine
competition policy which will have to be enforced vigorously. The
urgency with which the new Labour Government passed the Competition Act 1998 is remarkable and reflects not only the priorities of the
DTI, which has, in truth, become a peripheral department of government, but also the priorities of the Treasury. Officials in the Treasury

were in favour of reinforcing the competitive pressures in the economy before the election, and their views were reinforced by Gordon Brown and his entourage. Chapter 9 examined the background to the new Act in terms of the inadequacy of British law, the influence of European law, and the steady acceptance of the arguments for reform. In more grand historical terms, however, it can be seen that the 'old' model of British competition policy was an aberrant hangover from an earlier model of industrial politics. In reality it should have died when the post-war settlement died, and the policy was ripe for reform in the early 1980s. The delays in reform were fully reviewed in chapter 9 and they left the OFT and the MMC coping with abusive behaviour in the market with wholly inadequate tools. The intensity of work undertaken by the MMC and by the OFT in the late 1980s and early 1990s, while trying to apply the old system to new conditions, is quite remarkable.

The new Act provides the competition agencies with new tools. All the pointers are that they will be used vigorously. Here we briefly summarise the main features of the new regime before comparing it with the old. The Act is complex and quite technical.[22] Very simply, it introduces four essential principles into UK law:

- A prohibition on agreements which restrict competition and on conduct by firms which amounts to abuse of a dominant position. This is expressed as a 'chapter I' prohibition which reproduces Article 85 of the Rome Treaty (now Article 81[23]). It prohibits agreements between undertakings which 'have as their object or effect the prevention, restriction or distortion of competition within the UK'.[24] This is therefore an 'effects based' rather than a 'form based' prohibition. Chapter II contains the prohibition on abuse of a dominant position and virtually reproduces Article 86 (now 82).

- Substantial penalties for committing these new offences of up to 10 per cent of UK turnover.

- The harmonisation of UK law with EC law through a novel and important 'governing principles' clause which requires the authorities and the courts to ensure consistency of treatment with EC law and jurisprudence (and to 'have regard' to the decisions of the European Commission). This is contained in section 60 and requires a major shift in the UK statutory approach, from reliance on the wording of the UK Act, to reliance on the development of EC law. The practical effects are likely to be complex.

- A full appeal by the interested parties to the appeals tribunals of the new Competition Commission. Parties can appeal the substance of the decision and the level of penalties, as well as some of the processes.

This is a truly comprehensive and revolutionary transformation in British law. The Act repeals the Restrictive Trade Practices and the Resale Price Maintenance Acts, and substantial sections of the Fair Trading Act and the Competition Act 1980 (but not section 11). Of course, it retains the Fair Trading Act provisions controlling scale and complex monopolies and mergers, and the European law itself has unchanged effect in the UK.

These are exciting times for the UK competition authorities, which show every intention of applying the new Act with zeal. The OFT is required to issue guidelines on the application of the Act and a raft of guidelines were issued over 1998–99. Not only do the guidelines indicate that the OFT has thought through the administration requirements, they also give some indication of intention. Thus, 'the Director General intends ... to ensure that penalties have the necessary deterrent effect to prevent the occurrence and repetition of infringements'.[25] It is doubtful that British industry has taken on board the extent of the changes or the likely impact of a well-designed policy forcefully implemented. A survey of awareness of the Act was conducted by the OFT in the spring of 1999 concentrating on small and medium-sized businesses. Only 2 per cent of business managers had a good knowledge of the Act and 77 per cent were unaware of it.[26] Awareness among larger companies will be better and the OFT has advised companies on their compliance programmes. At the same time, when fines are first imposed after the Act comes into effect on 1 March 2000, then there is likely to be a shock wave running through boardrooms.

What of the Commission? The Act reproduces the MMC's existing functions on the 'reporting panel' side of the new Competition Commission although there are some adaptations in the detail of the provisions. To hear appeals it creates a new post of President of the Competition Commission Appeal Tribunals and a panel of appeal tribunals chairmen. These will all be legally qualified but the other members of the three-person tribunals could either be specially appointed or drawn from the reporting panel members. A cross-fertilisation between the two arms of the Commission is envisaged. The Commission will also be equipped with a formal management Board made up of the Chairman, the President, the Secretary and other members appointed by the Secretary of State. In March 1999 it was announced that Stephen Byers had appointed Judge Christopher Bellamy QC to be President of the Appeal

Tribunals. This was something of a coup. Judge Bellamy is a leading specialist in UK and European competition law and was the British judge in the Court of First Instance. It would have been hard to visualise a more suitable appointment.[27]

It is not at all clear how much work the new legislation will generate. The OFT has predicted as many as 600 cases a year requiring guidance and 400 requiring decisions, and it has taken on new staff. How many fines and how many appeals this will produce is even more uncertain. Predictions that all fines will be appealed promise a substantial caseload for the appeal tribunals, perhaps up to seventy cases a year. The merger and utility aspects of the Commission's work will continue but it is unclear whether there will be further monopoly cases. It would seem likely that the OFT would prefer to keep the Fair Trading Act provisions very much in reserve, but ministers may be more inclined to exploit the powers they still enjoy. For merger control it will be interesting to see what impact the European principles have. The merger regulation provides for control of large European mergers (concentrations) using the criterion of 'whether or not they are compatible with the common market'. The European Merger Task Force has developed its own approach to negotiation with undertakings and has created a substantial case law.[28] The European approach to market definition is particularly important and the law is operated in light of the principles of Article 86; in other words, whether a dominant position will be created and whether it would lead to restriction of competition.[29] When the rest of British competition law is consciously looking to European jurisprudence it would be odd if there was not a spillover effect into merger control. Thus the treatment of market definition, dominance and abuse could all be affected. Vertical restraints provides another area where European and British law are going to be permissive under the new legislation. It would be contradictory not to take an equally permissive approach to the potential effects of vertical restraints in merger cases. Such pressures for conformity are likely to reinforce arguments for an early reform of British merger control.

In considering the new legislation in relation to the system it replaces there is a complex mix of continuity and change. There is residual legislative continuity. In addition there is the administrative continuity of agencies and it is notable that the European procedural rules and practices are not imported under section 60.[30] Officials see the new system as replacing the tripartite system that prevailed from 1973 to 1999. It is equally possible to see the reforms as a major re-balancing of powers within the existing organisations. The test of the radicalism of the new system will lie in the activism, the determination and the competence with which it is implemented. The continuity of agencies and of personnel is particularly important although one potential source of change may come from the increased employment of lawyers and economists in the Competition Commision and the OFT.

The extent of change can be evaluated by reference to the key features of the traditional system which were listed on p. 340 above:

- Bi-partisan origins. This feature of the system remains. There was quite vigorous debate on the 1998 Bill but it was not ideological[31] and Labour has enacted a Bill based substantially on a Conservative draft.
- Civil service design and discretion. There is substantial change in this respect. The Act is based on a European and a judicial design, and the discretionary power of ministers and DTI civil servants is largely eliminated.
- An agnostic position on monopoly, restrictive practices and mergers. A total transformation has taken place here. The Act has plentiful sources of exclusions, exemptions and *de minimis* thresholds but the thrust of the Act is prohibitive and it upholds the principle of competition. This is a very far cry from the 1940s.
- A voluntaristic basis. Here again the transformation is marked. The new Act is centred on a judicial process and on clear powers of investigation and penalties for infringement. It expects voluntary compliance but based on a calculation of self-interest, not on the basis of bargained co-operation. The tests of conformity with the law are legal and objective, not administrative and subjective.
- A judgement of 'the public interest'. The public interest test as a formal criterion for decision meets its nemesis in the shape of 'effective competition'. This does not, however, mean that the idea of the public interest disappears from the administration of policy. The concept of 'effective competition' is most difficult to pin down. George Yarrow observed, in a perceptive lecture, that 'effective competition is competition that serves the public interest'. Hence, 'focusing competition policy on the notion of promoting effective competition ... is not therefore, in and of itself, a major advance relative to the public interest criteria of the [Fair Trading Act]'.[32] An ingenious argument, sympathetic to the continuity remarked upon in this book.

Final thoughts

Looking back over the fifty years in which the MMC has engaged in the elusive pursuit of the public interest what is striking is the uncertainty of the undertaking. The MMC and its members embarked with dedication and not a little introspection on a task for which they were given very little guidance by politicians or Parliament. The results of their deliberations are contained in over four hundred reports, which often portray with candour the arguments, contradictions and compromises which they were obliged to accept. No clear distillation of the public interest emerges from the reports and it would be foolish to expect it to. The public interest is a judgement which varies with the issues, the times, the state of knowledge and the contemporary character of responsible opinion.

The members of the MMC have adapted their understanding of the public interest over the decades. In the early years it was actually concerned with the need for, and design of, competition policy itself. In later years it became attuned to responsible business behaviour and more recently it has taken on a far more economistic coloration and a concern with efficiency and welfare. Despite the complaints of firms about the procedures the MMC emerges as a 'business friendly' mode of economic organisation, a body that, at times uniquely within British government, was prepared to engage with the details of competitive activity and to see matters from the perspective of the company. It is, however, in its relationship with the civil service, rather than with business, that the mainspring of the MMC is to be found. Its definitions of the public interest and its prominence in economic life have fluctuated in parallel to the fortunes of the free-trade-orientated officials in the BoT and successor departments. Chapter 2 dealt with the ups and downs in the history of the MMC. The periods of innovation and growth are all associated with civil service activism.

It is fitting to end with the new Competition Act, which exemplifies the transformation in the MMC and in competition policy since about 1985. In the nature of a history this book has emphasised continuities – from prosaic procedural continuities to grand norms such as the public interest test itself. History is a powerful tool to explain the present (and even to predict the future) and it underlines the magnitude of change as well as the features of continuity. An ancient dialectical principle is the shift from quantitative to qualitative change. Both the MMC and competition policy have undergone qualitative change. It is a change that is integral to the shift in Britain to a regulated market economy. In its origins the role of competition policy was to sustain a respect for the market and competitive principles within a mixed economy. Since the mid 1980s Britain has become a market economy in which regulation defends both economic efficiency and social goals. Competition policy and the MMC have become part of the framework of the new market economy and therefore an institutional component of the system. The role of competition policy will take on a central historical significance in the analysis of the new industrial politics and the new political settlement when the history of the 1990s comes to be written. Change of this magnitude is epochal, almost millennial; appropriate to the coincidental publication of this book on the eve of the new century.

Notes

1 See J. A. Farmer, *Tribunals Government* (London, Weidenfeld and Nicolson, 1974); T. J. Cartwright, *Royal Commissions and Departmental Committees in Britain* (London, Hodder and Stoughton, 1975). Some bodies have been extremely long lasting, such as the Alkali Inspectorate created in 1863.

2 Adam Smith, *The Wealth of Nations*, Books I–III, with an introduction by Andrew Skinner (Harmondsworth, Penguin, 1979, first published 1776).

3 A. Knight, *Private Enterprise and Public Intervention: The Courtaulds Experience* (London, Allen and Unwin, 1974). He devotes a fascinating chapter to merger and monopoly investigations.

4 Farmer, *Tribunals and Government*, p. 134.

5 B. G. Peters, *Institutional Theory in Political Science: The 'New Institutionalism'* (London, Pinter, 1999). He distinguishes seven institutional perspectives.

6 For 1956 see J. J. Richardson, 'The making of the Restrictive Trade Practices Act 1956 – a case study of the policy process in Britain', *Parliamentary Affairs*, 20 (1967); for 1973 see ch. 6 above; for 1998 there is no good study as yet but a sense of the complexity can be gained from P. Freeman and R. Whish, *A Guide to the Competition Act 1998* (London, Butterworths, 1999).

7 As examples see R. Floud and D. McCloskey (eds), *The Economic History of Britain Since 1700: Volume 3: 1939–1992* (Cambridge University Press, second edn, 1994), where competition policy is treated in only a small section in Bob Millward's chapter; and J. Tomlinson, *Government and the Enterprise Since 1900* (Oxford, Clarendon, 1994).

8 R. Shaw and P. Simpson, *The Monopolies Commission and the Market Process* (London, Institute of Fiscal Studies, 1989), p. 23.

9 R. Clarke, S. Davies and N. Driffield, *Monopoly Policy in the UK: Assessing the Evidence* (Cheltenham, Edward Elgar, 1998), p. 186.

10 K. George, 'UK competition policy: issues and institutions', in A. Jaquemin (ed.), *Competition Policy in Europe and North America: Economic Issues and Institutions* (Chur, Switzerland, Harwood, 1990), pp. 124–6.

11 D. A. Hay and D. J. Morris, *Industrial Economics and Organization: Theory and Evidence* (Oxford University Press, second edn, 1991), p. 613.

12 See, for instance, the special issue of the *Oxford Review of Economic Policy* on 'Competition Policy', 9:2 (Summer 1993); or, for a lucid introduction, G. Yarrow, 'Competition policies and industrial policies', in M. Mackintosh *et al.*, *Economics and Changing Economies* (London, Open University and International Thomson,

1996), pp. 251–83.

13 H. Mercer, *Constructing a Competitive Order: The Hidden History of British Antitrust Policies* (Cambridge University Press, 1995), pp. 94–5.

14 See also G. B. Doern and S. Wilks, 'Introduction', in G. B. Doern and S. Wilks (eds), *Comparative Competition Policy: National Institutions in a Global Market* (Oxford, Clarendon, 1996).

15 J. P. Cunningham, *The Fair Trading Act 1973: Consumer Protection and Competition Law* (London, Sweet and Maxwell, 1974), p. 107.

16 C. Lindblom, *Politics and Markets: The World's Political-Economic Systems* (New York, Basic Books, 1977), p. 162.

17 A. Sutherland, *The Monopolies Commission in Action* (Cambridge University Press, 1970), pp. 46–7.

18 K. Middlemas, *Power, Competition and the State. Volume 3, The End of the Postwar Era: Britain Since 1974* (London, Macmillan, 1991), p. 478.

19 See the brilliant exposition by Andrew Gamble in *The Free Economy and the Strong State: The Politics of Thatcherism* (London, Macmillan, 1988).

20 See S. Wilks, 'The Conservatives and the Economy, 1979–1997', *Political Studies*, 45:2 (September 1997).

21 G. Kelly, D. Kelly and A. Gamble (eds), *Stakeholder Capitalism* (London, Macmillan, 1997).

22 The best study published thus far is Freeman and Whish, *A Guide to the Competition Act 1998*. There is a range of good articles in the *ECLR* and the OFT has published an extensive and important series of guidelines explaining the operation of the Act, for instance OFT 400, *The Major Provisions*, 22 pp. and OFT 407, *Enforcement*, 14 pp. (London, OFT, March 1999 and OFT web site).

23 The Articles have been renumbered in the Treaty of Amsterdam, 1999, as Articles 81 (old Article 85) and Article 82 (old Article 86).

24 Section 2(1)(b), *Competition Act 1998*.

25 OFT, *The Competition Act 1998, Enforcement* (London, OFT 407, March 1999), 4.2.

26 OFT, Press Release, 19 April 1999.

27 Judge Bellamy spoke on the Act at several forums indicating, for instance, the potential for the EC law to be influenced by the national courts; and the possibility that the UK appeal process would be more flexible and appropriate than the Court of First Instance principles of judicial review. See for instance, 'The role of Community law in the application of domestic competition law: some reflections', at a Conference on The Europeanisation of UK Competition Law, University College, London, 10 September 1998. Judge Bellamy was fifty-two at the the time of his appointment and receives the remuneration of a High Court Judge.

28 A very useful account is given in D. Neven, R. Nuttall and P. Seabright, *Merger in Daylight: The Economics and Politics of European Merger Control* (London, CEPR, 1993); a more recent descriptive treatment is R. Celli and M. Grenfell, *Merger Control in the United Kingdom and European Union* (London, Kluwer, 1997).

29 For detail see D. Goyder, *EC Competition Law* (Oxford, Clarendon, third edn, 1998), ch. 18; and S. Eyre, 'The politics of merger control in the EU and UK' (PhD thesis, University of Exeter, 1999).

30 A point made, significantly, by Margaret Bloom, 'The OFT's role in the new regime', paper to a conference on The Europeanisation of United Kingdom Competition Law, p. 14.

31 The exception would be John Redwood's principled opposition to the European pedigree of the Bill.

32 G. Yarrow, 'MMC: retrospect and prospect', lecture on regulation, IEA/LBS series (27 October 1998), p. 7.

Appendix: the public interest test

Section 84 of the Fair Trading Act 1973 specifies the public interest test as follows:

> In determining for any purposes to which this section applies whether any particular matter operates, or may be expected to operate, against the public interest, the Commission shall take into account all matters which appear to them in the particular circumstances to be relevant and, among other things, shall have regard to the desirability –

> (a) of maintaining and promoting effective competition between persons supplying goods and services in the United Kingdom;

> (b) of promoting the interests of consumers, purchasers and other users of goods and services in the United Kingdom in respect of the prices charged for them and in respect of their quality and the variety of goods and services supplied;

> (c) of promoting, through competition, the reduction of costs and the development and use of new techniques and new products, and of facilitating the entry of new competitors into existing markets;

> (d) of maintaining and promoting the balanced distribution of industry and employment in the United Kingdom; and

> (e) of maintaining and promoting competitive activity in markets outside the United Kingdom on the part of producers of goods, and of suppliers of goods and services, in the United Kingdom.

Select bibliography

Aaronson, R., 'Do companies take any notice of competition policy?', *Consumer Policy Review*, 2:3 (1992).

—— *The Future of UK Competition Policy*, London, IPPR, 1996.

Allen, G. C., *The Structure of Industry in Britain*, London, Longmans, second edn, 1966.

Amato, G., *Antitrust and the Bounds of Power: The Dilemma of Liberal Democracy in the History of the Market*, Oxford, Hart, 1997.

Audretsch, D., *The Market and the State: Government Policy towards Business in Europe, Japan and the USA*, London, Harvester Wheatsheaf, 1989.

Auerbach, P., *Competition: The Economics of Industrial Change*, Oxford, Basil Blackwell, 1988.

Baillieu, C., *The Lion and the Lamb*, London, Wilfred Street Publications for the Conservative 2000 Foundation, 1996.

Baldwin, R. and C. McCrudden, 'The rise of regulatory agencies', in R. Baldwin and C. McCrudden (eds), *Regulation and Public Law*, London, Weidenfeld and Nicolson, 1987.

Barnett, C., *The Audit of War: The Illusion and Reality of Britain as a Great Nation*, London, Macmillan, 1986.

Barr, F., 'Has the UK gone European: is the European approach of the Competition Bill more than an illusion?', *ECLR*, 19:3 (1998).

Beesley, M. E., *Privatisation, Regulation and Deregulation*, London, Routledge, 1992.

—— and S. Littlechild, 'The regulation of privatised monopolies in the United Kingdom', *RAND Journal of Economics*, 20:3 (1989).

Bork, R. H., *The Antitrust Paradox: A Policy at War with Itself*, New York, The Free Press, expanded edn, 1993.

Borrie, Sir Gordon, 'Restrictive practices control in the United Kingdom: big bangs and lesser detonations', the Travers memorial lecture, in *Journal of Business Law*, September 1986.

—— 'Reflections of a retiring Director General', *Annual Report of the Director General of Fair Trading, 1991*, HC 38, London, HMSO, 1992.

Boswell, J. and J. Peters, *Capitalism in Contention: Business Leaders and Political Economy in Modern Britain*, Cambridge University Press, 1997.

Bow Group, *Monopolies and Mergers*, London, Conservative Political Centre, 1964.

Broadberry, S. N. and N. Crafts, 'The post-war settlement: not such a bargain after all', *Business History*, 40:2 (1998).

Burke, T., A. Genn-Bash and B. Haines, *Competition in Theory and Practice*, London, Croom Helm, 1988.

Burton, J., 'The competitive order or ordered competition? The "UK model" of utility regulation in theory and practice', *Public Administration*, 75:2 (1997).

Buxton, T., P. Chapman and P. Temple (eds), *Britain's Economic Performance*, London, Routledge, 1994.

Cabinet Office, Efficiency Unit, *Improving Management in Government: The Next Steps*, London, HMSO, 1988.

Cairns, Sir David, 'Monopolies and restrictive practices', in M. Ginsberg (ed.), *Law and Opinion in England in the 20th Century*, London, Stevens, 1959.

Campbell, J., *Edward Heath: A Biography*, London, Pimlico, 1993.

Carsberg, Sir Bryan, 'Reflections of an incoming Director General', *Annual Report of the Director General of Fair Trading, 1992*, HC 719, London, HMSO, 1993.

—— *Competition Regulation the British Way: Jaguar or Dinosaur?*, Wincott memorial lecture, London, IEA, 1996.

Cartwright, T. J., *Royal Commissions and Departmental Committees in Britain: A Case Study in Institutional Adaptiveness and Public Participation in Government*, London, Hodder and Stoughton, 1975.

Castle,. B., *The Castle Diaries 1964–70*, London, Weidenfeld and Nicolson, 1984.

Celli, R. and M. Grenfell, *Merger Control in the United Kingdom and European Union*, London, Kluwer, 1997.

Chandler, A. D., *Scale and Scope: The Dynamics of Industrial Capitalism*, Cambridge, Mass., Belknap, 1990.

Chapman, R., 'Commissions in policy making', in R. Chapman (ed.), *The Role of Commissions in Policy Making*, London, Allen and Unwin, 1973.

Clarke, R., S. Davies and N. Driffield, *Monopoly Policy in the UK: Assessing the Evidence*, Cheltenham, Edward Elgar, 1998.

Command papers, *Employment Policy*, Cmd 6527, London, HMSO, 1944.

—— Board of Trade, *Monopolies, Mergers and Restrictive Practices*, Cmnd 2299, London, HMSO, 1964.

—— *The Nationalised Industries*, Cmnd 7151, London, HMSO, 1978.

—— Department of Prices and Consumer Protection, *A Review of Monopolies and Mergers Policy*, Cmnd 7198, London, HMSO, 1978.

—— Department of Prices and Consumer Protection, *A Review of Restrictive Trade Practices Policy: A Consultative Document*, Cmnd 7512, London, HMSO, 1979.

—— *The Role of the Comptroller and Auditor General*, Cmnd 7845, London, HMSO, 1980.

—— DTI, *Review of Restrictive Trade Practices: A Consultative Document*, Cm 331, London, HMSO, 1988.

—— DTI, *Opening Markets: New Policy on Restrictive Trade Practices*, Cm 727, London, HMSO, 1989.

—— Nolan Committee, *Report of the Committee on Standards in Public Life*, Cm 2850-I, London, HMSO, 1995.

—— *Your Right to Know: Freedom of Information*, Cm 3818, London, Stationery Office, 1997.

—— *A Fair Deal for Consumers: Modernising the Framework for Utility Regulation*, Cm 3898, London, Stationery Office, 1998.

—— *Our Competitive Future: Building the Knowledge Driven Economy*, Cm 4176, London, Stationery Office, 1998.

Committee of Public Accounts, *Efficiency of Nationalised Industries: References to the Monopolies and Mergers Commission*, 1986–87, HC 26, London, HMSO, 1987.

Craig, F., *British General Election Manifestos 1900–1974*, London, Macmillan, second edn, 1975.

Craig, P., 'The Monopolies and Mergers Commission: competition and administrative rationality', in R. Baldwin and C. McCrudden (eds), *Regulation and Public Law*, London, Weidenfeld and Nicolson, 1987.

Crosland, A., *The Future of Socialism*, London, Jonathan Cape, 1956.

Cunningham, J. P., *The Fair Trading Act 1973: Consumer Protection and Competition Law*, London, Sweet and Maxwell, 1974.

David, P., 'Clio and the economics of QWERTY', *American Economic Review*, 75, (1985).

Davies, S. W., N. L. Driffield and R. Clarke, *Monopoly in the UK: What Determines Whether the MMC Finds Against the Investigated Firm?* Discussion paper 9808, School of Economics and Social Studies, UEA, 1998.

Deakin, S., T. Goodwin and A. Hughes, *Co-operation and Trust in Inter-Firm Relations: Beyond Competition Policy?* Cambridge, ESRC Centre for Business Research, WP 79, 1997.

Denhardt, R. D., *In Pursuit of Significance: Strategies for Managerial Success in Public Organisations*, London, Harcourt Brace, 1993.

DTI, *Mergers Policy: A DTI Paper on the Policy and Procedures of Merger Control*, London, HMSO, 1988.

—— *Tackling Cartels and Abuse of Market Power: A Consultation Document*, London, DTI, 1996.

—— *Tackling Cartels and Abuse of Market Power: A Draft Bill: An Explanatory Document*, London, DTI, 1996.

—— *A Fair Deal for Consumers: Modernising the Framework for Utility Regulation – the Response to Consultation*, London, DTI, undated but 1998.

Dumez, H. and A. Jeunemaitre, 'The convergence of competition policies in Europe: internal dynamics and external imposition', in S. Berger and R. Dore (eds), *National Diversity and Global Capitalism*, Ithaca, Cornell University Press, 1996.

Dunleavy, P., *Democracy, Bureaucracy and Public Choice*, Brighton, Harvester Wheatsheaf, 1991.

Dyson, K., *The State Tradition in Western Europe: The Study of an Idea and an Institution*, Oxford, Martin Robertson, 1980.

Edwards, C. D., *Control of Cartels and Monopolies: An International Comparison*, Dobbs Ferry, Oceana, 1967.

Eisner, M., *Regulatory Politics in Transition*, Baltimore, Johns Hopkins University Press, 1993.

Ellis, T. S., 'A survey of the Government control of mergers in the United Kingdom – Part I', *Northern Ireland Legal Quarterly*, Autumn (1971).

Evans, R., *In Defence of History*, London, Granta, 1997.

Eyre, S., 'The politics of merger control in the EU and the UK', PhD thesis, University of Exeter, 1999.

Fairburn, J., 'The evolution of merger policy in Britain', in J. A. Fairburn and J. A. Kay (eds), *Mergers and Merger Policy*, Oxford University Press, 1989.

Farmer, J. A., *Tribunals and Government*, London, Weidenfeld and Nicolson, 1974.

Fels, A., *The British Prices and Incomes Board*, Cambridge University Press, 1972.

Finbow, R. and N. Parr, *UK Merger Control: Law and Practice*, London, Sweet and Maxwell, 1995.

Fisher, F. M., J. J. McGowan and J. E. Greenwood, *Folded, Spindled, and Mutilated: Economic Analysis and U.S. v. IBM*, Cambridge, Mass., MIT Press, 1983.

Fishwick, F., *Making Sense of Competition Policy*, London, Kogan Page, 1993.

Foster, C., *Privatization, Public Ownership and the Regulation of Natural Monopoly*, Oxford, Blackwell, 1992.

Franks, J. and R. Harris, 'The role of the Mergers and Monopolies Commission in merger policy: costs and alternatives', *Oxford Review of Economic Policy*, 2:4 (1986).

Frazer, T., *Monopoly, Competition and the Law*, London, Harvester Wheatsheaf, second edn, 1992.

Freeman, P. and R. Whish, *A Guide to the Competition Act 1998*, London, Butterworths, 1999.

Freyer, T., *Regulating Big Business: Antitrust in Great Britain and America 1880–1990*, Cambridge University Press, 1992.

Friedrich, C. (ed.), *The Public Interest*, New York, Atherton, 1962.

Galbraith, J. K., *The New Industrial State*, Harmondsworth, Penguin, 1969, first published 1967.

Gamble, A., *The Free Economy and the Strong State: The Politics of Thatcherism*, London, Macmillan, 1988.

Garner, M., 'Auditing the efficiency of the nationalised industries: enter the Monopolies and Mergers Commission', *Public Administration*, 60:4 (1982).

George, K., 'UK competition policy: issues and institutions', in A. Jaquemin (ed.), *Competition Policy in Europe and North America: Economic Issues and Institutions*, Chur, Switzerland, Harwood, 1990.

Gerber, D. J., *Law and Competition in Twentieth Century Europe: Protecting Prometheus*, Oxford, Clarendon, 1998.

Gerschenkron, A., *Economic Backwardness in Historical Perspective*, Cambridge, Mass., Harvard University Press, 1962.

Gowan, P., 'The origins of the administrative elite', *New Left Review*, 162 (1987).

Goyder, D. G., *EC Competition Law*, Oxford, Clarendon, third edn, 1998.

Graham, C., 'The Office of Telecommunications: a new competition authority?', in G. B. Doern and S. Wilks (eds), *Changing Regulatory Institutions in Britain and North America*, University of Toronto Press, 1998.

Grant, W. and D. Marsh, *The CBI*, London, Hodder and Stoughton, 1977.

—— and J. Sargent, *Business and Politics in Britain*, London, Macmillan, second edn, 1993.

Gribbin, J. D., 'The operation of the Mergers panel since 1965', *Trade and Industry*, 17 January 1974.

—— *The Postwar Revival of Competition as Industrial Policy*, Government Economic Service Working Paper 19, London, Price Commission, 1978.

—— 'The contribution of economics to the origins of UK competition policy', in P. de Wolf (ed.), *Competition in Europe*, Dordrecht, Kluwer, 1991.

Grout, P., 'The cost of capital and asset valuation', in P. Vass (ed.), *Regulatory Review 1997*, London, CIPFA, 1997.

Grove, J. W., *Government and Industry in Britain*, London, Longmans, 1962.

Guenault, P. and J. Jackson, *The Control of Monopoly in the United Kingdom*, London, Longmans, 1960.

Hadden, T., *Company Law and Capitalism*, London, Weidenfeld and Nicolson, second edn, 1977.

Hannah, L., *The Rise of the Corporate Economy*, London, Methuen, second edn, 1983.

Hansard Society and the European Policy Forum, *The Report of the Commission on the Regulation of Privatised Utilities*, London, Hansard Society, 1996.

Harris, N., *Competition and the Corporate Society: British Conservatives, the State and Industry 1945–1964*, London, Methuen, 1972.

Hay, D. 'The assessment: competition policy', *Oxford Review of Economic Policy*, 9:2 (1993).

—— and D. J. Morris, *Industrial Economics and Organization: Theory and Evidence*, Oxford University Press, second edn, 1991.

—— and J. Vickers, 'The reform of UK competition policy', *National Institute Economic Review*, August (1988).

Hayward, J. (ed.), *Industrial Enterprise and European Integration: From National to International Champions in Western Europe*, Oxford University Press, 1995.

Heath, E., *The Course of My Life*, London, Hodder and Stoughton, 1998.

Hennessy, P., *Whitehall*, London, Secker and Warburg, 1989.

Heseltine, M., *Where There's a Will*, London, Hutchinson, 1987.

Hirschman, A., *Exit, Voice and Loyalty*, Cambridge, Mass., Harvard University Press, 1970.

Hobsbawm, E., *Industry and Empire: An Economic History of England since 1750*, London, History Book Club, 1968.

Hogwood, B., 'Regulatory institutions in the United Kingdom: increasing regulation in the "shrinking state"', in G. B. Doern and S. Wilks (eds), *Changing Regulatory Institutions in Britain and North America*, University of Toronto Press, 1998.

Hood, C., 'Keeping the centre small: explanations of agency type', *Political Studies*, 26 (1978).

Hoover, K. and R. Plant, *Conservative Capitalism in Britain and the United States: A Critical Appraisal*, London, Routledge, 1989.

Hornsby, S., 'Judicial review of decisions of the UK competition authorities: is the applicant bound to fail?', *ECLR*, 14:5 (1993).

Howe, G. (Lord Howe of Aberavon), 'The birth of an Office: a midwife's view', collected papers from a conference on fair trading at the Café Royal, OFT, 1992.

Howe, M., 'Rethinking British merger policy', *The Antitrust Bulletin*, 17 (1972).

—— 'Efficiency and competition policy', in C. Bowe (ed.), *Industrial Efficiency and the Role of Government*, London, HMSO, 1977.

Hughes, A., 'Research annex', in NEDO (ed.), *Competition Policy*, London, NEDO, 1978.

—— 'The impact of merger: a survey of empirical evidence for the UK', in J. Fairburn and J. Kay (eds), *Mergers and Merger Policy*, Oxford University Press, 1989.

Hutton, W., *The State We're In*, London, Vintage, revised edn, 1996.

Ingham, G., *Capitalism Divided? The City and Industry in British Social Development*, London, Macmillan, 1984.

James, O., 'Explaining the Next Steps in the Department of Social Security: the bureaushaping model of central state reorganisation', *Political Studies*, 43:4 (1995).

Jay, D., *Change and Fortune*, London, Hutchinson, 1980.

Jewkes, J., 'British monopoly policy 1944–56', *Journal of Law and Economics*, 1:1 (1958).

John, P., *Analysing Public Policy*, London, Pinter, 1998.

Johnston, A., *The City Takeover Code*, Oxford University Press, 1980.

Kay, J. A. and T. Sharpe, 'The anti-competitive practice', *Fiscal Studies*, 3 (1982).

Kelly, G., D. Kelly and A. Gamble (eds), *Stakeholder Capitalism*, London, Macmillan, 1997.

Kerse, C. S., *EEC Antitrust Procedure*, London, European Law Centre, second edn, 1988.

Kilroy, A., 'The task and methods of the Monopolies Commission', *The Manchester School*, XXII (1954).

Kipping, N., *Summing Up*, London, Hutchinson, 1972.

Knight, A., *Private Enterprise and Public Intervention: The Courtaulds Experience*, London, Allen and Unwin, 1974.

Lawson, N., *The View from No. 11*, London, Transworld, 1992.

Le Quesne, Sir Godfray, 'The role of the MMC', paper to a *Financial Times* conference, collected papers, October 1983.

—— 'The Monopolies and Mergers Commission at work', in K. George (ed.), *Macmillan's Merger and Acquisition Yearbook*, London, Macmillan, 1988.

Lindblom, C., 'The science of "muddling through"', *Public Administration Review*, 19 (1959).

—— *Politics and Markets: The World's Political-Economic Systems*, New York, Basic Books, 1977.

Lipworth, Sir Sydney, 'Development of merger control in the UK and the European Community', the Denning lecture 1990, in R. Miller (ed.), *The Monopolies and Mergers Yearbook*, Oxford, Blackwell, 1992.

Littlechild, S. C., *Regulation of British Telecommunications' Profitability: Report to the Secretary of State*, London, DTI, 1983.

—— 'Myths and merger policy', in J. Fairburn and J. Kay (eds), *Mergers and Merger Policy*, Oxford University Press, 1989.

Locke, S., 'A new approach to competition policy', *Consumer Policy Review*, 4:3 (1994).

—— and K. Scribbins, 'Cars and the MMC report: a fair deal for consumers?', *Consumer Policy Review*, 2:3 (1992).

MacKerron, G. and I. Biora-Segarra, 'Regulation', in J. Surrey (ed.), *The British Electricity Experiment: Privatization: The Record, the Issues, the Lessons*, London, Earthscan, 1996.

Maitland-Walker, J., 'Ice cream wars', *ECLR*, 16:8 (1995).

Maloney, W. and J. Richardson, *Managing Policy Change in Britain: The Politics of Water*, Edinburgh University Press, 1995.

Marquand, D., *The Unprincipled Society*, London, Fontana, 1988.

Maxwell-Fyfe, D. (Lord Kilmuir), *Political Adventure*, London, Weidenfeld and Nicolson, 1964.

Meeks, G., *Disappointing Marriage: A Study of the Gains from Merger*, Cambridge University Press, 1977.

Mercer, H., 'The Monopolies and Restrictive Practices Commission: a study in regulatory failure', in G. Jones and M. Kirby (eds), *Competitiveness and the State: Government and Business in Twentieth Century Britain*, Manchester University Press, 1991.

—— *Constructing a Competitive Order: The Hidden History of British Antitrust Policies*, Cambridge University Press, 1995.

Merkin, R. and K. Williams, *Competition Law: Antitrust Policy in the UK and EEC*, London, Sweet and Maxwell, 1984.

Methven, J., 'Keynote address', in K. George and C. Joll (eds), *Competition Policy in the UK and EEC*, Cambridge University Press, 1975.

Meynell, Dame Alix, *Public Servant, Private Woman*, London, Gallancz, 1988.

Middlemas, K., *Industry, Unions and Government: Twenty-One Years of NEDC*, London, Macmillan, 1983.

—— *Power, Competition and the State. Volume 1: Britain in Search of Balance 1940–61*, London, Macmillan, 1986.

—— *Power, Competition and the State. Volume 2: Threats to the Postwar Settlement: Britain 1961–74*, London, Macmillan, 1990.

—— *Power, Competition and the State. Volume 3: The End of the Postwar Era: Britain Since 1974*, London, Macmillan, 1991.

Millward, R., 'Industrial and commercial performance since 1950', in R. Floud and D. McCloskey (eds), *The Economic History of Britain Since 1700. Volume 3: 1939–1992*, Cambridge University Press, second edn, 1994.

Morgan, E. V., *Monopolies, Mergers and Restrictive Practices: UK Competition Policy 1948–87*, Hume paper 7, Edinburgh, The David Hume Institute, 1987.

National Audit Office, *The Work of the Directors General of Telecommunications, Gas Supply, Water Sevices and Electricity Supply*, 1995–96, HC 645, London, HMSO, 1996.

National Consumers' Council, *Competition and Consumers*, London, NCC, 1995.

Neale, A. D. and D. G. Goyder, *The Antitrust Laws of the U.S.A.: A Study of Competition Enforced by Law*, Cambridge University Press, third edn, 1980.

Neven, D., R. Nuttall and P. Seabright, *Merger in Daylight: The Economics and Politics of European Merger Control*, London, CEPR, 1993.

—— P. Papandropoulos and P. Seabright, *Trawling for Minnows: European Competition Policy and Agreements between Firms*, London, CEPR, 1998.

North, D., *Institutions, Institutional Change and Economic Performance*, Cambridge University Press, 1990.

O'Brien, D. P., 'Competition policy in Britain, the silent revolution', *The Antitrust Bulletin*, Spring (1983).

Opie, R., 'A perspective on UK competition policy', in C. Moir and T. Dawson (eds), *Competition and Markets*, London, Macmillan, 1990.

Parkinson, J. E., *Corporate Power and Responsibility: Issues in the Theory of Company Law*, Oxford, Clarendon, 1993.

Parsons, W., *Public Policy*, Aldershot, Edward Elgar, 1995.

Pass, C. Y., 'Horizontal mergers and the control of market power in the UK', *The Antitrust Bulletin*, 17 (1972).

—— and J. R. Sparkes, 'Dominant forms and the public interest: a survey of the reports of the British Monopolies and Mergers Commission', *The Antitrust Bulletin*, XXV:2 (1980).

Peritz, R. J. R., *Competition Policy in America 1888–1992: History, Rhetoric, Law*, Oxford University Press, 1996.

Peston, M., 'A new look at monopoly policy', *Political Quarterly*, 41 (1970).

Peters, B. G., *Institutional Theory in Political Science: The 'New Institutionalism'*, London, Pinter, 1999.

Pickering, J., 'The implementation of British competition policy on mergers', *ECLR*, 2 (1980).

Pickrill, D. A., *Ministers of the Crown*, London, Routledge and Kegan Paul, 1981.

Pimlott, B., *Harold Wilson*, London, Harper Collins, 1992.

Pollard, S., *The Wasting of the British Economy*, London, Croom Helm, 1982.

Poole Committee, *Monopoly and the Public Interest*, London, Conservative Political Centre, 1963.

Porter, M. E., *The Competitive Advantage of Nations*, London, Macmillan, 1990.

Prais, S., *The Evolution of Giant Firms in Britain*, Cambridge University Press, 1976.

Price, C., 'Gas regulation and competition: substitutes or complements?', in M. Bishop *et al.* (eds), *Privatization and Economic Performance*, Oxford University Press, 1994.

Prosser, T., *Law and the Regulators*, Oxford, Clarendon, 1997.

Ramsey, I., 'The Office of Fair Trading: policing the consumer market place', in R. Baldwin and C. McCrudden (eds), *Regulation and Public Law*, London, Weidenfeld and Nicolson, 1987.

Rhinelander, L., 'The Roche case: one giant step for British antitrust', *Virginia Journal of International Law*, 16:1 (1974).

Richardson, J. J., 'The making of the Restrictive Trade Practices Act 1956 – a case study of the policy process in Britain', *Parliamentary Affairs*, 20 (1967).

Ridley, N., *My Style of Government*, London, Hutchinson, 1992.

Robinson, C., 'Gas: what to do after the MMC verdict', in M. Beesley (ed.), *Regulating Utilities: The Way Forward*, London, IEA, 1994.

Rowley, C., *The British Monopolies Commission*, London, Allen and Unwin, 1966.

—— 'Mergers and public policy in Great Britain', *Journal of Law and Economics*, 11 (1968).

Scott, W. R., *Organizations: Rational, Natural, and Open Systems*, Englewood Cliffs, Prentice Hall, third edn, 1992.

—— *Institutions and Organizations*, London, Sage, 1995.

Seldon, A., *Major: A Political Life*, London, Weidenfeld and Nicolson, 1997.

—— and S. Ball (eds), *Conservative Century: The Conservative Party since 1900*, Oxford University Press, 1994.

Select Committee on Estimates, *Monopolies and Restrictive Practices Commission*, 1952–53, HC 177, London, HMSO, 1953.

Selznick, P., *Leadership in Administration*, New York, Harper and Row, 1957.

Sharpe, T., 'British competition policy in perspective', *Oxford Review of Economic Policy*, 3:1 (1985).

Shaw, R. and P. Simpson, 'The Monopolies Commission and the process of competition', *Fiscal Studies*, 6:1 (1985).

—— *The Monopolies Commission and the Market Process*, London, Institute of Fiscal Studies, 1989.

Shonfield, A., *Modern Capitalism: The Changing Balance of Public and Private Power*, Oxford University Press, 1965.

Soames, T., 'Merger policy: as clear as mud?', *ECLR*, 12:2 (1991).

Stedman, G., *Takeovers*, London, Longman, 1993.

Stern, J., 'Gas – regulation and the MMC review 1993', in P. Vass (ed.), *Regulatory Review 1994*, London, CIPFA, 1994.

Stevens, R. B. and B. S. Yamey, *The Restrictive Practices Court: A Study of the Judicial Process and Economic Policy*, London, Weidenfeld and Nicolson, 1965.

Stewart, M., *Politics and Economic Policy in the UK Since 1964: The Jekyll and Hyde Years*, Oxford University Press, 1977.

Strickland, P., 'Telecommunications regulation in 1996–97', in P. Vass (ed.), *Regulatory Review 1997*, London, CIPFA, 1997.

Sturm, R., 'The German cartel office in a hostile environment', in G. B. Doern and S. Wilks (eds), *Comparative Competition Policy: National Institutions in a Global Market*, Oxford, Clarendon, 1996.

Sutherland, A., *The Monopolies Commission in Action*, Cambridge University Press, 1970.

Swann, D., D. O'Brien, P. Maunder and S. Howe, *Competition in British Industry: Restrictive Practices Legislation in Theory and Practice*, London, Allen and Unwin, 1974.

Swift, J., 'Merger policy: certainty or lottery?', in J. Fairburn and J. Kay (eds), *Mergers and Merger Policy*, Oxford University Press, 1989.

Thatcher, M., *The Downing Street Years*, London, Harper Collins, 1993.

Tomlinson, J., 'British economic policy since 1945', in R. Floud and D. McCloskey (eds), *The Economic History of Britain Since 1700. Volume 3: 1939–1992*, Cambridge University Press, second edn, 1994.

—— *Government and the Enterprise Since 1900: The Changing Problem of Efficiency*, Oxford, Clarendon, 1994.

Trade and Industry Committee, *Takeovers and Mergers*, 1991–92, HC 90, London, HMSO, 1991.

—— *Takeovers and Mergers: Minutes of Evidence*, 1990–91, HC 226, London, HMSO, 1991.

—— *UK Policy on Monopolies*, 1994–95, HC 249-I, London, HMSO, 1995.

—— *Government Observations on the Fifth Report from the Trade and Industry Committee (Session 1994–95) on UK Policy on Monopolies*, 1994–95, HC 748, London, HMSO, 1995.

Trebilcock, C., *The Industrialisation of the Continental Powers 1780–1914*, London, Longmans, 1981.

Utton, M. A., 'On measuring the effects of industrial mergers', *Scottish Journal of Political Economy*, 21 (1974).

—— *The Political Economy of Big Business*, Oxford, Martin Robertson, 1982.

—— *Profits and the Stability of Monopoly*, Cambridge University Press, 1986.

Vickers, G., *The Art of Judgement*, London, Chapman and Hall, 1965.

Vogel, D., *National Styles of Regulation: Environmental Policy in Great Britain and the United States*, Ithaca, Cornell University Press, 1986.

Waldenstrom, M., 'Foreword', in S. Gray and M. McDermott, *Mega-Merger Mayhem*, London, Mandarin, 1990.

Walshe, J. G., 'Industrial organization and competition policy', in N. Crafts and N. Woodward (eds), *The British Economy Since 1945*, Oxford, Clarendon, 1991.

Waterson, M., 'Vertical integration and vertical restraints', *Oxford Review of Economic Policy*, 9:2 (1993).

Whish, R., *Competition Law*, London, Butterworths, third edn, 1993.

Whittington, G., 'Regulatory asset value and the cost of capital', in M. Beesley (ed.), *Regulating Utilities: Understanding the Issues*, London, IEA, 1998.

Wilks, S., *Industrial Policy and the Motor Industry*, Manchester University Press, revised edn, 1988.

—— *The Office of Fair Trading in Administrative Context*, London, CIPFA, 1994.

—— 'The prolonged reform of United Kingdom competition policy', in G. B. Doern and S. Wilks (eds), *Comparative Competition Policy: National Institutions in a Global Market*, Oxford, Clarendon, 1996.

—— 'The Conservatives and the economy, 1979–1997', *Political Studies*, 45:2 (1997).

—— and L. McGowan, 'Disarming the Commission: the debate over a European Cartel Office', *Journal of Common Market Studies*, 33:2 (1995).

—— with L. McGowan, 'Competition policy in the European Union: creating a federal agency?', in G. B. Doern and S. Wilks (eds), *Comparative Competition Policy: National Institutions in a Global Market*, Oxford, Clarendon, 1996.

Williams, M., 'The effectiveness of economic policy in the United Kingdom', *Oxford Review of Economic Policy*, 9:2 (1993).

Williamson, O. E., 'Economics as an antitrust defense: the welfare trade-offs', *American Economic Review*, 58 (1968).

—— *Antitrust Economics: Mergers, Contracting and Strategic Behaviour*, Oxford, Basil Blackwell, 1987.

Wilson, H., *The Labour Government, 1964–70*, London, Weidenfeld & Nicolson and Michael Joseph, 1971.

Wraith, R. and P. Hutchesson, *Administrative Tribunals*, London, Allen and Unwin, 1973.

Wright, M., 'City rules OK? Policy community, policy network and takeover bids', *Public Administration*, 66:4 (1988).

Wright, V., 'Conclusion: the state and major enterprises in Western Europe', in J. Hayward (ed.), *Industrial Enterprise and European Integration: From National to International Champions in Western Europe*, Oxford University Press, 1995.

Yarrow, G., 'Competition policies and industrial policies', in M. Mackintosh *et al.* (eds), *Economics and Changing Economies*, London, International Thomson, 1996.

Young, D. (Lord Young of Graffham), *The Enterprise Years: A Businessman in the Cabinet*, London, Headline, 1990.

Young, J. W., 'The Heath government and British entry into the European Community', in S. Ball and A. Seldon (eds), *The Heath Government 1970–1974: A Reappraisal*, London, Longman, 1996.

Young, S. with A. V. Lowe, *Intervention in the Mixed Economy: The Evolution of British Industrial Policy 1964–72*, London, Croom Helm, 1974.

Archives

Public Records Office, Kew

Files of the:
> Board of Trade PRO, BT
> Cabinet and Cabinet Committees PRO, CAB
> Department of Employment and Productivity PRO, BT
> Department of Trade and Industry PRO, BT; and PRO, FV
> Lord Chancellor's Office PRO, LCO

DTI archives

Files studied in DTI archives are referenced as PRO with their DTI file reference. They will become open to the public as the thirty-year rule applies.

Modern Records Centre, University of Warwick

CBI Predecessor Archives MRO, MSS200
CBI Archives MRO, MSSS200

Index